WOMEN
and LITERACY

Local and Global Inquiries for a New Century

NCTE–LEA Research Series

Series Editors

Literacy
David Bloome, The Ohio State University
Arlette Ingram Willis, University of Illinois at Urbana-Champaign

Composition
Malea Powell, Michigan State University
Duane Roen, Arizona State University

Alsup • *Teacher Identity Discourses: Negotiating Personal and Professional Spaces**

Banks • *Race, Rhetoric, and Technology: Searching for Higher Ground**

Daniell/Mortensen, Eds. • *Women and Literacy: Local and Global Inquiries for a New Century**

The NCTE–LEA Research Series, co-published by the National Council of Teachers of English and Lawrence Erlbaum Associates/Taylor & Francis Group, comprises two distinct strands: (1) literacy studies in P–12 classroom and related contexts and (2) composition studies. Volumes in this series are invited publications that are primarily authored or co-authored works that are theoretically significant and hold broad relevance to their respective audiences. The series may also include occasional landmark compendiums of research.

The scope of the series includes qualitative and quantitative methodologies; a range of perspectives and approaches (e.g., sociocultural, cognitive, feminist, linguistic, pedagogical, critical, historical, anthropological); and research on diverse populations, contexts (e.g., classrooms, school systems, families, communities), and forms of literacy (e.g., print, electronic, popular media).

For additional information about the NCTE–LEA Research Series and guidelines for submitting proposals, visit www.taylorandfrancis.com or www.ncte.org.

*Titles acquired and developed under Series Editors Andrea A. Lunsford and Beverly J. Moss (2002–2005)

WOMEN
and LITERACY

Local and Global Inquiries for a New Century

Edited by

Beth Daniell
Kennesaw State University

Peter Mortensen
University of Illinois at Urbana-Champaign

Routledge
Taylor & Francis Group
LONDON AND NEW YORK

NCTE National Council of Teachers of English
1111 W. Kenyon Road, Urbana, Illinois 61801-1096

Cover design by Tomai Maridou.

Cover art by Safia El-Wakil.

First published by Lawrence Erlbaum Associates
10 Industrial Avenue, Mahwah, New Jersey 07430

This edition published in 2012 by Routledge
2 Park Square, Milton Park, Abingdon, Oxon OX14 4RN
711 Third Avenue, New York, NY 10017, USA

Routledge is an imprint of the Taylor & Francis Group, an informa business

© 2007 by Taylor & Francis Group, LLC

International Standard Book Number-13: 978-0-8058-6007-8 (Softcover) 978-0-8058-6006-1 (Hardcover)

Library of Congress Cataloging-in-Publication Data

Women and literacy : local and global inquiries for a new century / edited by Beth
    Daniell and Peter Mortensen.
       p. cm.
    (NCTE-LEA research series)
    Includes index.
    ISBN 978-0-8058-6006-1 (hbk)
    ISBN 978-0-8058-6007-8 (pbk.)
    1. Woman--Education. 2. Literacy. 3. Women--Books and reading. I. Daniell, Beth,
1947- II. Mortensen, Peter, 1961-

LC1481.L646 2006
302.2'244082--dc22   2006025578

Visit the Taylor & Francis Web site at
http://www.taylorandfrancis.com

Visit the National Council of Teachers of English Web site at
http://www.ncte.org

For
Maggie, Nancy, and Rae
and
Sarah and Ellen

Contents

II. WOMEN'S LITERACIES IN A GLOBALLY
INTERDEPENDENT WORLD

Preface

The calligraphy on the cover of this book was created by Safia El-Wakil, one of the contributors to *Women and Literacy: Local and Global Inquiries for a New Century*. Safia teaches at the American University in Cairo along with Kate Coffield, and both are co-authors with Gail Hawisher and Cynthia Selfe of "Women and the Global Ecology of Digital Literacies," a chapter that examines how two women, Safia and Kate, learned to use computers to write and to teach writing. But El-Wakil also uses the computer to create intricate calligraphy, an example of which she has generously shared with us. El-Wakil explains:

> The vortex recapitulates the whirling dance movement performed by the mystic dervishes of the thirteenth-century Mevlevi Sufi Order of Konya (Turkey) founded by Jalaluddin Rumi .... As the Mevlevi dervish whirls and rotates in celebration of his Creator, he represents the earth revolving on its own axis while orbiting the sun. His dance thus aspires to capture the splendor of the creation, to spread the rapture of love, and to evoke the feelings of joy and compassion that will ultimately unite him with his spiritual essence.

> The written words at the center of the vortex are "He is Alive" (meaning God, the Creator), and the rose petals flowing out of the vortex and beyond are the symbolic petals of love. (Private correspondence, 9 Feb. 2006)

El-Wakil tells us that the whirling movement of the dervishes recreated in her calligraphy imitates "the fundamental condition of our existence from the cosmic swirl of stars and planets above to the minutest rotation of the protons and electrons around the nucleus of an atom."

El-Wakil's artwork is an appropriate cover for this collection of essays about women and literacy, for, as you will find, the women readers and writers whose stories, tragedies, and hopes are told in this volume are indeed part of the swirling life of the universe. Yet it was not so long ago, we remember, that women's stories were not told, that they were not considered a part of the universe. We hope you will discover, as we have, that the women whose stories are told here use their literacies in the service of life—to make life better for themselves, other women, their families, their communities, their nation, and their world. This is not to say that all of the women documented in this book have prevailed. Nonetheless, we would argue that they have used their literacies to join the cosmic swirl El-Wakil writes of so eloquently.

We hope you will see, as well, the love that brought the essays we have collected to fruition. The contributors to *Women and Literacy* committed not just to telling stories or theorizing about them, but also to the women whose stories they report and analyze. The researchers have come to feel what Jacqueline Jones Royster calls "passionate attachments" to their subjects, whether historical figures like Louisa May Alcott, Dorothy West, Ethel Azalea Johnson, the Appalachian women of Depression-era Virginia, or feminist writers of the sixties and seventies; or women in other parts of the world, such as those in Vietnam struggling with English and Japanese or in South Africa dealing with the legacy of apartheid; or contemporary women in the mountains of North Carolina, the plains of Nebraska, the cities of Tunisia; or women in the aftermath of war, such as college students at Western College in Ohio meeting peers from around the globe, or old women in Korea finally telling stories of their sexual exploitation during World War II.

We are grateful to the scholars whose work we present here. They have been good-natured about our requests for revisions, especially our pleas to trim and compress. In addition, they have been enormously patient with the sheer time the editorial process has taken. Making this book occurred through one birth and two interstate moves, in addition to our usual tasks running composition and rhetoric programs. We thank all the contributors for sticking with us, and we hope that our readers will see the effort, the time, the love these researchers have expended in writing about research that is dear to them.

We are grateful as well to Andrea Lunsford and Beverly Moss for their commitment to include *Women and Literacy* in the NCTE–LEA Research Series. They found two anonymous manuscript readers who not only appreciated our effort, but also asked hard questions of us and of our contributors. These readers, along with Beverly and Andrea, offered valuable suggestions for making the volume better. Too, editors at both NCTE and Erlbaum have guided us in important ways, and we thank Zarina Hock and Naomi Silverman for their keen advice. Others whose early interest in the project was most encouraging are Jean Ferguson Carr, Angela Crow, Suellynn Duffey, Karl Kageff, Mary P. Sheridan-Rabideau, Christine Skolnik, and Katherine Kelleher Sohn.

Our British colleagues who study literacy—David Barton, Roz Ivanič, and Anna Robinson-Pant—were helpful as well, offering thoughtful suggestions at a critical juncture. Two of Peter's colleagues at Illinois, Susan Koshy and Zohreh Sullivan, were similarly generous with advice when consulted.

Graduate students in Writing Studies at the University of Illinois at Urbana-Champaign checked sources for us, and we are grateful to them: Patrick Berry, Samantha Looker, Christa Olson, Janine Solberg, and Martha Webber. And it was Berry who applied his extraordinary graphic talents to the task of designing a cover that would showcase El-Wakil's calligraphic artwork.

The idea for this collection originated at the annual convention of the Conference on College Composition and Communication in 2001. After participating in several panels at CCCC about literacy research, we realized—at the 2001 WPA Breakfast, to be precise—that we knew enough people doing research on women's literacy to make a book. We began immediately by organizing a roundtable for the 2002 meeting in Chicago, calling it "Advances in the Study of Women's Literacies: New Directions on Current Research." In addition to Kim Donehower, Keith Walters, Rhea Estelle Lathan (who all show up in this volume), and the two of us, we also included Janet Carey Eldred, Mary Trachsel, and Gesa Kirsch. In the summer of 2001 we wrote a call for papers, which we sent to a list of possible contributors.

But then September 11 happened.

Like many other Americans, we began to see how crucial it is that we begin to think more comprehensively—some would say "globally"—if we are to appreciate how our culture and our interests are connected to those of our fellow human beings around the world. Stories about women in Afghanistan who risked the wrath of the Taliban to provide literacy for their daughters moved us to consider the price women around the world have been willing to pay for literacy. Our notion of diversity expanded. We still believed that looking at the literacy practices of various U.S. women was very important, but now we wanted to broaden our vision to include studies of women's literacy in other parts of the world.

So we revised the call for papers and sent copies to everyone we knew who was working on literacy. We asked our colleagues in literacy studies to pass our flyers on to their graduate students. Both Deborah Brandt and Robert Brooke did so, and we are pleased to present here the work of some exciting young scholars. We also circulated our flyers at conferences. We soon had confirmation of what we had hoped: that a vital group of researchers within CCCC takes seriously the idea of examining not just literacy in general but specifically the literacy practices of women and girls.

And so we ended up with far more papers than any publisher would allow us to present. It was a genuine heartbreak to lose some essays, but we are confident that they will find their way into print elsewhere. We want to thank all those researchers who answered our initial call. And we want to encourage those scholars, as well as all whose work appears in this volume, to continue looking at what happens when women read and write.

This encouragement, this invitation, extends of course to those who read this volume. We wish you to join the researchers whose work we present here—and the women they write about—in the whirl of active inquiry that emulates both the cosmic course of the stars and the invisible dance of the slightest small matter.

—*B. D., Kennesaw, Georgia*
—*P. M., Urbana, Illinois*

Contributors

Kate Coffield, an English major, was introduced to computers while working at MIT in the early 1970s. Later, she earned an MA in Teaching English as a Foreign Language and taught first-year composition at the American University in Cairo, where she was also coordinator of the computer classroom in the English department. As a participant at Computers and Writing conferences, she met Gail Hawisher and Cindy Selfe and became interested in their research. She is currently director of web communications at AUC.

Ilene Whitney Crawford is associate professor of English and women's studies at Southern Connecticut State University in New Haven, where she teaches undergraduate courses in rhetoric and composition and graduate courses in feminist and rhetorical theory. Her previous work on the intersecting rhetorics of race and emotion appears in *Composition Forum, JAC*, and, with Donna Strickland, in the collection *A Way to Move: Rhetorics of Emotion and Composition Studies*. Her work in progress includes a piece with Donna Strickland on feminist WPA work, as well as an essay on how metaphors emergent in her research on Vietnam inform her composition pedagogy.

Beth Daniell is associate professor of English and director of composition at Kennesaw State University in the Atlanta suburbs. She teaches a variety of graduate and undergraduate courses in writing, rhetoric, and literacy theory. Her work has appeared in *Pre/Text, College Composition and Communication, JAC*, and the *Journal of Teaching Writing*, as well as in various collections, most recently *Teaching Rhetorica, Rhetorica Teaching*, edited by Kate Ronald and Joy Ritchie. She is the author of *A Communion of Friendship: Literacy, Spiritual Practice, and Women in Recovery*, a study of the uses of literacy among women in one Al-Anon group; the book appeared in the CCCC Studies in Writing and Rhetoric series, published by Southern Illinois University Press.

Mary K. DeShazer is professor of English and women's studies at Wake Forest University. She is the author *of Fractured Borders: Reading Women's Cancer Literature* (2005), *A Poetics of Resistance: Women Writing from El Salvador, South Africa, and the United States* (1994), and *Inspiring Women: Re-Imagining the Muse* (1987). She edited *The Longman Anthology of Women's Literature* (2001). Her current research focuses on literature written in response to hearings conducted by South Africa's Truth and Reconciliation Commission.

Kim Donehower is assistant professor of English at the University of North Dakota, where she directs the Red River Valley Writing Project. She has researched rural literacy in Southern Appalachia and in North Dakota and Minnesota. Her book *Rural Literacies*, co-written with Charlotte Hogg and Eileen Schell, is forthcoming in the CCCC Studies in Writing and Rhetoric series from Southern Illinois University Press. She is currently at work on a project on rural autodidacts.

Safia El-Wakil holds three degrees in English language and literature: a BA from Cairo University, Egypt; an MA from the American University of Beirut, Lebanon; and an MLitt from St. Hugh's College, Oxford University, UK. Her teaching experience has been at the American University of Beirut, the Arab University of Beirut, and the American University in Cairo, where she helped initiate and develop computer and web-based instruction in the writing program. El-Wakil practices the art of calligraphy and illumination (both traditional and digital) and holds exhibitions in Cairo. She has most recently trained to deliver a Cisco Systems Business Essentials online course for trainers and learners.

Kathryn T. Flannery is professor of English and director of women's studies at the University of Pittsburgh, where she enjoys teaching courses in literacy studies (including first-year writing), women's studies, and literature. She is the author of *Feminist Literacies, 1968–1975* (2005), *The Emperor's New Clothes: Literature, Literacy, and the Ideology of Style* (1995), and articles on literacy, performance pedagogy, and teaching women writers.

Gwendolyn Gong is a professor in the English Department at The Chinese University of Hong Kong and founding editor of the *Asian Journal of English Language Teaching*. She teaches discourse analysis, sociolinguistics, gender, psycholinguistics, and writing courses. With Sam Dragga, she wrote *Editing: The Design of Rhetoric*, recipient of the 1990 NCTE Achievement Award for Best Book of the Year. Gong and Dragga have also published *A Writer's Repertoire* and *A Reader's Repertoire*.

Gail E. Hawisher is professor of English and founding director of the Center for Writing Studies at the University of Illinois at Urbana-Champaign. Her work probes the many connections between literate activity and new information technologies and is reflected in her most recent book with Cynthia Selfe, *Literate Lives in the Information Age*. In 2004, she was honored to receive the Lynn Martin Award for Distinguished Women Faculty and the Campus Award for Excellence in Undergraduate Teaching. In 2005, she was named a University Distinguished Teacher/Scholar.

Catherine L. Hobbs is professor of English at the University of Oklahoma, where she teaches in the composition/rhetoric/literacy program and directs the first-year composition program. She most often writes on historical issues in literacy, having edited and introduced *Nineteenth-Century Women Learn to Write* (University Press of Virginia, 1995) and published *Rhetoric on the Margins of Modernity* (Southern Illinois University Press, 2002). She has also published *Elements of Autobiography and Life Narrative* (Longman, 2005).

Charlotte Hogg is assistant professor of English at Texas Christian University. Her work includes *From the Garden Club: Rural Women Writing Community* (University of Nebraska Press, 2006) and, with Kim Donehower and Eileen Schell, the forthcoming *Rural Literacies*, a part of the CCCC Studies in Writing and Rhetoric series, published by Southern Illinois University Press. Her work has been published in *Western American Literature, Great Plains Quarterly,* and elsewhere.

Rhea Estelle Lathan is an assistant professor at Michigan State University in the Writing, Rhetoric, and American Cultures Department. She is developing a manuscript entitled *Writing a Wrong: A Case of African American Adult Literacy Action in South Carolina, 1957–1962*, which investigates how literacy is defined and the way it functions in the context of the Adult Literacy Campaign of the civil rights movement. Her research interests include literacy in non-academic communities, writing instruction, African American studies, and women's studies.

Min-Zhan Lu is professor of English at the University of Louisville, where she teaches courses in composition theory and pedagogy, life writing, critical and cultural theory, and creative nonfiction. Her work includes "The Politics of Critical Affirmation" (*CCC*, 1999), *Shanghai Quartet: The Crossings of Four Women of China* (Duquesne University Press, 2001), and "An Essay on the Work of Composition: Composing English Against the Order of Fast Capitalism," which received the 2005 CCCC Richard Braddock Award for best article in *CCC*.

Peter Mortensen is an associate professor of English at the University of Illinois at Urbana-Champaign, where he was director of rhetoric from 1999 to 2006. He is co-author, with Janet Carey Eldred, of *Imagining Rhetoric: Composing Women of the Early United States* (2002) and co-editor, with Gesa E. Kirsch, of *Ethics and Representation in Qualitative Studies of Literacy* (1996). Currently, he is completing a book on rhetorics of illiteracy.

Katrina M. Powell is associate professor at Virginia Tech. She teaches courses in rhetorical theory, literacy studies, feminist autobiography, and pedagogy. The research in this collection is part of a larger project, *Rhetorics of Displacement: The Politics of Literacy, Letters, and Relocation in Shenandoah National Park*, forthcoming from University of Virginia Press in 2007. Based on this project, she received a National Endowment for the Humanities Fellowship for 2005–2006.

Kate Ronald is the Roger and Joyce L. Howe professor of English at Miami University, where she teaches graduate and undergraduate courses in composition and rhetoric and directs the Howe Writing Initiative in the School of Business. Her recent publications include *Reason to Believe: Romanticism, Pragmatism, and the Possibility of Teaching*, co-authored with Hephzibah Roskelly (State University of New York Press, 1998), and *Available Means: An Anthology of Women's Rhetoric(s)* (University of Pittsburgh Press, 2001), and *Teaching Rhetorica: Theory, Pedagogy, Practice* (Boynton/Cook, 2006), both co-edited with Joy Ritchie.

Hephzibah Roskelly is professor of English at University of North Carolina at Greensboro where she teaches courses in women's rhetoric, composition theory, and American literature. She directs the undergraduate program in women's and gender studies. Her most recent book is *Everyday Use: Rhetoric at Work in Reading and Writing* with David Jolliffe. She is from Louisville, Kentucky, and received her PhD from the University of Louisville in 1985. She is a former high school English teacher.

Cynthia L. Selfe is Humanities Distinguished Professor in the Department of English at The Ohio State University and co-editor of *Computers and Composition: An International Journal*. Selfe is an EDUCOM Medal award winner—the first woman and the first English teacher ever to receive this award for innovative computer use in higher education. Her numerous publications about computer use in educational settings include *Literacy and Technology in the 21st Century: The Perils of Not Paying Attention*. Selfe has served as the chair of the Conference on College Composition and Communication and the chair of the college section of the National Council of Teachers of English.

Bonnie Kathryn Smith is assistant professor of English at Belmont University in Nashville, Tennessee. She received her BA from the University of the South in 1997 and her PhD from the University of Wisconsin–Madison in 2003. Both her teaching and her research explore ways literacy informs life in community. Currently, she is investigating literacy among a group of women who are in recovery from prostitution and drug abuse.

Donna Strickland is assistant professor of English at the University of Missouri-Columbia. Her work has appeared previously in a variety of journals, including *College English, JAC*, and *Works and Days*, as well as in the collections *A Way to Move: Rhetorics of Emotion and Composition Studies* and *Tenured Bosses, Disposable Teachers: Writing Instruction in the Managed University*. She is currently completing a book on the managerial affect of composition studies.

Keith Walters, a sociolinguist, teaches in the Applied Linguistics department at Portland State University. Much of his research focuses on language and identity in North Africa, and Tunisia in particular. He is co-author of two textbooks, *Everything's an Argument, with Readings* and *What's Language Got to Do with It?* Volunteer work with a local hospice helps remind him that the world is larger than the view from his office window.

Shevaun Watson is assistant professor of English at the University of South Carolina where she teaches advanced writing, rhetorical theory and criticism, American literature, and African American rhetoric. Her current book project explores the role of testimony in the A.M.E. Church in Philadelphia in the late-eighteenth century and the Denmark Vesey slave conspiracy in Charleston in 1822. Her other research interests include slave/plantation literacy, rhetoric in the eighteenth-century South, writing centers, and writing program administration.

Morris Young is associate professor of English at Miami University in Oxford, Ohio, where his research and teaching focus on composition and rhetoric, literacy studies, and Asian American literature. His book *Minor Re/Visions: Asian American Literacy Narratives as a Rhetoric of Citizenship* (Southern Illinois University Press, 2004) received the 2004 W. Ross Winterowd Award for the most outstanding book in composition theory from *JAC* and the Association of Teachers of Advanced Composition; and in 2006, it received the Outstanding Book Award from the Conference on College Composition and Communication.

Introduction—
Researching Women and Literacy:
Usable Pasts, Possible Futures

Peter Mortensen
Beth Daniell

I.
HERE AND NOW

Several years ago, Patricia Bizzell characterized the preceding decade of historical work in rhetorical studies as one that had yielded astounding new knowledge about women rhetors. This resulted, she argues, as much from the savvy application of "traditional tools of research" as from the use of "methods which violate some of the most cherished conventions of academic research" ("Feminist" 16). We believe the same is true of the scholarship on women's literacy that appeared in the final years of the twentieth century. Those years saw publication of such path-breaking books as Caroline Heller's *Until We Are Strong Together* (1997), Anne Ruggles Gere's *Intimate Practices* (1997), Shirley Wilson Logan's *"We Are Coming"* (1999), and Jacqueline Jones Royster's *Traces of a Stream* (2000), as well as important edited collections such as Catherine Hobbs's *Nineteenth-Century Women Learn to Write* (1995).[1] All demonstrate a sustained intellectual commitment to understanding women's literacy by both observing established conventions of research in literacy studies and by advancing innovative methods that push the making of knowledge into new spaces of inquiry.

Taking these accomplishments as a point of departure, this collection of original essays emphasizes the variety of approaches and subject matter that will characterize the next generation of research on women and literacy. Building on and critiquing scholarship in literacy studies, composition studies, rhetorical theory, gender studies, postcolonial theory, and cultural studies, contributors necessarily discuss at length what literacy is—or, rather, what literacies are. Yet their strongest interest is in documenting and theorizing women's lived experience of these literacies. In the chapters that follow, contributors answer questions that focus on:

- the expansive diversity of women's literacies within the United States, including, but not limited to, the dynamic relations that exist among women, literacy, economic position, class, race, sexuality, and education;
- relations among women, literacy, and capitalism in the United States and abroad, including changes in women's private and domestic literacies, the evolution of technologies of literacy, and women's experience of the commodification of literacies; and
- the emergent role of women in a globally interdependent world, including the global commercialization of literate experience, the possibility of generalizing about women's literacy, and covert scenes of literate activity achieved despite huge obstacles.

We have arranged the collection's fifteen chapters in two parts: "Women's Literacies Situated Locally: Past, Present, and Future" and "Women's Literacies in a Globally Interdependent World." In doing so, we do not mean to suggest that there exists a significant boundary between the local and the global, conceptually or materially. Rather, we see the division as heuristic. It emphasizes possible articulations between the complexities we encounter when we choose to study seemingly indigenous performances of gender and literacy, and those complexities that become apparent when we consider the social, economic, and political networks that link place to place and time to time.

It is commonplace to arrange an edited collection into sections, with chapters sequenced appropriately therein. To be sure, such sequencing encourages one way of reading while discouraging others. Consequently, the logic of the table of contents should not be trusted as the best guide to a truly generative encounter with chapters whose arguments emerge from the multiple intelligences of contributors who are themselves far from one mind on the subjects of gender and literacy. Thus, we provide three additional ways into the chapters that follow, two of them elaborated in the remainder of our introduction, and one that appears in the book's afterword.

In the next section, Usable Pasts, we examine antecedents to the scholarship represented in *Women and Literacy*. We do this with a two-fold purpose. First, we track trends in composition and rhetoric that have, over the past half-century, either enabled or disabled the study of women and literacy in relation to one another. We also selectively survey relevant influences exerted by other disciplines in the humanities and humanistic social sciences. Our account of the past often moves briskly; it is a prolegomenon to a more extensive history of women and literacy yet to be written. But it is sufficient for an immediate purpose: to help readers locate the contributions to this collection in a larger project of disciplinary "self-understanding," a project that demonstrates, as Thomas Miller and Joseph Jones have put it, that "the discipline has changed as it has become more broadly engaged with the arts of exercising power through language in everyday life" (434).

In the introduction's third section, Possible Futures, we read the book's chapters with and against one another. This happens in two ways. First, we illuminate two critical problems emergent across chapters. We are particularly interested in how authors take up, modify, and critique Deborah Brandt's notion of literacy sponsorship as it relates to women and gender. And in a similar vein, we explore how contributors treat the rewards of literacy, comparing accounts of emotional and material change. Second, we provide a comparative analysis of our authors' treatment of major issues in literacy studies: economy, technology, language, geography, and politics. The introduction culminates with a subsection that speculates on next steps for research on women and literacy.

Min-Zhan Lu extends this speculation in her provocative afterword. She searches out the connections contributors make to the processes of "fast capitalism" that are rapidly reshaping the global economy. In many chapters she finds evidence that it is not just literacy, and not just English-language literacy, but English-language literacy of a very specific type, that is influencing the life prospects of women and girls in developing nations worldwide. Lu is dubious of claims that mastery of English in oral and written forms will bring these women anything like the material wealth or emotional succor they deserve. She doubts, too, that scholars of literacy and gender can be of much practical help in improving the situation. Still, she asserts, only when the rhetoric of development and the logic of fast capitalism are pried apart—as many authors in this collection do—can we find the conceptual space for inquiry that might lead women to leverage literacy (not necessarily in English) against social and economic forces that run counter to their best interests.

II.
USABLE PASTS

Locating Histories

When the journal *College Composition and Communication*—and, argu-ably, the field of composition studies—celebrated its golden anniver-sary in 1999, *CCC* editor Joseph Harris filled two issues with articles he hoped would "construct a *usable past*" that might aid in "reshaping our actions as writers, teachers, intellectuals, activists, and administrators" (343). Certain keywords recur across the pages of both issues: literacy and gender are among the most prominent. In fact, literacy is referenced directly in all but three of the 17 articles Harris assembled, and two of those three invoke the word in a related form. Likewise, gender is wo-ven into a majority of the articles that make up the *CCC* retrospective. Yet these terms, so important now, were not yet part of the field's regu-lar lexicon a half-century before.[2] A brief foray into the *CCC* archive sets the stage for rereading two articles in Harris' special issues.

Literacy, as such, did not enter the literature of composition and rhetoric until Dudley Bailey complained in 1954 of the "overwilling-ness of English departments to assume the responsibility for college-level literacy" (40), and then it was many more years before literacy (apart from "writing" and "reading") became an object of analysis. Fleeting mention of Richard Hoggart's *The Uses of Literacy* in James Steel Smith's "Popular Culture and the Freshman: Three Questions" (*CCC*, December 1959) and his "Readership Scholarship" (*CCC*, Octo-ber 1964) presage the serious questions about literacy raised at the 1971 CCCC Annual Meeting in Cincinnati. At that meeting, partici-pants in a workshop titled "Is Literacy Enough?" sought to describe the "relative contributions of literacy to life," in which discussion "it became clear that the word 'literacy' needed itself to be defined" (284). Working toward a definition, participants agreed that "functional lit-eracy" should be understood "as distinct from cultural literacy," and all participants reportedly "accepted the idea that everyone—not just English instructors—be challenged constantly to push upward to-ward new frontiers of literacy" (284). With regard to this challenge, one participant suggested that all persons preparing for teaching ca-reers should minor in English, and that "all English majors should be required to take a minor in anthropology" (284). This latter recommen-dation resonates with scholarship informed by anthropological and sociological notions of literacy whose influence began to be felt throughout the field a decade later.

Gender has a more conspicuous early history in composition studies, though strictly as a term of art in discussions of English grammar.[3] Yet it is precisely these discussions that turned, in the late 1970s and early 1980s, to sexist language, and specifically to the use of the male pronoun to refer to collectivities that included women; for example, see Mary DeShazer's "Sexist Language in Composition Textbooks: Still a Major Issue?" (*CCC*, February 1981). Laying the groundwork for such arguments, however, were earlier deliberations, such as those in a workshop at the 1971 Annual Meeting that grew out of "[i]nformed papers about the Women's Liberation Movement in general, and about women in the academic profession in particular" that were delivered by Marian Musgrave and Florence Howe ("The Position" 283). Making gender inclusive on the page and in the profession was formidable and defining work, indeed. In 1960, Edwin Sauer could quote with approval—and without printed rejoinder—a student composition in which the author asserted, "The woman that works is the neuter gender in a language that doesn't recognize one" (8). By 1978, when William Coles bristled that passages in the "man(or woman)uscript" of his "Teaching the Teaching of Composition" had been subjected to "desexing or unsexing or non-sexing" (207), Julia Stanley and Susan Robbins Wolfe could reply by claiming, "Since Coles evidently equates gender and sex, his continual use of the masculine pronoun amounts to little more than homosexual prose; the editor's annoying intrusion of the feminine pronoun must have resulted in *coitus interruptus*" (405). Stanley and Wolfe's indictment of Coles' conflation of gender and sex, not to mention the sexual politics of the insult they hurl, foreshadow theoretical contributions to the literature of composition studies that would reach critical mass after a decade's more work.

The "usable pasts" commemorated in the fiftieth volume of *CCC* are significant for their explicit theorizing of those pasts, theorizing that draws extensively from critical vocabularies that had evolved in the field over the preceding fifteen years or so. Of particular interest in this regard, and germane to the aims of this book, are two articles: Joy Ritchie and Kathleen Boardman's "Feminism in Composition: Inclusion, Metonymy, and Disruption," and Beth Daniell's "Narratives of Literacy: Connecting Composition to Culture." It would be a stretch to say that these articles are in dialogue, yet there is an unmistakable, though largely implicit, confluence of interest in the authors' theorizing of gender and literacy. Making this confluence visible, as we do in the remainder of this section, is an important step toward our later framing of contributors' approaches to gender and literacy.

The thirty-year history of feminism in composition that Ritchie and Boardman survey is characterized by compositionists' encounters with social constraints on women *qua* women, followed by the naming of these constraints, followed by collective efforts to disrupt the language and logic that normalize such constraints.[4] They conclude that, in composition studies, "feminism has been most challenging and disruptive and also provided a sense of alliance and inclusion when it has maintained a dialogical relationship between theory and experience" (602). Ritchie and Boardman round out their retrospective by remarking that colleagues in composition, particularly feminist colleagues, "have only begun to explore effective ways to connect our research to wider public concerns and debates about literacy" (603). We understand these debates to be social forums in which the terms of women's gendered performance as writers and readers are negotiated. What is being negotiated are answers to questions of agency: Who writes and is read? What is writing allowed to do—when and for whom? The agency defined by answering these questions entails, according to Ritchie and Boardman, "inclusion and proliferation of difference, multiplicity, and uncontainable excess"—all of which is embodied and localized, judging by the examples they offer (603). Thus, when Ritchie and Boardman posit "accounts of agency that exceed limited ideas of the determined subject," we appreciate these accounts as narratives of literacy that construct realities whose complexity owes much (but certainly not all) to the particularities of place and time (603).

Daniell, for her part, expresses distrust of literacy narratives that are not carefully located in place and time. In this spirit, she critiques the "great leap" theory of orality and literacy that composition studies appropriated from anthropology, sociology, classics, and literary theory. The "great leap" theory suggests that so-called primitive and modern peoples (and their cultures) differ fundamentally owing to the cognitive and social transformations that occur when oral language practices yield to literate ones. Daniell describes efforts within composition studies to refute the great leap theory, but she worries that compositionists' cultural materialist remedy risks substitution of one grand narrative for another, the new narrative touting to extremes the liberatory promise of literacy. As a counter to both great leap and liberatory narratives, Daniell offers the notion of "little narratives," which "seldom make theoretical statements that claim to be valid for literate persons in general or literate cultures in general" (403). Instead, studies that advance little narratives of literacy assume "that literacy is multiple, contextual, and ideological," and that the "relationship between literacy and oppression or freedom is rarely as simple" as great leap or liberatory narratives insist (403). Such studies, Daniell observes, tend to take gender seriously: "many of the little narratives—but not all—are written by women, and many of their subjects—but not all—are women" (403). In contrast, we would add, liberatory narratives often end up subordinating gender to class, and great leap theorizing typically ignores gender altogether—though, as Marianna Torgovnick reminds us, "Sooner or

later those familiar tropes for primitives become the tropes conventionally used for women" (17).

Reflecting on the intersection of Daniell's argument with Ritchie and
Boardman's, then, we see how composition studies' current theorizing
of gender and literacy occupies overlapping conceptual space, wherein
both constructs are mutually constituted in relation to power, and
where power is conditioned in part by local and temporal circumstances of enormous complexity.

Borrowing Histories

Many of the articles in the *CCC* fiftieth anniversary issues take notice of
particular ideas—questions and methods—that have been adapted
from other disciplines. Some of these ideas have had a lasting influence
on how colleagues treat gender and literacy in their research. It is therefore worth scrutinizing these ideas, as well as the processes by which
they have been borrowed and put to use. This section examines borrow-
ings that have been well documented; the next section takes up borrow-
ings that are less frequently recognized. In both sections, the links
between gender and literacy are not always obvious, so they must be
teased out with some analytical effort.

Like themed issues of scholarly journals, edited essay collections
are usually intended to intervene in ongoing disciplinary conversations: to summarize, interpret, evaluate, forecast, and connect. As artifacts viewed retrospectively, essay collections also reflect particular
moments of intellectual ferment. Such is the case with *Perspectives on
Literacy* (1988), edited by Eugene Kintgen, Barry Kroll, and Mike Rose.
The editors express concern that "[l]iteracy as a cover term is so broad
that it must almost be defined for each occasion on which it is used," to
which they add, "Just as a single definition of literacy is insufficient, so
is scrutiny from within the confines of a single academic discipline"
(xv). They explain that the collection isolates "essential background
reading" (xix), while advancing no "privileged perspective, but rather
various ways of investigating a complicated and multidimensional
topic" (xix).

Prominent in the first two sections of *Perspectives on Literacy* are
works from beyond the realm of composition studies that either advance or critique the "literacy thesis."[5] It is introduced by its primary
exponents: Eric Havelock in "The Coming of Literate Communication
to Western Culture," a 1980 *Journal of Communication* article that extends an argument begun in *Preface to Plato* (1963), and Jack Goody and
Ian Watt in their 1963 *Comparative Studies in Society and History* article,
"The Consequences of Literacy." Goody and Watt begin by observing
that "man's biological evolution shades into prehistory when he

becomes a language-using animal; add writing, and history proper begins" (304), and conclude that "[i]t is probable that it is only the ana-
lytic process that writing itself entails, the written formalization of
sounds and syntax, which make possible the habitual separating out
into formally distinct units of the various cultural elements whose in-
divisible wholeness is the essential basis of the 'mystical participation' ... characteristic of the thinking of non-literate peoples" (345).

There is little in these foundational expressions of the literacy thesis
that speaks directly to gender, save the ubiquity of male pronouns and
the occasional sexist reference. Still, it is possible to draw some infer-
ences. For example, Goody and Watt maintain, "on the whole there is
less individualization of personal experience in oral cultures" compared with literate ones, such that "the techniques of reading and writing are undoubtedly of very great importance" in establishing the
"complicated set of complementary relationships between individuals in a variety of roles" that is characteristic of literate cultures (339).
Further, Goody and Watt venture that "writing, by objectifying words,
and by making them and their meaning available for much more pro-
longed and intensive scrutiny than is possible orally, encourages private thought," a type of cognition that is essential to "personal
awareness of individualization" (339). For evidence that Goody (if not
Watt) might have imagined such individualization as governing the
lived experience of gender, consider Goody's contemporaneous "On
Nannas and Nannies," in which he reports on how the terms in his title
evolved in literate English culture to structure related roles for grandmothers (tied by kinship) and nannies (female caregivers situated in a
labor market). Further, Goody asserts that the derivative term
"nancy," when applied to men, is meant to impugn their masculinity. It
would seem, then, that among the consequences specified by the literacy thesis are linguistic constructs that have the power to impose and
enforce a gendered social order.

Some years later, Walter Ong adopted this line of reasoning in his fu-
sion of humanistic and social scientific theorizing of literacy. In *Interfaces of the Word* (1977), for example, Ong associates literacy with the
rational cognition he believes is characteristic of men, and ascribes the
emotion and immediacy of orality to women (22–29). Then, in *Fighting
for Life* (1981), published a year before *Orality and Literacy,* Ong contends
that the agonistic rhetoric of antiquity that persists in literate cultures
today arose "to counterbalance the overwhelming femininity of earlier
stages of human existence" (188). Indeed, Ong positions "[f]ulsome
public praise" as "a kind of public mothering ... in oral and residually
oral cultures around the globe" (110).

As we hope is obvious by now, linking literacy to gender in the context of the literacy thesis is a strenuous activity that pays marginal re-

turns, and so it is unsurprising that gender is not foregrounded in the texts that *Perspectives on Literacy* presents as critical responses to Havelock, Goody, and Watt.[6] Indeed, most critical engagements with their work, as well as with important elaborations by Walter Ong and David Olson, downplay gender as a category of analysis.

Forgotten Influences

But what do we see when we look back before the years of the field's engagement with the literacy thesis, roughly 1963 through the early 1990s? We see, in a word, women. Not in abundance, of course, but over the decades from 1900 through the early 1960s, women do in fact populate a number of studies wherein literacy and gender matter together. A good starting point for a brief retrospective is the sociolinguist Dell Hymes' critique of "The Consequences of Literacy," which characterized Goody and Watt's argument, and several others, as "oversimplified, where not simply wrong, in the light of what little ethnographic base we have" (25). Typifying this base for Hymes is Leonard Bloomfield's "Literate and Illiterate Speech" (1927), an essay widely remembered in composition studies for the irritating claim that "writing, of course, is merely a record of speech" (433). Bloomfield contends that in distinguishing between "good" and "bad" language—that is, "literate" and "illiterate" speech—it is "by a cumulation of obvious superiorities, both of character and standing, as well as of language" that "some persons are felt to be better models of conduct and speech than others. Therefore, even in matters where the [linguistic] preference is not obvious, the forms which these same persons use are felt to have the better flavor" (439). Bloomfield anchors this argument in his study of the Menomini of Wisconsin, a "compact" community of 1,700 with no written language, among whom the most "literate" (according to Bloomfield's reckoning of literacy) was Red-Cloud-Woman, a woman in her sixties. She "speaks a beautiful and highly idiomatic Menomini. She knows only a few words of English, but speaks Ojibwa and Potawatomi fluently, and, I believe, a little Winnebago. Linguistically, she would correspond to a highly educated American woman who spoke, say, French and Italian in addition to the very best type of cultivated, idiomatic English" (437).

Bloomfield, though dismissive of writing, makes several instructive points. First, he imagines an ethos inherent in literacy: whether one is deemed literate depends in part on who one is, not merely how one speaks. Second, in Bloomfield's view, a woman can possess the ethos requisite to be appraised the most literate person in her community. A third point, enabling of the first two, is that the operative binary in Bloomfield's structural analysis is literacy versus illiteracy, not literacy versus orality. The difference is significant, for with the ascendancy of the literacy thesis in the 1960s, the literacy/orality dichotomy eclipsed the literacy/illiteracy distinction, thereby darkening a conceptual space in which Bloomfield and later researchers were able to situate literacy and gender in relation to one another. Typical explorations of the relationship are evident in the following examples.

In the early twentieth century, many—perhaps, most—comments on gender or women and literacy occur in the context of academic research on the working conditions of immigrants, poor whites, and (to a lesser extent) African Americans. A suggestive example is Nellie Mason Auten's "Some Phases of the Sweating System in the Garment Trades of Chicago," which appeared in the *American Journal of Sociology* in 1901. In this condensed version of her University of Chicago master's thesis, Auten reports detailed statistics on the literacy of Italian immigrants, noting that "[a]mong the women … seem to be the extremes of both literacy and illiteracy, while nearly all the men seem to have some education or at least to be able to speak English" (607). She ultimately ties her observations about literacy to a call for Chicago's public schools to accommodate the children of immigrants so that they might have the opportunity to learn "American ideas and ideals" by rubbing shoulders with "American children" (644). Literacy here is positioned as lubricating the social machinery of assimilation, machinery that functions inefficiently so long as there persists a striking disparity between men's and women's English-language literacy. Auten's article received immediate attention in *Literary Digest* (the forerunner of *Time* magazine), where it was noticed by author and activist Jack London, who mentioned it in a speech before an August 1901 meeting of the Socialist Democratic Party, a speech was subsequently collected in his *War of the Classes* (1905). But Auten's observation about the literacy of immigrant Italian women was lost in translation; London never mentioned it.[7]

Auten strongly implies that the workplace exploitation of Italian immigrant women extends to denial of access to educational resources. In her estimation, the women's poverty is not a consequence of their supposed illiteracy; it is the other way around. This argument is worked out more explicitly a decade later by sociologist (and social activist) Florence Kelley, also in the *American Journal of Sociology*, who insists that the "cotton industry everywhere, and at all times, pays such low wages that wives and children must eke out the family subsistence," one inevitable result being the "illiteracy" of women (309). Kelley's demand that communities underwrite "night-schools for illiterate adults" is part of a plan aimed at forcing the industry to take responsibility for the welfare of its female employees. As did Auten before her, Kelley understands that unfair labor practices produce what she calls illiteracy; she sees no evidence that poverty is a consequence of illiteracy.

Not surprisingly, academic discourse on labor, especially immigrant labor, often touched on questions of citizenship and literacy's relationship to it. Take, for example, political scientist Finla Crawford's analysis of data gathered in the first decade after New York began, in 1923, to require "certificates of literacy" of new voters. He concludes that "half of the women" eligible by age to vote "are not interested in the suffrage," but notes that women who do wish to qualify for voting pass the state's literacy test at a much higher rate than their male counterparts (344). Because of the "increased efficiency of the evening schools and special schools for foreign-born women," Crawford surmises that it is not literacy holding women back from the ballot box, but rather a lack of interest in political affairs (344). For Crawford, women's literacy certainly bears scrutiny, but ultimately is not labeled a cause of the social problem he examines.

In retrospect, the social-class analyses presented by Auten, Kelley, and Crawford may seem thin, but the value of their innovation—thinking about women and literacy in relation to their economic circumstances—should not be underestimated. This value becomes more apparent when we compare their writing with accounts of women and literacy that routinely circulated in the popular press. The press, from mass circulation daily newspapers to weekly news magazines, was awash in reporting that blamed women's poverty and vice on their inability to read and write. That blame was often sensationalized by racist innuendos. The *New York Times* took this approach with some regularity, especially in its coverage of African American women and poor white women in the South. For example, in reporting on an annulment trial in 1925, the *Times* repeatedly labeled "illiterate" the letters that Alice Jones Rhinelander wrote to her husband, Leonard Kip Rhinelander, after her African American heritage was disclosed to him. The *Times'* stories were structured to convey the strong impression that Mrs. Rhinelander's illiteracy, evident in the sometimes "unpleasant, crudely expressed sentiments" of her letters, indexed a type of mental deficiency informed by racist assumptions about African Americans" ("Loved Rhinelander" 1; see also Lewis and Ardizzone).

To be sure, literacy as a racialized construct runs through certain strains of academic scholarship in the early twentieth century, most notably that published by researchers influenced by sociobiological theories such as eugenics. Witness the characterization as illiterate of Deborah Kallikak in Henry Goddard's *Kallikak Family* (1912). Such characterizations tended to fix on the ill judgment of illiterate, "mentally defective" women, the likelihood being that they would bear the children of equally defective men. But by and large, for the better part of the century, academic scholarship that linked U.S. women and literacy tended to challenge prevailing popular assumptions on the subject. Much the

same can be said for scholarship that discusses the literacy—specifically, the cultural literacy—of women elsewhere in the world. For instance, in a 1931 international affairs journal, it is reported that M. K.
Gandhi, challenged as to why women's illiteracy was so much higher in
Kashmir and Hyderabad than in British India, replied "that if the illiteracy was greater there it was due to the negligence of the ruler or because
the population was predominantly Mohammedan" (735). And by mid-
century, scholars such as sociologist Robert Lynd were curious—
though hardly certain—about how women's literacy shaped the transforming cultural and political economies of the People's Republic of
China and the Soviet Union.

About this time, in late 1955 to be exact, E. E. Evans-Pritchard delivered a lecture at Bedford College, University of London, entitled "The
Position of Women in Primitive Societies and In Our Own." In it he challenged the arguments of Margaret Mead and Simone de Beauvoir, who
had recently asserted, in Evans-Pritchard's words, "that the tempera-
mental and social differences between the sexes are simply a product of
cultural conditioning" (55). He labeled this thinking "a reification that
explains nothing—certainly not so universal a feature of social life as
the leading role men play in it" (55). When the lecture appeared in print
for the first time a decade later, anthropologist Ruth Landes took
Evans-Pritchard to task for his narrowness. Contrasting the volume of
Evans-Pritchard's collected writing with the essays by various authors
collected in *Women in the Modern World* (1967), Landes notes that
"[w]omen scholars who approach the subject ... may offer glimpses into
an unofficial woman's subworld that is freer" than a male anthropologist can access (576). She praises the contributors for documenting
women's various advancements, literacy being one of them, but she
laments that men make certain that "these advances largely benefit the
ruling groups and so remain shelved for most of the population" (576).
Indeed, Landes believes that the chapter on the United States, which
features a full section on women's literacy education, reproduces this
problem in that it "ignore[s] Negro and American Indian women, and
... also ignores Spanish speakers" (576). The contributors to *Women in
the Modern World* may not make generalizations, as does Evans-
Pritchard, about women and women's literacy based on a masculinist
experience of culture, but they are inheritors of his tendency to ignore
race and ethnicity in the analysis of gender.

Landes' critique of this shortcoming anticipates the more systematic
appraisals of anthropological studies of women that would soon be assembled by Michelle Zimbalist Rosaldo and Louise Lamphere in
Women, Culture, and Society (1974) and Rayna Reiter in *Toward an Anthropology of Women* (1975). A number of chapters in these collections consider what it means for a woman to be literate under particular cultural

circumstances at a particular moment in time. But Rosaldo and Lamphere's and Reiter's collections were exceptional in their day. General academic inattention to the subject of women's literacy was the norm before the appearance of the explicitly feminist sociological and anthropological scholarship of the late 1980s and 1990s, scholarship to which researchers in composition studies now often turn in their work on literacy.[8]

Much the same can be said of scholarship in literature and literary history. As late as 1980, Annette Kolodny could remark, "A creature from Mars seeking knowledge of the Earth through reading journals like this one [*New Literary History*], for example, might, with some difficulty, eventually surmise that there are, in fact, two sexes inhabiting the planet. But that creature might never divine that women, like men, were literate and had enjoyed some measure of literary activity" (591). It took books like Janice Radway's ethnography, *Reading the Romance* (1984/1991), and Cathy Davidson's literary history, *Revolution and the Word* (1986), to confirm that serious scholarship on women's literacy had to begin, in deference to Kolodny's Martian, by establishing women as writers and readers.

Crossing the Divide

As we have suggested, access to a modest "usable past" was lost when composition studies turned toward Havelock's and Goody and Watt's literacy thesis. The field's subsequent engagement with E. D. Hirsch's writing on "cultural literacy" was largely received as an extension of the literacy thesis, especially by those who objected to Hirsch's constrained vision of culture and normative sense of literacy. Yet, as Patricia Bizzell argued in 1988, Hirsch's formulation of cultural literacy has served as "a corrective to 'Great Divide' literacy theories" (144). In and of itself, the corrective is modest; after all, both theories assume a unitary culture that must be protected from corruption. However, Bizzell's assertion pointed the way—along with other poststructuralist urgings—toward scholarship that would expand the meanings of "culture" and "literacy," along with exploring gender and literacy as interanimating concepts in lived experience.

But how best to explore these concepts? How best, following Shirley Brice Heath, to "estimate" their meaning? As the field contended with Hirsch's unitary notion of cultural literacy, with its emphasis on consuming rather than producing culture, Heath reminded scholars of the "power of history" and "ethnography" to provide "data-based comparisons" across boundaries of time and place that simply cannot be accomplished by argument in the realm of theory alone (97). Heath was responding favorably to Anne Ruggles Gere's "Kitchen Tables and Rented Rooms: The Extracurriculum of Composition," in which Gere explored, among other things, the practices of nineteenth-century women who, while excluded for the most part from higher education, built institutions—women's clubs—in which literacy was central to women's "cultural work" (85). Also among the respondents to Gere's article, which was based on her 1993 CCCC chair's address, was Jean Ferguson Carr. Carr encouraged scholars to embrace Gere's research agenda, but urged them to do so while continuing to study schooled literacy curricula, especially curricula authored by and for women, this because "[t]he academic and the extracurricular can never fully be quarantined from each other" (95). For Carr, the "academic world," like the extracurriculum, was and remains the site of "alternative literacies" and "resistant or differential uses for reading and writing" (96). Like Gere, Carr calls us to "rethink the notion that influence and tradition are produced in straight lines," while also recognizing that "interference" in the transmission of tradition "can come from within the academy" (97).

With their emphasis on women's literacy as productive of culture, Gere and her respondents gave encouragement to the slow but steady emergence of historical research on women and literacy that has continued to this day. But at the time they wrote, as English studies journals and edited collections filled pages that explored cultures of literacy new and old, explicit and sustained attention to gender and literacy was still quite scant. One exception is Jacqueline Jones Royster's "Perspectives on the Intellectual Tradition of Black Women Writers" in *The Right to Literacy* (1990), which grew out of a presentation at the 1988 Right to Literacy conference cosponsored by the Modern Language Association, The Ohio State University, and the Ohio Humanities Council.[9] Other exceptions include Gere's "Literacy and Difference in 19th-Century Women's Clubs" in *Literacy: Interdisciplinary Conversations* (1994), and Susan Miller's "Things Inanimate May Move: A Different History of Writing and Class" (1994), the latter a response to Gere's "Kitchen Tables" essay. And among the many excellent chapters in Catherine Hobbs' edited collection, *Nineteenth-Century Women Learn to Write* (1995), is Shirley Wilson Logan's "Literacy as a Tool for Social Action among Nineteenth-Century African American Women." We name these four essays because each evolved into a book that explores the social processes by which literacy defines cultural spaces that are marked primarily by gender. We look briefly at how Logan, Royster, and Gere situate women in relation to literacy before turning to consider how Miller implicates literacy in the formation of gender.

Logan, in *"We Are Coming": The Persuasive Discourse of Nineteenth-Century Black Women* (1999), and Royster, in *Traces of a Stream: Literacy and Social Change Among African American Women* (2000), study a number of African American women who were affiliated with clubs locally and nationally, while clubs themselves are the central focus of Gere's *Intimate Practices: Literacy and Cultural Work in U.S. Women's Clubs* (1997).[10] Logan analyzes speeches and essays by such clubwomen as Fannie Barrier Williams, finding in them particular rhetorical strategies—primarily, what Kenneth Burke called "identification"—aimed at forming a community that could be mobilized to produce "race uplift" (110). For her part, Royster, at a critical juncture in her book, engages in similar analysis, but then strives to show how the prolific literate activities of Williams, as well as Mary Church Terrell, Anna Julia Cooper, Charlotte Forten Grimké, and others, follow in a tradition dating back to the earliest years of the Republic— and earlier still. Calling her approach *"historical ethnography,"* Royster argues for situating African American women's literate practices in a continuum of cultural developments that reach back before the African diaspora and that survive the unremitting violence of slavery in the United States as well as the intense racism of "free" existence in the antebellum North (11). Doing so allows Royster "to assign the women" she studies "a point of view, authority, and agency in their intellectual work" as a means of accounting for their cultural productivity (274). And although the women Royster studied worked together—some closely— toward collective ends, she is insistent that her "examination of African American women's literate experiences" demonstrates that "African American women are not monolithic in terms of either personhood or literate practices" (7). Moreover, she contends that only through developing "'thick descriptions' of the literate practices of a particular group in the company of similar descriptions of other groups" will we arrive at a much-needed "concrete sense of human variety in the use of literacy" (6).

Gere looks deep into the archives of various women's clubs to fashion her own thick descriptions of the concrete practices to which Royster refers. And like Royster, Gere explains why these practices have not been widely visible and accorded value. Ironically, she writes, "The highly social nature of clubwomen's literacy may help account for its receiving only slight attention; because it does not fit the dominant model, it is harder to see" (37). For example, while "clubwomen's reading and writing about philanthropy introduced new themes to the nation's public policy discourses," evidence of such remained in archives to which access was tightly controlled (15). According to Gere, "These controls made intimacy possible; by insisting on keeping information about themselves and their activities out of public view, clubwomen created the spaces in which they could develop intimate relationships with one another," with the consequence that women's clubs emerged at the turn of the century as "sites of both cultural production and calibration" (45, 176).

While Logan, Royster, and Gere foreground *women* in their archival studies of literacy, Miller, in her work, stresses *gender* as a central category of analysis. Miller appreciates Gere's focus on the "ordinary texts" produced by clubwomen, but, in her response to the "Kitchen Tables" essay, she is wary about using the term "extracurriculum" because it and similar terms "imply that their opposites have always and everywhere been privileged sites of cultural formation" ("Things Inanimate" 106). It is Miller's contention, in *Assuming the Positions* (1998), that such sites are narrative constructions whose maintenance over time depends heavily, if not exclusively, on how gender figures into lessons on ordinary writing, wherever they occur and whomever they involve. "Writing gender," she contends, "is a literate diversion that symbolically enacts entitlement. Ordinary writing organizes gender to fund the exchange of its ready sexual currency for yet another cultural property, discursive assurances of class superiority" (149).[11] Consequently, this "gender doxa," as Miller calls it, "never articulates the categories of men and women apart from its primary purpose, to manage anxieties about class standing" (172). Consistent with this *doxa*, Miller found in her archive—centuries-old commonplace writing held by the Virginia Historical Society—that lessons in literacy were never separate from lessons on the expectations of gender. Narratives of gender, bonded inextricably to narratives of literacy, amounted to a "cultural pedagogy" that helped produce, then reproduce, distinctly American "men" and "women" as axiomatic categories of knowledge and discrete loci of social performance (172).

Miller's intensive theorizing of gender and literacy in relation to social class is unusual among scholars who address women and literacy in historical perspective. True, Gere delves into the class tensions evident in middle-class clubwomen's outreach to their working-class sisters, and she studies working-class women's clubs as well, just as Royster does. But the contention that gender is deployed in literacy lessons as a way of normalizing class stratification (and thereby mollifying class antagonism) is by far strongest in Miller's historical inquiry.

A similar array of theoretical positions on gender and literacy is apparent in the other major strand of "empirical" (in Heath's sense) research on literacy: ethnographic inquiry. For example, in "On the Subjects of Class and Gender in 'The Literacy Letters,'" Linda Brodkey takes up a position akin to Miller's as she examines how educational discourse in the context of an adult literacy tutorial inscribes class-stratified subject positions in correspondence that is seemingly about a middle-class tutor and a working-class student's "shared concerns as mothers" (100). Brodkey's approach, like Miller's, affords a view of literacy practices in which the agency one exercises as a reader and writer—especially from a socially subordinate position—may be illusory, or at least less powerful than one imagines.[12] Other ethnographic studies in the field that seek to understand how apparent limits on agency are resisted as people assemble literate strategies that enable them to produce cultural spaces in which they can redefine their lives.

Such is the case in Ellen Cushman's *The Struggle and the Tools: Oral and Literate Strategies in an Inner City Community* (1998), which foregrounds the efforts of women to secure the services they need to live with dignity. Cushman features women and their children prominently for two reasons: "my own gender made it easier for me to interact with the females in the study" and "[b]eyond this, though, there just weren't many adult males in this area and my access to them was limited" (xi). She found that because of women's numerical dominance in the community she studied, they "held the power and status in this community, positions that made them the cultural brokers of knowledge needed to negotiate public service institutions" (xii). The access granted to Cushman enabled her to see how the women used this power and status: on one level, they made collective efforts to share strategies for filling out and filing forms that would bring them resources, but they also used literate strategies to theorize and critique the institutional systems from which they sought resources. The latter, political uses of literacy would not have been visible to someone who had not adopted the participant-observer stance that Cushman's gender- and class-inflected subjectivity allowed her to inhabit with authenticity. In other words, documentary evidence alone could not have led Cushman to her conclusions about the women's literate agency. She had to be present with them in their daily lives in order to see critical documents in use.

Caroline Heller's ethnography of San Francisco's Tenderloin Women Writers Workshop, *Until We Are Strong Together* (1997), witnesses the production of cultural agency not in everyday documentary transactions, but in the concerted effort of a group of women to compose in genres that permit the critique of both self and institutions. The interpretive burden placed on the ethnographer in such a situation is not trivial. As Heller puts it, "It became clear to me that to look at the workshop through a lens that focused too broadly on the political functions of the workshop or too narrowly on the obvious literacy activity occurring would leave out far too much" (17). It was only after spending a considerable amount of time in the workshop that Heller recognized its political functions, and it took still longer to understand the purpose of that critique: the women "came to be reassured that they had lived lives that were of value and that could be—through the precision of their own words—felt, understood, and remembered by others" (18). Writing from this position of empowerment, the women of the workshop created a permanent record of the circumstances, large and small, surrounding their existence in one of the "roughest" of San Francisco's "rough neighborhoods" (6).

In view of Heller's findings, literate practices calculated to surrender cultural power might seem an ironic reversal of achievements made by women like those whose literacies Cushman and Heller describe. This is not the case for women seeking the spiritual surrender intrinsic to twelve-step recovery. In *A Communion of Friendship: Literacy, Spiritual Practice, and Women in Recovery* (2003), Beth Daniell prefers to characterize this surrender as paradoxical, not ironic. True, the reading and writing that women of the Mountain City Al-Anon meeting engage in leads to spiritual development marked by acceptance of powerlessness over all worldly things that a person cannot change. But, as Daniell argues, this acceptance is, in fact, empowering, even liberating, in the material realm. Some women use this power to "transform" their circumstances, others to "endure" them (144, 151). But what is most important to notice, Daniell claims, is that whatever change literacy brings does not happen "automatically"—it happens by way of a continuous stream of social literacy events—and it happens in ways that have meaning and effects in a "limited and local sense" (151, 144).

This is not to say, however, that the "little" or "local" narratives of gendered literacy characterized by Cushman, Heller, and Daniell are not resonant with larger discourses that attend, for example, to forces that implicate the local in material and political economies of region, nation, and globe. Documenting and interpreting this resonance is the work Deborah Brandt accomplishes in *Literacy in American Lives* (2001). Although Brandt does not focus exclusively on the literacy of women, she does use gender as a category of analysis to illuminate the differential access people have to resources that enable them to gain and use literacies as gateways to economic advancement (or at least survival). For example, she tells what Daniell would call "little narratives" about Raymond Branch and Dora Lopez, both born in 1969, "whose differences in family background and literacy achievement embody the familiar breakdown along categories of gender, race, and class" (172). While Brandt is certainly interested in the particular differences that distinguish Raymond from Dora (she refers to them by first name), her larger project is to demonstrate how such differences are generations in the making, and how current economic and cultural conditions draw on global resources to maintain invidious differences—gendered differences among them—whose origins reach deep into the nation's past. Reading Brandt's study, with its blend of historical and qualitative inquiry, reminds us, as Royster's historical ethnography does, that much is gained by linking detailed local narratives of women and literacy with accounts of the networks of resources that enable and constrain people's use of literacy in their lives.

Expanding Horizons

The historical and ethnographic scholarship just reviewed, and the larger body of literature it represents, focus primarily on the literacy of women in the United States. But not entirely so. Both Royster and Brandt make deliberate gestures toward women whose literate practices are valued according to economies that extend historically and geographically beyond the nation's borders. It is exceptionally important that literacy researchers in composition studies continue to make these gestures—and make them with care and respect. We say this for two reasons. First, we see value in reconnecting with the tradition of research on women and literacy in the humanistic social sciences that was interrupted by the great leap theorizing of the 1960s, 1970s, and early 1980s. Second, so much of the contemporary discourse on women and globalization—and, in particular, the popular and policy strands of that discourse—would benefit greatly by an infusion of research that attends to, rather than makes unsubstantiated claims about, the literate practices of women around the world.

The literature on women and literacy prior to the 1960s is not abundant, yet it explores a range of questions that remain relevant today. For example, what conditions do recently emigrated women face in the U.S. workplace? Such women today generally are not from Italy, Sweden, or Poland, as they were in Auten's day a century ago. Rather, they hail from countries around the globe, many with ties to the United States created by decades of aggressive military and economic posturing abroad. A century ago, Auten wondered how literacy functioned for Italian immigrant women at home before they sailed for American shores. The same question could be asked about women from Vietnam, Guatemala, and Nigeria who, in recent years, have sought refuge and work in the United States. An adequate answer to this question requires knowledge of cultures around the globe and, specifically, knowledge of what literacy means to women's production of culture in those places. It would seem foolish, then, not to connect with a tradition of sociological and anthropological inquiry—to which scholars such as Auten, Lynd, and Landes contributed over the years—that has something to say about women and literacy in global contents.

The exigency is clear. Theorizing about the global expansion of U.S. cultural and economic power by the likes of Michael Hardt and Antonio Negri pays little attention to women, let alone literacy. Lee Quinby argues that Hardt and Negri's *Empire*, in which the authors advance the

notion of "multitude" as a globalized proletariat, overlooks the organized power of women's groups throughout the developing world.
Quinby points to Amartya Sen's *Development as Freedom* as a less
totalizing inquiry into globalization, in part because Sen is attuned to
the various roles literacy—especially women's literacy—can play in local democratic deliberation. At the same time, popular treatments of
globalization, such as Ted Fishman's best-selling *China, Inc.*, document
the effects of women's differential access to literacy along an urban/ru-
ral axis, but books like Fishman's have little to say about the cultural
conditions that have sustained such differences, and how they might
now be changing. Fishman's emphasis, instead, is on how increasingly
skilled labor in China will undoubtedly have implications (mostly negative) for business and labor in the United States.

Writing of the future of U.S. workers in a global economy, David
Shipler, in *The Working Poor: Invisible in America*, quotes statistics from
the National Adult Literacy Survey to make the case that low literacy in
the U.S. workforce will hasten the export of unskilled work to Sri Lanka,
India, and Mexico (139–40). And Jason DeParle, in *American Dream*, has
little more to say than Shipler does about literacy in his study of three
women and their families in the aftermath of the welfare reform undertaken by the federal government in the mid-1990s. Even Barbara
Ehrenreich, in her terrifically popular *Nickel and Dimed*, makes fairly
predictable assertions about women's literacy and its relation to the
work they perform.

How unfortunate that the subject of women and literacy gets short
shrift in theoretical and popular treatments of conditions attendant
upon the spread of global capitalism. Scholarly critique is certainly
warranted, yet, in our estimation, such critique best serves women as
the catalyst for next steps, among them research that we know must be
done, that we know how to do, but that is far from accomplished. A first
step in this regard: In 2001, when Ellen Cushman joined Kintgen, Kroll,
and Rose in updating *Perspectives on Literacy* as *Literacy: A Critical
Sourcebook* (2001), the editors added a chapter devoted to women's literacy outside the U.S. In that chapter, Lalita Ramdas concludes her argument with this powerful statement:

> When literacy can enable every woman and girl to walk fearlessly and
> confidently, alone and with her head held high, then and only then will
> she opt for literacy voluntarily. Reading and writing skills would then
> truly become a weapon with which each woman could be empowered to
> read and write her world, analyze and understand it, and where neces-
> sary transform it. That alone is true justice. (643)

We look forward to new work in our field that pursues the challenge to
researchers implicit in Ramdas' definition of social justice in global per-

spective. Already, scholars such as Bruce Horner and John Trimbur, in "English Only and U.S. College Composition" (*CCC,* 2002) and Min-Zhan Lu, in "An Essay on the Work of Composition: Composing English against the Order of Fast Capitalism" (*CCC,* 2004) are examining heretofore overlooked global-local tensions in composition's past and present. Many contributors to Andrea Lunsford and Lahoucine Ouzgane's *Crossing Borderlands* (2004) do the same, as do Gail Hawisher, Cynthia Selfe, Yi-Huey Guo, and Lu Liu in "Globalization and Agency" (2006), a study of women whose lives have been profoundly shaped by information technologies. It is imperative, we think, that this new trajectory sustain attention to women and literacy, and so we offer this volume as contributions to that effort.

III.
POSSIBLE FUTURES

Little Narratives of Women and Literacy

Informed by the literature reviewed in the previous section, *Women and Literacy: Local and Global Inquiries for a New Century* assembles chapters that stake out new territory—intellectual, ideological, geographical, and linguistic territory—for the study of literacy in composition and rhetoric. In Part I, we present eight chapters that focus on literacy and women in the United States. The first two chapters, "Feeling Literate: Gender, Race, and Work in Dorothy West's 'The Typewriter' " by Donna Strickland and "Crusader: Ethel Azalea Johnson's Use of the Written Word as a Weapon of Liberation" by Rhea Estelle Lathan, give vivid glimpses into the complexity of literacy among African American women. The next two chapters, Katrina Powell's "Virginia Mountain Women Writing to Government Officials: Letter of Request as Social Participation" and Kim Donehower's "Reconsidering Power, Privilege, and the Public/Private Distinction in the Literacy of Rural Women," are about the uses of literacy by Appalachian women during, respectively, the 1930s and contemporary times. Charlotte Hogg's contribution, "Sponsoring Clubs: Cultivating Rural Identities through Literacy," also concerns rural women, but this time older women residing in Hogg's native Nebraska. The last three chapters discuss literary reading and writing. Hephzibah Roskelly and Kate Ronald's "Literacy on the Margins: Louisa May Alcott's Pragmatic Rhetoric," Kathryn Flannery's "'Diverse in Sentiment and Form': Feminist Poetry as Radical Literate Practice, 1968–1975," and Bonnie Kathryn's Smith's "Branding Literacy: The Entrepreneurship of Oprah's Book Club" all show the variety of roles that literary writing can play for women writers and readers.

In Part II, we offer seven chapters about women's literacy in global contexts. The first of these chapters, "Professing 'Western' Literacy: Globalization and Women's Education at the Western College for Women" by Shevaun Watson and Morris Young, focusing on the international programs at Western College in Oxford, Ohio, serves as a segue from literacy in the U.S. to literacy in other parts of the world. The next two chapters recount stories of women's literacy in Northern Africa. Keith Walters' "Considering the Meanings of Literacy in a Postcolonial Setting: The Case of Tunisia" takes up the history of women's schooling in Tunisia, while Gail Hawisher, Cynthia Selfe, Kate Coffield, and Safia El-Wakil's "Women and the Global Ecology of Digital Literacies" reports on the literacy and digital expertise of two women at American University in Cairo, Egypt. The fourth chapter in Part II, Ilene Crawford's "The Emotional Effects of Literacy: Vietnamese Women Negotiating the Shift to a Market Economy," continues the interest in digital literacies, but this time from the perspective of younger women. The next two chapters, "Post-Apartheid Literacies: South African Women's Poetry of Orality, Franchise, and Reconciliation" and "Gender and Literacies: The Korean 'Comfort Women's' Testimonies," take up overtly political dimensions of literacy. Like contributors in the second section's last chapters in Part I, Mary DeShazer turns her attention to literary composition and its many uses by women in South Africa. Gwendolyn Gong explores the complexity and contradictions of literacy in regard to the sexual enslavement of Korean women by the Japanese army during World War II. In the last chapter, "The Outlook for Global Women's Literacy," Catherine Hobbs surveys demographic studies of women's literacy around the world. We think readers will find compelling Hobbs' commentary on the statistical data. *Women and Literacy* ends with an afterword by Min-Zhan Lu, "Reading Literacy Research Against the Grain of Fast Capitalism," wherein she takes up the question of reading the research we present here at a time when the United States exerts influence over many nations' economies.

As the remainder of our introduction unfolds, we discuss the critical issues and major themes that recur across chapters, survey the variety of research methods authors have adapted to their needs, and, finally, comment on lines of inquiry suggested by the research and researchers represented herein.

Critical Problems

The Continuum of Sponsorship

Many of our contributors either make passing reference to, or explicitly invoke, Brandt's notion of literacy sponsorship. In her influential article, "Sponsors of Literacy," Brandt defines sponsors as any agents, local or distant, concrete or abstract, who enable, support, teach, model, as well as recruit, regulate, suppress, or withhold literacy— and gain advantage by it in some way .... [They] lend their resources or credibility to the sponsored but also stand to gain benefits from their success, whether by direct repayment, or indirectly, by credit of association. ("Sponsors" 166–67)

But readers will notice that our contributors use this concept in ways that recast Brandt's formulation. As they do so, they stretch literacy sponsorship across a provocative conceptual continuum.

Watson and Young, for example, discuss a collaborative essay "sponsored," if you will, not only by a particular writing teacher, but also by the ideals of Western College for Women. Smith's research reveals a communal literacy, with individual readers of the same text sharing their written comments on a public website; the website is ostensibly sponsored by Oprah Winfrey and her company, but also by the readers who supply the content. Hogg's chapter first asserts that extension and garden clubs sponsor the literacy of the rural women in her small Nebraska hometown, but then argues that these women use the identities they forge to cultivate their own literacy, by way of researching and writing family histories. This literate activity in turn sponsors the literacy of younger women, including Hogg herself. Another example of self-sponsored literacy can be found in the mountain women whom Donehower observed and interviewed. Using literacies not required by outside sponsors, the women of Haines Gap employ their literacy to define their relations with family, community, spirituality, and self; for these women, literacy's rewards are not material prizes, but rather enhancements of what Donehower calls the "relational" self.

By using Brandt's concept of sponsorship, we see—perhaps more easily than we otherwise might—the literacies presented in other chapters in *Women and Literacy* as grounded in material and historical conditions. Flannery's research shows women whose poetic and political literacies are sponsored by feminist magazines and writing workshops of the 1970s. The chapters by DeShazer and Lathan discuss women's literacies that could be said to be sponsored by liberation movements, asking women to write in the service of social change for, respectively, indigenous peoples in South Africa and African Americans. Walters, Crawford, and Gong demonstrate how complicated sponsorship can be, insofar as the women, who are the focus of their respective inquiries, acquire and use literacies in complex colonial and postcolonial configurations in Tunisia, Vietnam, and Korea. Hawisher and Selfe's chapter also illustrates this complexity: Who sponsors the technological literacies of their co- authors and research participants, Coffield and El-Wakil? American University in Cairo? The Conference on Computers and Writing? Selfe and Hawisher? The women themselves? These chapters in *Women and Literacy* both use and complicate Brandt's theoretical concept of sponsorship.

The Rewards of Literacy: Emotional versus Material Change

Similarly, other chapters draw on and challenge the literacy myth, so named by Harvey Graff, a concept that manifests differently in the inquiries we present here. According to Graff, literacy promises economic advancement, political empowerment, and cultural capital, but those promises are inequitably fulfilled (*The Literacy Myth*). An example of the phenomenon Graff describes occurs in Jean Duitsman Cornelius' *"When I Can Read My Title Clear."* Cornelius recounts stories of slaves and freed blacks in the antebellum South who learned to read and write, sometimes at quite a high level, but who received neither economic, political, or cultural advantage. In our volume, Strickland explicitly uses Graff's explanation of the literacy myth to present a compelling portrait of the gendered and racialized literacies in Dorothy West's short story, "The Typewriter." But the myth is powerful, as we see in a number of chapters in this volume—for example, in the Vietnamese women about whom Crawford writes and in the women whose experiences with computer literacies Hawisher and Selfe recount. These women, both the protagonist in the West story and the research participants in Vietnam and Egypt, believe that acquiring the right kinds of literacy will grant them economic security. For their part, Crawford and Hawisher and Selfe write persuasively of what can be gained by strategically substituting what we might call literacy hope for the literacy myth.

Other contributors show how little literacy can offer in increasing women's economic or political well-being: witness the women studied by Powell, Donehower, and Hogg. Instead, these contributors highlight the emotional benefits of literacy that we must attend to. In their chapters, reading and writing figure prominently in building women's sense of self, often in ways that can only be described as empowering. Some scholars might be inclined to dismiss such empowerment as delusional in the face of dire material conditions. We take issue with this critical stance because it wrongly posits the emotional realm as a retreat from reality rather than an inescapable feature of reality itself. Thus, to whatever extent literacy can be said to fortify emotional health, it becomes an asset of great personal value. And social value, too, if we believe that emotionally self-aware individuals are more effective at sustaining the community ties and intimate relationships by which well-being is shared.

In addition, we might surmise from many of the chapters in *Women and Literacy,* including Watson and Young's, and perhaps Strickland's as well, that the material rewards of literacy, such as they are, often accrue to the descendents of the women who have themselves fought for access to reading and writing. And while it might not be fashionable these days to talk about women's literacies benefitting their families, that may in fact be one of the important lessons of research into women's literacies. Hobbs certainly makes this point in her survey of women's literacies around the globe. Indeed: how many of us are educated today because our mothers or grandmothers supported—or sponsored—the literacies of family members? Graff's notion of the literacy myth, like Brandt's sponsorship concept, is expanded, complicated, and challenged by some of the chapters that follow.

Major Issues

Economics

While acknowledging that the literacy myth has been debunked in much of the field's scholarship on literacy, our contributors understand that nuanced relationships exist between the possession of certain literacies by certain people at a certain historical moment, and attainment by these individuals of a particular standard of living. For reasons that several contributors explore, this is especially true when literacies are considered in gendered perspective. Take the case of Louisa May Alcott, for example. In their chapter, Roskelly and Ronald discuss how she applied her highly developed talent as a writer to make a living for herself and her family, all the while encoding in her fiction stories about the nontraditional paths that girls and women in the nineteenth century might follow to achieve a literacy that they could put to creative use. Consider, too, the condition of women's literacy in sub-Saharan Africa, Southern Asia, and Arab states in the Middle East. Hobbs cites research showing that, during a fifteen-year period beginning in 1980, the absolute number of illiterate persons increased in 50 of 63 countries in these regions, with women in the majority in every instance. She suggests that the resultant gender gap can be ascribed at bottom to the influence of gender ideologies. In daily practice, though, these ideologies can by turns be amplified, masked, or mitigated by an array of external forces, including those exerted by such formidable institutions as the World Bank and the International Monetary Fund. Unfortunately, a precise understanding of these forces and their effects is elusive, for worldwide surveys of literacy often depend on self-report, and variable definitions of literacy and illiteracy are very much in play. Perhaps more certain is the fact that schooling can rather quickly increase literacy rates for both women and men—if equal access to schooling is allowed. Indeed, as Hobbs shows, studies indicate that investment in women's education pays extra dividends, insofar as it appears that literate women, enjoying better health than their illiterate sisters, are positioned, to support the acquisition of basic literacy by other family members, an outcome not necessarily registered when male family members become readers and writers.

But even women who attain high levels of literacy in their native language are not immune to the instability that results when nations move to align their economies with global capital. Crawford illustrates what is happening in Vietnam as that country slowly opens its planned economy to world markets. Crawford's interviewees report feeling compelled to acquire competence in English and Japanese, but toward ends that are not clearly defined. Reporting on Oprah's Book Club, Smith shows how the branding of a particular kind of fiction became foundational to a corporate enterprise that has persuaded hundreds of thousands—perhaps millions—of readers, the vast majority women, that just as knowledge in an information economy builds wealth, self-knowledge gleaned by reading Oprah-branded fiction can also be profitable.

Technology

While all literacies rest on technologies—styluses and clay tablets, ink and parchment, ballpoint pens and notebook paper—new technological developments alter literacy practices, adding value to some and subtracting from others. Featured in Hawisher and Selfe's chapter, Kate Coffield and Safia El-Wakil were able to capture momentum from certain evolving social trends so as to become early adopters of computer technology in the college composition classroom. In El-Wakil's case, the rise of secular feminism in Egypt cleared the way for her to establish how vital computers and writing might be to the project of advancing her nation's economic standing in the region and the world. It may be, however, that the convergence of social and technological forces experienced by El-Wakil was exceptional. Several generations younger, Thuy Nga, about whom Crawford writes, faces Vietnam's embrace of technology with mixed emotions. For her, acquiring technological literacies is something of a gamble. Doing so may improve her standard of living, but maybe only temporarily—until global corporations can find a cheaper technical workforce elsewhere. As Smith shows, the Oprah readers use online forums to find substantial audiences for personal expression: the testimonials that foreground the liberatory potential of literacy and thus resonate best with Winfrey's brand of literacy get top billing on her high-traffic website. Curiously, though, Winfrey's site provides little room for exploration of why a new media technology— the web—is rendered transparent in order to promote consumption of the most conventional of literate technologies—books.

Language

While many scholars in composition and rhetoric study English-language literacy, several contributors to *Women and Literacy*, especially those whose work appears in Part II, consider literacy in languages other than English. Walters, for instance, examines the historical complexity of literacy and language for women in Tunisia, where the question of agency as it relates to literacy has been, and still is, vexed. Walters demonstrates that many, if not most, Tunisian women are subject to the oppressive force of their country's colonial past as they are steered toward or away from literacy in French, Arabic, or English. For her part, Crawford focuses on pressures on women's literacy in the aftermath of failed U.S. colonial domination in Southeast Asia and the assertion of Japanese economic hegemony in the vacuum left after the United States' exit from the region. Again the question: literate in what language—in this instance, Vietnamese, French, English, or Japanese—and for what purpose? Crawford illustrates the material consequences that may follow from the literacy and language choices made by her Vietnamese research participants.

Gong's study of the languages and literacies involved in finally bringing to light the stories of Korean women's sexual exploitation during World War II points our attention first to these poignant testimonies, but then to the problem of their translation from oral to literate form, from various Korean dialects to standard Korean, and finally from standard Korean into written English. Like Gong, DeShazer takes up not only the issue of translation from orality to literacy, but specifically oral and written poetry composed in indigenous languages of South Africa, Afrikaans, or English. These chapters ultimately speak to the profound influence of language choice on the formation of political, cultural, and personal identity.

Age

In addition to these complicated language situations, the rich diversity of women's literate experiences is signaled in *Women and Literacy* in chapters that take up such issues as age, region, race, and ethnicity. Chapters by Gong, Hogg, and Donehower, for example, focus on older women, while Crawford turns her attention to young women. According to Gong, the Korean women who were systematically subjected to sexual violence by the Japanese military during World War II, now feeling their mortality, were able finally to tell the stories of their horrific exploitation. In their case, age changed the stakes of expression and motivated literate activity. Hogg celebrates the independence of older women in her Nebraska hometown who use their literacy skills to enhance not only community life, but also their own sense of self-worth. Similarly, Donehower's research in Haines Gap shows us older women whose literacy has enriched their own lives and those of their family members, though it seldom brought economic rewards. And even when literacy seems to offer choices, socioeconomic stability may not be among them. To wit, the young Vietnamese women in Crawford's chapter feel the need to become literate in languages and with technologies that will allow them to participate in the new global economies—but their doing so is not likely to calm the volatility of their national economy.

Locale

Because of sparse population and distance from urban centers that concentrate cultural production and consumption, certain regions—both in the United States and abroad—are routinely drawn into public discourse on literacy (and, more to the point, illiteracy). These regions tend to be classified as "rural," although what counts as rural has long been reckoned in metropolitan terms that are insensitive to social, economic, and even geographical differences from one actual place to another. Likewise literacy: it often becomes conceptually flat when studied in rural contexts. Two chapters in the collection challenge this problem with their treatment of women's literacy in the Appalachian South. Powell's chapter tells us that when the federal government sought to establish the Shenandoah National Park in Northwestern Virginia, numerous families were to be moved off their land and onto substitute homesteads miles away. Resistance to this relocation took many forms: among the most interesting, letters written by women on behalf of their families. Some letter writers outright rejected the government's condemnation of their property, but most demanded—with varying success—a kind of justice aimed at mitigating the coming hardship. What is most striking about these letters is that their writers imagine a world beyond the local, and they do so in a way that betrays metropolitans' claims that rural life necessarily isolates and impoverishes the imagination. The other chapter on Appalachia, Donehower's, substantiates the claim that it is best to set aside the private/public dichotomy and to see rural women's literacy as relational. The relation in question might be to one's place, spirituality, neighbors, or country, but in all cases it involves a performance that draws from and contributes to a social fabric whose edges extend far beyond the confines of the Southern mountains.

The notion that literacy functions relationally is, of course, relevant beyond the Appalachian locales described by Powell and Donehower. The rural Nebraska women featured in Hogg's chapter, for example, used literacy in the service of family and community, and also self. The generations of women who attended the Western College in Oxford, Ohio, accumulated literacies that were, in their day, radically relational. As Watson and Young show, the international curriculum at Western, initially with a strong domestic flavor, pushed women's reading and writing out into a world of international relations that long was reserved for men—and typically men from sophisticated metropolitan areas. According to Watson and Young, the women at Western wrote their way into personal relationships with international visitors as a means of understanding foreign (and especially non-Western) cultures.

Race and Ethnicity

In addition to issues of age and locale, contributors to this volume show the diversity of women and their literacies in terms of race and ethnicity. Both Strickland and Lathan recount literacy narratives of African American women. In Strickland's reading of "The Typewriter," writer Dorothy West uses a literary form to comment on and try to change the kinds of literacies allowed African Americans. In her chapter, Lathan highlights literacy during the civil rights movement of the 1950s and 1960s. In *The Crusader,* a black newspaper published in Union County, North Carolina, Ethel Azalea Johnson variously protests the treatment of black women, teaches African Americans their history, and deconstructs forms of white oppression. In South Africa, DeShazer argues, women's oral indigenous poetry combines with written poetic forms to testify to the fears and aspirations of both black and white women after apartheid. Gong and Crawford show Asian women dealing with the personal, cultural, and economic consequences of two wars. The chapters by Walters and by Hawisher and Selfe take up the complex situation of literacy in colonial and postcolonial Northern Africa.

Agency to Effect Political and Social Change

Many women whose stories are told in these chapters use their writing—sometimes translated from oral composition—to protest political oppression and to empower groups they represent. In Lathan's study, Johnson uses her writing in service of the American civil rights movement. According to Strickland, West also writes to protest the social and economic conditions of African Americans in the first half of the twentieth century. Chapters by Roskelly and Ronald and by Flannery show women applying their literacies to bring about their own and other women's liberation in a strict patriarchal culture. DeShazer's poets write to come to terms with oppression, to celebrate the franchise, to effect forgiveness—in short, to bring about social change. Gong writes of women who after decades of silence speak out against the abusive treatment they had suffered at the hands of their country's oppressors. Both Gong and DeShazer show us how speaking one's experience can be freeing for the individual and how the inscription of one's testimony for the protection and well-being of future generations adds value to the literate record: this is what Audre Lorde has called "the transformation of silence into language and action" (40). The contributors to this book remind us that Lorde's words are not a theoretical construct, but in fact a description of the experiences of actual women. Yet as Donehower argues, literacy does not assure liberation.

For the women whose stories Donehower reports, literacy is "a power used to keep them in their cultural place," teaching them to "better assimilate to the status quo, rather than to try to change it." Powell shows us the courageous writing of the Appalachian women removed from their ancestral homes by the federal government, writing that sought to protect their families by protesting unfair rules and asking permission from the powerful to use the fruits of their own labors. What we know is that while some individuals' petitions may have won concessions, the literacies of these mountain women and those since have not prevented further exploitation by outsiders who conspire to exploit the natural wealth of the Appalachian mountains.

The young Vietnamese women Crawford writes about underscore the demands of literacies changing rapidly in response to the technological developments brought on by a global economy few seem to understand. Gong shows that literacy can, in fact, contribute to the most horrific kinds of exploitation of women: Korean girls who wanted education were often easy targets for kidnappers, who then sold them to the imperial Japanese army.

And so while *Women and Literacy* appreciates the various literacies of women in the United States and elsewhere, this volume also recognizes that literacy is a complex social practice, contributing to oppression on the one hand and giving people tools for fighting it on the other. What we want to emphasize is that even when women's literacies do not change material conditions, acts of reading and writing can enable women to become agents in their own lives. Political, economic, and social forces still constrain women's choices, but being able to read and write "against" these forces, having the tools to voice one's own concerns, allows women a kind of agency that researchers often miss or misunderstand.

Future Research

It is customary to conclude chapters that introduce edited collections like ours with a call for further research, and this we do. Above all, we

hope that the work assembled here encourages more archival and ob-
servational inquiry into the literacy of women, both in the United States
and across the broader international scene. Opportunities for such inquiry abound. Literate activity that is constitutive of gendered identity
unfolds all around us all the time—in public institutions, in workplaces,
in domestic spaces, in locations marked sacred and profane, in places
that provide refuge from violence, and so on—and yet it is barely understood in specific relation to the socioeconomic and cultural particularities of these venues.

It is by design that each chapter in this book raises more questions
than its author or authors can possibly answer in 6,000 words. In many
cases, our authors are pursuing fuller answers in long-term, book-
length projects. Even so—and this almost goes without saying—there
will always be ample opportunity for more inquiry: no one scholar
owns exclusive rights to study, say, women's literacies in Southern
Appalachia, or the literacies that African American women cultivated
in the fight for federal civil rights legislation, or the literacies of women
in Vietnam or Tunisia.

The visibility of such projects in this volume is, of course, suggestive
of others paths of inquiry that might have been—but finally are
not—represented herein. We trust, however, that other researchers are
already following these paths, or soon will be. It is a good thing: we
need to learn more about the literacy practices of Latinas involved in
current struggles to win social justice for their sisters and brothers,
about American Indian women's efforts to sustain a tradition of written
resistance to interference in sovereign tribal affairs, about immigrant
girls of various nationalities using reading and writing both to resist
and to assimilate into U.S. culture, and on and on. We need to learn
about women whose particular literacies are conditioned by the cultural and material contours of the Midwest, the Deep South, and the Pa-
cific Northwest; by life in cities, suburbs, small towns, and the
countryside. This accumulation of knowledge about gendered literacy
is not aimed at constructing generalizations about women *per se*. Rather,
the effort must be about putting diverse representations of women's literate practice on display so that we can begin to understand how literacy rewards women *and* what it costs them. And it must be about doing
this at all times with the utmost care and respect. This ethical imperative
calls researchers to approach literacy both as the complex social construct that it is, and as a force felt individually and therefore differently
by women in the course of their everyday lives.

As a number of contributors remind us, it is far too easy to imagine
the literacies of women's everyday lives solely within the confines of
Eurocentric academic discourse and the norms of North American
white, heterosexual, suburban, middle-class culture. We especially

hope, then, that the experiences of literate women outside the United States capture the interest of our readers. How could we ask for less at a time when the United States asserts its economic superiority abroad so violently, when such assertions provoke violent response, and when the resultant suffering is borne disproportionately by women and girls. We need, then, to know far more than we do about what it means for women to read and write in countries and cultures beyond U.S. borders.

Examinations of women's literacy in Central and South America seem to us to be of crucial importance. How, for example, have regional free-trade agreements influenced the work and home conditions of women, and how have these influences compelled or constrained women's reading and writing? In eastern and central Europe, cultural changes precipitated by political transitions should be of interest. How has access to literacy for women in the former Soviet-bloc changed since the fall of the Berlin Wall? What roles have women's literacies played in restructuring the economies and social institutions of Bosnia and Serbia or Slovakia and the Czech Republic? Looking beyond the Americas and Europe, several chapters in *Women and Literacy* whet our appetites for more studies of women and literacy in Southeast Asia, North Africa, sub-Saharan Africa, and the Middle East. In addition, it is imperative that research in literacy studies take account of the varying traditions of literacy that women experience in the Middle East and the Islamic world beyond, as well as in the heterogenous cultural landscape of South Asia.

As we turn our research in these directions, we acknowledge scholarship by colleagues whose questions and methods may differ from our own, but from whose interest in women and literacy we have much to learn. The contributors to Anna Robinson-Pant's edited collection, *Women, Literacy and Development* (2004), offer one point of departure: a set of inquiries that push against narrow definitions of literacy inherent in narratives of "development," such as one finds in the World Bank's *Gender and Development in the Middle East and North Africa* (2004). A similar sentiment can be found in the work of Valentine M. Moghadam, whose scholarship challenges state-centered models of development and "view[s] the state and social structure as equally determinant of social change processes" in areas such as women's education ("A Tale" 449; see also *Globalizing; Modernizing;* Moghadam and Senftova; Momsen). To better appreciate revisionist interpretations of Middle Eastern and South Asian women's literacy, we need to acquaint ourselves with histories of the regions that account for women as social actors possessed of agency to effect cultural change. Feminist scholars such as Afsaneh Najmabadi, whose focus is Iran, and Ayesha Jalal, whose focus is South Asia, are doing this critical work. Providing a theoretical frame within which to situate these new histories is Chandra Talpade Mohanty, who not only documents how literacy functions in efforts to forge solidarity among women under the regime of postcolonial globalization, but also calls for a "[f]eminist literacy" that "necessitates learning to see (and theorize) differently—to identify and challenge the politics of knowledge that naturalizes global capitalism and business-as-usual in North American higher education" (171). As more scholars in our field acquire Mohanty's sense of feminist literacy, we can pursue projects abroad that document the contours of literacies that have been formed under a multiplicity of traditional, colonial, and postcolonial pressures—some ultimately liberating, but many quite oppressive.

Apropos of such oppression, in *Reading Lolita in Tehran,* Azar Nafisi tells of her role as sponsor of the complicated literacies of several women who had been her students at universities in Tehran after the Islamic revolution. In weekly meetings in Nafisi's home, these young women took off their heavy robes and veils and, dressed in jeans and T-shirts, defied the ayatollahs by reading Western novels. Together, Nafisi and her students examined tyranny in Nabokov and discovered democracy in Austen. They wrote journals and papers explaining their own relations to these texts and the relations of the texts to the political status of women in Iran. While Nafisi's students' sense of themselves as individuals increased as they read and discussed the texts set before them, their literacies created dissonance as well. This enhanced sense of self conflicted with the restrictions imposed on them by those in power in Iran and often, as well, with their families' expectations for them. Some of these young women, like Nafisi herself, finally left Iran because the limits on their behavior became unbearable. Nafisi's students—and Nafisi, too—paid a high price for the self that was formed through reading and writing. Yet it is important to remember the privileged status of Nafisi's "girls": These young women were, after all, able to attend not only university but also graduate school; as well, they were able to find ways out of the country when they chose to do so. What of the women who had no sponsors for their literacy except the government, whether because they were from small towns or because their families simply could not afford to school their daughters?

The point is that the literacies described in this volume, whether in Tehran or Tunisia, in Haines Gap or Union County, in Vietnam or Egypt, whether constructing websites or writing poetry or composing letters to government officials, are merely glimpses into phenomena we sense but seldom see. All of us, as researchers, need to see these literacies, to see what it means for women in many cultures and sub-cultures to be or become literate. If we can see these literacies, then we can, as teachers, help others to see them, too. And if we teach others to see and understand, we will have achieved a collectivity of understanding that, as a citizenry, can be moved to celebrate the rewards conferred by literacy while at the same time appreciating the costs—sometimes dear—that women must pay to claim that reward.

NOTES

Many thanks to Elizabeth Baldridge, Janet Carey Eldred, John Hudson, Lance Massey, Kim Hensley Owens, Janine Solberg, and Amy Wan for responding to drafts of this introduction.

1. Recent book-length studies of women's literacy include Katherine Adams' *A Group of Their Own: College Writing Courses and American Women Writers, 1880–1940* (2001), Wendy Sharer's *Voice and Vote: Women's Organizations and Political Literacy, 1915–1930* (2004), Karyn Hollis' *Liberating Voices: Writing at the Bryn Mawr Summer School for Women Workers* (2004), and Sarah Robbins' *Managing Literacy, Mothering America: Women's Narratives on Reading and Writing in the Nineteenth Century* (2004). Related work on women's rhetoric often attends to the acquisition and uses of literacy: see Cheryl Glenn's *Rhetoric Retold: Regendering the Tradition from Antiquity through the Renaissance* (1997), Susan Kates' *Activist Rhetorics and American Higher Education, 1885–1937* (2001), Janet Carey Eldred and Peter Mortensen's *Imagining Rhetoric: Composing Women of the Early United States* (2002), Nan Johnson's *Gender and Rhetorical Space in American Life, 1866–1910* (2002), Carol Mattingly's *Appropriate(ing) Dress: Women's Rhetorical Style in Nineteenth-Century America* (2002), and Roxanne Mountford's *The Gendered Pulpit: Preaching in American Protestant Spaces* (2003).

2. The meaning of literacy in contemporary use—both everyday and scholarly—is perhaps as unstable as ever. There are good reasons and bad for this state of affairs. On the one hand, we agree with historian David Vincent that "the term 'literacy' has become attached to too many disparate practices" and that "renewed attention needs to be paid to how the acquisition and use of skills of written communication are conditioned by the core structures of the home, the classroom, and the state" (341). On the other hand, we acknowledge that we have gained immeasurably from scholarship that looks beyond conventionally schooled literate practices that occur in the most accessible public venues (which have been and continue to be marked by the oppressive logic of white, male, bourgeois, heterosexual privilege). Throughout this introduction, then, we argue for more discerning use of the term "literacy": it is best used when referring to the production and reception of written communication. But we also argue that literacy research must embrace more robust conceptions of home, classroom, and state, in addition to other socially structured venues—churches, clubs, unions, and so on—in which reading and writing take place.

3. On defining gender, see Joan Wallach Scott's "Gender: A Useful Category of Historical Analysis." Scott contends that "gender must be redefined and restructured in conjunction with a vision of political and social equal-

ity that includes not only sex but class and race" (50). Doing this, we will "recognize that 'man' and 'woman' are at once empty and overflowing categories. Empty because they have no ultimate, transcendent meaning. Overflowing because even when they appear to be fixed, they still contain within them alternative, denied, or suppressed definitions" (49). When the terms "woman" and "women" are used in this volume, it is with the intention of indexing these alternative definitions—and the politics in which they are enmeshed.

4. Among the earliest monographs reviewed by Ritchie and Boardman are two that look closely at U.S. women's academic literacies: Susan Miller's *Textual Carnivals* (1991) and Gesa Kirsch's *Women Writing the Academy* (1993). For more on how literacy figures in feminist composition scholarship, see *Feminism and Composition: A Critical Sourcebook*, edited with commentaries by Kirsch and Faye Spencer Maor, Lance Massey, Lee Nickoson-Massey, and Mary P. Sheridan-Rabideau.

5. Complementing what is presented in *Perspectives on Literacy*, Halverson offers a provocative definition of the "literacy thesis," as do Collins and Blot 9–33; see also Daniell's related discussion of the "great leap theory" ("Against"), Frake's commentary on the "great cognitive divide" addressed by Scribner and Cole in their research, and Street's critique of the "autonomous model of literacy and rationality" (*Literacy* 19–65).

6. One chapter in *Perspectives on Literacy*, Kyle Fiore and Nan Elsasser's "'Strangers No More': A Liberatory Literacy Curriculum," gives sustained attention to women enrolled in a liberatory literacy curriculum in the Bahamas.

7. London, for example, speculated on the outrage of "the class-conscious worker when he learns through his class literature that among the Italian pants-finishers of Chicago[,] the average weekly wage is $1.31" (254–55). No direct mention of women or women's literacy here, only the gendered implication that class-conscious male workers possess the literate wherewithal to read and learn about their own exploitation.

8. See, for example, Micaela di Leonardo's edited collection, *Gender at the Crossroads of Knowledge: Feminist Anthropology in the Postmodern Era* (1991), and Kamala Visweswaran's *Fictions of Feminist Ethnography* (1994).

9. The Right to Literacy conference, held September 16–18, 1988, in Columbus, Ohio, was co-directed by Andrea A. Lunsford, Helene Moglen, and James Slevin, all members of the MLA Commission on Writing and Literature (see Lunsford, Moglen, and Slevin; and "Report"). MLA Executive Director Phyllis Franklin reported that the conference "brought together 645 people from 42 states, the District of Columbia, Canada, the United Kingdom, and South Africa to talk about issues affecting literacy education both within and outside schools and colleges" (364). She noted, too, that "[t]his was the first conference the MLA organized that was directed at and open to a public beyond the MLA membership" (364). Although the conference's call for papers made no explicit mention of women or gender, it did prompt "explorations of the relations between … literacy and culture," as well as "explorations of attempts to achieve literacy in different historical periods and different cultures" ("The Right"). Not only did a number of the presentations, like Royster's, address gender

and literacy together, gender and literacy became an informal topic of conversation among "a very diverse group of participants, including school teachers, college and university professors, literacy program directors, and literacy workers" ("Professional" 240). This is nowhere more evident than in the postconvention testimonial offered by Nancye Brown Gaj, director of Motheread, a then-fledgling program based in North Carolina that encourages women to improve their reading abilities as they share literature with their children:

> I had never before heard literacy discussed in a humanities context. In fact, in my sixteen years as an adult educator, I have never heard literacy discussed in a public forum in terms other than political or functional. It is rare for literacy educators to feel that their work has a theoretical base. I have always known that mine has. My struggle has been to define and communicate what that base is. With your assistance, I have become better able to articulate the humanities-based core of Motheread and allow the program to grow from the strength of that knowledge. (Qtd. in Franklin 364)

A decade after attending the conference, Gaj was awarded the National Humanities Medal for her work with Motheread and for her leadership in the field that has come to be known as family literacy (Guy). Even more community literacy leaders like Gaj were involved in a follow-up conference, Responsibilities for Literacy, held September 13–16, 1990, in Pittsburgh, which aimed to "promote conversation and encourage the exchange of ideas among people from communities, schools, and workplaces" ("Responsibilities").

10. Elizabeth McHenry also studies the literate practices of nineteenth-century African American women in *Forgotten Readers: Recovering the Lost History of African American Literary Societies* (2002); see especially her chapter on "Reading, Writing, and Reform in the Woman's Era" (187–250).

11. For a very different treatment of ordinary writing, see Jennifer Sinor's *The Extraordinary Work of Ordinary Writing*, which strives to connect one woman's daily writing from the mid-nineteenth century to its reception today by readers whose interests are both academic and intensely personal.

12. Similarly, in *Something in My Mind Besides the Everyday*, Jennifer Horsman recounts stories of women in rural Nova Scotia who were enrolled in adult literacy classes. Horsman argues that without other support and opportunities, literacy instruction can actually perpetuate the status quo.

WORKS CITED

Adams, Katherine H. *A Group of Their Own: College Writing Courses and American Women Writers, 1880–1940*. Albany: State U of New York P, 2001.

Auten, Nellie Mason. "Some Phases of the Sweating System in the Garment Trades of Chicago." *American Journal of Sociology* 6 (1901): 602–45.

Bailey, Dudley. "The Graduate Assistant and the Freshman English Student." *College Composition and Communication* 5 (1954): 37–40.

Bizzell, Patricia. "Arguing about Literacy." *College English* 50 (1988): 141–53.

——. "Feminist Methods of Research in the History of Rhetoric: What Differences Do They Make?" *Rhetoric Society Quarterly* 30.4 (2000): 5–17.

Bloomfield, Leonard. "Literate and Illiterate Speech." *American Speech* 2 (1927): 432–39.

Brandt, Deborah. *Literacy in American Lives.* New York: Cambridge UP, 2001.

——. "Sponsors of Literacy." *College Composition and Communication* 49 (1998): 165–85.

Brodkey, Linda. "On the Subjects of Class and Gender in 'The Literacy Letters.'" *College English* 51 (1989): 125–41. Rpt. in *Writing Permitted in Designated Areas Only.* Minneapolis: U of Minnesota P, 1996. 88–105.

Carr, Jean Ferguson. "Rereading the Academy as Worldly Text." *College Composition and Communication* 45 (1994): 93–97.

Coles, William E., Jr. "Counterstatement: Response to William E. Coles, Jr., 'Teaching the Teaching of Composition: Evolving a Style.'" *College Composition and Communication* 29 (1978): 206–09.

Collins, James, and Richard K. Blot. *Literacy and Literacies: Texts, Power, and Identity.* Cambridge, UK: Cambridge UP, 2003.

Cornelius, Janet Duitsman. *"When I Can Read My Title Clear": Literacy, Slavery, and Religion in the Antebellum South.* Columbia: U of South Carolina P, 1991.

Crawford, Finla G. "Operation of the Literacy Test for Voters in New York." *American Political Science Review* 25 (1931): 342–45.

Cushman, Ellen. *The Struggle and the Tools: Oral and Literate Strategies in an Inner City Community.* Albany: State U of New York P, 1998.

Cushman, Ellen, Eugene R. Kintgen, Barry M. Kroll, and Mike Rose, eds. *Literacy: A Critical Sourcebook.* Boston: Bedford/St. Martin's, 2001.

Daniell, Beth. "Against the Great Leap Theory of Literacy." *Pre/Text* 7.3–4 (1986): 181–93.

——. *A Communion of Friendship: Literacy, Spiritual Practice, and Women in Recovery.* Carbondale: Southern Illinois UP, 2003.

——. "Narratives of Literacy: Connecting Composition to Culture." *College Composition and Communication* 50 (1999): 393–410.

Davidson, Cathy N. *Revolution and the Word: The Rise of the Novel in America.* New York: Oxford UP, 1986.

DeParle, Jason. *American Dream: Three Women, Ten Kids, and a Nation's Drive to End Welfare.* New York: Viking, 2003.

DeShazer, Mary K. "Sexist Language in Composition Textbooks: Still a Major Issue?" *College Composition and Communication* 32 (1981): 57–64.

di Leonardo, Micaela, ed. *Gender at the Crossroads of Knowledge: Feminist Anthropology in the Postmodern Era.* Berkeley: U of California P, 1991.

Ehrenreich, Barbara. *Nickel and Dimed: On (Not) Getting By in America.* New York: Henry Holt, 2001.

Eldred, Janet Carey, and Peter Mortensen. *Imagining Rhetoric: Composing Women of the Early United States.* Pittsburgh: U of Pittsburgh P, 2002.

Evans-Pritchard, E. E. *The Position of Women in Primitive Societies and Other Essays in Social Anthropology.* New York: Free Press, 1965.

Fiore, Kyle, and Nan Elsasser. "'Strangers No More': A Liberatory Literacy Curriculum." Kintgen, Kroll, and Rose 286–99.

Fishman, Ted C. *China, Inc.: How the Rise of the Next Superpower Challenges America and the World.* New York: Scribner, 2005.

Frake, Charles O. "Did Literacy Cause the Great Cognitive Divide?" Rev. of *The Psychology of Literacy,* by Sylvia Scribner and Michael Cole. *American Ethnologist* 10 (1983): 368–71.

Franklin, Phyllis. "Report of the Executive Director." *PMLA* 104 (1989): 363–71.

Gandhi, M. K. "The Future of India." *International Affairs* 10 (1931): 721–39.

Gender and Development in the Middle East and North Africa: Women in the Public Sphere. Washington, DC: The World Bank, 2004.

Gere, Anne Ruggles. "Kitchen Tables and Rented Rooms: The Extracurriculum of Composition." *College Composition and Communication* 45 (1994): 75–92.

——. "Literacy and Difference in 19th-Century Women's Clubs." *Literacy: Interdisciplinary Conversations.* Ed. Deborah Keller-Cohen. Cresskill, NJ: Hampton P, 1994. 249–65.

——. *Intimate Practices: Literacy and Cultural Work in U.S. Women's Clubs, 1880–1920.* Urbana: U of Illinois P, 1997.

Glenn, Cheryl. *Rhetoric Retold: Regendering the Tradition from Antiquity through the Renaissance.* Carbondale: Southern Illinois UP, 1997.

Goddard, Henry Herbert. *The Kallikak Family: A Study in the Heredity of Feeble-Mindedness.* New York: Macmillan, 1912.

Goody, Jack. "On Nannas and Nannies." *Man* 62 (1962): 179–84.

Goody, Jack, and Ian Watt. "The Consequences of Literacy." *Comparative Studies in Society and History* 5 (1963): 304–45. Rpt. in Kintgen, Kroll, and Rose 3–27.

Graff, Harvey J. "The Legacies of Literacy." Kintgen, Kroll, and Rose 82–91.

——. *The Literacy Myth: Literacy and Social Structure in the Nineteenth-Century City.* New York: Academic P, 1979.

Guy, Andrew, Jr. "And the Literacy Advocate Lived Happily Ever After." *Raleigh News and Observer* 8 November 1998: A1.

Halverson, John. "Olson on Literacy." *Language in Society* 20 (1991): 619–40.

Hardt, Michael, and Antonio Negri. *Empire.* Cambridge: Harvard UP, 2000.

Harris, Joseph. "A Usable Past: CCC at 50." *College Composition and Communication* 50 (1999): 343–47.

Havelock, Eric A. "The Coming of Literate Communication to Western Culture." *Journal of Communication* 30 (1980): 90–98. Rpt. in Kintgen, Kroll, and Rose 127–34.

——. *Preface to Plato.* Cambridge: Harvard UP, 1963.

Hawisher, Gail E., and Cynthia L. Selfe, with Yi-Huey Guo and Lu Liu. "Globalization and Agency: Designing and Redesigning the Literacies of Cyberspace." *College English* 68 (2006): 619–36.

Heath, Shirley Brice. "Finding in History the Right to Estimate." *College Composition and Communication* 45 (1994): 97–102.

Heller, Caroline E. *Until We Are Strong Together: Women Writers in the Tenderloin.* New York: Teachers College P, 1997.

Hirsch, E. D., Jr. *Cultural Literacy: What Every American Needs to Know.* Boston: Houghton Mifflin, 1987.

Hobbs, Catherine, ed. *Nineteenth-Century Women Learn to Write.* Charlottesville: UP of Virginia, 1995.

Hollis, Karyn L. *Liberating Voices: Writing at the Bryn Mawr Summer School for Women Workers.* Carbondale: Southern Illinois UP, 2004.

Horner, Bruce, and John Trimbur. "English Only and U.S. College Composition." *College Composition and Communication* 53 (2002): 594–630.

Horsman, Jennifer. *Something in My Mind Besides the Everyday: Women and Literacy.* Toronto: Women's Press, 1990.

Hymes, Dell. "Introduction: Toward Ethnographies of Communication." *American Anthropologist* 66.6, pt. 2 (1964): 1–34.

"Is Literacy Enough?" [Workshop Report from the 1971 CCCC Annual Meeting]. *College Composition and Communication* 22 (1971): 284.

Jalal, Ayesha. *Democracy and Authoritarianism in South Asia: A Comparative and Historical Perspective.* Cambridge, UK: Cambridge UP, 1995.

——. *Self and Sovereignty: Individual and Community in South Asian Islam since 1850.* New York: Routledge, 2000.

Johnson, Nan. *Gender and Rhetorical Space in American Life, 1866–1910.* Carbondale: Southern Illinois UP, 2002.

Kates, Susan. *Activist Rhetorics and American Higher Education, 1885–1937.* Carbondale: Southern Illinois UP, 2001.

Kelley, Florence. "Minimum-Wage Boards." *American Journal of Sociology* 17 (1911): 303–14.

Kintgen, Eugene R., Barry M. Kroll, and Mike Rose. Introduction. Kintgen, Kroll, and Rose xi–xix.

Kintgen, Eugene R., Barry M. Kroll, and Mike Rose, eds. *Perspectives on Literacy.* Carbondale: Southern Illinois UP, 1988.

Kirsch, Gesa E. *Women Writing the Academy: Audience, Authority, and Transformation.* Carbondale: Southern Illinois UP, 1993.

Kirsch, Gesa E., Faye Spencer Maor, Lance Massey, Lee Nickoson-Massey, and Mary P. Sheridan-Rabideau, eds. *Feminism and Composition: A Critical Sourcebook.* Boston: Bedford/St. Martin's, 2003.

Kolodny, Annette. "Reply to Commentaries: Women Writers, Literary Historians, and Martian Readers." *New Literary History* 11 (1980): 587–92.

Landes, Ruth. Rev. of *The Position of Women in Primitive Societies and Other Essays in Social Anthropology,* by E. E. Evans-Pritchard, and *Women in the Modern World,* ed. Raphael Patai. *American Anthropologist* 70 (1968): 575–76.

Lewis, Earl, and Heidi Ardizzone. *Love on Trial: An American Scandal in Black and White.* New York: Norton, 2001.

Logan, Shirley Wilson. "Literacy as a Tool for Social Action among Nineteenth-Century African American Women." Hobbs 179–96.

——. *"We Are Coming": The Persuasive Discourse of Nineteenth-Century Black Women.* Carbondale: Southern Illinois UP, 1999.

London, Jack. *War of the Classes.* London: Macmillan, 1905.

Lorde, Audre. *Sister Outsider: Essays and Speeches.* Trumansburg, NY: Crossing P, 1984.

"Loved Rhinelander, Wife's Letters Say." *New York Times* 13 November 1925: 1, 3.

Lu, Min-Zhan. "An Essay on the Work of Composition: Composing English against the Order of Fast Capitalism." *College Composition and Communication* 56 (2004): 16–50.

Lunsford, Andrea A., Helene Moglen, and James Slevin. Introduction. *The Right to Literacy.* New York: Modern Language Association, 1990. 1–6.

Lunsford, Andrea A., and Lahoucine Ouzgane, eds. *Crossing Borderlands: Composition and Postcolonial Studies.* Pittsburgh: U of Pittsburgh P, 2004.

Lynd, Robert S. "Planned Social Solidarity in the Soviet Union." *American Journal of Sociology* 51 (1945): 183–97.

Mattingly, Carol. *Appropriate(ing) Dress: Women's Rhetorical Style in Nineteenth-Century America.* Carbondale: Southern Illinois UP, 2002.

McHenry, Elizabeth. *Forgotten Readers: Recovering the Lost History of African American Literary Societies.* Durham, NC: Duke UP, 2002.

Miller, Susan. *Assuming the Positions: Cultural Pedagogy and the Politics of Commonplace Writing.* Pittsburgh: U of Pittsburgh P, 1998.

——. *Textual Carnivals: The Politics of Composition.* Carbondale: Southern Illinois UP, 1991.

——. "Things Inanimate May Move: A Different History of Writing and Class." *College Composition and Communication* 45 (1994): 102–07.

Miller, Thomas P., and Joseph G. Jones. "Review: Working Out Our History." *College English* 67 (2005): 421–39.

Moghadam, Valentine M. *Globalizing Women: Transnational Feminist Networks.* Baltimore: Johns Hopkins UP, 2005.

——. *Modernizing Women: Gender and Social Change in the Middle East.* 2nd ed. Boulder: Rienner, 2003.

——. "A Tale of Two Countries: State, Society, and Gender Politics in Iran and Afghanistan." *The Muslim World* 94 (2004): 449–67.

Moghadam, Valentine M., and Lucie Senftova. "Measuring Women's Empowerment: Participation and Rights in Civil, Political, Social, Economic, and Cultural Domains." *International Social Science Journal* 57 (2005): 389–412.

Mohanty, Chandra Talpade. *Feminism without Borders: Decolonizing Theory, Practicing Solidarity.* Durham: Duke UP, 2003.

Momsen, Janet Henshall. "Backlash: Or How to Snatch Failure from the Jaws of Success in Gender and Development." *Progress in Development Studies* 1.1 (2001): 51–56.

Mountford, Roxanne. *The Gendered Pulpit: Preaching in American Protestant Spaces.* Carbondale: Southern Illinois UP, 2003.

Nafisi, Azar. *Reading Lolita in Tehran: A Memoir in Books.* New York: Random House, 2003.

Najmabadi, Afsaneh. *Women with Mustaches and Men without Beards: Gender and Sexual Anxieties of Iranian Modernity.* Berkeley: U of California P, 2005.

Olson, David. "From Utterance to Text: The Bias of Language in Speech and Writing." *Harvard Educational Review* 47 (1977): 257–81. Rpt. in Kintgen, Kroll, and Rose 175–89.

Ong, Walter J. *Fighting for Life: Contest, Sexuality, and Consciousness.* Ithaca: Cornell UP, 1981.

——. *Interfaces of the Word: Studies in the Evolution of Consciousness and Culture.* Ithaca: Cornell UP, 1977.

——. *Orality and Literacy: The Technologizing of the Word.* London: Methuen, 1982.

——. "Some Psychodynamics of Orality." Kintgen, Kroll, and Rose 28–43.

Patai, Raphael, ed. *Women in the Modern World.* New York: Free Press, 1967.

"The Position of Women" [Workshop Report from the 1971 CCCC Annual Meeting]. *College Composition and Communication* 22 (1971): 283–84.

"Professional Notes and Comments." *PMLA* 104 (1989): 234, 236, 238, 240, 242.

Quinby, Lee. "Taking the Millennialist Pulse of *Empire's* Multitude: A Genealogical Feminist Diagnosis." *Empire's New Clothes: Reading Hardt and Negri.* Ed. Paul A. Passavant and Jodi Dean. New York: Routledge, 2004. 231–52.

Radway, Janice A. *Reading the Romance: Women, Patriarchy, and Popular Literature.* 1984. Rev. ed. Chapel Hill: U of North Carolina P, 1991.

Ramdas, Lalita. "Women and Literacy: A Quest for Justice." Cushman, Kintgen, Kroll, and Rose 629–43.

Reiter, Rayna R., ed. *Toward an Anthropology of Women.* New York: Monthly Review P, 1975.

"Report of the Commission on Writing and Literature." *Profession* (1988): 70–76.

"Responsibilities for Literacy: Communities, Schools, and Workplaces" [Call for Proposals]. *PMLA* 104 (1989): 773.

"The Right to Literacy" [Call for Papers]. *PMLA* 102 (1987): 884.

Ritchie, Joy, and Kathleen Boardman. "Feminism in Composition: Inclusion, Metonymy, and Disruption." *College Composition and Communication* 50 (1999): 585–606.

Robbins, Sarah. *Managing Literacy, Mothering America: Women's Narratives on Reading and Writing in the Nineteenth Century.* Pittsburgh: U of Pittsburgh P, 2004.

Robinson-Pant, Anna, ed. *Women, Literacy and Development: Alternative Perspectives.* London: Routledge, 2004.

Rosaldo, Michelle Zimbalist, and Louise Lamphere eds., *Women, Culture, and Society.* Stanford, CA: Stanford UP, 1974.

Royster, Jacqueline Jones. "Perspectives on the Intellectual Tradition of Black Women Writers." Lunsford, Moglen, and Slevin 103–12.

——. *Traces of a Stream: Literacy and Social Change among African American Women.* Pittsburgh: U of Pittsburgh P, 2000.

Sauer, Edwin H. "The Advanced Placement Program—Advantages and Cautions." *College Composition and Communication* 11 (1960): 7–12.

Scott, Joan Wallach. "Gender: A Useful Category of Historical Analysis." *Gender and the Politics of History.* Rev. ed. New York: Columbia UP, 1999. 28–50.

Scribner, Sylvia, and Michael Cole. "Unpackaging Literacy." Kintgen, Kroll, and Rose 57–70.

Sen, Amartya. *Development as Freedom.* New York: Anchor Books, 1999.

Sharer, Wendy B. *Voice and Vote: Women's Organizations and Political Literacy, 1915–1930.* Carbondale: Southern Illinois UP, 2004.

Shipler, David K. *The Working Poor: Invisible in America.* New York: Random House, 2004.

Sinor, Jennifer. *The Extraordinary Work of Ordinary Writing: Annie Ray's Diary.* Iowa City: U of Iowa P, 2002.

Smith, James Steel. "Popular Culture and the Freshman: Three Questions." *College Composition and Communication* 10 (1959): 253–59.

——. "Readership Scholarship." *College Composition and Communication* 15 (1964): 153–57.

Stanley, Julia P., and Susan Robbins Wolfe. "Counterstatement: Response to William E. Coles, Jr." *College Composition and Communication* 29 (1978): 404–06.

Street, Brian V. *Literacy in Theory and Practice.* Cambridge, UK: Cambridge UP, 1984.

Torgovnick, Marianna. *Gone Primitive: Savage Intellects, Modern Lives.* Chicago: U of Chicago P, 1990.

Vincent, David. "Literacy Literacy." *Interchange* 34 (2003): 341–57.

Visweswaran, Kamala. *Fictions of Feminist Ethnography.* Minneapolis: U of Minnesota P, 1994.

PART I

Women's Literacies Situated Locally:
Past, Present, And Future

Feeling Literate: Gender, Race, and Work in Dorothy West's "The Typewriter"

Donna Strickland

The "literacy myth," the belief that the acquisition of written language leads to social progress and individual economic betterment, has been one of the enduring legacies of the Enlightenment, according to Harvey Graff (*Literacy* and *Legacies*). Graff, who introduced this term to describe the largely unwarranted faith in literacy's ameliorating potential, has demonstrated that literacy alone has not been a reliable predictor of economic success in western societies; rather, social class, race, and gender have been more reliable determinants of occupational and economic status than literacy level. In particular, the historical record shows that "[e]ducation conferred greater material benefits on whites" in postbellum America:

> As levels of literacy among blacks rose, race became more important, and literacy less so, in determining occupational levels. The contradiction between the promise of literacy and its reality was stark. Educational efforts had a dramatic impact on literacy, but they could not influence the place of blacks in the social order. (Graff, *Legacies* 363)

Because history demonstrates that the direct material benefits of literacy have been limited by such factors as race and gender, Graff hopes that literacy might be "reformulated and reconceptualized" to displace the literacy myth (*Legacies* 398). Literacy *does* have the potential to be one factor "linked to change and action"—a factor which, in no small part, helps to explain the faith that marginalized groups of people have often placed in literacy—and thus needs to "take its place among other fundamental human needs and rights" (*Legacies* 398). In other words, literacy needs to lose its mythic status and become fundamental, like life itself.

This chapter begins here, with the hope that literacy might come to function primarily as a life-enhancing enabler of action rather than simply as a form of cultural capital, a mark of social distinction (see Bourdieu). To realize such a hope, however, will require more than a different way of thinking about literacy: it will require a different way of *feeling*. The burden of my argument, in other words, will be to demonstrate that feelings attached to literacy—produced through the hegemonic work of a stratified capitalist society—contribute powerfully to the perpetuation of the literacy myth. Literacy tends to emerge attached to feelings of pride; illiteracy, conversely, tends to be attached to feelings of shame, feelings that contribute to an "identity kit," to use James Paul Gee's term (7). According to Gee, to be literate is not simply to acquire technical proficiency in language; rather, to become literate is to acquire "Discourses," which provide access to language along with "ways of being in the world; ... forms of life which integrate words, acts values, beliefs, attitudes, and social identities as well as gestures, glances, body positions, and clothes" (6–7). The "identity kit" of Discourses, according to Gee,

> comes complete with the appropriate costume and instructions on how to act, talk, and often write, so as to take on a particular role that others will recognize .... [E]xamples of Discourses [include] (enacting) being an American or a Russian, a man or a woman, a member of a certain socioeconomic class, a factory worker or a boardroom executive .... (7)

If, as Lynn Worsham has argued, one's identity, one's sense of oneself, emerges through the organization of "an emotional world," including "patterns of feeling that support the legitimacy of dominant interests, patterns that are especially appropriate to gender, race, and class locations," then a key role of Discourse is to inculcate patterns of feeling appropriate to a given identity (223). The feelings of pride and approval that accompany Discourse acquisition—what I will call "feeling literate"—are part and parcel of Discourses, of literacies.

Historical studies of literacy, however, have tended to provide little access to ways of feeling about literacy, offering conceptual sweeps of literacy's development more often than "little narratives" of individuals' actual experiences with literacy (Daniell 393). Janet Carey Eldred and Peter Mortensen's work, however, suggests a fruitful source for the study of literate feelings: literacy narratives found in literary works. "When we read for literacy narratives," Eldred and Mortensen explain, "we study how the text constructs a character's ongoing, social process of language acquisition" (512). If, as I have suggested, emotion makes possible and reinforces this process, then literacy narratives should offer discursive glimpses of characters' literate feelings. To ground my argument, then, I will focus on a short story that offers two intertwined and gender-specific literacy narratives. First published in 1926, Dorothy West's "The Typewriter" deals, in part, with a young African American woman's desire to obtain—and, in fact, success in getting—a job as a typist by acquiring clerical literacy. She is aided in this process of acquisition by her father, who simultaneously takes on new literacies himself. At the center of the story, then, are these two gender-coded and emotionally schooled performances of literacy acquisition, performances that demonstrate the extent to which emotion serves as a certain kind of "sponsor" of literacy, along with the uneven consequences of that sponsorship. As a literate performance itself, however, the story enacts the potential of a different way of feeling about literacy, thus offering grounds for imagining alternative definitions of literacy, along with alternative futures.

EMOTION AS A SPONSOR OF LITERACY

Emotion, as I have suggested, serves as an important sponsor of literacy. Deborah Brandt, who introduced the concept of literacy sponsors, describes them as "agents, local or distant, concrete or abstract, who enable, support, teach, and model, as well as recruit, regulate, suppress, or withhold, literacy" (19). While the sponsors she refers to tend to be people—"older relatives, teachers, religious leaders, supervisors, military officers, librarians, friends, editors, influential authors"—attached to these material sponsors are immaterial ones that work at the level of emotion, persuading the sponsored to identify her- or himself with the cultural meanings and cultural projects associated with that institutional site (Brandt 19).

I offer the concept of immaterial sponsors as an extension of the concept of immaterial labor, which Michael Hardt describes as "labor that produces an immaterial good, such as service, knowledge, or communication" (94). Affective labor—"the production and manipulation of affects"—is one type of immaterial labor; by extension, then, emotion is one type of immaterial sponsor (Hardt 97–98). In fact, the production and manipulation of affects is also the work of emotional sponsorship. Of course, the sponsored emotion may or may not "stick." Thus, even as pride in literacy may seem to produce docile subjects—à la Foucault—it may also produce subjects who resist, whose pride moves them to subvert the very institution that sponsors their literacy. Be that as it may, the lure of feeling literate—along with the threat and potential drawbacks of such feeling—remains an under-investigated site of literacy research.

The study of the emotion of literacy seems especially necessary, however, as literacy studies move to focus on what Beth Daniell has called the "little narratives" of literacy—on lived experiences. Even as a nuanced understanding of literacy is impossible apart from a study of actual people who acquire literacy and put it to use, it remains important to tie these little narratives to larger ones. David Harvey argues that we cannot choose "between particularity or universality in our mode of thinking and argumentation" because "[w]ithin a relational dialectic one is always internalized and implicated in the other" (16). The emotion of literacy, I maintain, is a particularly important site for the simultaneous study of the local and the global, of the relationship between the individual and social networks of meaning. "The particularity of the body," explains Harvey, "cannot be understood independently of its embeddedness in socio-ecological processes," including the labor process (16). Conversely, the contemporary labor process, shaped as it is by globalization, "is about the socio-spatial relations between billions of individuals" (16).

Because emotions are performed by/in individual bodies, they have often been neglected in critical studies; as Worsham points out, dominant schooling "mystifies emotion as a personal and private matter and conceals the fact that emotions are prevailing forms of social life" (223). Similarly, literacy has traditionally been conceived as an "autonomous," cognitive skill that can be individually measured, rather than recognized as ideological, embedded in a social context (see Street 1–2). Reconnecting feelings associated with literacy, feelings that might initially be overlooked as nothing more than subjective individual responses, to the social networks of meaning in which they are embedded, would allow literacy studies to focus simultaneously on the individual *and* the cultural work of that individual's orientation toward literacy— another way of demonstrating that the personal, as the slogan says, is the political. Reading literacy narratives with attention to the ways in which literacy is felt and how those feelings both contribute to and complicate the labor process, then, has the potential to contribute to both the "little narratives" of literacy and to more general questions concerning the production and reproduction of cultural values in a capitalist society. West's "The Typewriter" offers an exemplary narrative for just such a reading, a reading that will focus on particular performances of gendered emotions that both perpetuate and complicate the literacy myth and the capitalist labor process supporting it.

GENDERED PERFORMANCES OF LITERACY

The central characters in West's narrative are a young woman, Millie, and her father, who as a young man in the early twentieth century migrated from the South to Boston. Like West's own father, this fictional father had come to the city full of optimism and ambition to become a businessman, but secured instead a series of service-sector jobs, finally working as a janitor. Though a janitor, he is described as a "humble little middle-class man" ("Typewriter" 13). He is financially secure enough to own his own flat, and he is able (although reluctant) to rent a typewriter for his daughter, who is practicing to become a clerical worker. Millie asks her father to "dictate a letter" for her one evening; he obliges and is plunged into a fantasy of actually being a businessman. For many nights, this performance—in which he pretends to be J. Lucius Jones, executive, and she pretends to be his secretary—continues, until Millie secures a job and so returns the typewriter. Adelaide Cromwell has described the "fragile black community" in pre-war Boston as a place "where janitors and caterers were the leaders" (358). The central characters appear to be part of this fragile black community, and, as such, are not struggling in particular with "the blatant racism in [for example] the Chicago of Bigger Thomas" (Cromwell 362). In fact, rather than race, what at first seems most striking are the gendered divisions of literacy in the story.

The story's plot revolves around a series of literate performances, performances that are gender-coded and emotionally schooled. The gendered divisions become apparent when, one evening, Millie asks her father to help her enact a literacy event:

> Dictate me a letter, Poppa. I c'n do sixty words a minute. You know, like a business letter. You know, like those men in your building dictate to their stenographers. Don't you hear 'em sometimes? (13)

The daughter needs to enact a particularly feminized sort of literacy: the typing of a dictated letter. In order to do so, she needs her father to perform a masculinized literate act: the dictating of a business letter. The father reluctantly complies, but soon finds that the act of dictating a letter temporarily transforms him:

> A light crept into his dull eyes. Vigor through his thin blood. In a brief moment the weight of years fell from him like a cloak. Tired, bent, little old man that he was, he smiled, straightened, tapped impressively against his teeth with a toil-stained finger, and became that enviable emblem of American life: a businessman. (14)

What particularly interests me in this scene is the transforming power, not of literacy itself, but of the cultural significance of a certain performance of literacy—a performance that is gender-coded and emotionally schooled. The father knows that he must hold his body differently, that he must reject the way in which "the weight of years" have inscribed themselves on his body. He must enact a different kind of emotion, a different way of feeling: he must tap "impressively against his teeth" if he is to successfully perform the Discourse of a businessman. Indeed, he takes on a new identity to signify this transformation:

> Every night thereafter in the weeks that followed .... there was the chameleon change of a Court Street janitor to J. Lucius Jones, dealer in stocks and bonds. (14)

Quite dramatically and thoroughly, the father takes on a new "identity kit" by taking on a new Discourse. He is persuaded to continue this Discursive performance for several weeks because it provides the *feeling* of importance: taking on the Discourse of business allows him to forget that he is a janitor.

For the father, then, the act of dictating is a productive act that allows him to enact the socially powerful role assigned primarily to middle-class white men. For Millie, however, who does not compose but types, the performance is not primarily productive but reproductive, a feminized activity. She does not produce, as her father does, "compositions of [the] brain" but facsimiles of those compositions (16). She seems, however, to be emotionally detached from the consequences of this distinction. Or, rather, she is emotionally moved by a gendered pride in her ability—a pride that doesn't detect the distinction. The ability to mechanically reproduce words is, for a young woman, a mark of intelligence: her teacher, Mr. Hennessy, "had promised the smartest girl in the class a position in the very near future. And she, of course, was smart as a steel trap" (15). To be "smart as a trap" implies that her intelligence is based on what her brain can hold onto, rather than on what her brain can create.

This sort of mechanical literacy, coded as feminine, functions as both a sponsor of the father's more creative use of literacy, which is coded as masculine, and as a threat of sorts to the father's masculinity. Mechanical literacy leads eventually to more success for the girl, even though historically black women, like black men, were not rewarded with what their literacy levels would have suggested they deserved. Let me turn now to the threat posed by this "mechanical" literacy.

The story opens with the father's dread of going home to the sound of the typewriter. At this point, he has not begun the performance that dominates the story. Rather than enabling the performance of his own literacy, he first experiences the machine as an emotional and economic threat. On his way home, unaware of the transformation in store for him that night, he thinks of the typewriter:

> He knew quite suddenly that he hated his flat and his family and his friends. And most of all the incessant thing that would "clatter clatter" until every nerve screamed aloud, and the words of the evening paper danced crazily before him, and the insane desire to crush and kill set his fingers twitching. (9)

He experiences his daughter's act of mechanically reproducing words as an aural and psychic disruption of the leisure of reading—one kind of literacy disrupting another. The typewriter, which gives the story its name, represents a new literacy technology, one that marked a shift in the "meaning and status of individual literacy" (Brandt 1). As Brandt points out, "individual literacy exists only as part of larger material systems," and, with the advent of corporate capitalism, the ability to write—whether conceptually or mechanically—achieved a new level of importance in the coordination of work in hierarchically organized businesses (1; see also Yates; Strickland). This shift from reading to writing as the privileged form of literacy disrupts the father's relationship to his own literate practice, causing him to feel threatened, and, later, ashamed.

If the typewriter disrupts the leisure of his own ritualized literacy, the machine also represents for the father an unnecessary luxury, a threat to the economic stability that maintains his status as a member of the middle class. He tells his wife "that they couldn't afford" the typewriter, to which she responds with a challenge to his masculinity:

> You're a poor sort of father if you can't give that child jes' three dollars a month to rent that typewriter. Ain't 'nother girl in school ain't got one. An' mos' of 'ems bought an' paid for. (11)

His masculinity is challenged in other ways, as he sees himself as not quite a man, someone who doesn't use language in a manly way and who allows masculine and feminine roles to blur in his home. After being berated by one of his tenants for leaving the tending of the furnace to his wife during the day—"Tending a furnace ain't a woman's work. I don't blame you wife none 'tall" (12)—he considers enforcing a strict division of labor, a determination brought on by an uncharacteristic language performance:

> He wondered uneasily if he dared say "damn." It was taken for granted that a man swore when he tended a stubborn furnace. And his strongest interjection was "Great balls of fire!"

> The cellar began to warm, and he took off his inadequate overcoat that was streaked with dirt. Well, Net would have to clean that. He'd be damned! It frightened and thrilled him. (10)

Although momentarily "thrilled" by his manly swearing, he soon abandons his determination to enforce gendered divisions of labor, "telling himself, a little lamely, that it wouldn't take him more than a minute to clean it up himself after supper …. he hated men who made slaves of their womenfolk" (12).

With his masculinity threatened, the father's psyche is primed to take on a new identity kit, a new Discourse that would allow him to perform masculinity. His daughter, then, functions as a sponsor of this literacy, enabling, through her own performance of a feminized literacy, her father's performance as a businessman. She functions, in other words, as a situational sponsor, providing a concrete exigence that calls forth his literate performance. Given his initial reluctance to enact the role of a businessman, however, it seems unlikely that Millie's situational sponsorship would be enough to maintain her father's interest in acquiring this literacy. Millie's performance of feminine subordination, then, serves not simply as a situational sponsor, but perhaps more importantly, as an emotional sponsor of her father's literacy. Insofar as she feels literate, she also participates in affective labor, producing and reproducing emotional ties to literacy in others.

These gender-specific feelings of literacy, further, are performed through certain ways of holding and using the body—on the one hand, the (masculine) business executive taps "with impatient fingers" as he speaks his compositions, "importantly flicking imaginary dust from his coat lapel"; on the other, the (feminine) secretary announces that she is "ready for dictation, sir" and speaks no more, silently typing the letters dictated to her (14). These performances, sponsored by gender-specific emotion, reinforce the rightness and naturalness of literacies that are ultimately sponsored by corporate capitalism, a sponsor that relies on the reproduction of the literacy myth.

LITERACY'S UNEVEN CONSEQUENCES

Although both father and daughter properly perform gendered Discourses, taking pride in their gender-coded abilities, the consequences of racial coding prevent the father from benefitting from his own increasingly complex performances of literacy. The father, moreover, had long been denied the opportunity to make use of his literacy. Early on in the story, as the father is introduced, we learn that he came to Boston as part of the migration of African Americans from the South and that, upon his arrival, he had been full of ambition:

> He thought of that eager Negro lad of seventeen who had come North to seek his fortune .... he had thrown up his head and promised himself: "You'll have an office here some day. With plate-glass windows and a mahogany desk." (10–11)

Clearly, he arrived in Boston with a great deal of pride, but, we are told, "he was not the progressive type" (11). The "progressive type," it seems, must be white. For what other reason could a young person, clearly educated and full of desire, not find suitable employment in economically prosperous times? The Progressive era, however, was a time of stark contradictions: even as socially progressive legislation was being made in the early years of the twentieth century, racial violence was rampant in both the Northern and Southern states. While "progressive" in some ways, the Progressive era still left much to be desired in terms of racial equality. The ideals of the Progressive era, moreover, reinforced faith in the literacy myth: Progressive reformers like John Dewey promoted education as the answer to individual betterment and social change. In West's story, however, the uses to which literacy can be put are limited by race.

Men who are other than white, it seems, can enter the corporate office only to clean it, despite the evidence that the father clearly can perform the corporate Discourse. Rather than becoming a business executive, the father "became successively, in the years, bell boy, porter, waiter, cook, and finally janitor in a downtown office building" (11). He was full of ambition, and full of ability, as is clear when he performs later as J. Lucius Jones. The letters he dictates—"the compositions of his brain"—we're told, "were really the work of an artist" (16). Moreover, despite the fact that his performance is not economically significant, he works to improve it:

> He was growing very careful of his English. Occasionally—and it must be admitted, ashamedly—he made surreptitious ventures into the dictionary. He had to, of course. J. Lucius Jones would never say "Y'got to" when he meant "It is expedient." And, old brain though he was, he learned quickly and easily, juggling words with amazing facility. (15)

It can't be his literate abilities or his ambition that has caused him to clean offices rather than preside over them. As long as he dictates the letters to his daughter each night, however, he can maintain a fantasy of having fulfilled his potential. When the typewriter is returned after Millie secures a job, he is overwhelmed with the reality of his situation: the silence that had previously been filled with the noise of the typewriter "crowded in on him … blurred his vision, dulled his brain" (17). In the final line of the story, we are told, "Against the wall of that silence J. Lucius Jones crashed and died" (17). Whether this death is literal or figurative, it is clear that the unfulfilled promise of his own literacy devastates him.

In this sense, then, the story is a literacy myth narrative, an account of the economic and, significantly, the emotional price paid by those who are unable to reap the rewards of their literacy. The potential danger of the literacy myth, this little narrative suggests, comes when literacy performances are driven by corporate-endorsed emotion without being economically sponsored or rewarded. And, according to Graff's account in *The Legacies of Literacy*, this narrative is an accurate one. Graff maintains that African Americans who migrated from the South to Boston tended to be from cities and "to have above-average literacy" (365). "But despite their levels of literacy and preparation," Graff continues, "Boston blacks fared poorly economically. No other ethnic or racial group was as concentrated at the bottom of the occupational hierarchy" (366). Insofar as the story represents an accurate picture of racial discrimination and its economic effects, it functions to expose the contradictory consequences of feeling literate: on the one hand, acquiring literacy leads to feelings of pride, feelings that tend to support the literacy myth; on the other, unfulfilled literate abilities can lead to emotional (and, potentially, physical) devastation, as the promises of literacy prove to be, indeed, a fiction.

How one reads this story, moreover, is an effect of the literacy myth and the gendered schooling of emotion. That is, the dominant culture might ask us to react with pity for the father, who is capable of language performances appropriate to a man, but only in the context of his home, a feminized site. The literacy myth conspires with this gendered schooling of our emotions to suggest that the problem was inadequate ambition: he was not, we are told, the "progressive type." Moreover, the gendered schooling of the dominant culture might ask us to see the women in his life as "emasculating": his daughter gains a job at his expense, by building and then destroying his hyper-masculine fantasy. His wife "nags" him into renting a typewriter. His tenant taunts him for expecting his wife to do a man's job.

At the same time that the literacy myth and the dominant schooling of emotion suggests this reading, however, the story pushes against any possibility of so seamless (and, for me, troubling) a reception. After all, it *is* clear that the father has ambition and a high-level of literacy, thus complicating the reading of him as inadequately "progressive." Moreover, his daughter *does* get a job, at a time when white women dominated clerical work. As the historian Jacqueline Jones has documented:

> During the 1920s, four out of every ten new white women workers went into "clean work" as sales clerks or secretaries (some of them immigrants' daughters who had completed commercial courses of study in public high schools), but only 5 percent of all new black women workers found . similar jobs, and those were hired primarily in black businesses or in mail-order operations, out of sight of white customers. (324)

By evading the institutionalized racism that kept African American women out of clerical positions, Millie is able to put her literacy to use, and thus challenges the dominant culture's articulation of clerical work with a racialized gender-coding. To a certain extent, then, Millie represents a positive example of putting corporate sponsorship, even if gender-specific, to use. She is more than a docile body performing a me-chanical task: she is taking it upon herself to take on new literacies, in particular, literacies that can be exchanged in the labor process by a fe-male body.

In putting her gendered literacy to use for economic advantage, how-ever, Millie automatically enters into a social relationship, in that the significance of literacy takes shape only in relation to others (see Street; Brandt). To perform gendered literacy, she must enter into a relation-ship of subordination that temporarily revitalizes her father. Simulta-neously, she participates in a socioeconomic system that refuses to recognize the literacy performed by her father's racialized body. She is rewarded for her gendered performance, but must subordinate herself to a masculinized and racialized corporate space and witness her father's demise. As Harvey points out:

> Trade-offs plainly exist between how laborers submit to or struggle with the dictates of capital at one moment to enhance their powers at another. Abject submission to the dictates of capital within production, for exam-ple, may for some be a reasonable price to bear for adequate pleasures and fulfillments of desires …. But what dictates whether that price is judged too high? (117)

Millie, along with similar women who take on clerical and other service positions, trade submission for a job; feeling literate is one way in which adequate pleasure in the job is maintained, making the cost of submis-sion seem reasonable.

TOWARD A DIFFERENT WAY OF FEELING

This story, then, could be said to represent the "pessimism of the intel-ligence" that leftist scholars since Gramsci have traditionally deemed essential for hegemonic struggle, dramatizing as it does the uneven economic advancement brought by literacy acquisition, despite the apparent promises of the literacy myth. Gramsci made "[p]essimism of the intelligence, optimism of the will" an imperative in his work, ad-vocating the necessity "to direct one's attention violently towards the present as it is, if one wishes to transform it" (175). The literacy narra-tives in West's story—like other literacy narratives that "both drama-tize and critique" the literacy myth—realistically expose the symbolic violence of a society that holds out the promise of self-advancement through education while severely limiting the ability of whole groups of people to trade on this cultural capital (Eldred and Mortensen 514; see also Bourdieu). As Eldred and Mortensen point out, "the left posits a version of literacy that, short of political revolution, always results in the unfinished, the displaced" (534). Insofar as West's story offers a pessimistic tale of displaced literate feelings, it remains unfinished—a narrative that calls into question existing social conditions, but that seems to offer no clear alternative.

Harvey, working out of this leftist tradition of intellectual pessimism, has recently argued that the "inability to find an 'optimism of the intellect' with which to work through alternatives has now become one of the most serious barriers to progressive politics" (17). As a theoretical alternative to pessimism, Harvey offers the concept of "dialectical utopianism," a utopianism "rooted in our present possibilities at the same time as it points towards different trajectories for human uneven geographical developments" (196). Dialectical utopianism never loses sight of the violence of the present, but it strives to move beyond that violence, using the present as material for "thought experiments about alternative possible worlds" (Harvey 199). In order to be optimistic about literacy, then, in order to find a different way of feeling about literacy, it will be essential to imagine alternatives without losing sight of the emotional and economic hazard of the failure of literacy's promise. Linked as they are to the failure of education to lead to economic betterment, literacy narratives that expose the literacy myth certainly serve as fodder for a pessimism of the intelligence and offer a useful reminder of the material and immaterial limits of literacy. The challenge is to find a way to use these pessimistic conditions as the point of emergence of a new possibility.

Insofar as West's story itself stands in as a literate performance that seeks to educate our emotions, and thus makes use of literacy as a critical tool for potential social change, it offers an opportunity for imagining materially grounded alternatives for literacy. If we think of the young woman writing the story as a version of the young woman written in the story, we begin to glimpse the potential of literacy as a tool that can work in new ways only through a re-schooling of literate feelings. West was only seventeen years old when "The Typewriter" tied for second-place (with a story by Zora Neale Hurston) in *Opportunity* magazine's 1926 literary contest, sponsored by the Urban League (Washington xiv). In the 1995 introduction to her collection of stories and sketches, *The Richer, The Poorer*, however, West recalls winning a prize sponsored by *The Crisis*, the NAACP's magazine. She apparently was confusing the two important Harlem Renaissance-era magazines, but her comments on *The Crisis* are nonetheless instructive:

> My mother, who had heard of *The Crisis*, was dismayed when the magazine appeared in our mail slot. The young members in our extended family, all born and raised in Boston, had little if any knowledge of lynching and other obscenities. To see them graphically depicted might discourage us from pursuing our ambition in a world stacked against us. (2)

In linking her story with *The Crisis*, West suggests that she regards "The Typewriter" itself to be a depiction of a "world stacked against" black people. Although West was raised in an affluent, middle-class home and "never had to struggle with want," and although her father, a former slave, had achieved his dream of becoming a wholesale produce merchant in Boston, West was able to *imagine* and depict a middle-class black family whose success was less secure ("Gift" 178, 179). In using literacy to imagine lives unlike her own, West is enacting literacy as defined by Jacqueline Jones Royster: "the ability to gain access to information and to use this information variously to articulate lives and experiences and also to identify, think through, refine and solve problems, sometimes complex problems, over time" (45). According to Royster, "African American women writers across genres ... evidence a desire ... to 'move' the audience, that is, to inspire change—in thinking, feeling, and behavior" (21). Royster's definition moves literacy away from the literacy myth and traditional ways of feeling literate, to emphasize instead literacy's very real potential for social change. If feeling literate is one way in which the capitalist life-world is produced and reproduced, a different way of feeling about literacy should hold the potential for altering that world (see Hardt 100). Although neither the father nor daughter in the story seem to be emotionally moved by literacy's potential for collective action, the story itself performs literacy as defined by Royster. By demonstrating both the limits and the potential of feeling literate, West uses her own literacy to "articulate lives and experiences" and thus "to move" her readers, so that her writing "both reflects and critiques the attitudes and ideals of the black bourgeoisie"(Washington xii). Although her family's and her own economic success exceeded that of the family in the story, West was nonetheless able to use her own literacy to, as Royster says, gather information and see outside of herself. While the critique enacted in the story's literacy narratives holds firmly to a pessimism of the intelligence, West's own use of literacy points toward optimism: the belief, the feeling that literacy is one avenue toward social change.

Through vivid demonstrations of the emotional thread that connects gendered and racialized identities, literate performances, and labor processes, West's story raises important questions for literacy scholars and educators. In part, these questions are pessimistic: as educators who regularly sponsor performances of literacy, what ways of feeling literate does our sponsorship evoke? What uses of literacy do these feelings resist or reinforce? West's story suggests that, more often than not, sponsored literacy plays into the literacy myth, which, in turn, supports a labor process that violently marginalizes and feminizes. West's story, however, also supports Michael Hardt's tentative optimism: if affective labor, together with literacy, is a "necessary foundation for capitalist accumulation and patriarchal order," then affect and literacy also offer enormous potential as the foundation for resistance and change, since, as Foucault has taught us, "[w]here there is power, there is resistance"

(Hardt 100; Foucault 95). Critically examining emotion as a literacy sponsor thus serves as more than a moment of intellectual pessimism: it also marks the potential point of emergence of literacies that may themselves sponsor different ways of feeling and new deployments of affective labor.

WORKS CITED

Bourdieu, Pierre. *Language and Symbolic Power*. Trans. Gino Raymond and Matthew Adamson. Cambridge: Harvard UP, 1991.

Brandt, Deborah. *Literacy in American Lives*. New York: Cambridge UP, 2001.

Cromwell, Adelaide M. Afterword. *The Living Is Easy*. By Dorothy West. New York: Feminist P, 1982. 349–64.

Daniell, Beth. "Narratives of Literacy: Connecting Composition to Culture." *College Composition and Communication* 50 (1999): 393–410.

Eldred, Janet Carey, and Peter Mortensen. "Reading Literacy Narratives." *College English* 54 (1992): 512–39.

Foucault, Michel. *The History of Sexuality, Volume I: An Introduction*. Trans. Robert Hurley. New York: Random House, 1978.

Gee, James Paul. "Literacy, Discourse, and Linguistics: Introduction." *Journal of Education* 171 (1989): 5–25.

Graff, Harvey J. *The Legacies of Literacy: Continuity and Contradictions in Western Culture and Society*. Bloomington: Indiana UP, 1987.

——. *The Literacy Myth: Literacy and Social Structure in the Nineteenth-Century City*. New York: Academic P, 1979.

Gramsci, Antonio. *Selections from the Prison Notebooks*. Ed. and trans. Quintin Hoare and Geoffrey Nowell Smith. New York: International, 1971.

Hardt, Michael. "Affective Labor." *Boundary 2* 26 (1999): 89–100.

Harvey, David. *Spaces of Hope*. Berkeley: U of California P, 2000.

Jones, Jacqueline. *American Work: Four Centuries of Black and White Labor*. New York: Norton, 1998.

Royster, Jacqueline Jones. *Traces of a Stream: Literacy and Social Change Among African American Women*. Pittsburgh: U of Pittsburgh P, 2000.

Street, Brian V. *Literacy in Theory and Practice*. New York: Cambridge UP, 1984.

Strickland, Donna. "Taking Dictation: The Emergence of Writing Programs and the Cultural Contradictions of Composition Teaching." *College English* 63 (2001): 457–79.

Washington, Mary Helen. Preface. *The Richer, the Poorer: Stories, Sketches, and Reminiscences*. By Dorothy West. New York: Anchor/Doubleday, 1995. xi–xv.

West, Dorothy. Introduction. *The Richer, the Poorer: Stories, Sketches, and Reminiscences*. New York: Anchor/Doubleday, 1995. 1–6.

——. "The Gift." *The Richer, the Poorer: Stories, Sketches, and Reminiscences*. New York: Anchor/Doubleday, 1995. 177–79.

——. "The Typewriter." *The Richer, the Poorer: Stories, Sketches, and Reminiscences*. New York: Anchor/Doubleday, 1995. 9–17.

Worsham, Lynn. "Going Postal: Pedagogic Violence and the Schooling of Emotion." *JAC: A Journal of Composition Theory* 18 (1998): 213–45.

Yates, JoAnne. *Control through Communication: The Rise of System in American Management*. 1983. Baltimore: Johns Hopkins UP, 1993.

Crusader: Ethel Azalea Johnson's Use of the Written Word as a Weapon of Liberation

Rhea Estelle Lathan

Like the dead-seeming, cold rocks, I have memories within that came out of the material that went to make me. Time and place have had their say. So you will have to know something about the time and place where I came from, in order that you may interpret the incidents and directions of my life.
                                    —Zora Neale Hurston, "Dust Tracks on A Road"

Black liberation struggle must be re-visioned so that it is no longer equated with maleness. We need a revolutionary vision of black liberation, one that emerges from a feminist standpoint and addresses the collective plight of black people.
                                    —bell hooks, *Yearning: Race, Gender and Cultural Politics*

Within their roles as mothers, sisters, spiritual leaders, and instructors, African American women have commanded positions as cultural, social, and political leaders. Through multiple intellectual and literate activities, they have maintained their presence in American crusades for social justice. Both Shirley Wilson Logan and Jacqueline Jones Royster have developed frameworks through which to consider how nineteenth-century African American women, struggling under the double burden of racism and sexism, acquired and incorporated literate and rhetorical tools as a means of empowerment and resistance (Logan, *Coming*; Royster, *Traces*). Working from these studies, I explore how this tradition is both continued and transformed in the twentieth century by women involved in the civil rights movement. Particularly, I explore

59

these continuities and changes by looking at the writing of the late civil rights activist Ethel Azalea Johnson, in an effort to expand representations of African American women's literacies. I follow Deborah Brandt by illustrating how individual ways of writing, knowing, interpreting, and being are connected to larger social systems.

Ethel Azalea Johnson was co-founder, editor, business manager, and columnist for *The Crusader,* a weekly newsletter she published along with Robert and Mabel Williams in Monroe, North Carolina, in the late 1950s and early 1960s. Monroe is located in Union County, which spans the borders of North and South Carolina. *The Crusader* was primarily developed as an answer to the white press and to what Johnson and the Williamses considered an accommodationist black press. Johnson was exasperated with the manner in which incidents regarding Monroe's black community were altered by outside publications and she saw the newsletter as an opportunity to express a homegrown grassroots perspective of black Southern radicalism, which emerged from local African American traditions and communities of resistance. Another goal of the publication was to challenge *The Crisis,* the national but more conservative newsletter targeting black readers published by the National Association for the Advancement of Colored People (NAACP).

ETHEL AZALEA JOHNSON: A BRIEF BACKGROUND

Johnson was born on January 31, 1916, in Abbeville, South Carolina, and died June 26, 1985, in Baldwin, Michigan. The granddaughter of enslaved African Americans, she included in her column in *The Crusader* the horrific stories of captivity passed down to her by her mother, Hilliard Johnson. Johnson's mother also taught her about her African heritage and nurtured Johnson's belief in basic human rights. *The Crusader* and her column served as an opportunity for Johnson to publish some of the stories passed on by her mother. For example, Johnson's father had to flee for his life from their home because he called a white man a liar, an incident that resulted in a late-night visit from the Ku Klux Klan. According to Johnson, this incident produced physical and psychological scars for her mother, ultimately helping to formulate Johnson's own direction in life:

> I remember the sorrow of my mother, when my father had to flee for his life, because he'd called a white man a liar. How she tried to keep us from seeing the white hooded men at the door. But we saw them and heard the awful threats too. From then on, my mother had to work so hard to support us. She lost her eyesight later in life, due to (said the doctor) "years of eye strain." I remember the dime kerosene lamps and the huge pile of white folks' clothing to be ironed. (29 Apr. 1961)[1]

Consequently, Johnson became extremely active in the struggle for civil rights; she served as Secretary of the Union County Branch of the NAACP. Johnson was affiliated with the Southern Christian Leadership Conference and in the 1960s was trained as a voter registration organizer at the Highlander Folk School, a center in New Market, Tennessee, for labor union and civil rights activism and home to the famous Highlander Freedom Schools. At Highlander she received training in adult literacy education from Septima Clark, best known for her high profile role as Educational Director for Highlander and the Southern Christian Leadership Conference. According to her co-publisher Mabel Williams, Johnson was intensely aware of her African roots, while organizing and teaching adult literacy classes throughout Union County, in various subjects, including African and African American history.

"DID YOU KNOW?"

From 1959 through 1961, Johnson wrote a weekly column in *The Crusader*, called "Did You Know?" Similar to earlier generations of African American women such as those analyzed by Royster, Johnson employed her literacy and her rhetorical practices to express a traditional value system while aggressively disrupting an ideology of racist oppression. She joins a tradition of African American women who use inventive and resourceful critical thinking strategies to make life better for themselves, and in doing so, make life better for others. However, unlike some of the elite African American women in studies like Royster's and Logan's, Johnson was a working-class, single mother. She was an African American woman with no formal instruction in journalism or the conventions of public writing. Even more distinctive is Johnson's grassroots activism. As a local resident, she tells the story from inside the community.

Using the column as an instructional tool, Johnson employed a form of persuasive meaning-making to dismantle racist ideologies. The title and Johnson's editorial work positioned "Did You Know?" as a challenge, and its tone implies that she is going to tell you what she has to say regardless of what you already know. It also implies that what you know may be distorted and you need to be re-taught. Johnson used her "Did You Know?" column systematically to provide a counter-reality to Jim Crow oppression. One way she did this was by boldly challenging contradictions in language used to tyrannize black people. In the following passage, she launches a direct attack on white supremacist language by carefully and systematically challenging specific words. She asks her readers to think differently about the uses and meanings of these words.

> *Did You Know* ... The word 'Negro' was made by white supremacists for the definite purpose of separating the minds of black people from any

land, country or nation, and from dignity of manhood. All races of men are named by two things: The land or country to which they belong and by the race to which they belong. The word Negro does not refer to any land or country. There is not now, nor has there ever been a place in the whole wide world called "Negro-land." There is no such thing as a Negro race. White people schemed to keep black people from calling themselves black men and black women (just as white people proudly call themselves white men and white women) by making the word *black* a bad word. This brainwashing scheme starts in early childhood when children first learn to talk. They are taught that a black cat is a bad-luck cat; black Friday was a terribly bad day in America (Sept. 24, 1869). Blackmail is a bad crime and white means pure, clean, good, spotless and Caucasian people. One leading dictionary follows the pattern by defining the word *black*: "Negro. Dirty, filthy"—This is not accidental. Out of all this confusion that white people made, many black people are ignorantly ashamed of the word "black" and gladly accept the caste name "Negro." (11 July 1959)

Johnson critically deconstructs the language supporting Jim Crow ideologies by offering an interpretation of the social and economic biases against which a struggle for liberation must be aimed. She makes a conscious effort to teach her readers about the ideas connected to something as important as naming. Armed with the knowledge of the ways in which the English language is used to oppress the African American community, Johnson responds by using the oppressors' language against the oppressor. In other words, she uses the Master's tools to dismantle the Master's house (cf. Lorde). She begins by instructing the reader to resist historically racist definitions and then re-presents racially oppressive language from an African American perspective. She projects a clear message that black pride must transcend the psychologically confining paradigms that limit black thought and achievement. In turn, she attacks socially accepted language, labels, and titles placed on black people. For example, by unpacking the race-based terms, *Negro* and *black*, she frames them to connote an alternate, less degrading meaning. Johnson carefully sets up her writing to inform her readers of an alternate way of thinking and making meaning.

Here we see that Johnson's pedagogical aim is similar to Paulo Freire's notion of *conscientização,* a term referring the process of "learning to perceive social, political, and economic contradictions, and to take action against the oppressive elements of reality" (35). Like Freire, Johnson draws attention to the consciousness of the oppressed. She uses a teaching style that compels the reader to see the contradictions within the language of a society that has created a vocabulary to dehumanize African American people. Freire argues that the process of interpreting language includes critically exploring its ideological significance. What we see here is Johnson's creative meaning-making strategies that clearly convey the relationship between language and political realties. This approach promotes and encourages resistance to the system of oppression.

LOCAL CONDITIONS

Another pedagogical strategy for Johnson was the use of history and narrative to confront *The Crusader*'s readers with local conditions so that they could no longer ignore or deny the social, economic and political realities in their community. As Royster and Logan have demonstrated, significant traumatic events can be motivating incidents for participation in crusades against oppression. For instance, the brutal lynching of a good friend catapulted Ida B. Wells into the arena of writing for liberation. Johnson utilized her position within the group, as a resident of the community, to report on local social, political, and economic events that had a direct impact on the lives of black women as domestic workers and mothers. Johnson recounts in "Did You Know?" the lived experience of a woman doing domestic work:

> It was a beautiful fall day in Abbeville, South Carolina. The parsonage was a galaxy of lovely fall flowers, the old furniture showed the results of many hours of polishing, and the floors were waxed in readiness, awaiting the arrival of the new minister of the local white church and his family. The ladies of the church were nervously seeing that the planned elaborate meal was just right. The perspiring Negro cook kept assuring them that the dinner was all right, even though she had prepared everything without any additional help. The cook felt rather proud of the dinner, proud to show her culinary skill to the new family. The expected group finally arrived. They had four children and a dog.
>
> After the dinner was over, some of the ladies came into the kitchen showing the pastor's wife around and giving her an opportunity to meet her cook. The pastor's wife mentioned the feeding of the dog, then she and the other Christian white ladies began raking the leftovers into two plates, and told the cook to take one of the plates of food and give it to the dog, and then to "sit down and eat your dinner" (which to the amazement of the cook, was the other plate of leftovers). And after she'd cleaned up the kitchen, she was "free to go home."
>
> After the ladies had gone into the other part of the house, the cook sat down at the kitchen table and stared at the leftover food. Tears began to run down her smooth black cheeks. After all the long hours she'd spent preparing the dinner, to think she was only allowed the leftovers. She was being treated like the dog, only the dog had to be given his dinner before she could eat hers. (1 Oct. 1960)

Johnson finishes this narrative by relating how this woman walked home to her hungry children with tears in her eyes, knowing that she would have to choose between rejecting this dehumanizing treatment and being able to feed her own children. Johnson knew that episodes like this were common for black women confined by the straight jacket of Jim Crow. Johnson recounts such incidents so that the local community can connect to the misery and humiliation of their own situations. She inserts Christian commentary as an appeal to the consciousness of the members of her community who claim a religious alliance to Christianity. Her story gives readers evidence with which to examine their individual and collective culture. It also provides readers a means to weigh what they have been led to believe about Christianity against the reality of racist ideologies engrained in the consciousness of some practitioners of that faith. Johnson's appeal also demonstrates, again, that a large part of the success of the civil rights movement derives from the traditional intersection, within African American communities, between religious and secular organizations that formed around shared goals.

Johnson also demonstrated that she recognized the value of economic independence and sociopolitical sovereignty, a philosophy she acquired through personal experience. She was a self-taught business woman and an advocate for local black-owned businesses. She always owned a station wagon or pickup truck and, according to Mabel Williams, it was not uncommon to see Johnson driving around Union County selling merchandise from her automobile. While writing for *The Crusader*, Johnson supported herself by selling life insurance to black people. Self-taught, she passed the trade on to others. Insurance sales facilitated her access to the African American community, supported her pursuit of community activism, and virtually eliminated white economic retaliation. Her commitment to the economic freedom of black people was evident in the number of *Crusader* advertisements that promoted local businesses. She used her column to bring attention to white-owned businesses that supported the liberation movement along with a call to boycott those businesses that did not support the crusade. For example, she writes:

> Did you know that some Afro-Americans here would not patronize the new ultra-modern laundry-mart until the "colored only" sign was removed? Now another launderette has opened in the same Afro-American neighborhood with "white only" signs prominently displayed under both windows of the G. B. Mangum owned building in this same neighborhood, which has flourished and grown because of Afro-American patronage. (6 June 1961)

Johnson goes on to report that the owner of this business spoke publicly in favor of "tearing down colored homes" in the African American section of town. Her goal is to expose the racist and oppressive behaviors of "white-operated" businesses and advocate the support of black-owned businesses.

Focusing her columns on events throughout Union County, Johnson reported on the activities of local churches, businesses, and community projects. She helped organize a relief program called the Crusaders Association for Relief and Enlightenment (CARE), which provided food, clothing, and money to poor people in the community. In several of her columns she illustrated her frustration with the limited support from local church members. She also used the column to inform her readers of the ways in which the "Christian" community's minimal concern left many children unable to attend school because of a lack of food and clothing. Johnson used these situations as learning opportunities for herself, transferring her consciousness to readers by framing the facts of oppressive conditions.

JOHNSON AND HER AUDIENCES

Most effectively Johnson used her column to remind her readers of local injustice and of the dangerous environment in which they lived. In fact, at the fevered height of the civil rights movement, the acquittal of two white men who in separate incidents assaulted two black women actually vaulted *The Crusader* into production.

Accounts of the incidents state that Georgia Davis White, a mother of five and a black maid at the Hotel Monroe, interrupted the sleep of Brodus F. Shaw, a railroad engineer, while attending to her duties. Shaw, angered by what he perceived as her intrusion, severely beat White and threw her down a flight of stairs. He was acquitted without even bothering to make his court appearance. On the same day Shaw was scheduled to appear in court, the trial of Lewis Medlin, a white mechanic accused of attempting to rape a pregnant black woman, was set to begin. Medlin was accused of entering the home of Mrs. Ruth Reid in an inebriated state and attempting to rape her in front of her children. Eight months pregnant, Reid resisted him, running into the street with her six-year-old son defending her with a stick. With the assistance of a white neighbor, Reid escaped. Taking a courageous stand, Reid pressed charges against Medlin, even though, as sharecroppers, she and her husband risked eviction (or worse) as retaliation. This effort to fight Jim Crow proved fruitless, and Medlin was acquitted and released into the community to continue terrorizing the black women of Monroe. Johnson considered the theatrics acted out in the courtroom an attack against the integrity of *all* black women, especially when the defense attorney argued that Medlin was drunk and merely attempting to amuse himself. The *New York Post* of May 7, 1959, reported that during the trial several of the white jurors laughed out loud. Medlin's attorney stressed the social differences between Mrs. Reid and Medlin's wife, who was deliberately positioned next to her husband during the court proceedings to give the appearance that Mrs. Medlin was also on trial. The defense attorney stated, "This woman, this *white* woman is the pure flower of life. She is one of God's lovely creatures, a pure flower of life." Continuing with his theatrics he stated, "[D]o you think he would have left this pure flower ... for *that?*" Medlin was acquitted (Tyson 148). Of this incident, Johnson wrote:

> It had been a hot and tiring day of court trials in Monroe, many Negroes had stated from the onset that there would be no justice in the court, and that it behooved our cause to render justice to the offenders. The court freed one white Seaboard Railroad engineer, for kicking a Negro hotel maid down a flight of stairs. When the white man was set free for attempting to rape a pregnant Negro woman (I've often wished the National officers of the NAACP could have talked with her as we did) the faces of Negroes in the court room, reflected the type of anguish that demands reassurance or positive action. (17 Oct. 1959)

She continues to give voice to the outrage of black women in Monroe writing, "The virtue of Negro women and Negro rights must be defended as all rights of other races are defended" (17 Oct. 1959). *The Crusader* was a means to give voice to the outrage of black women of Monroe.

Johnson emphasized that she was fed up with the Jim Crow system of oppression and seized an opportunity to be one of the liberating voices of and for black women in Monroe. She illustrated her intellectual aptitude by developing her writing into a tool for expressing her liberatory consciousness. In a column of September 12, 1959, Johnson demonstrates how her thoughts and language converge with a larger sociopolitical significance. She frequently takes up the problem of black accommodationist writing: "The Negro must use all of his facilities, if he is to prove himself. He must stop imitating others; he must be nonconformist to an oppressed caste system, if he expects to leave his footprints on the sands of Time." In this passage she is clearly addressing an audience—black accommodationists—that may not subscribe to her beliefs. However, she uses language that calls attention to the specific actions that support the racist ideologies. Johnson typically expressed theses ideas using religious illustrations, arguing that "imitating" the oppressor only further supports that oppressive philosophy. She calls attention to the fact that accommodating behavior and attitudes will not change oppressive conditions for black people in the United States:

> Some of our Negro Ministers have accumulated great wealth on the theory that the Negro masses must pray[,] keep quiet[,] and turn the other cheek to their oppressors. They have preached that in time, God will change the

white folks' hearts, and then the whites will treat us fairly. They have preached that if we pay our last dollar to them, two more dollars will come back to us from somewhere. Prayer, nonresistance and money, these three things our Negro ministers have pounded in our heads for generations. Of course, men aught always to pray, but to me, this nonresistance is misused and intentionally so by our ministers. (17 Sept. 1960)

She denounces the acceptance of the notion of white people as superior to Negroes and calls upon people to act. Johnson does this by first requesting that the community respond by not accepting conventional racist language supported by racist ideologies: "American Negroes must stop conforming to oppressive customs. The American Negro must ignore the whirlwind of words, whispered by men who will conform, men who will give up the spark of perception, for their own comfort" (12 Sept. 1959). Johnson encourages African American people to use their intellect, asserting that the result of ignoring their own abilities will make black people "like everyone else," and she counsels, "will never enable you to speak your convictions, never enable you to believe in yourself and you will forever need the soothing, lying praise of the masses" (12 Sept. 1959). She employs her knowledge of language and its usefulness in achieving particular rhetorical effects to obligate the reader to respond.

As a grassroots, working-class, self-employed black woman, Ethel Azalea Johnson applied her considerable intellectual resources in addressing various segments of the black community from her stance as a public writer. She usually focused her writing on a poor working-class black readership. However, within this group she recognized multiple guiding philosophies, including, but not limited to, Christianity. Johnson often directed her writings toward African American ministers, especially those in her own denomination, the African Methodist Episcopal Church. She also addressed the traditional civil rights leadership, including the NAACP and SCLC, as well as like-minded white ministers. She included black accommodationists as well. In one column she specifically addressed the white racist who was reading her column and making life-threatening phone calls to her home. Johnson wrote to young people in her community to encourage them to become economically independent. Her intellectual creativity is especially interesting because of the ways she used her knowledge of a range of attitudes and beliefs within her community.

IMPLICATIONS

The argument I wish to make about African American women's literacies is indicated by the words from Zora Neale Hurston, words

that open this chapter. Like Hurston, I argue that black women's critical intelligence is part of the African American tradition and must be
recognized in order to give a fuller understanding of the world in
which we live. Hurston's concepts of memory, material, incidents, and
direction call for re-interpreting literacy's history, instruments, and
context. I follow Royster in the belief that: "People Who Do Intellectual Work Need to Understand Their Intellectual Ancestry" (*Traces*
265). In other words, exploring Johnson's literate activities adds to the
legacy of African American women's experience, strength, and hope
in the struggle for liberation. Like Royster and Jean Williams in their
essay "History in the Spaces Left: African American Presence and Narratives of Composition Studies," I am working from the theory that
"unnoticed" stories of composition history can "interact with official-
ized narratives and tell a reconfigured, more fully textured story than
we now understand" (581).

I suggest a mutually dependent relationship between literacy learning and a social political movement, while simultaneously challenging essentialist assumptions of African American women's
intellectual achievements. Moreover, Johnson's crusade confronts
conventional patriarchal histories of the civil rights movement and the
types of nonviolent expressive protest, such as marches and sit-ins,
commonly connected to it. This project builds on the work of Afrafem-
inists who argue that African American women were central to the
civil rights movement. Further, it calls attention to African Americans
who, in the mid-twentieth century, contributed to knowledge-making
as a means to advance social justice and action. As Royster has stressed, these women are not a lone phenomenon, but rather are part of
African American tradition.

Royster and Logan have called attention to an African American
women's tradition that draws upon creative intellectual strategies in order to stake a claim to power and autonomy. Both Royster and Logan
emphasize the variety of literate styles and content used by African
American women across generations. We have learned that elite black
women played a primary role in African American communities, but
Johnson's life illustrates that African American women's intellectual
work is not restricted to the elite. Johnson is an example of a grassroots,
working-class black woman using literacy as an instrument for change.
Her story provides material for researching the relationship between
literacy and economic, political, and social changes from the perspective of people living through those changes. My work on Ethel Azalea
Johnson is an attempt to deepen the well of African American women's
intellectual enterprise and to show that critical intelligence also runs
through the literate practices of black women not trained or educated in
mainstream institutions.

NOTE

1. Unless otherwise indicated, all quotations are from "Did You Know?," a column that appeared in *The Crusader,* located in the Wisconsin State Historical Society's Library Pamphlet Collection. *The Crusader* issue dates are listed parenthetically in the text.

WORKS CITED

Brandt, Deborah. *Literacy in American Lives.* New York: Cambridge UP, 2001.

——. "Literacy." *The Encyclopedia of Rhetoric and Composition.* Ed. Theresa Enos. New York: Garland, 1996. 392–94.

Freire, Paulo. *Pedagogy of the Oppressed.* 1970. Trans. Myra Bergman Ramos. New York: Continuum, 2000.

hooks, bell. *Yearning: Race, Gender, and Cultural Politics.* Boston: South End P, 1990.

Hurston, Zora Neale. "Dust Tracks on a Road." *Folklore, Memoirs, and Other Writings.* Ed. Cheryl A. Wall. New York: Library of America, 1995. 557–808.

Logan, Shirley Wilson. *We Are Coming: The Persuasive Discourse of Nineteenth-Century Black Women.* Carbondale: Southern Illinois UP, 1999.

Lorde, Audre. *Sister Outsider: Essays and Speeches.* Trumansburg, NY: Crossing P, 1984.

Royster, Jacqueline Jones. "Perspectives on the Intellectual Tradition of Black Women Writers." *The Right to Literacy.* Ed. Andrea A. Lunsford, Helen Moglen, and James Slevin. New York: MLA, 1990. 91–103.

——. *Traces of a Stream: Literacy and Social Change among African American Women.* Pittsburgh: U of Pittsburgh P, 2000.

Royster, Jacqueline Jones, and Jean C. Williams. "History in the Spaces Left: African American Presence and Narratives of Composition Studies." *College Composition and Communication* 50 (1999): 563–84.

Tyson, Timothy. *Radio Free Dixie: Robert F. Williams and the Roots of Black Power.* Chapel Hill: U of North Carolina P, 1999.

Williams, Mabel. Personal interview. 16 Oct. 2002.

Virginia Mountain Women Writing to Government Officials: Letters of Request as Social Participation

Katrina M. Powell

> ... let me no if I ante eot the same write to git apples on this place ....
> —Mrs. Charley Dyer, Letter to the Superintendent
> of the Shenandoah National Park, May 8, 1936

> We have realized that there is no such thing as "the" southern woman, for she came in many varieties of class, race, and ability. The reality, we have discovered, is neither so simple nor so glamorous as the myth.
> —Anne Firor Scott, "Historians Construct the Southern Woman"

When the Shenandoah National Park (SNP) was formed in the early 1930s, more than 500 families were displaced from their homes in Virginia's Blue Ridge Mountains. Once the land became federal property, the Resettlement Administration, together with local social workers, began a complicated process of evaluating people for their eligibility for homesteads. While the homesteads were being built, families remained on parkland until their new homes were ready, some for as many as five years. During this waiting period, federal law required residents who continued to live on parkland to obtain a special use permit. This permit stated that any activities such as grazing cattle, collecting wood, and removing building materials be done only with written permission of the superintendent of SNP. So during this interim, from the time their land became federal property until the time they were removed to homesteads, mountain residents wrote to park officials requesting various permissions. Today, the park's archive holds over 300 letters (only recently available to the public) written by mountain residents during this time. The letters, mostly handwritten in pencil (see Fig. 3.1), reveal a complex relationship between the displaced families of the mountains and the state and federal government agencies responsible for their displacement into homesteads.

Approximately twenty percent of the letters were written by women.[1] I examine the letters' significance in light of the writers' education and literacy, noting how the writers' act of engaging officials (primarily men) suggests a powerful assertion of agency under seemingly hopeless circumstances. The contents of the letters, in terms of language and rhetoric, reveal the complex identities of mountain women, identities that counter and complicate dominant discourses about women and about mountaineers.

"Mountaineers" are culturally inscribed as uneducated, illiterate, and pointedly male (Shapiro). The fact that women wrote the letters to government officials during this time suggests a counter-narrative of the mountaineer and reveals interesting economic, political, and social factors shaping this moment wherein women were contributing rhetors in their communities. The gendered concept of the mountaineer is contradicted through these letters, and the specific contents of the letters suggest the women were literate "enough" to write, to assert an agency not only within their homes and communities, but also through the larger social participation of resisting the federal government's decision to establish a park on their homeland. As Barton and Hall suggest in *Letter Writing as a Social Practice*, "An important aspect of literacy practices is the roles and identities which *participants* assume. In letter writing there are distinct roles, beginning with the writer and the reader" (7). The women writing letters to government officials assumed roles counter to those expected of them, and consequently obliged officials to consider them in different ways.

REPRESENTATIONS OF THE MOUNTAINEER

The people of Appalachia have long been represented as primarily poverty stricken, uneducated, and isolated (Fisher; Foster; Horning; Perdue and Perdue; Whisnant). As studies by Peter Mortensen and by Katherine Sohn demonstrate, countering past representations and consequent attitudes is an ongoing struggle for contemporary Appalachian communities. Historical constructions that can be ascribed to authorities long dead continue to affect life and education in contemporary Appalachia. As both Mortensen and Sohn recommend, it is important to trace conduits of power that link the region's past to its present, and this I do by contrasting metropolitan representations of mountain women's literacy with their own self-representation in high-stakes argumentative prose.

One of the earliest representations of the park and its inhabitants is *Hollow Folk*, written by Mandel Sherman and Thomas Henry, and pub-

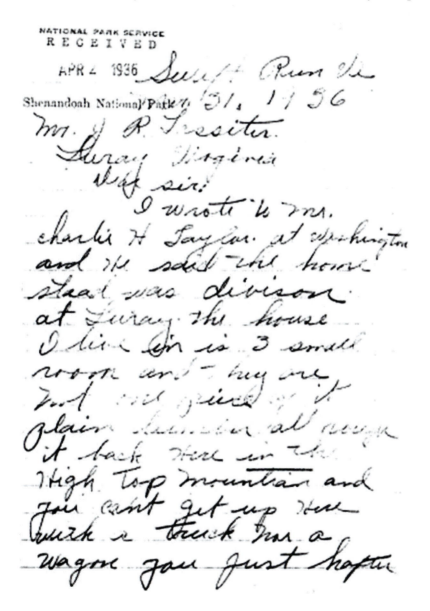

Figure 3.1.   Photocopy of the first page of a letter written by Rebecca Baugher, 31 Mar. 1936 (Luray, VA: Shenandoah National Park Archive).

lished in 1933. Sherman, the director of the Washington Child Research Centre, hired several psychologists and sociologists to conduct surveys about the living conditions, mental states, and nutrition of families living in a hollow within the park's proposed boundaries. Sherman was an associate of George Pollock, a prominent businessman who owned the Skyland resort and was a proponent of the park's development (his reminiscences were written in *Skyland*). Pollock employed schoolteacher Miriam Sizer, a graduate student at the University of Virginia, and encouraged her to participate in the surveys conducted by the Centre. According to archaeologist Audrey Horning, Sizer's survey coincided with the debate over the removal of park residents (*In the Shadow* 100). In addition to her work with the Centre, Sizer's conclusions were used by Virginia officials to recommend ways to solve problems created by the relocation of mountain families. In her "Tabulations" Sizer was genuinely concerned, it is clear, with the mountain folk and their well-being. Based on her interviews with families in several mountain hollows and on her training as a Progressive Era educator, she was concerned that people largely did not understand the "significance of the changes in their lives, and that few have made any plans for this change. This means that the problems of family placement of park residents are practically unsolved" (49). However, her tone was patronizing and patriarchal, and focused primarily on the poverty stricken. Based on her survey results, several months of teaching at a school near Old Rag Mountain, and interviews with families in several hollows, Sizer concluded that because mountain people were "steeped in ignorance, wrapped in self-satisfaction and complacency, possessed of little or no ambition, little sense of citizenship, little comprehension of law or respect for law," they "present a problem that demands and challenges the attention of thinking men and women" ("Suggestions").

As a local schoolteacher, Sizer would have had access to families. The families in this area worked for Pollock and initially trusted the schoolteacher as she asked them questions about their education, work, and social habits. She was sympathetic to their plight, and suggested to those in power that assistance be given to families because of the "limited educational, business, and social opportunities of these mountain people. They live in a medieval age to a large extent, and hence need assistance in making satisfactory adjustments to a modern age" ("Tabulations" 44). Sizer was later despised by the local community because of her condescending and inaccurate descriptions (Horning, *In the Shadow* 100).

Sizer's generalities coincided with misrepresentations of residents in Washington, D.C. newspapers. As the park's development was reported, mountaineers were described as "a community of perennial starvation and penniless squalor ... [where] sisters and brothers have intermarried," a community in which residents were illiterate and therefore unable to communicate with the outside world. "They speak a queer, Chaucerian English, almost un-understandable. They say 'holpen' for 'to help,' and 'withouten' for 'without'" ("U.S."). A *New York Times* article also depicted dire living conditions, asserting that mountain residents were living in "bleak simplicity" and that "there are no social activities, no toys, no group diversions" (Weil). These served as a denigrating misrepresentation of the more complex social, economic, and political systems that existed in the mountains. Sizer's documents and letters to government officials did implore them to establish programs for the mountain people: it is clear she thought she was helping them. However, her paternalistic attitudes about the residents influenced the decisions and policies made by the Secretary of the Interior, the Director of the National Park Service, and the Governor of Virginia. The emphasis on the poverty stricken in the mountains ignored the multiple levels of self-sufficiency, wealth, and education of the population as a whole.

Scholars such as Horning and historian Darwin Lambert have recognized the limited representations of the residents removed from the area that is now the park, and have theorized about how those limited representations have affected our cultural and collective memories about a specific place (see also Powell). When *Hollow Folk,* was published, readers were only presented with images of "unlettered folk ... sheltered in tiny, mud-plastered log cabins and supported by a primitive agriculture" (1). The written images of poverty in *Hollow Folk,* together with photographs within the official documents of the government of the late 1920s and early 1930s, had a lasting effect on the assumed identity of the mountaineer, an identity that included poverty, illiteracy, and dependence. (Many of the photographs of park residents, their homes, and their lands, were taken by Arthur Rothstein, a Farm Security Administration photographer commissioned to take photographs as part of the Federal Writers Project to document rural life.) A direct result of these representations included the physical displacement of mountain families from their homes. Local community members and their political leaders were persuaded by the dominant rhetoric about mountaineers' lack of education and self-sufficiency; consequently, their resistance to the park was minor. The resistance that did exist was unorganized, and it was ultimately inconsequential insofar as the park was established and people lost their homes. However, as the letters I discuss here indicate, Virginia mountain women engaged in a social act that pointedly resisted those dominant representations. While they were not necessarily consciously resisting inscribed identities, their self-constructions reflect identities counter to those provided for them, identities that include education, literacy, rhetorical awareness, strength, hard work, caring for others, and a sense of justice.

EDUCATION OF WOMEN IN RURAL VIRGINIA

According to William Link, a prominent historian of Virginia's progressive education movement, "Local power over education was most apparent in rural schools, which, between the mid-nineteenth century and World War I, flourished in isolation from their urban counterparts" (6). Standardized curricula were a rarity in rural schools, although it is likely that many used primers such as *The McGuffey Reader* and *Harvey's Grammar*. The Commonwealth of Virginia enacted compulsory education for children ages 5–18 in 1908. However, several schools existed in the mountains before this legislation, schools that were funded primarily by parents and local communities. Changes in public education at the turn of the century paralleled the general changes in attitudes about social programs and reform. Link says that, "in a region that more than any other valued individualism, familial identity, and personal honor among white males, hostility toward public control of youth socialization was a virtual certainty. In the antebellum Southern belief system, education remained a matter of private choice and an area in which central, outside government had no place" (7). When Progressive Era reformers moved toward making changes in rural education at the turn of the century, they thought that the "regional uplift" depended on educating white Southerners (88). Link highlights reformers like Hollis Burke Frissell and Robert Frazer, who described poor whites as "semi-civilized" and "poor and ignorant," respectively (88).[2] The reformers' elitist attitudes about poor whites influenced politicians and businessmen, like those interested in establishing the national park in Virginia. As a result, rhetorics of paternalistic reform were used to persuade local communities that moving people out of their isolated locations and close to education was not only good for them as individuals but also good for the region.

Not much research exists about poor women's education in the South or in Appalachia; most historical studies of women's education in the South focus on women of middle and upper classes (Hawks and Skemp; Farnham), although Hawks and Skemp call for studies of women's education that pay more attention to the working classes. Some contemporary research focuses on Southern working-class women who have resisted industry and working conditions (Anglin; Friedman; Kahn; Sohn). The letters written by the women of the Blue Ridge mountains during the 1930s tell an untold story: they are a written record of the kinds of issues faced by working and poor women as social and educational reform shaped their destinies and relocated their homes. As acts of literacy, they provide insight into poor and working class women's education.

Only twenty percent of the letters in the collection were written by women, yet as census data show, women were literate at a higher rate than men, and more girls attended school than did boys. What might account for this discrepancy? While the discrepancy is difficult to account for, several factors may be responsible. First, many of the women living in this area may not have been willing to write to persons in authority, particularly because those authorities were men. Second, their husbands tended to be listed as owners of the land and perhaps the women did not feel in a position to ask for resources. Finally, several of the letters indicate that women wrote for their husbands and signed their husbands' names. In addition to these possible reasons, the women's letters themselves generally varied in content and length from the men's. Many of the women wrote several times while men tended to write only once. In addition, most of the letters written by women were longer and contained more personal information—disclosures that supported the rationales they offered for their requests. Their letters tended to address their values and sense of themselves more often than the ones written by men. As the following analyses suggest, the women writing letters possessed literacies that challenged conventionally accepted notions. Deborah Brandt, among others, reminds us that literacy consists of social meaning-making through language. This definition broadens literacy from reading and writing to wider contextual communicative acts. Donehower asserts that in addition to Scribner's metaphors of adaptation, power, and state of grace, literacy is also relational (see pg. 92 this volume). Scholars like Daniell and Brandt, among others, have already argued for the ways that literacy is key to "identity formation" (Daniell 404). I would add to this conversation that participating in a literacy event such as writing a letter to a government official is a radical shift in a sense of one's self. It does not simply involve forming an identity. The consequences can be devastating as participants re-see themselves in relation to the world around them. The identities constructed in their letters reflect ones they possessed, yet also ones that they had to present to those in power. Consequently, their literacy suggests complex identities that challenged not only the dominant culture's views of them, but also the very political movement used to remove them from their homes. The following analyses ask questions about what literacy or literacies women possessed to challenge inscribed identities.

WOMEN WRITING TO GOVERNMENT OFFICIALS

During the years that the women wrote to the Shenandoah National Park Service, the staff was primarily male, including administration officials and rangers. While mountain families interacted with some women in positions of authority, including teachers, missionaries, and welfare agents, the federal employees charged with managing the land

and the people living on parkland were men. At the archives, nearly all the files with residents' letters include a response from either Park Superintendent James Lassiter, or his rangers, or Ferdinand Zerkel, the projects manager for the Division of Homesteads.[3] The superintendent, together with his park rangers, took great care in answering residents' requests.[4] As the letters indicate, there was much face-to-face interaction between the rangers and the residents; therefore, in the instances where a written response is not included in the files, I assume that a reply was made verbally. Of the letters written by women to government officials during the 1930s, most fell into the following categories: requests, advocacy, demands, and resistance. In the sections that follow, I highlight several letters that illustrate these categories and how they reflect women's literacy at this time.

Simple Requests

Not much collective resistance to the federal takeover of the land occurred, partly because the people were not informed of plans by powerful Virginia businessmen to purchase the land and donate it to the federal government.[5] By the time people wrote letters to park officials, they were not demanding return of their property, but were instead requesting various material goods or assistance based on their individual circumstances. Given the situation, many residents wanted to retain certain materials or harvest crops even though the land was no longer theirs. It is clear from the letters that local park rangers recommended that residents direct their requests in writing to the superintendent of SNP. Following this procedure, apparently, ensured residents' staying out of trouble and thus not receiving an admonishment letter in return. The mountain residents were subjected to the documents of bureaucratic agencies like Virginia's Commission on Conservation and Development (SCCD), the Virginia Department of Public Welfare, the Resettlement Administration, and the National Park Service. While many residents—and nonresidents as well—took materials without permission, residents were encouraged by officials to seek permission and thereby comply with federal regulations.

For instance, Ardista Lamb asked in her letter that she be able to remain on her farm an additional year, as her special use permit had expired before her homestead was ready. The homesteads often took years to complete and many residents were forced to extend their special use permits, often multiple times. In September, 1935, Lamb wrote to Zerkel, "I am very anxious to know if I may stay on my farm for another year. I wasn't to sow grain this fall if I may stay on to harvest it, and I also wish to know if I may have the privilege of having the boxwood on this farm trimmed and sell the trimmings." Lamb explained that if allowed to stay another year, she would be able to harvest her crops, but she would not do so until permission was granted. She also requested that she be able to sell boxwood trimmings. This seems a trivial request, but one that was necessary given park regulations about not destroying or cutting any vegetation on parkland. In her letter, she mentioned that William Carson, the former director of the State Commission on Conservation and Development, saw her at her home (she did not indicate why or how that visit came about). According to Lamb, Mr. Carson planned to "have the boxwood taken up and taken away." She requested that she be able to trim the boxwood beforehand so that she could earn some money from them. Asking for permission this way indicates that Lamb was willing to follow the rules.

Similarly, Rebecca Baugher's request reveals a person interested in salvaging what she can from her property. Her letter sought to persuade the superintendent to allow her to use the materials from the house she lived in to build another when she moved outside the park's boundaries. She first appealed to Superintendent Lassiter's logic, saying, "The house I live in is 3 small room and they are not one piece of it plain lumber all rough." The wood is rough, and not useful to the "CCC boys" who would "burn it up and I hope you Had rather give it to me then for them to burn it up." Baugher referred to President Roosevelt's initiative, the Civilian Conservation Corps, which conducted most of the labor in establishing the park. Primarily young men from Northeastern cities, these "boys" built the Skyline Drive, planted vegetation, and razed the houses deemed of "no value" to the park. Indicative of the mountain families knowing much of the situation among neighbors, Baugher knew that the CCC employees had been directed to burn any lumber that was not deemed useful to the park. Rather than burn and waste the lumber, she argued, give it to her to use in a modest rebuilding of her home. She then commented on her own character: "I wouldn't go ahead and take thing and not ask you all for them." She referred to Mr. Burt, a park ranger, who could vouch that she had been a good citizen by helping him save windows for other residents. Finally, Baugher appealed to Lassiter's emotions: "My Husband was a Vutirn in the World War and He never has got a thing." Because her husband was a veteran, who did not receive any aid from the government, she suggested that it was not too much to ask for this lumber. While her tone at times was pleading, she was also assertive in her postscript: "Answer at once." Baugher's letter reveals what many of the other letters do—that there are resources that could be used, and that CCC employees have been directed to destroy them. While she asked for lumber, many others asked for permission to harvest crops such as apples, chestnuts, and potatoes—crops that in some cases were planted before the residents were evicted. Baugher did not elaborate on her husband's current condition, but she was the one who initiated the request through written permissions so that she and her family might have lumber to build in a different location.

The simple requests that Lamb and Baugher make reflect a large majority of the requests made by both men and women who resided in the park area. They understood that they must follow park regulations, and within the established system of rules, they wrote letters to gain permission for what they needed. However, though their requests were simple, they constructed letters that sought to persuade SNP officials, by ethical appeal, of the reasons they should be granted their requests.

Advocacy for "Nabors"

In addition to requesting materials for their own use, several women wrote on behalf of their neighbors.[6] Interestingly, in the surrounding community, many women in positions of authority wrote to SNP on behalf of mountain residents. Several teachers from mountain schools, social workers from Virginia's Department of Public Welfare, attorneys from local townships, and missionaries from small churches wrote letters to suggest that the park help particular residents because they were "good citizens" or had "never given the park any trouble." The commitment to sustaining community, made visible in care for one's neighbors, was a strongly held value in the mountains, as several residents' letters imply.

One particular letter writer, Daisy Nicholson (Mrs. Haywood Nicholson), wrote to Superintendent Lassiter several times, imploring him to let the residents living near a large commercial orchard have fruit for their own "family use," a term used by Lassiter in letters to other residents regarding collecting fruit in other areas of the park.[7] In her letter written in April 1936, Nicholson suggested that the residents left in the park needed the fruit more than the orchard owners, who no longer lived in the park. She explained in her letter that the orchard owners continued to make a profit from the apples, while she and some other residents depending on relief funds had no fruit for their families. While the Nicholson brothers no longer operated the orchard (as it belonged to the park at this point), they did have a special use permit to continue harvesting the apples. Many residents were no longer allowed to gain commercially from their land, and therefore Lassiter often directed residents to share the fruit available from the many orchards located within the park's boundaries. In her letter, it is clear that Nicholson was aware of this practice, as she referred to "family use" of fruit, one example of several where residents employed the language of the government. She pleaded with Lassiter to let the people living near the orchard have the fruit because they were poor and had difficulty getting food and clothes. In fact, she said, the children went to school with no shoes or new clothes. As an advocate for her neighbors, Nicholson directed Lassiter to visit the school himself so that he might see their plight and agree to let them have the fruit.

Lassiter replied to Nicholson, saying that "[I] wish to advise that I am not in a position at this time to turn over the apples on this place to anyone. Without bias to any of the people, not only your section but in all of the park last year, it was my desire that all of you obtain sufficient apples from the trees within the area needed for family use, and it will be my aim again this fall to try to make a suitable division of the fruit." Lassiter's vague reply did not provide Nicholson with any direction or specific answer to her question. Lassiter's rhetoric reflected much of the correspondence among state and federal officials as policies changed and responsibility for specific decisions and rules were tenuous. Nicholson and others were forced to decode this rhetoric, and navigate the ambiguity. She wrote later that year, and again pleaded with Lassiter that the residents, instead of the orchard owners, be allowed to collect the apples. Nicholson reiterated that while some families had plenty, others had nothing. She appealed to Lassiter's sense of what was right, suggesting that since the apple trees were on public land, the surrounding residents should have access to them. In response to this second letter by Nicholson, Chief Ranger Hoskins wrote for Lassiter, explaining that the original owners of the orchard had the government's permission to collect the apples:

> Your letter of August 29 addressed to Superintendent Lassiter has been referred to me for an answer. If you recall on the same day that your letter was mailed, I called by to see you relative to a request that you had previously made to get apples from the orchards that were formerly owned by Peter and Paul Nicholson. The Nicholson Brothers have permission to get apples from these orchards through this season.

Hoskins and Nicholson apparently had a conversation about the orchard so his letter was likely a formality, a written record of their oral conversation. Many of the residents' letters refer to meetings in residents' homes, the general store, or the park's headquarters in Luray. In this letter, Hoskins referred to their previous conversation, and then told Nicholson that the former owners had a special use permit to continue to harvest apples from the orchard they owned before it was turned over to the park. Nicholson's letters, however, suggested that the owners had everything they needed while she and others suffered. While she acknowledged the response from Lassiter earlier in the year, she made it clear that the situation remained unsatisfactory in her estimation and that it was unfair for the former owners to continue to gain profit from the apples while she and other families would surely suffer during the winter without the fruit.

Nicholson's request was ultimately denied. However, whether a resident's rhetoric was persuasive or not seems to have had little to do with whether a request was granted. Park officials were dealing with a complex situation in which the land shifted ownership (it was first "purchased" by the state of Virginia from landowners, then "donated" to the federal government) and where policies were constantly being negotiated. Given the amount of communication among neighbors, it must have been known that requests were often denied. However, people like Nicholson continued to write letters anyway, resisting the park's policies and calling attention to their unfairness. Nicholson made her plea a matter of record, using her literacy skills to create historical documentation. In addition, she used her literacy to write for others who either were unable or unwilling to write for themselves, so that their positions might be heard by those in authority.

Demands for Assistance

Like Lamb, Baugher, and Nicholson, many of the letter writers were accommodating, asking politely for various materials and information. Some, however, were more assertive, demanding not only that the park grant their requests, but also that the government acknowledge that the requests were valid. For instance, Ida Lillard wrote to Lassiter, "I want a little information and I know you can give it." Rather than the typical polite request that many residents used (e.g., "just a few lines," "I hate to bother you"), Lillard explicitly stated what she wanted and let Lassiter know that she was aware of his access to information. In her letter she asked, using a hypothetical example, whether or not "the party that sold the land [can] still claim that fence and move it away ...." Lillard bought land adjacent to the park and some of the fence line extended into the park's boundaries. The "party" apparently still lived on parkland and continued to pasture cattle there. This party informed Lillard that he was going to move the fence because it was his and the result would be that his cattle would "come in on me." In her letter, Lillard insisted that Lassiter settle her dispute with her neighbor/seller. Because residents continued to live within park boundaries, park officials frequently served as mediators in this kind of disagreement.

Residents often had problems with neighbors whose animals grazed on their land. This kind of dispute was common before the park was established, and local law enforcement settled various arguments. But once the park assumed authority of the land, residents sought help from park rangers who usually deferred authority to the superintendent. For instance, Mrs. Charley Dyer (Lizzie Nicholson Dyer) wrote to Ranger

Hoskins, "Will you plese come Down and git [my neighbor] to put His Hogs up all Drop Him a letter we Been wating all the spring and He want put them up We hovent put out a Bit of girden yet they aer sraying the green zaud [sod] Dawn Here we aer Both living on the zame Farm you come Dawn at once." Because of her neighbor's hogs, Dyer was unable to put in a garden. She suggested the park should force her neighbor to restrain his livestock and demanded that the Ranger come to her place at once to settle the dispute.

In another example, Teeny Nicholson (see Fig. 3.2) also wrote to Ranger Hoskins to settle a dispute. She told him in her March 13, 1937, letter that her neighbors "just keeps milking my cows and I give them milk every time they come after it .... They done my cows bad last year[,] they would milk them and take thire bells off and pull a part thire tails off and made other threats."

She asks the ranger to move the family as soon as possible because "if you leave it to him he wont move at all .... Please Mr. Hoskins don't mention this to [him] or any one that would tell him Because if he knew it no telling what kind of private injure he would do to me, and please have my house fix up as soon as you can for it is in sorely bad shape. Remember me to your wife." Like Dyer, Teeny Nicholson recognized the park service's authority and therefore demanded protection from its

Figure 3.2.   This photograph of Teeny Nicholson was taken by Arthur Rothstein, a Farm Security Administration photographer, outside her home in October, 1935 (Library of Congress, Prints and Photographs Division, FSA/OWI Collection, LC-USF3301-002173-M1).

employees. While she was insistent that they help her, her letter reflected a familiarity with the ranger. She said "remember me to your wife," positioning herself as one who knew him personally and one who could follow letter convention.

In all of these women's letters, there is an urgency, directness, and demand that Lassiter or Hoskins attend to their concerns. While in many letters the grammar and diction were nonstandard, the authors' understanding that the situation deserved a government official's attention is clear. These women were unafraid of informing officials of their duty to provide assistance. The assertion in the letters demanding assistance is also echoed in letters that directly resist the authority of the park. In the following letters, women defied convention as they continued to seek access to resources.

Resistance to Park Authority

In several cases, when mountain residents were not successful in their various requests, they wrote letters to other officials, either within the state or federal government. Lula Haney's house, for instance, was scheduled to be razed because of its proximity to the proposed Skyline Drive. Park officials, and director of the National Park Service, Arno Cammerer, in particular, wanted all evidence of human habitat to be done away with. Therefore all houses within one to two miles of the proposed Skyline Drive were to be destroyed or moved. In an effort to save her home from razing, Lula Haney wrote to President Franklin D. Roosevelt after park officials were unable (or unwilling) to help her. She told the President in her January 13, 1936 letter, "We had a 100 acres here on top of the 'Blue Ridge' now the entrance of the 'Park' on Swift Run Gap. I am not ashamed of the old house, tho it does look kinda weather beaten. I always loved my 'mountain home' and never wanted to sell it, but as you know how it all happened, guess it is 'gone' now." Haney was certain Roosevelt knew about the park (he dedicated it in 1935) and her letter suggested that if he knew her personal attachment to the house he would do something for her. She also told him that the limited range of options for relocation was unacceptable. While she and her family had signed for a homestead, their current home would be torn down before the homestead house was ready. She asked Roosevelt where her family was supposed to stay in the interim. While she acknowledged that she would ultimately lose her home to the park, she asked to remain there until her homestead was ready. She concluded her letter saying, "I know there is some other 'authority' perhaps I should have asked, but I did not know to whom to go, so in humble simplicity I come to you for directions and information. May I hear from you at an early date? May God bless and keep you as one who leads our 'nation.'

Fraternally yours, Lula A. Haney." While she affected humility in "bothering" the President, she also deemed her situation and the situation of the park as a whole as something with which he should be concerned. Nearly all requests were denied, yet women like Lula Haney wrote because it seemed to be their only recourse. Haney resisted through documenting her frustration, and by bypassing Lassiter's authority and writing directly to the President.

While Haney's letter was polite and urged the President to answer her request as the leader of the nation, Lillie Herring's letter vehemently defended her identity as an upstanding citizen. Herring's letter is one of the most passionate letters contained in the SNP archives, written by a woman whose family was forced from its land in 1936. Like many of the letters, there is no resistance to the loss of her home and property but rather resistance to the park's procedures. In this letter in particular, Herring defended her honor: she was angry and insulted that Zerkel had assumed wrongdoing on her part. She said,

> I'm now answering your letter I recived from you. so called a Copy to Boss Morris. I'm very mutch suprised to get a thang like that. I have not said or even thraught of tearing dawn any thang up there. that is some of Boss Morrises lies he reparted to you. his wife told me she had a wretten permett to stay there tell fall and said you had given them the buildings to move a way this fall. and I do know the CCC boys has been giving a way the buildings. and I can proved this to you they gave the George Shifflett house and all to Aubry Mawbray. and the also gave GM Shifflett buildings to Bernard & Warren Shifflett and the also got NC Herrings buildings and the gave Mr. CJ Begoon buildings to William Sullivan. and Mr. Sellars buildings to ame Shifflett. and I wretten to W C Hall Chairman Richmond and he said you all had no right to give a way the buildings. and I say if you were a goning to give them a way wouldent it be more nicer to give it to the one who awned the property and Boss Morris moved from his house he taken the windows & doors I do not know what he did with them.

Herring was quite angry and referred to activities common to the area during the establishment of the park. Many residents (and nonresidents for that matter) "stole" materials from the park; that is, they removed various buildings, fence rails, and crops that were either abandoned or actually part of their original property. These activities became stealing once the federal government owned the land. However, in some cases with written request and permission, residents were allowed to remove materials. In her letter, Herring suggested she was accused of stealing and chastised Zerkel for "sending me your harble letters." Her letter signals that she was aware of the power of her literacy, that it could change Zerkel's assumptions about her and, consequently, decisions he may made about her and her family.

This kind of passion was generally not included in the letters in the park's archives. Herring's letter, however, does reflect some general sentiment about the officials' attitudes toward the mountain families. It was assumed they were lazy and not able to be trusted. Lassiter's letters to other government officials (particularly to social workers) contain disparaging comments about mountain residents as a whole. Herring's rhetoric vehemently resisted that construction. Through her complex rendering of events she refused to be called a liar and demanded that the park cease its wrongs toward her and her family. She took her subjectivity into her own hands, constructing an identity counter to the one Zerkel had apparently provided for her.

CONCLUSIONS

The patterns I have identified in the letters include simple requests, advocacy for "nabors," demands for assistance, and resistance to park authority. But a rhetorical analysis reveals something more than the patterns in the contents of the letters: a complex negotiation of identity with those in power. The women's sense of value and morality is also reflected in the letters, a sense of what is right, sharing the wealth, using materials wisely, and an awareness of literacy and its power. Indeed, their letters are constructed much as early twentieth-century composition textbooks would have directed. According to Lucille Schultz, letter-writing instruction not only taught students "how to write business and social correspondence," it also "inculcat[ed] children with the manners and morals of polite society in 19th century America" (110). We can see this sense of manners in some of the letters, but not all. Schultz also suggests that while in some cases letters were an occasion to reflect these classed values, they were also an occasion "for resisting dominant social codes" (111). The anger, passion, sarcasm, and shrewd understanding of the situation in some of the women's letters were in direct opposition to what was expected of polite society, and certainly of women in the 1930s.

The community members Cushman interviews in *The Struggle and the Tools* were similarly able to analyze their rhetorical situations. Her conclusions about their negotiations with bureaucratic documents, including correspondence, are crucial to understanding the mountain residents' negotiations with park officials. Cushman's participants "understood all too well how odious gatekeepers were," yet they "pressed each other into playing up to, but not necessarily into, [their] ideologies" (80). Similarly, the rhetoric contained in the letters suggests their rhetorical knowledge of what park officials might value in determining permissions. While interviews like Cushman's are not available from the mountain residents, their written literacy evidences rhetorical knowledge and strategies similar to that Cushman found in the community she studied. Some of the women may have believed that their rhetorical power could change SNP policy; indeed, some of their requests were granted. More importantly, though, is that documenting their identity through literacy showed women counter to the representations of them by those who had the power to make decisions affecting their lives. The letters indicate that those living in the mountains of Virginia were not necessarily innocent pawns manipulated by the park, but rather savvy rhetoricians, capable of engaging powerful officials. The act of writing itself indicates a certain kind of resistance. As Barton and Hall point out, "[L]imitations with literacy skills did not mean that people were cut off from using literacy in powerful and moving ways" (11). Furthermore, everyday letter writing was often self-taught (8) and "complete command of reading and writing skills is not necessary for the effective assertion of agency through the use of literacy" (9). The fact that women wrote to men in authority meant they were willing (at least rhetorically) to enter a bureaucratic, male world to make an argument or express a need. Since their requests were mostly not granted, it may seem on the surface that their literacy failed. Rather than view literacy and its power as achievement or success-based, the women's letters reflect that literacy's power lies in its interactive nature. The act of engaging those in positions of power is more salient than whether or not their requests were granted. Their letters reveal their abilities to use complex language, when those in power believed they had none. Their literacy poignantly records their values, ethics, and critical awareness, all aspects not recognized by those who had the power to determine their fates and displace them from their homes.

NOTES

1. This count is based on the letters in this specific collection. There are, however, other letters written by people from this region to officials in Virginia's state government (located in the Virginia State Library in Richmond, Virginia), the National Park Service (located at the National Archives at College Park, Maryland), and President Roosevelt (located at the Library of Congress in Washington, D.C.). The extended version of this project examines all documents related to Shenandoah National Park.
2. In this letter, Link quotes from Hollis Burke Frissell's letter to Julius D. Drehr, March 27, 1899, and Robert Frazer's manuscript report to the Southern Education Board, "Conditions Relating to Public Education in Virginia," March 24, 1903. Both are contained in the Papers of Hollis Burke Frissell, Hampton University Archives, Hampton, Virginia.
3. The Resettlement Administration was part of the U.S. Department of Agriculture. Authority for moving families shifted twice during the development of the park. Originally the Division of Homesteads in the

Department of the Interior was in charge, then the Resettlement Administration, and then the Farm Security Administration. These bureaucratic moves resulted in huge shifts in policy and administration during the middle of resettling mountain families. Consequently, much confusion, miscommunications, and broken promises occurred between park officials and residents.

4. The archives include meticulous records. Together with the letters from residents are carbon copies of responses by government officials.

5. Various accounts of the history of Shenandoah National Park have been written. See, for instance, both Engle and Michaud. The author wishes to thank historian Carolyn Janey-Lucas for her invaluable insights into the history of Shenandoah National Park.

6. I have gained permission to quote directly from the letters from many descendants of mountain families who wrote government officials. Several families, however, wish that their ancestors' letters not be quoted directly. Therefore, in the case of Daisy Nicholson's letters, I briefly paraphrase.

7. Many women signed their husband's names. For example, based on the 1930 Census, Daisy Nicholson, living in Nethers, Virginia, wrote several times to park officials, signing her name, "Mrs. Haywood Nicholson." The handwriting in the letters that are signed "Haywood Nicholson" is very similar to that in the ones signed "Mrs." Indeed, in one of the letters signed "Haywood Nicholson," there is a reference to "my husband."

WORKS CITED

Anglin, Mary K. *Women, Power, and Dissent in the Hills of Carolina.* Urbana: U of Illinois P, 2002.

Barton, David, and Nigel Hall. Introduction. *Letter Writing as Social Practice.* Ed. David Barton and Nigel Hall. Philadelphia: John Benjamins, 2000.

Baugher, Mrs. Lloyd (Rebecca Jane Powell Baugher). Letter to James R. Lassiter, SNP Superintendent. Mar. 1936. Resource Management Records. Luray, VA: Shenandoah National Park Archives.

Brandt, Deborah. *Literacy in American Lives.* New York: Cambridge UP, 2001.

Cushman, Ellen. *The Struggle and the Tools: Oral and Literate Strategies in an Inner City Community.* Albany: State U of New York P, 1998.

Daniell, Beth. "Narratives of Literacy: Connecting Composition to Culture." *College Composition and Communication* 50 (1999): 393–410.

Dyer, Mrs. Charley (Lizzie Nicholson Dyer). Letter to James R. Lassiter, Park Superintendent. 8 May 1936. Resource Management Records. Luray, VA: Shenandoah National Park Archives.

Engle, Reed. "Shenandoah National Park: A Historical Overview." *Cultural Resource Management* 21.1 (1998): 7–10.

Farnham, Christie Anne, ed. *Women of the American South: A Multicultural Reader.* New York: New York UP, 1997.

Farr, Sidney Saylor. *Appalachian Women: An Annotated Bibliography.* Lexington: UP of Kentucky, 1981.

Fisher, Stephen L., ed. *Fighting Back in Appalachia: Traditions of Resistance and Change.* Philadelphia: Temple UP, 1993.

Foster, Stephen. *The Past Is Another Country: Representation, Historical Consciousness, and Resistance in the Blue Ridge.* Berkeley: U of California P, 1988.

Friedman, Jean E. "Women's History and the Revision of Southern History." *Sex, Race, and the Role of Women in the South.* Ed. Hawks and Skemp. Jackson: UP of Mississippi, 1983. 3–12.

Haney, Lula A. Letter to Franklin D. Roosevelt. January 13, 1936. Resource Management Records. Luray, VA: Shenandoah National Park Archives.

Hawks, Joanne V., and Sheila L. Skemp, eds. *Sex, Race, and the Role of Women in the South.* Jackson: UP of Mississippi, 1983.

Herring, Lillie Coleman. Letter to Ferdinand Zerkel. March 17, 1935. Resource Management Records. Luray, VA: Shenandoah National Park Archives.

Horning, Audrey J. "Archaeological Considerations of 'Appalachian' Identity: Community-Based Archaeology in the Blue Ridge Mountains." *The Archaeology of Communities: A New World Perspective.* Ed. Canuto and Yaeger. London: Routledge, 2000. 210–30.

——. "Beyond the Shenandoah Valley: Interaction, Image, and Identity in the Blue Ridge." *After the Backcountry: Rural Life in the Great Valley of Virginia 1800–1900.* Ed. Kenneth E. Koons and Warren R. Hofstra. Knoxville: U of Tennessee P, 2000. 145–66.

——. *In the Shadow of Ragged Mountain: Historical Archaeology of Nicholson, Corbin, and Weakley Hollows.* Luray, VA: Shenandoah National Park Association, 2004.

Kahn, Kathy. *Hillbilly Women.* Garden City, NY: Doubleday, 1973.

Lamb, Ardista. Letter to James R. Lassiter. Resource Management Records. Luray, VA: Shenandoah National Park Archives.

Lambert, Darwin. *The Undying Past of Shenandoah National Park.* Boulder: Roberts Rinehart, 1989.

Lassiter, James R. Letter to Mrs. Haywood Nicholson. Apr. 1936. Resource Management Records. Luray, VA: Shenandoah National Park Archives.

——. Letter to Mrs. Lloyd Baugher. Apr. 1936. Resource Management Records. Luray, VA: Shenandoah National Park Archives.

Lillard, Ida O. Letter to James R. Lassiter. 18 July 1936. Resource Management Records. Luray, VA: Shenandoah National Park Archives.

Link, William A. *A Hard Country and a Lonely Place: Schooling, Society, and Reform in Rural Virginia, 1870–1920.* Chapel Hill: U of North Carolina P, 1986.

Michaud, Karen A. "Shenandoah National Park: A Sense of Place." *Cultural Resource Management* 21.1 (1998): 11–12.

Mortensen, Peter. "Representations of Literacy and Region: Narrating 'Another America.'" *Pedagogy in the Age of Politics: Writing and Reading (in) the Academy.* Ed. Patricia A. Sullivan and Donna J. Qualley. Urbana, IL: NCTE, 1994. 100–20.

Nicholson, Mrs. Haywood (Daisy Sisk Nicholson). Letter to James R. Lassiter. 1 Apr. 1936. Resource Management Records. Luray, VA: Shenandoah National Park Archives.

——. Letter to Taylor Hoskins. 29 Aug. 1936. Resource Management Records. Luray, VA: Shenandoah National Park Archives.

Nicholson, Teeny. Letter to James R. Lassiter. 13 March 1937. Resource Management Records. Luray, VA: Shenandoah National Park Archives.

Perdue, Charles, and Nancy Perdue. "Appalachian Fables and Facts: A Case Study of the Shenandoah National Park Removals." *Appalachian Journal* (1979–80): 84–104.

Pollock, George Freeman. *Skyland: The Heart of the Shenandoah National Park.* Ed. Stuart E. Brown, Jr. Berryville, VA: Chesapeake Book Company, 1960.

Powell, Katrina M. "Writing the Geography of the Blue Ridge Mountains: How Displacement Recorded the Land." *Biography: An Interdisciplinary Journal* 25.1 (2002): 73–94.

Reynolds, George P. "The CCC: The Road to Recovery." *Foxfire 10*. New York: Anchor-Doubleday, 1993. 240–302.

Schultz, Lucille. "Letter-Writing Instruction in 19th Century Schools in the United States." *Letter Writing as Social Practice*. Ed. David Barton and Nigel Hall. Amsterdam: John Benjamins Publishing Company, 1999. 109–30.

Scott, Anne Firor. "Historians Construct the Southern Woman." *Sex, Race, and the Role of Women in the South*. Ed. Hawks and Skemp. Jackson: UP of Mississippi, 1983. 95–110.

Scribner, Sylvia. "Literacy in Three Metaphors." *Perspectives on Literacy*. Ed. Eugene R. Kintgen, Barry M. Kroll, and Mike Rose. Carbondale: Southern Illinois UP, 1988. 71–81.

Shapiro, Henry D. *Appalachia on Our Minds: The Southern Mountains and Mountaineer in the American Consciousness, 1870–1920*. Chapel Hill: U of North Carolina P, 1978.

Sherman, Mandel, and Thomas Henry. *Hollow Folk*. New York: Thomas Crowell and Company, 1933.

Sizer, Miriam. "Suggestions Concerning Some Types of Mountain People in the Proposed Shenandoah National Park." 1932. Shenandoah National Park Group. College Park, MD: National Archives II.

——. "Tabulations: Five Mountain Hollows." 1928. Shenandoah National Park Group. College Park: National Archives II.

Sohn, Katherine Kelleher. *Whistlin' and Crowin' Women of Appalachia: Literacy Practices since College*. Carbondale: Southern Illinois UP, 2006.

Special Use Permit. Resource Management Records, 1934. Luray, VA: Shenandoah National Park Archives.

United States. Department of Commerce. Bureau of the Census. *Fifteenth Census of the United States: 1930. Population, Volume III, Part 2*. Washington, DC: Government Printing Office, 1932.

"U.S. Will Move Village Where Soap is Unknown and Chaucer English Is Spoken." *Washington Herald* 2 May 1932: B2.

Weil, Elsie. " 'Lost' Communities in Blue Ridge Hills: Centres Where Intelligence Practically Is Missing Reported by Psychologists." *New York Times* 19 October 1930. 16.

Whisnant, David. *All that is Native and Fine: The Politics of Culture in an American Region*. Chapel Hill: U of North Carolina P, 1983.

Reconsidering Power, Privilege, and the Public/Private Distinction in the Literacy of Rural Women

Kim Donehower

Rural women, worldwide, are often the targets of literacy programs. This makes it incumbent on us to understand the powers literacy might offer rural women. In the United States, the rural region that has most been targeted for literacy intervention is Southern Appalachia. In the late 1990s, I studied the effects of these literacy interventions on members of one Appalachian community, which I call "Haines Gap."[1] Haines Gap has been visited by three distinct purveyors of literacy: Northern teachers working in the local public schools and area colleges, Presbyterian missionaries, and government workers in the Civilian Conservation Corps and VISTA programs.[2] These groups of Northern, mostly urban literacy workers who worked in Haines Gap, and throughout much of Appalachia, promoted their ways of practicing and valuing literacy according to fairly standard models of literacy's power.

Sylvia Scribner documents these traditional notions of the "powers" of literacy in her classic essay, "Literacy in Three Metaphors." "Literacy as adaptation" describes models of "functional" literacy—reading and writing skills necessary to get and hold jobs, to engage in legal and economic communications, and to participate in society. "Literacy as power" adherents see literacy as a prerequisite and catalyst for social change. Under "literacy as a state of grace," literacy transforms the self through exposure to the intellectual traditions of high culture. All three metaphors suppose that the motivations for pursuing literacy are rooted in the desire to alter one's relationship to broad-based economic, political, and cultural structures.

This echoes the influence on the field of literacy studies of two major theorists: Paulo Freire and Pierre Bourdieu. Freire's literacy work is situated in the social and political contexts of Brazil; Bourdieu is a theorist of language, not literacy, and bases his work on the sociopolitical and economic contexts of France. Nonetheless, these two are often referenced in academic discussions about the powers of literacy. Freire's work is used to argue for the power of literacy to dismantle oppressive social and political structures; Bourdieu's theories are adapted to show the ways literacy operates in already-established hierarchies of power. I have been influenced by both. However, as I analyzed the interview transcripts from my research in Haines Gap, particularly my interviews with women, I found that understanding literacy as either a tool to challenge the dominant class, or to "pass" as a member of it, did not fully explain the functions of literacy in these women's lives.

In this chapter, I argue that to understand these women's motivations to pursue literacy, we must redefine (1) the traditional concepts of the powers of literacy, (2) the privileges it provides, and (3) the public/private distinction that has often been made to distinguish between the power of literacy in men's lives and women's lives. Ultimately, I suggest that understanding literacy as both a "performance," in the folkloric sense, and as a relational tool best describes the power literacy can have in the lives of the women I interviewed in Haines Gap. I have also seen literacy serving this function for women in my current research study, in rural North Dakota and Minnesota, but for the purposes of this chapter, I refer only to interviews I conducted in Haines Gap.

HAINES GAP AND THE STUDY PARTICIPANTS

In Haines Gap, I interviewed ten people who attended the area public schools and mission school during a period of great missionary literacy activity in Appalachia from 1920 to 1965. Public schools often recruited teachers from the North, and used a "great books" curriculum with a strong emphasis on learning the conventions of standard American English in both speaking and writing. The Presbyterian mission school recruited students from the more remote areas outside the town. It also had a staff who were mostly from the Northern United States, and its curriculum included instruction in "hygiene," agriculture, and home economics as well as more traditional academic subjects. The mission school's literacy instruction centered around Biblical study, which emphasized memorization of key scriptures and interpretation according to conservative Presbyterian theology.

Of the people I interviewed in Haines Gap, I discuss seven women in this chapter. Four are mother-daughter pairs.[3] Irma was in her nineties when I first interviewed her in 1995. She was born in a small community outside Haines Gap, and attended the mission school. After she graduated, she married, farmed with her husband, and raised three children. One of these is Deana, who attended public schools and an area college, and became a teacher and school principal in a community near Haines Gap. Pearl was born in 1905 a few miles outside Haines Gap. She attended the local one-room school through the seventh grade, when she got married. She and her husband raised six children, whom she cared for while he worked on the railroad. Pearl's daughter, Eliza, was born in 1928. Eliza left Haines Gap after high school and eventually joined the military so she could pay for a college degree. After a career as an English teacher and guidance counselor, Eliza retired to Haines Gap. Pearl's niece, Ida, was also interviewed for this study. Ida attended the local public schools and, briefly, a Catholic boarding school in a nearby city. After high school, she obtained a cosmetology license and opened a beauty shop in Haines Gap. Now in her eighties, she has served as the town librarian and is the author of three books on local history. Margaret, who runs the public housing office, attended local public schools and an area college that recruited Appalachian students. Lucinda is a retired public elementary school teacher who also attended area public schools.

POWER, PRIVILEGE, AND THE PUBLIC/PRIVATE DISTINCTION IN HAINES GAP

As I pored over the transcripts from my interviews with these women, I found some connections to Scribner's three metaphors in my informants' stated reasons for studying literacy. But there were many more reasons given by the women in the study that were not adequately explained by the ways of understanding and valuing literacy that Scribner documents.

I felt that "power" needed to be redefined. Some of the most profound stories of literacy's power were not tales of its ability to help women remake their economic, political, or cultural status. The differences that reading and writing practices brought to these women's lives did not always produce changes in privilege or status visible to the outside observer. Instead, the regular performance of certain kinds of reading and writing created other changes in these women's lives. It is tempting to think of these as "private" powers of literacy, to contrast with the more public, or visible sorts of changes literacy can bring. Yet these internal changes often affected women's public voice and ability to affect public matters. The line between public and private literacy in these women's lives became so blurred as to be irrelevant.

It is important to remember that the specific context in which I am investigating literacy is rural. Rural areas have been somewhat overlooked in studies of community literacy, and the material conditions of rural life, to which reading and writing activities must be fit, are markedly different than those in urban areas. The structure of leisure time, the accessibility of literacy resources, the specialized literacy demands of agricultural and other rural occupations, and the need to use literacy activities to build community differ significantly in rural places.

The status of women in rural areas differs as well. In Haines Gap, as in much of Appalachia, literacy has traditionally been gendered female (Puckett). It is not unusual, even today, for the women in a family to have higher levels of literacy than the men. Dual-career families are common, and usually an economic necessity. While the necessities of rural life enforce certain kinds of equality for women in Haines Gap, traditional ideas about "women's place" as subservient to men, often understood as having a basis in Christian scripture, are held in parts of this community.

Within this context, the women of Haines Gap do use literacy as adaptation, to improve their job status and economic condition. For a few, literacy does provide a means to speak out for social change, as the "literacy as power" metaphor suggests. Many find a spiritually transformational role for reading and writing in their lives, using literacy as a means to a state of grace. But social, political, and economic structures limit the kinds of privileges these sorts of literacy can bring. There are other reasons, then, that drive these women to pursue literacy and find power in it. Before turning to these reasons, it is worth considering the ways literacy can, and cannot, confer privilege in the lives of rural women.

LITERACY'S PRIVILEGE-MAKING POWERS

Literacy's primary "powers" have traditionally been viewed as either conferring privilege or as allowing systems of privilege to be dismantled or altered. In *Language and Symbolic Power*, Bourdieu describes how forming a "standard" language is integral to nation-building (48). Once a "legitimate language" for the nation is established, linguistic practices of the right sort can confer social privilege or profit. Therefore, members of marginalized groups can learn to linguistically "pass," and thereby participate in the privileges of mainstream society.

It has been tempting to take Bourdieu's claims about linguistic practices and apply them to the potential status-making powers of literacy. E. D. Hirsch's cultural literacy project argues that reading a common set of texts and being able to acquire and use knowledge from those texts in particular ways grants one membership in the class of educated Americans. But can literacy really function according to Bourdieu's arguments about language, privilege, and power?

Appalachia provides an interesting laboratory in which to investigate these ideas. Henry Shapiro, Peter Mortensen, Allen Batteau, David Whisnant, and others have documented the ways in which the de-legitimization of Appalachian language and literacy, as well as missionary efforts to rescue the literacy of Appalachian people, were influenced largely by efforts to build a unified, Anglo-Saxon American nation in the late nineteenth century. Missionary literacy workers who flooded the region as part of government, educational, and religious programs imagined that the powers of the reading and writing they would confer would entitle Appalachian men and women to greater participation in what they believed to be legitimate American culture and society (Shapiro 159). Did Appalachian women reap the social and economic profits of literacy according to this model of literacy's power?

Certain kinds of literacy training could allow Appalachian women to "pass," linguistically, in mainstream U.S. society as non-Appalachian. But these women were still women of limited economic resources, and literacy could not erase other markers of their social status. Here is Ida, explaining why she left St. Catherine's, a prestigious Catholic boarding school in a nearby city:

> That fall I enrolled at St. Catherine's, in Carville. But I didn't stay the year out there.... Those girls were nearly all from wealthy families, the boarding girls. And they had money to spend, and at that time they didn't wear uniforms.... And I just sort of—Dad was on a low income, and I thought, well, I'd better go back home.... See, I was mostly raised on a farm.... This—sister she was so old, you wouldn't think she could do any work. And she was sweeping the hall, and shoving some of the trunks down the hall. And I said, "Sister, may I help you?" I wanted to do some work, after hours. I would have loved to have worked in the kitchen. But they wouldn't let me! ... My roommate was friendly and she hated for me to leave. But the others—I don't know, they weren't too friendly.... Well you know, they first invited me with them to go to town. Well, you had to go on the bus. And then they'd buy all of these things to eat and everything. And I couldn't afford it, so I had to turn it down. And they quit asking.

Far more than literacy skills are required for Ida to participate in the privileges of middle-class city life. Even if she does have the financial and cultural resources to match her literacy skills, she is still a woman in the 1940s South, and the privileges to which her literacy might entitle her are limited. As it happens, Ida chooses to return to her hometown, where she becomes a successful entrepreneur without the need to "pass" in the world outside Haines Gap.

Ida finds that she does not wish to engage in the privileges to which her literacy skills might entitle her. The way of life that St. Catherine's represents is not for her. Similarly, other women felt that choosing to live outside Haines Gap was not the privilege their teachers represented it to be. Responding to a question from me, Margaret describes her reaction to a college teacher who criticized her language skills:

A: Well, I was taking, I don't remember what course at Berry Hill College, and, she was from, I guess up North some place. Away from here, and … she had asked me, how then would I say a Model T, or a T Model. And I don't even remember my answer to her but she asked me a couple of other questions, and she said, "You know, to be well-rounded and educated, you've got to watch what you say, of course." Which I realized that. And I guess maybe she saw the glint in my eye was not too favorable. But anyway, she came back the next week and she said "I have been listening to other mountain people." And she said, "I have come to the conclusion that, you probably are—is not going to change your way of speaking. And, you probably are not going to move away from here, so, this is the dialect of the mountains."

Q: So she decided—

A: She decided it was okay. Right.

Q: And well, what was your reaction to all of that?

A: … I had never, I never had really gave it any thought at all.… I just thought, you know, "What in the world is she talking about?" You know, "She's out of her league." I guess that's what I thought.

In this exchange, Margaret reverses the linguistic privilege. She mocks the teacher's pompous way of speaking: "I have come to the conclusion that …." The teacher believes that she has the privilege to determine that Margaret's way of speaking is inferior, but to Margaret, the teacher is on Margaret's turf now, and has no linguistic rights to make this kind of decision. Instead, it is the teacher's language that is out of place. The kind of privilege the teacher's language represents is, to Margaret, no privilege at all.

For these women, literacy did not confer significant privilege outside their home communities. However, literacy was a useful tool to renegotiate their status within Haines Gap. Ida offers an example: The self-appointed town historian, Ida has published three books on local clubs and on the wealthy Cuthbertson family, for whom Ida's family tenant farmed. Through writing, Ida aligns herself with groups—clubwomen (and men), and the local elite—to which her birth as a tenant farmer's child might not entitle her. Since the representatives of these groups are long gone, Ida uses writing to inscribe herself into their company.

Reading also lets Ida control her position in the community. Ida's tastes run to religious books and histories of the British royal family—another way to associate herself with wealth and privilege. Ida is known as a devout Catholic, which marks a certain kind of status in the hierarchy of religious denominations in Appalachia. When she checked out a book from the public library by Andrew Greeley, knowing only that he was a Catholic priest, she was shocked by its salacious content. She returned the book immediately. Because the library's check-out records were public, she insisted that the librarian white-out her name on the check-out register. Ida sees public awareness of her reading preferences as a signal of her place in the community. And, despite their small size, rural communities can contain as many different social groups, within which one might locate oneself, as suburban and urban areas.

A contemporary of Ida's, Deana came to Haines Gap from "the country," a term locals use to describe less desirable areas outside of town. Deana pursued literacy vigorously, getting a master's degree and becoming principal of one of the area schools. After she was fired for falsifying attendance records to gain more state funding for her school, Deana went into real estate and began an active career as a local politician and occasional editorialist. Deana turned the critical literacy she had learned in graduate school against the injustices of her local community:

A: There has been a great deal of emphasis in the past fifty years on local women and men going away to school for four years, and coming back. And I feel that this is one thing that's responsible for the low ebb of learning now.... We need teachers from outside ... to challenge.... Most people who come in, value honesty. And truth.... But it's not the same brand of honesty and truth that we have. This area probably got a good dose of Baptist religion at some time. And that's a little different brand of honesty and truth.... What would be oppression to one family, keeping a family poor, because they work for you and not giving them very much advantage, still might be honesty to you, and then a person coming from another area would see that they needed a bathroom, or they needed more clothes, or they needed more books—they needed a greater reward for their labor. And—still, yet the local person would say that he was being fair, if the family did not have a bathroom, if they had no books, [as long as] they were warm and had clothing.

Q: So it's good to have people come in from the outside to sort of—

A: Challenge…. I think that we really needed our values—our—
livelihoods, our outlook challenged. Because we were pretty
narrow.

Deana used her literacy skills to make herself into one who challenged
the status quo of her community, and in this way she laid claim to the
role of community iconoclast. Deana's local origins, along with her con-
trary views, entitled her to the iconoclast position—one that has some
status to it in many small rural communities. Deana used the literacy of
the dominant culture to transform from an anonymous "country child"
to a central figure in the political life of the town.

Deana's case illustrates both the abilities and limits of literacy to
confer status in women's lives. While Deana has been able to use literacy to alter her position within the community, literacy has not functioned to alter her status within her family. While Deana became a
practitioner of a kind of critical literacy, her family, particularly her
mother, Irma, practiced a literacy influenced by fundamentalist Christianity, instilled at one of the area mission schools. By choosing a different kind of literacy than that of her family, Deana had lowered her
status within her family. This was clear during my interview with
Irma, who ignored Deana's accomplishments and bemoaned the fact
that Deana did not regularly attend church. Kathy Sohn's work in Appalachia similarly shows ways in which increased literacy training
may not confer status on women within their families, and can even
lead to spousal abuse (438–40).

But among the Haines Gap women, being the most literate in the family did not necessarily bring negative repercussions. As a child, Pearl
served as her family's reader and scribe. The youngest of thirteen children of illiterate parents, Pearl was taught to read and write by her siblings. As they left the family to find work, Pearl took over the roles of
nightly Bible-reading and letter-writing. She assisted her mother, a
midwife who also attended the dying, by filling out birth and death certificates to be mailed to the state records office.

The idea that literacy is perceived as "women's work" in many societies is not new. Michael Smith and Jeffrey Wilhelm review research that
argues that "hegemonic versions of masculinity are not consistent with
being literate" (12). Anita Puckett has documented the ways literacy
has been gendered female in Appalachia. Being more literate than the
men in their community does not necessarily improve rural women's
status, especially within their families. Nonetheless, a marital situation
in which the wife is literate, and the husband is not, confers some advantage to the literate partner. One Haines Gap woman reported her
suspicions that a local man, who was illiterate, had been taken advantage of for years by his wife, who could read and write.

LITERACY'S PRIVILEGE-TAKING POWERS

While Bourdieu-inspired theories look at literacy's power to create privilege, Freirian models investigate the ways literacy deconstructs systems of privilege. Scribner documents this model as "literacy as power," in which "expansion of literacy skills is often viewed as a means for poor and politically powerless groups to claim their place in the world" (11–12). This is not accomplished through adopting the linguistic habits of the dominant culture; rather, it is through using critical literacy to unmask and deconstruct hegemony.

The influential Freirian paradigm asserts that literacy has the power to create social change. Freire and Macedo argue that literacy is both a prerequisite and catalyst for changing the social order (156–59). Scribner, among others, has argued that while this potential power of literacy exists in theory, it has not been so widely documented in practice. She notes that in many cases, social change has been the prerequisite for increased literacy, instead of the other way around (12).

In fact, in the lives of many women (and men) from stigmatized groups, literacy's power serves primarily to reinforce existing social structures that keep them at a cultural and economic disadvantage. Literacy instruction in Appalachian schools reinforced stereotypes about Appalachian culture to keep Appalachians "in their place." The excerpt from the interview with Margaret, previously cited, offers one example. In addition, the most striking finding among the transcripts of my work in Haines Gap was that, without exception, every single interviewee's first memories of school literacy were ones of physical and/or psychological abuse. Beatings for writing left-handed, being forced to wear a dunce cap for the inability to recite the alphabet backwards, teachers "accidentally" bumping one's hand while practicing lines and lines of Palmer-method exercises—these were the types of responses to the question, "What's the first thing you remember about learning to read and write in school?"

In this model, the power of literacy first appears in these women's lives as a force arrayed against them. It is a power used to keep them in their cultural place. It is not surprising, then, that many of the women I interviewed saw a potential power of literacy in their lives as a means to better assimilate to the status quo, rather than to try to change it. Lucinda, a grade school teacher, offers a striking example:

Q: Tell me why you think the grammar is important.
A: In the way one speaks.
Q: Okay. Because—that's how people—
A: Right.
Q: Make decisions about you?

A: Right.... Absolutely. And it was drilled into me, and I *drilled* it into my students, I guess.... You know your grandparents, and my grandparents and—people who didn't have English grammar stressed at home, their pronunciation and the use of the word like, "have went," those little helping words, we call them helping words, down in third grade, and expressions like that, you know, and the pronunciation of "brush," instead of "bresh," and "frush" instead of "fresh," and then—the correct usage of the verb, that—meant *so* much. And when they hear it at home, day in and day out, they come to school and they're wearing that there, and it's hard, you have to go over and go over, repetition, repetition, repetition, to get that out, and then, I had a child tell me once, I had been hammering on something that I was trying to get into them, one of the students came back and said, "Ms. Sykes, they made fun of me at home, because I did so and so." You know? And I said, "Well, you just stick to it because you *are* right." They said that he was trying to put on the dog. Yeah, you know, using the correct form of the verb or something. But—it was fun, I enjoyed it.

The key point in her statement is the one about verb forms: "they mean *so* much." This teacher does not believe in following grammar rules solely for the sake of "correctness," but rather as a means of controlling what others think of you in a world that maintains rigid hierarchies of class and status. For her, grammar and dialect are something you "wear," like a suit of clothes, that shapes how other people view you. One of the most powerful signals in this system is verb forms—one of the most obtrusive markers of incorrect grammar, and an esoteric code system, since English has so many irregular verbs. The power of knowing and using this system is so important for this teacher that her students are made to practice it even if it provoked ridicule at home. For Lucinda, literacy is a means of assimilating to the status quo, not a tool for changing it.

Contrast her view with Deana's, who sees literacy as a critical tool. But Deana did not turn literacy's critical powers on the larger society that stigmatized her home community and that, by her admission, conspired to keep economic and educational resources from Appalachia. Instead, she focused her critique on Appalachia itself, specifically, on her own county.

When studying the literacy of rural women, particularly from this time period, it is important to note that many of these women fully expect, and desire, to live out their lives in their rural communities. Eliza, the one woman I interviewed who made her life outside Appalachia, returned to Haines Gap when she retired and ran for local office. The sphere in which many rural women, and men, practice their literate skills is the local one. Like Margaret, they must come to terms with what the outside world thinks of them and their literacy.[4] But their priority is to find the ways literacy will best serve them in their home communities.

The local nature of everyday literacy practices, then, weighs against the kind of sweeping social change desired by "Freireistas," as Villanueva calls them, or the kind of social mobility a Bourdieu-influenced researcher might expect to see. But within this local context, a whole other range of literacy's powers emerge.

LITERACY'S OTHER POWERS: LITERACY AS PERFORMANCE

In the lives of the women of Haines Gap, literacy is a powerful tool to manage their relationships—with others, with themselves, with their spirituality, and with the nature of their everyday lives. Reading and writing can function as a means to build, shape, and deconstruct relationships if we understand each individual act of literacy as a kind of performance, in the folkloric sense, that reveals aspects of identity. Folklorist Dorothy Noyes notes that "folklorists have long been aware that certain kinds of identity are derived from performance" (467) and that "performance, sanctioned and unsanctioned, becomes a key means of boundary construction and maintenance" (454). In other words, folk performances are a way of marking social territory, defining the boundaries between social groups. Folk performances have long been understood to do this through what William Hugh Jansen describes as the "esoteric–exoteric factor." Esoteric performances seek to define the group in terms of itself—as in, "this is us." Exoteric performances define the group by contrasting it with others—in essence, "this is not us." Folklorist Deborah Kapchen extends these notions of performance and identity to individuals as well as groups, when she defines performances as "aesthetic practices—patterns of behavior, ways of speaking, manners of bodily comportment—whose repetitions situate actors in time and space, structuring individual and group identities" (479).

Can literacy be considered a "performance" in this way? More specifically, can the literacy acts of the women described here, most of whom conducted their reading and writing in private, without an audience, be understood as "performance?" I believe so. Kapchen explains that performances "provide an intricate counterpoint to the unconscious practices of everyday life insofar as they are stylistically marked expressions of otherness, lifting the level of habitual behavior and entering an alternate, often ritualized ... interpretive 'frame' wherein different rules apply" (479). In other words, an "aesthetic practice" can only be considered a performance if it is done consciously, with an awareness that there are other ways to perform the task.

The women of Haines Gap grew up in a community steeped in stereotypes of rural and Appalachian illiteracy. No fewer than three different groups came to the community to try to "fix" the literacy "problem" that was presumed to exist there. These were Northern teachers recruited to work in Appalachian schools, the Presbyterian mission school, and government programs.

Each of these different literacy "sponsors," to use Deborah Brandt's term, offered a particular way of doing literacy—a how, what, and why to read and write.[5] At the same time, each promoted the message that the ways the people in the community already read and wrote represented another distinct, and inferior, way of doing literacy. If different options are clearly present about what, how, and why to read and write, and each option represents the worldview of distinct groups, then choices about how to read and write, even if there is no audience to receive the "performance," can serve to position the reader or writer in relation to the groups these forms of literacy represent.

Reading and writing allowed women such as Ida and Deana to redefine their relationships to their communities: in Ida's case, by associating herself with a wealthy local Catholic family far above her own socioeconomic status, and in Deana's, by taking public stands against positions shared by much of the community. Similarly, Eliza, when asked to describe the literacy of those around her as she was growing up in Haines Gap, replied, simply, "They weren't." However, Eliza's mother, Pearl, was one of the most active readers and writers in the study, her father read the Bible nightly, and one of her brothers is also an avid reader. To maintain the view that the people around her "weren't" literate, Eliza must consider that her way of practicing literacy is significantly different from the kinds of reading and writing that went on around her. It is the kind of literacy Eliza practices that sets her apart, in her mind, from others.

LITERACY'S OTHER POWERS: LITERACY AND SELF-CONCEPT

Acts of literacy provided many women in the study with a distinct sense of self. Eliza recalls how her early writing proficiency brought her both local and self-recognition:

> The year the war started, I remember—you know, the Japanese bombed Pearl Harbor—the Carville paper had all the schools sponsor a writing contest, of what students' impressions of this act was, and then they quoted several. And one line of mine was quoted.... I remember going in

the grocery store downtown, and [?] was in there and she said, "Oooh I sure did like that line of yours...." But you know, that was a really good experience for me, I mean, that was really a treat.... It felt wonderful, even though it's just that one line. I can just remember coming out of the store and just walking so proud down the street.

Eliza further explains that her developing handwriting style also connected to her sense of self:

I would experiment with writing.... It just didn't end with penmanship. I remember at one point I wrote slanting the other way.... Back-slant. You know. And it was really—the handwriting at some point or other became my identity.... That's probably not unique.

Literacy could also provide a means to define and support one's spiritual self-concept. This is amply illustrated in this quote from Irma, Deana's mother:

Well, who do you believe is going to be in heaven? Now we've got to love all the churches. Even ... the Catholics too. No matter. Who do you think? ... Those [whose] names are written in the lamb's book of life.... What's going to surprise you the most, if you study the Word, as you get older, when you, when you open that Bible, there'll be something that'll be talking back to you.... Oh, sometimes I read and it'll slap me in the face, I've not been living like I ought to.

Irma uses scriptural study to question and alter the direction of her own life. But, in addition, Irma's relationship to "the lamb's book of life" confers on her a kind of spiritual power that, for her, trumps other powers of education or class. During the interview, Irma interrogated my own spiritual status, as well as raising questions about that of her educated daughter, Deana. For Irma, spiritual literacy made her impervious to the hierarchies of privilege that might be imposed upon her by others, that might label her as lower class in terms of her economic, social, or educational status. Spiritual literacy protected Irma from feeling acutely these judgments that might be placed on her by those both outside and inside the community, and she could rest assured in her belief that her literate practices were paving the way for her to join a most privileged group in the afterlife.

LITERACY'S OTHER POWERS: COPING WITH EVERYDAY LIFE

A literate self-concept also provided a means to cope with the extreme material hardships of life. Eliza's mother, Pearl, who raised six children during the Great Depression while her husband was away working on the railroad, described reading as a counterweight to the immediate pressures or her everyday life: "Something to—get my mind interested in, y'know. Cause that was a hard life then. You know." When asked why she liked to write poetry and songs and stories, Pearl responded, "That's just the way I felt. I was a romantic person. I had a romantic mind." Literacy both supported Pearl's strong self-concept—as someone with "a romantic mind," and therefore a writer—and helped her find meaning from the everyday surroundings of her life. Pearl's poetry and songs took as their subject her surroundings. In this way literate practices offered Pearl a means to deepen and enrich her relationship with the physical setting in which she lived out a very long and sometimes arduous life.

Literacy could also offer a relationship with the world beyond the local setting. Here is Pearl's explanation of how and why she reads so much:

Q: Of the reading that you've done, through the years, was there any special thing you wanted to get from it? Or get out of it?

A: Knowledge. I like to know things, y'know, and understand—And now when I read, I have a dictionary, and I lay on my bed, and, and I read words that I don't know the meaning of, and I go to the dictionary, and find out what it means …. Then I understand my reading better.

Q: So you, you wanted to read to find out things about people, and other places, other things—

A: The whole world—

For many rural women, isolation is a fact of life that must be dealt with. Reading helps Pearl bring the world to her.

Pearl's daughter Eliza used reading as a means to cope with a different sort of life path than her mother's. Unlike Pearl, Eliza planned to leave Haines Gap and explore the world. In preparation, she read avidly, making her way through the tiny public school library as well as the better equipped mission school library. Eliza left Haines Gap after high school and eventually joined the Air Force as a way to pay for college. She described her reading activities as a way to construct for herself a "philosophy of life," which would then give her a basis for understanding others' philosophies of life. Reading, for Eliza, was preparation to interact with others who had different ideas and values than the people of Haines Gap. It was also a way to equip herself with a system for understanding and directing her own life choices.

PUBLIC/PRIVATE INDISTINCTION

In *Intimate Practices*, Anne Ruggles Gere notes that the traditional distinction made by some academic feminists between the public and private arenas of women's lives has begun to break down (13). The assumption has typically been that women's literacy tends to function more within the private sphere, and that male literacy tends to be more public. Gere documents the ways literacy practices in late nineteenth- and early twentieth-century women's clubs connected women both to one another and to larger cultural and political issues.

The lives of Ida, Deana, Margaret, Eliza, and Pearl support the dismantling of the private/public distinction. As family reader and scribe, Pearl's reading of the local newspaper within the "private" family circle influenced her father's voting in the public sphere. Deana's practice of critical literacy informed both her public life as a politician and her private sense of self. Pearl's poetry-writing may seem wholly personal and private, yet members of her family were known locally as people who valued literacy and education. (One interviewee explained why his mother had applied for him to attend college without his knowledge by saying, "She was a Sykes, you know." Pearl's family are Sykes.) Pearl's private literacy affected the family's public face.

In addition, in communities where literacy becomes gendered female, women take on a more public role than their urban contemporaries at a similar time. Katrina Powell's examination of letters of request from displaced Appalachians to Shenandoah National Park officials shows that a significant minority of letter writers were women (see p. 71, this volume). When the park boundary encompassed their communities, residents had to ask permission of park officials for any changes in their living circumstances. Since women were, for the most part, more literate than men, they composed these letters. The gendering of literacy in this community mandated a public role for these women's literacy. In Haines Gap, a legacy of female-gendered literacy makes it unremarkable, even today, that many more local political offices are held by women than in large, progressive urban areas. Many rural communities, especially Appalachia, simply do not fit a model of private female literacy and public male literacy.

LITERACY AS RELATIONAL

A conception of literacy that crosses the public/private distinction to encompass all the many powers of literacy just enumerated is that of literacy as relational. I submit that we add this metaphor to others that have been proposed as ways of understanding literacy (Scribner; Barton; Brandt, *Involvement*), especially when we try to understand the roles of literacy in women's lives. Since different groups value and practice literacy in different ways, conscious choices about what, how, and why to read and write can make literacy a tool to configure one's relationship with various groups and individuals, in both "private" and "public" spheres. The potential of literacy to support a self-concept affects one's relationship with oneself. The ways reading and writing provide a means to respond to the conditions of life offer a way to structure one's relationship with material circumstances. The deep connection between literacy and religion—most religions feature, at center, a relationship with a text—allows a means to shape one's relationship to the divine.

If we think of literacy practices as constituting the kind of performances Noyes and Kapchen describe, we can see how reading and writing function relationally for Ida, Deana, Eliza, Irma, and Pearl. Their literacy practices let them take certain stances with, against, or between various cultural entities. Ida's reading and writing help her renegotiate her status within the local community. Deana uses critical literacy to assert an iconoclastic relationship with the rest of Haines Gap. Eliza used her literacy practices to align herself with the world outside her hometown. Irma's spiritual literacy distinguishes her attainments from the educational accomplishments of her daughter and the beliefs of those academic outsiders who stigmatize the literacy of the local community. Pearl's literacy demonstrates her "romantic mind," justifying her hours of isolation away from community and family as she reads and writes poems.

The complex uses these women have for literacy demonstrate the benefit of the kinds of research that Beth Daniell refers to as "little narratives of literacy":

> [T]he little narratives show that the modernist promise of literacy—economic security, upward mobility, political freedom, intellectual achievement, middle-class values, personal fulfillment—is inequitably fulfilled. But they also show that some people use literacy to make their lives more meaningful, no matter what their economic and political circumstances are. (404)

Daniell's premise is amply demonstrated by the interviews with the women—and men—in this study. The privileges which literacy granted these women were not sufficient to explain the depth and breadth of their reading and writing practices. Distinctions between private and public powers of literacy were blurred completely. In this small rural community, it is impossible to tell where the private ended and the public began. For these women, and perhaps for many women and men, much of literacy's power lies in its ability to define and enhance the relationships through which they find meaning in their lives.

NOTES

1. All place and personal names are pseudonyms.

2. In "Literacy Choices in an Appalachian Community," I discuss the effects of the efforts of these three groups on the attitudes and choices about literacy made by Haines Gap residents. Some of the analysis in this chapter is drawn from my conclusions in that article.

3. In referring to interviewees by their first names, I mean no disrespect. Many of the participants in this study are related and share surnames, making it confusing for the reader were I to refer to them by last name only.

4. "Outside" and "outsiders" were terms informants themselves used to refer to places and people beyond their section of the county.

5. Brandt defines sponsors of literacy as "any agents, local or distant, concrete or abstract, who enable, support, teach, model, as well as recruit, regulate, suppress or withhold literacy—and gain advantage by it in some way.... Sponsors ... set the terms for access to literacy and wield powerful incentives for compliance and loyalty" ("Sponsors" 166–67).

WORKS CITED

Barton, David. *Literacy: An Introduction to the Ecology of Written Language*. Oxford: Blackwell, 1994.

Batteau, Allen. *The Invention of Appalachia*. Tucson: U of Arizona P, 1990.

Bourdieu, Pierre. *Language and Symbolic Power*. Cambridge: Harvard UP, 1991.

Brandt, Deborah. *Literacy as Involvement: The Acts of Writers, Readers, and Texts*. Carbondale: Southern Illinois UP, 1990.

——. "Sponsors of Literacy." *College Composition and Communication* 49 (1998): 165–85.

Daniell, Beth. "Narratives of Literacy: Connecting Composition to Culture." *College Composition and Communication* 50 (1999): 393–410.

Donehower, Kim. "Literacy Choices in an Appalachian Community." *Journal of Appalachian Studies* 9 (2003): 341–62.

Freire, Paulo, with Donaldo Macedo. *Literacy: Reading the Word and the World*. London: Bergin and Garvey, 1987.

Gere, Anne Ruggles. *Intimate Practices: Literacy and Cultural Work in U.S. Women's Clubs, 1880–1920*. Urbana: U of Illinois P, 1997.

Hirsch, E. D., Jr. *Cultural Literacy: What Every American Needs to Know*. New York: Houghton Mifflin, 1987.

Jansen, William Hugh. "The Esoteric–Exoteric Factor in Folklore." *The Study of Folklore*. Ed. Alan Dundes. Englewood Cliffs, NJ: Prentice-Hall, 1965. 43–51.

Kapchen, Deborah. "Performance." *Journal of American Folklore* 108 (1995): 479–508.

Mortensen, Peter. "Representations of Literacy and Region: Narrating 'Another America.'" *Pedagogy in the Age of Politics: Writing and Reading (in) the Academy*. Ed. Patricia A. Sullivan and Donna Qualley. Urbana, IL: NCTE, 1994. 100–20.

Noyes, Dorothy. "Group." *Journal of American Folklore* 108 (1995): 449–78.

Puckett, Anita. " 'Let the Girls Do the Spelling and Dan Will Do the Shooting': Literacy, the Division of Labor, and Identity in a Rural Appalachian Community." *Anthropological Quarterly* 65.3 (1992): 137–47.

Scribner, Sylvia. "Literacy in Three Metaphors." *American Journal of Education* 93.1 (1984): 6–21.

Shapiro, Henry. *Appalachia on Our Mind: The Southern Mountains and Mountaineers in the American Consciousness, 1870–1920*. Chapel Hill: U of North Carolina P, 1978.

Smith, Michael, and Jeffrey Wilhelm. *Reading Don't Fix No Chevys: Literacy in the Lives of Young Men*. Portsmouth, NH: Heinemann, 2002.

Sohn, Katherine Kelleher. "Whistlin' and Crowin' Women of Appalachia: Literacy Practices since College." *College Composition and Communication* 54 (2003): 423–52.

Villanueva, Victor. "Considerations for American Freireistas." *Cross-Talk in Comp Theory: A Reader*. Ed. Victor Villanueva. Urbana, IL: NCTE, 1997. 621–38.

Whisnant, David. *All That Is Native and Fine: The Politics of Culture in an American Region*. Chapel Hill: U of North Carolina P, 1983.

Sponsoring Clubs: Cultivating Rural Identities through Literacy

Charlotte Hogg

At [the town's] heart are the widows. They are the ones who know [the town] best, who daily feed its pulse. It is thought by the townspeople that these women are without power, that the deaths of their husbands have rendered their lives meaningless and without purpose. Yet they are the ones who hold the town together, cutting across so many families as each of them does, reaching into every corner of the small community, knowing collectively all that takes place and guessing the rest.
— Sharon Butala, *The Fourth Archangel*

My mom recently told me about a visit my paternal grandparents made to see us in Minneapolis in the mid-1970s. At the time, my mom had just become a Tupperware consultant (then called a Tupperware lady) and attended a meeting led by Ora Lee, a unit leader from Texas. Mom took Grandma along with her, and they sat in someone's living room—no doubt with refreshments like a punch with 7-Up served in Tupperware glasses—while Ora Lee began asking each woman in the group to discuss her motivations for becoming a Tupperware lady. Ora Lee first explained that she became unit leader because of a need for her own identity, something she could claim herself that was separate from her husband and children. Each woman at the meeting told a similar story about selling Tupperware, including my mom. When Ora Lee came to my grandma, a guest at the meeting, Grandma said: "I am Dorlis Hogg. Mrs. George Hogg. I'm a wife, mother, and grandmother. That's all the identity I've ever needed."[1]

Instead of feeling disappointed, this story first made me laugh, as I can think of very few people who have such a strong sense of self as my grandma. But then, I've really known her best since my granddad died.

He died in 1980, and until she went to the nursing home in 1997, her name in the phone book was listed as Mrs. George Hogg. Yet the woman I know is far more complicated than the one who appeared to label and define herself through her husband. The disappointment from the Tupperware story hit me only later when I thought about how my grandma and women like her are often assumed to have missed opportunities because they define themselves through their roles with others. There is also disappointment in knowing that some in their own agrarian context regard them as peripheral because their life work, raising families, is technically over. But growing up around Grandma and other older women in my hometown of Paxton, Nebraska (population about 500)—and later working with nine of them in an ethnographic study—gives me a different perspective.[2]

Catherine Hobbs reminds us that in researching women and literacy, the question is not just "how did literacy affect women?"—though this is a critical question to answer—but "how did women change literacy?" (3). Her question might best be read broadly as a call for research into women's literacy practices, and since Hobbs made this call a decade ago, researchers have challenged ideas of what counts as literacy, such as looking at the more "ordinary" and "private" spaces. Anne Ruggles Gere's work on women's clubs and Beth Daniell's study of spirituality, women, and literacy are two of many examples that consider the particular ways that gender shapes literacy. In thinking about the women in my hometown, the question took on a particular relevance as I considered what counts as literacy, how literacy is taught and shared, and how literacy connects to gendered identities.

These Paxton women's identities were made richer and more complex in often unacknowledged ways by their work as "sponsors" of literacy, to use Deborah Brandt's term. Taking a term like "sponsor" that has become economically charged (as in a TV show being sponsored by a company), Brandt defines literacy sponsors as "any agents, local or distant, concrete or abstract, who enable, support, teach, model, as well as recruit, regulate, suppress, or withhold literacy—*and gain advantage by it in some way*" (166, emphasis added). Brandt's construction of sponsorship is broad conceptually but allows for local and specific contexts; she provides a useful and multifunctional term that literacy scholars can use to contextualize literacies and show how they are supported, developed, and expanded within group settings. Her definition and discussion of sponsorship serve as a useful heuristic for more localized and specific literacy studies in addition to or within broader economies of literacy. She provides an opening for scholars to examine the ways in which the sponsored are shaped by sponsors, be they corporations or individuals.

While Brandt provides a strong theoretical framework for understanding the benefits of sponsorship, her examples center mainly on those who are sponsored rather than those who are sponsors. Researchers of literacy also need to understand motivations and negotiations that foster sponsorship, what rhetorical practices sponsors enact, and what the individual benefits of sponsorship are. Brandt explains that sponsor seems a fitting term for "the figures who turned up most typically in people's memories of literacy learning: older relatives, teachers, priests, supervisors, military officers, editors, influential authors" (167). As is discussed elsewhere in this volume, women are often positioned as literacy educators and purveyors in families and communities as, for example, teachers or librarians. So, just as we might investigate the ways women have been sponsored (or not), we must examine how women have been given—or taken on—roles as sponsors themselves.

"Usually richer, more knowledgeable, and more entrenched than the sponsored," Brandt argues, "sponsors nevertheless enter a reciprocal relationship with those they underwrite. They lend their resources or credibility to the sponsored but also stand to gain benefits from their success, whether by direct repayment or, indirectly, by credit of association" (167). In the rural town I come from, this type of sponsorship occurs through women's relationships and clubs that cultivate those relationships. I think of the older women in Paxton and the intergenerational legacies of literacy sponsorship that take place directly and indirectly in my Nebraska hometown. I illustrate here how on a smaller, but no less significant, scale, sponsorship occurs in the "ordinary" lives of women in a rural area, where women sponsors "deliver the ideological freight that must be borne for access to what they have" (168). Older rural women in Paxton use literacy to teach other townspeople, usually other women, how to create a sense of place and community. In the process, the older women "gain advantage" in their roles as sponsors through taking on more substantive roles in the community (166).

For example, older women pass on such things as written histories, club offices, and recipes to "younger" women. For these women, maintaining the culture of the community was of vital importance; through their community and club work, they sought to provide and model various literacies for those in the rural town of Paxton. But at the same time, the older women benefitted from the work meant primarily for those in the community. I want to extend Brandt's notion of sponsorship by exploring the role of sponsor in a more localized context, examining the term in a gendered framework to understand the negotiations experienced by women as they use and facilitate literacy, while at the same time constructing authority for themselves through their literacy work, challenging traditional patriarchal identities prevalent in their agrarian setting. In other words, I argue here that through the collaborative work of clubs and independent projects (family histories, for example) they were provided the space and authority to navigate more complicated identities as women in an agrarian culture, thus benefiting as sponsors while facilitating local knowledge for the sponsored in their hometown.

First I want to make clear how I'm using the term *literacy*. Rather than understanding literacy in static terms that don't account for particular contexts or histories (i.e., once one can functionally read and write, literacy is essentially fixed), I conceive of literacies—plural—as social, varied, specific, and complicated processes of reading—broadly defined here as gaining knowledge—and writing—broadly defined as making meaning with that knowledge in ways that are usually textual—or, as Beth Daniell also defines, "reading and writing *meaningfully*" (3, emphasis added). This meaningful reading and writing takes place within certain contexts, relationships, and power structures; thus I also draw upon Daniell's description of literacy "as event, as action, as ideological, as local, as gendered, as complying with structures of society, and as resisting those structures" (3). For older women in Paxton, their sense of place and the rural context of their lives influence their literacy, and in turn, their literacy practices allow them to influence their place through sponsorship of others in the town through acts such as leading club lessons and writing family and community histories. In the process, their roles as sponsors disrupt traditional roles for rural women. As anthropologist Deborah Fink explains, because rural women define(d) themselves and others define(d) them as "farm wives" and not farm owners (a male role), the difficult work they did was viewed as just "helping out." Fink's observation extends beyond studies done *about* people in rural areas to include the perceptions *within* the rural culture as well. Fink writes, "rural people have concurred in attributing greater importance to men than to women" (*Open Country, Iowa* 8; see also Fink, *Agrarian Women*). The agrarianist mind-set is a fixture in these women's and men's belief systems. What I discovered is that the women in Paxton neither completely subverted nor fully conformed to their roles as rural wives and mothers. Rather, identity is negotiated most visibly through their literacy practices—as researchers, writers, and speakers—in the community. Many of the women in my study worked informally as educators at home, at church, or in the country; some worked in the public school system. But it is their nontraditional literacy work—work outside of typical venues for education—that most illuminates how they assumed the sort of sponsorship that complicated their identities as rural women.

In this chapter, I focus on two enactments of literacy sponsorship involving older women in Paxton: participating in clubs and composing family histories. These enactments illustrate how Paxton's older women modeled and enabled others' access to local and regional literacies, all the while complicating what it means to be a rural woman for themselves and for those in the community whom they sponsored. As described in the following section, the more intellectually engaging the literacy endeavors, the more the women assumed roles as powerful citizens of their rural place, thereby influencing not only themselves but also those around them. For example, rather than constructing my grandma in a domestic role too narrow to encompass her identity as a researcher, public speaker, organizer, businesswoman, I, as one sponsored by her, thought of her as all of these growing up, because in my hometown in western Nebraska, I saw her thrive in all of these capacities through her local literacy practices.

SPONSORSHIP ABOUT TOWN: WOMEN'S CLUBS

In *Intimate Practices,* on the literacies of U.S. clubwomen from 1880–1920, Anne Ruggles Gere writes, "clubwomen developed ideologies of literacy that foregrounded intimate social interactions, symmetry between reading and writing, physicality, and gender equity" (52). For much of their adult life, women in Paxton founded and participated in many clubs of varying interests, for many an involvement that intensified after being widowed. These clubs served as sites of sponsorship, wherein involvement fostered, promoted, and showcased literacies. I turn now to the literacy work that highlights the importance of the engagement, interaction, and meaning making borne out of club activities. While the social aspect of club involvement is a crucial motivating factor for participation, I found that the Paxton women considered clubs a space in which they could engage in intellectual endeavors as well, many of which were explicitly connected to literacy. In these spaces, literacy sponsorship abounded as women gave lessons, planned activities, wrote histories, and held leadership positions. They derived authority from these acts of sponsorship. Indeed, as we will see, when the women could not act with authority, when they found themselves in the role of passive learners rather than active meaning-making sponsors, they found their roles uncomfortably constraining.

Extension Clubs

When I first began my research I knew little about extension clubs, as they were significantly dwindling in size by the time I lived in Paxton. Nationally and in Nebraska, extension clubs thrived in the earlier part of the twentieth century. While a smattering of programs began in the 1800s, the Smith-Lever Act of 1914 "authorized cooperative extension work between Land-Grant colleges and the USDA," which allowed for agricultural and home economics instruction and demonstration in rural areas ("Events"). From the early 1900s through 1940, rural extension information was distributed by the University of Nebraska by way of the Farmer's Institute movement, in which sessions on homemaking—"primarily on nutrition and food preparation"—were paired with those on agriculture (Arnold 4). By 1914, federal and state legislation allowed public funds for the Cooperative Extension Service, "which had as its mandate 'to extend' the University to people not enrolled in colleges" (4). In 1940, the Nebraska Council officially joined the National Council of Home Demonstration Clubs. It is perhaps an indication of the assumption about rural people that these lessons were only vocational—or some would say *a*vocational—in scope, involving "canning, soap making, making dress forms, millinery, and many other subjects," activities that, while useful and needed by some, were also likely redundant for many resourceful rural women who had learned these skills from earlier generations (4).

Lucy, my high school home economics teacher in the 1980s, had finished college and moved to Paxton as an extension agent in the 1950s. I asked Lucy to describe the work of extension clubs at the time she was an agent: "We'd have leader training and they'd come to take the training for the lessons they would take back to their class, and there were some of them I remember that I wrote myself .... I did one on Christmas wrapping, but it could be a variety of things, it could be sewing, child care, foods." For Lucy, doing extension club work was also fulfilling employment. But for others involved, like my aunt, who participated in the same extension club as my grandma in the 1950s, extension work was enjoyable, but perhaps not as fulfilling as it had been for Lucy, because some creative acts of literacy—such as preparing lessons—had been preempted by the state extension office, which had moved to centralize lesson preparation. Anyone participating in the extension club would go to the extension office and receive their lesson to teach when it was their turn to host a meeting. For Aunt Barbara, the exercises at extension club meetings could be a bit vacuous, as she mentioned in our interview:

> There was nothing to them. They were a little bit strange. I gave one on cookies one time, and we had question and answer .... [T]hey were dumb. questions, like are you supposed to wash your cookie sheets every time you use them? Well, yeah, you'd say yeah. Well no, they meant every time between batches. So we all answered it wrong .... [The questions] were already made out [by the state] .... A lot of the questions [were] just common sense stuff ... and I felt so dumb having to ask them.

For my aunt, then, the lack of ownership over the extended club programs led to a passivity toward the literacy work involved in preparing for the meetings; there was not the rewarding feeling of researching and then passing that knowledge onto others. Like Lucy, my aunt agreed that for the most part, while there was good information to be gained by extension clubs, the social aspect of meeting was most important, echoing Gere's point in *Intimate Practices* that "a number of clubs listed among their purposes the promotion of sisterhood, thus articulating the intentional nature of the warm friendships that developed among club members" (47). While extension clubs certainly promoted sisterhood, they appear to have underestimated rural women's abilities by assuming that their geographical isolation meant that they had never learned to cook well. And while women in these communities surely enjoyed preparing the recipes they received, they often already possessed excellent culinary skills, despite the isolation that extension officials perceived as limiting. My aunt's extension club materials included how-to booklets for various breads, cakes, pies, and candies, as well as one entitled "Foreign Foods We Enjoy in Nebraska."

Of the clubs the women in Paxton were involved with, extension clubs were valued and enjoyed but overall seemed less satisfying to these women who so vigorously took ownership of their own literacy practices. For many of them, the social aspect of meeting was important, but contributing their talents—literate and otherwise—to a worthwhile activity was a primary reason for involvement in clubs. The extension clubs were limiting when women served as transmitters or receivers of information, rather than choosing and shaping the information themselves. While the work still involves passing on information, it is something other—something less—than sponsorship where Paxton women foster knowledge for their peers through researching and creating lessons, and thus normative roles are left unchallenged. There is a difference between providing discrete information to help people accomplish a specific goal and sponsorship, which entails long-term, complex goals that demand considerable engagement, exploration, and discovery to accomplish.

Garden Club

In other kinds of activities, the women in Paxton exercised much greater ownership of their literacies. Thus they were able to derive satisfaction from their sponsorship of learning by club members and members of the wider community and through their literacy work, described below, in order to carve identities as integral contributors and purveyors of local authority in this rural community. For many of Paxton's older women, there is nothing unusual about where they practice literacy—

the town library, for example. And for the most part, these older women control literate spaces like the library. Yet through their literacy practices, by way of their profession, they also maintain institutions in town that are not immediately identified as such. Garden Club is the most obvious of these institutional spaces, as it is a space that allows older women in Paxton to nurture their growth as researchers, writers, and speakers who use literacy to share their horticultural expertise and, more importantly, sponsor others in the club to do the same.

In 1991, Garden Club's forty-year history was reported in the *Keith County News*. A member of the National Federation of Garden Clubs, the Paxton club's projects have included, but are not limited to: garden therapy programs with nursing home residents; hat parties "with bonnets created out of anything original and natural such as colanders and cabbage"; annual Labor Day garden shows at the Community Center; and making yearbooks (Lammers, "Garden Club"). Like extension clubs, Garden Club would meet regularly: part business meeting, part lesson, and part social time. The difference was that, in Garden Club, the women were responsible for creating the lessons themselves, such as how to attract butterflies or what flowers are edible, and thus they conducted research and prepared the lessons. Literacy endeavors such as planning meetings, giving lessons, keeping minutes, putting together programs, and corresponding with other state and national Garden Club organizations were central to the club. Garden Club is a site of sponsorship where social enjoyment is conjoined with a serious commitment to work. Unlike extension clubs, Paxton women take ownership of the club. Garden Club makes clear how activities that come as a part of club membership, including research, are pathways by which older women and subsequent generations sponsor others (and each other). It is in the exchange of knowledge through literate practices—whether it comes in the form of creating lessons at the monthly meeting, writing the history of Garden Club, or making scrapbooks—that the women exercise authority and reap the benefits of sponsorship, one of which is that they model for others a sense of self that presumes intellectual value in literacies that shape the community in nontraditional ways. Through an activity viewed as "just" domestic, older women in Paxton created a space in town where they had the most expertise and intellect—where others, the sponsored, could learn from them. Sandy, a teacher who joined Garden Club in her forties, describes her initiation into Garden Club and the ways in which it began to complicate her traditional ideas of gaining knowledge:

> I felt like a real idiot when I started Garden Club. My mother had gardened to some extent but she never used the botanical names of every-

thing. We had the common names of things and I knew some of them. A lot
of times the [older women in Paxton] knew the Latin names of things ...
and they'd done ... this and that and different things, and really in a lot of
ways they were quite well educated, considering ... I have no idea if any
of them had beyond high school education.

Eventually, Sandy became involved in many of the same clubs the older
women had been a part of, and now assumes leadership roles in book
clubs and the library board. For Garden Club, she's responsible for producing the yearbook detailing annual events. Now, many of the older
women are gone, and she is sponsoring others new to the club.

At the time I interviewed her in 1999, Cathy had been president of
Garden Club for six years and was about to move on to become Director
of the District 9 Garden Club. She has been a member of Garden Club
over three decades. But when she joined around 1960, she was a fresh
face to my grandma (a charter member who taught the first lesson on
irises in 1951). I asked Cathy about being involved in Garden Club, and
her answer illuminates the cycles of literacy sponsorship through
which women passed on their knowledge about gardens and flowers as
well as a model of leadership: "Your grandma was one that really encouraged me. She gave me so much help. Anytime I wanted to find out
something, I went to Dorlis. In fact, when I first joined Garden Club I
was scared of them. They know so much and here I'm just a little thing.
They were really looked up to."

Now, as President of Garden Club, Cathy finds herself in the leadership role, where she now encourages newer members and passes on her
gardening knowledge, acting as the sponsor rather than the sponsored.
She described for me her role as president:

You've got to have ideas; you've got to have enthusiasm .... We encourage and try to push Garden Club. I have taken ... I take slides of
wildflowers, and the best up in Yellowstone. With my camera I can get
this close [motions] with my subject. Up in Snowy Range, Northwest
or southwest of Laramie, there is a lily, perfect lily, that grows about
that high, and I've gotten so close to it you'd think it was this tall. And
I have given talks showing my slides to other garden clubs and
women's clubs.

In the process of sharing knowledge by researching and preparing lessons, Paxton women are sponsoring a kind of organic model for
research that legitimizes and intellectualizes what is too often disre-
garded by themselves, the community, and outsiders to the culture as
"women's work."

While ultimately not transgressing the agrarianist ideologies that
pervade their rural area through traditional positions of power that are

most recognizable, such as being a member of the school board or the mayor, these women do negotiate a kind of power in the community through being sponsors of literacy. As Kim Donehower has already suggested in this volume, and as Daniell explains in her study of a group of Al-Anon women, power is a term that usually connotes economic and political power. With regard to women's literacy, the word "power" is not so easily translatable but takes on a contextual complexity. As Daniell argues, for example, Scribner's well-known metaphors of literacy as adaptation, power, and state of grace must be reconfigured and reordered. For the women Daniell worked with, "their vernacular experiences and literacies take priority over their public experiences and literacies" (130). The women in my study, as sponsors, had certain power in rural, gendered, and domestic contexts that have long been considered less important, and thus, the literacies they employed would not fall into traditional notions of power. Still, for older women in Paxton, sponsorship brings to them a kind of recognition for their own literacy work—exemplified in the ways Sandy and Cathy talk of being a bit awed by the horticultural knowledge of their mentors, for instance—that gives them personal fulfillment and also allows them a greater sense of authority participating in community activities by feeling qualified and responsible for passing on information and history.

While not everyone in town was likely aware of the literacies that were a key component of Garden Club, other activities ultimately resulting from their literacy endeavors were visible to the entire community—the actual horticultural artifacts themselves. From the research, the meetings, and the lessons, one of the goals was to produce exemplary gardens and flowers, and this was how most of the rest of the town knew their work. Indirectly their literacy work became available to others and a source of community pride as the results of their research were displayed throughout the town. Through work like embroidery, cooking, and gardening, women are able to create cultural artifacts that stand as representations of their sites of learning and teaching. By "representations," I mean connections to and parts of literacy but not literacy in and of itself. I draw upon Anne Berthoff's use of I. A. Richards' definition of the term; she argues that to him the term "meant symbolization" and that "representation ... is mediation—the means of making meaning" (142–43). Flowers arranged throughout the town are not in and of themselves doing this work but serve as a symbol that can be interpreted as an artifact stemming from knowledge gained through literacy.

The idea of representation of literacy seems particularly useful for women's literacies, as scholars have paid more attention in recent years to cultural artifacts such as quilts. Heretofore ignored because of gender bias and high art/low art prejudices, suggests that these artifacts are beginning to be valued for what can be *read* from them (Elaine Showalter, cited in Bower 4). Through materials and artifacts, Anne Bower argues in *Recipes for Reading*, women "not only recorded and reflected the world around them, they worked to construct their world" (6). Thus, nontextual artifacts, such as the floral arrangements these women created and displayed in the Labor Day Garden Show, have been and continue to be "read" by members of the town. In describing how the work of Garden Club infuses the town, one member of the club, Sandy, told me:

> You knew that [the older women] planted those lilacs north of the school? This is the trouble—their product dies out [laughs] .... People don't realize the things we do, what it does for people. We've done baskets at graduation for years, barrels downtown by the post office and grocery store. The one thing I think people have noticed is Yard of the Week. People have said how nice Paxton looks because of it .... I know [Janice] said once when they were moving to this area ... they looked at these towns [surrounding the plant where her husband would work], and she said Paxton looked so nice because the lawns were green and kept up.

The primary mission of Garden Club members is for their work to make the town more beautiful. A result of that work, it seemed, was that the aesthetics also helped sustain their rural community. Part of the reason Janice chose Paxton rather than other towns closer to her husband's job was that she felt people in Paxton must have cared more about their town, as evidenced by meticulous and lovely lawns and gardens. Community beautification was an integral part of the town's pride and the research and creation of landscape was a respected practice; the women produced landscapes, which were visible throughout the town. This landscape was a direct result of the knowledge shared and received through the club's literacy practices; it was literally a product of sponsorship. To have the responsibility for the aesthetics of the town was a worthy endeavor, and to be able to train others in that aesthetic even more so.

What is apparent from talking with Sandy and Cathy is that older women created this space in which they were the experts, and products of that expertise could be seen around town. And through their work in Garden Club, they then moved into other more traditional public spaces where they were the experts and became sponsors themselves: Cathy, for example, using literate knowledge to become a public speaker, to share her Yellowstone slides with others. Having created spaces like Garden Club, the older women also carved a place to act as sponsors to others in the club and the larger community as a whole. From this sanctioned community space, these older women took their gained authority to become more independent researchers, acting as sponsors by modeling, through literacy practices, an identity that negotiated the gendered expectations of the town with intellectually fulfilling literacy endeavors.

SPONSORSHIP FROM HOME

Having participated in clubs and other organizations in Paxton for decades, and even founding some of these organizations, the older women I talked with had local knowledge that newcomers or younger residents didn't have. As those "more knowledgeable" and "more entrenched" in local history, these older women also acted as sponsors in another way outside the clubs: by sharing this knowledge through literacy work they researched and composed independently in the hopes that the information would be used by the sponsored (others in the community and visitors who wanted to learn about Paxton) (Brandt 167). Here I argue they acted as sponsors in two ways: modeling the identity of an independent researcher for townspeople (the sponsored), and providing literate artifacts designed to be a resource of local history and genealogy from which others could learn.

Paxton women's work as researchers is one facet of their role as sponsors that particularly elucidates their negotiation between gained authority and gendered community expectations and is a common thread along the varied kinds of sponsorship, both collaborative (through clubs) and independent, in which they engaged. Research is perceived as (and of course is) an intellectual enterprise, a scholarly practice that legitimizes the literacy endeavors undertaken by these women. For them, the act of researching—while I believe it was done primarily out of genuine intellectual inquiry—at the same time made more visible to others in the community the ways their literacy practices were valuable through sharing family histories with others. The *process* of their literacy endeavors, taking on the role of researcher (a role largely intended to share local knowledge and history with others through the documents they produced), gave older women in Paxton an authoritative space within the boundaries of accepted activities for women of their generation and in their agrarian setting. Once they established that authoritative space, the way was paved for subsequent generations of Paxton women and men (the sponsored) potentially to see that work as legitimate for learning. Further, the *product* of their various literacy endeavors—family histories, genealogies, and town histories for the library, for example—were documents meant to teach others in the town about local histories. Through such textual artifacts, the older women sponsor literacy as well, as interested parties could read and learn about older women's construction of family and town events.

Mona, an older woman in my study who still lives out on the family ranch, constructs authority through her role as a researcher, having completed a book on family history that required extensive research in the region. I looked back at our first interview transcript to see how her family history project motivated her, how it took shape and elicited her notions of expertise. In our first interview she explained the seeds of her desire to write the family history in a book she called *Echoes of Yesterday*:

> I was always interested in family history, always, ever since I can remember I've asked jillions of questions of my mother and she always said I could ask more questions than anybody she ever saw, but I remember them and I inherited some of the pictures and well. I just remembered or wrote down lots of the stories she told about her childhood, so I had more information about the family history than anybody else in the family did. Maybe because I was interested and kept the notes .... I kept notes for many years.

Her family asked her to record the stories she knew so well, and years later she began to put a text together while still living on the ranch but after selling the cattle. *Echoes of Yesterday* begins with an overview of the history of the area since the formation of the Sandhills. She describes attending a seminar in North Platte on writing histories and referring to/copying from *Stories from the Far West* by Joseph Masters for the general historical sections of her book. Her motivation for attending the seminar, she told me, was to figure out how to start the book. Then she began the family histories, research process and struggles of which she shared with me:

> But when you get to the family history, it's terribly hard to get those dates and all of that just down exactly right, and you know I thought [I made mistakes on it]. I tried not to, but when you get into it you'll see you probably will. No, that was aggravating in a lot of ways where I would try to get information out of them and [relatives] wouldn't answer. And I'd write and I'd call and I'd beg them. I spent two years getting one date on one of them. Two years on one date. He didn't remember the date so I had to look it up. I found it in the library, in the old *Keith County News* is where I found that one. I used any source I could find to get to the history of it. The old *Keith County News* sure helped.

Mona told me of two other book projects, *Sandhills Saga* and *Beyond Tomorrow*, that she didn't know if she'd get to. For *Sandhills Saga*, Mona also had extensive notes and thought this book would be about the people in the area she grew up in, stories about those who weren't family members but significantly shaped the area.

The writing Mona has completed as well as future projects she has planned is not uncommon for women (and some men) in Paxton. Projects regarding genealogy and family history are of great importance to many in Paxton. Acting as sponsors, they share their literacy work in order to provide future generations with historical information about what it means to be a Paxtonite. Grandma's niece, Liza, has dedicated her time for years to collecting and preserving the maternal heritage of the family. I witnessed what some of the research work entailed: Liza takes trips around the country to visit libraries to research records and regularly attends family reunions to share her genealogy research and talk with the relatives whose family she has researched. When my grandmother moved into the nursing home, my dad kept her many white three-ring notebooks filled with genealogy from the Hogg side. Since taking the notebooks a few years ago, my dad has begun extensive Internet research. I can also remember my grandparents taking trips to Iowa in search of genealogical records—for many members of my family, it is a consuming and rewarding practice, a clear benefit of the older women's sponsorship in that it is personally fulfilling to them. But women like Mona also used the authority of print and publication—and the research that led them there—to negotiate their identities beyond the stereotypical "women's role" in a rural setting. In their unquestioned beliefs that they had important information and ideas to share with others, they carved a distinct authoritative space in the community. This, built upon the authority gained from their powerful roles in clubs, allowed older women in Paxton to take their abilities as researchers, speakers, and writers to other places in town. No matter what the context, women in Paxton found ways to use literacy to contribute to the well-being of their community while at the same time negotiating their own power and authority in ways that disrupt easy conclusions made by both insiders and outsiders. More importantly, their literacy work challenged how they viewed themselves; though they did not violate the agrarian ideologies surrounding them, they acknowledged their strengths of intellect through research and local knowledge in which they demonstrated more expertise than others in the community.

Their work as sponsors also did more than affect their positions in the community: it influenced the many sponsored who worked with them directly; heard lessons at extension club; read their writing down at the library, church, and elsewhere; listened to their stories; and saw the visual artifacts representing their work. Understanding Paxton women in this way meant re-seeing my experience as a rural woman from the Great Plains, but it also meant revising my ideas about why and how we study women's literacy. Not only do the women have much to tell us about the value of studying lived experiences with literacy amid broad historical surveys, but (and aren't they still acting as sponsors here?) they can also teach us about the malleability of women's identities that can occur when their literacy practices allow them to define—rather than be defined by—their roles.

NOTES

1. With the exception of my grandma Dorlis, all participants/interviewees in this piece have pseudonyms.
2. My research took place between March 1997 and 2000, where I conducted interviews with nine older women who first contributed a chapter to "Early Paxton," a memoir on life in Paxton before 1925. I also spoke with one adult child of every woman who had children and a few women community members who worked closely with the older women in clubs or church. I obtained approval to research subjects from the Institutional Review Board at the University of Nebraska-Lincoln. This piece is part of a larger project on the literacies of these western Nebraska women.

WORKS CITED

Arnold, Roy. *A Golden Milestone, 1936–1986: A History of Nebraska Council of Home Extension Clubs, Inc.* Dallas: Taylor, 1985.

Berthoff, Anne. *The Sense of Learning.* Porstmouth, NH: Boynton/Cook, 1990.

Brandt, Deborah. "Sponsors of Literacy." *College Composition and Communication* 49 (1998): 165–85.

Bower, Anne, ed. *Recipes for Reading: Community Cookbooks, Stories, Histories.* Amherst: U of Massachusetts P, 1997.

Butala, Sharon. *The Fourth Archangel.* Toronto: HarperCollins, 1992.

Daniell, Beth. *A Communion of Friendship: Literacy, Spiritual Practice, and Women in Recovery.* Carbondale: Southern Illinois UP, 2003.

"Events Leading up to Smith–Lever Act and Cooperative Extension." *North Carolina State University Cooperative Extension.* 18 Dec. 2004 <http://www.ces.ncsu.edu/chatham/archived/HeritageDay/HDHistory.html>.

Fink, Deborah. *Agrarian Women: Wives and Mothers in Rural Nebraska, 1880–1940.* Chapel Hill: U of North Carolina P, 1992.

——. *Open Country, Iowa: Rural Women, Tradition, and Change.* Albany: State U of New York P, 1986.

Gere, Anne Ruggles. *Intimate Practices: Literacy and Cultural Work in U.S. Women's Clubs, 1880–1920.* Urbana: U of Illinois P, 1997.

Hobbs, Catherine. Introduction. "Cultures and Practices of U.S. Women's Literacy." *Nineteenth-Century Women Learn to Write.* Ed. Catherine Hobbs. Charlottesville: UP of Virginia, 1995. 1–33.

Lammers, Shelley. "Garden Club 40 Years Old." *Keith County News* n.d. [1991]: N. pag.

Literacy on the Margins: Louisa May Alcott's Pragmatic Rhetoric

Hephzibah Roskelly
Kate Ronald

Louis Menand's *The Metaphysical Club: A Story of Ideas in America,* became a surprising bestseller when it was published in 2001, perhaps in part because Menand chose to write his intellectual history as a narrative. In fact, the book has been both hailed and occasionally criticized for its storytelling bent.[1] In any case, its popularity has meant that many readers, general public as well as academic critics and philosophers, are rethinking the philosophical story Menand tells, the tale of a changing American culture and the rise of pragmatism in post-Civil War America. As Menand describes it, this period marked the birth of modern America:

> The Civil War discredited the beliefs and assumptions of the era that preceded it. Those beliefs had not prevented the country from going to war; they had not prepared it for the astonishing violence the war unleashed; they seemed absurdly obsolete in the new, postwar world. The Civil War swept away the slave civilization of the South, but it swept away almost the whole intellectual culture of the North along with it. It took nearly a half a century for the United States to develop a culture to replace it, to find a set of ideas, and a way of thinking that would help people cope with the conditions of modern life. That struggle is the subject of this book. (x)

To tell the story of an emerging modern America, Menand uses the lives and work of four influential men who were direct or indirect participants in the famous Metaphysical Club, Boston intellectuals who met to discuss philosophy and ideology and who altered American ideas and culture. Menand records the lives of the four men—Oliver

Wendell Holmes, Charles Sanders Peirce, William James, and John Dewey—as they struggle to find meaning, experience, faith, and purpose in the aftermath of the war. Menand claims that the group

> not only had an unparalleled influence on other writers and thinkers; they had an enormous influence on American life. Their ideas changed the way Americans thought—and continue to think—about education, democracy, liberty, justice, and tolerance. And as a consequence, they changed the way Americans live—the way they learn, the way they express their views, the way they understand themselves, and the way they treat people who are different from themselves. We are still living, to a great extent, in a country these thinkers helped to make. (xi)

Our recent project is to relate a parallel story of ideas in the United States to the one that Menand recounts, adding the perspective of women on the margins of the Metaphysical Club who, we claim, also altered American ideas and culture, especially in their devotion to the emergence of women's agency in the world of work. Since in this chapter we can't explore the work of all the women with connections to the Metaphysical Club—Margaret Fuller, Alice James, and Jane Addams among others—we focus here on one woman who used the radical ideas generated by the Club in her own life and work, in the process deepening and extending the Metaphysical Club's most famous and far-reaching idea, pragmatism. Taking Louisa May Alcott as a case study of how intellectual women worked in nineteenth-century America, it becomes clear that women just outside the Metaphysical Club's circle helped create and made use of the pragmatic ideas the Club became so celebrated for, and that their cultural position necessarily changed the character of those pragmatic ideas and actions.

Literacy, like knowledge itself, is contextual. An investigation into literate practices just outside the margins of power and prestige highlights alternate practices and comments on those more powerful strategies and stances. To understand Alcott's work and influence on the margin of the Metaphysical Club can therefore deepen and extend our understanding both of pragmatism and its rhetoric and of the literacy practices of women, typically on the margins. Louisa May Alcott succeeded as a writer; her own literacy practices worked to give her prestige and an income that supported her family. Readers knew her then and now as the author of *Little Women*, a novel that appears to reinforce traditional paths for women to follow in their personal and working lives. But subtly within her most famous stories, *Little Women* and its successors, and overtly within her recently discovered anonymous work, readers find an alternative vision of how women achieve literacy, and of how Alcott uses the tenets of pragmatism to assert a literacy of exigency, experiment, and experience for her women characters and for herself.

Living in a culture which did not believe in locating opportunities for women to achieve self determination and profoundly influenced by a father who believed in equality but in women's domestic sphere at the same time, Alcott, like other intellectual women of the era, was caught in a double bind. How might she aspire to be angel and guardian, and, at the same time, confront her own desire to influence and to experience? American individualism, especially as it was explored through Emersonian transcendentalism, required both experience and self-reliance, and women in America were denied both. As Alcott realized, women needed to understand and employ the pragmatic concept of exigency in order to locate their own kind of transcendental experience, to make their own contexts into experiences to draw on, to make their limitations strengths. Alcott's biography and work suggest how determinedly she used exigency to explore women's agency, as well as how clearly she followed and reshaped other pragmatic principles as she explored women's cultural condition and potential. Reading Louisa May Alcott as a contributor to pragmatic philosophy—putting her into "the Metaphysical Club"—reshapes pragmatism's American legacy. Since she did not have the luxury of writing in the array of fields open to Holmes, James, Peirce, and Dewey (who wrote textbooks, poetry, psychology, philosophy, and public policy), recognizing Alcott's contribution to this movement constitutes an expansion, not only of pragmatism, but of literate public practice.

PRAGMATISM AND THE CLUB

Although there were many differences among the men who made up the Metaphysical Club, they all shared an idea about ideas that proposed that ideas exist not out in the universe waiting to be discovered but instead within people's experience. Ideas, then, are completely dependent upon the people who think them up, and their effectiveness resides not in some outside notion of truth or immutability, but in their adaptability, in how they change to accommodate new environments and new thinkers. That meant for the pragmatists that ideas must always be uncertain, contingent, susceptible to change, and that those qualities constituted the only values ideas hold. Menand says that the essence of the Club's belief was "the belief that ideas should never become ideologies—either justifying the status quo, or dictating some transcendent imperative for renouncing it" (xii). Their skepticism helped people cope with modern life—the continual state of upheaval that capitalism thrives on—and freed them from thralldom to the official ideologies of the church, state, and academy.

The members of the Metaphysical Club changed the way America thought of itself, according to Menand, through the working out of ideas they came to call pragmatism. Briefly, the principles of pragmatic thought include these:

> Ideas are tools.
> Ideas are social.
> Ideas are dependent on circumstance.
> Ideas must be adaptable.

C. S. Peirce, credited with the invention of the term "pragmatism," stressed the importance of both action and consequence in the development of ideas. "A belief is only something upon which one is prepared to act," he argued (141). The truth of an idea and its meaning, then, come as a result of its actions or its consequences. Cornel West calls pragmatism the "American evasion of philosophy" in his book of that title because pragmatism moves away from first things to last things, from *a priori* assumptions about truth and ideas and toward the real-life consequences of those ideas.

The idea that received interpretations and behaviors were not particularly useful for a country redefining itself after its most extreme test in the Civil War was energizing for women who had been clamoring for new interpretations of their work and their roles in society since long before that war. But their pragmatic contingencies, their contexts of possibility, differed greatly from the members of the Club in spite of their intellectual abilities or accomplishments. Thus, women's work and influence were enacted in new ways, though, dramatically in Louisa May Alcott's case, both action and influence were certainly felt.

Why was this little Club able to change so much? Menand's book demonstrates, through its careful biographies of the men—and the cultural/intellectual context surrounding them—that the effect of the work of the Club had much to do with the men's background, education, upbringing, and experience. They were all influential: three of four from distinguished, wealthy Boston families and brought up to understand their importance in the cultural scheme of American life. They spoke together, gave lectures, wrote valuable discussions of their ideas, taught those ideas to students who themselves were brought up to influence and power. They *anticipated* their influence. The women who heard their words, lived beside them in the same post-Civil War climate, and worked in and out of the home to realize their own idea about ideas could not count on that kind of influence, could not anticipate being heard in the same way or at all.

LOUISA MAY ALCOTT'S PRAGMATIC ACTION

Pragmatically speaking, proximity to ideas is important, since it is the social and collaborative character of ideas that gives them weight and truth, and, as the pragmatists pointed out, circumstance or contingency determines beliefs and actions. Louisa May Alcott's circumstance as the oldest child of Bronson Alcott, the most eccentric of the eccentric group of Yankee intellectuals during the American Renaissance, put her in touch with the most important and difficult ideas of the time. Bronson Alcott, a fiery philosopher who spoke on women's rights, abolition, and educational reform, had helped establish a Concord circle where he, along with Thoreau, Emerson, and various other thinkers and writers, discussed important issues of the day, often in the Alcotts' parlor. Bronson knew Henry James Sr., William's father, and they sparred on occasion, finding little sympathy between them but sharing common ideas. The whole Alcott family were good friends of Emerson's, who inspired and influenced many of the Metaphysical Club's members, including Holmes who wrote that Emerson "set him on fire" when he first heard him speak as a student at Harvard. In some ways, the Metaphysical Club itself was an extension of the Concord circle, since so many of its members were affected and inspired by Emerson.

Bronson Alcott was in real ways a feminist, one of the only men among his associates who wanted women to achieve and to contribute in a public space: "Does any reasonable man question if there be not as many women having public gifts as there are men?" he asked (qtd. in Menand 8). His words strike a chord dramatically different from Club member Oliver Wendell Holmes on women's education: according to Menand, Holmes believed that "[t]here were a few women who had the capacity to profit from education, … but '[a] natural law is not disproved by a pickled monster'" (8). William James's father Henry was even more strident: "Woman is by nature inferior to man. She is man's inferior in passion, his inferior in intellect, his inferior in physical strength. Would any man fancy a woman after the pattern of Daniel Webster?" (Lewis 79–80). Yet although Bronson believed in women's agency, he also held idealized notions of women, admiring their "better natures," their purity, and their demure, calm demeanor. Louisa, very much like Jo in her best known novel *Little Women,* had few of these attributes and often was in conflict with her father about her own proper sphere and behavior.

Throughout most of her life, at least until she became famous and well paid, Alcott's family lived in extreme poverty. Bronson was never a provider, and it fell to the kindness of their friends, including Emerson, to help the family out of its frequent difficulties. Early in her life, Louisa became a contributor to the family purse, and she was the main source of support for her mother, father, and sisters for most of her life. From the beginning, writing was for her both an aesthetic expression and a source of income. When an early story, "Thoreau's Flute," brought her some acclaim from reviewers, she noted with characteristic practicality in her journal, "I liked the $10 nearly as well as the honor of being 'a new star' and a 'literary celebrity' " (*Journals* 119). The need of her family left Louisa little luxury for considering her role as "author" or as "lady."

Like Oliver Wendell Holmes, Louisa became a part of the Civil War shortly after the fighting broke out in 1861. Her work as a nurse in an army hospital outside Washington tested her strongly held belief in abolition, and it fed her hunger to experience directly the world that was reserved primarily for men. She wrote in her journal from the army camp about this desire: "I trot up and down the streets in all directions, some times to the Heights, then half way to Washington, again to the hill over which the long trains of army wagons are constantly vanishing and ambulances appearing. That way the fighting lies, and I long to follow" (115).

This desire to act on a belief both she and her family held fervently (a painting of John Brown hung in the family dining room, and Bronson enrolled a black child in his progressive school in Concord much to the disapproval of his community) characterizes Alcott's pragmatic determination. When she had to leave the war after becoming ill from the mercury (calomel) doctors had administered to cure her pneumonia, Alcott continued to work in the cause of Union victory and abolition, and long after the war was over, continued to write about slavery's evils and human rights.

THE DOUBLE LIFE AND NEW LITERACY

Still, acting on belief, a primary tenet of pragmatic thought, was a difficult task for a woman constrained by her society and family, as well as by her economic situation. Alcott adapted by living a double life in her writing, where she both carried the domestic banner for women and undercut it. The rhetoric she fashioned in her most well known writing appears to uphold traditional female virtue. But it also qualifies the idea of the domestic angel through the creation of characters like Jo March, who questioned that role throughout the novel, and through situations, like the March women without their patriarch, that demanded independence in women rather than reliance on others. She wrote of good and intelligent women who ask questions and struggle with their limitations in *Little Women* and its successors: *Rose in Bloom, Under the Lilacs Tree, Little Men, Jo's Boys,* and *Aunt Jo's Scrapbag.* In these novels, virtuous women teach others, especially other women, to behave in traditional, angelic Bronson-approved ways. But even in these novels, Alcott undercuts the traditional and asserts the feminist. In *Jo's Boys*, for example, Jo speaks out against the separate spheres of male and female:

> "Now, if you young people don't want England to get ahead of us in many ways, you must bestir yourselves and keep abreast, for our sisters are in earnest, you see, and don't waste time worrying about their sphere, but make it wherever duty calls them."

> "We will do our best, ma'am," answered the girls heartily, and trooped away with their work baskets, feeling that though they might never be Harriet Martineaus, Elizabeth Brownings or George Eliots, they might become noble, useful, and independent women, and earn for themselves some sweet title from the graceful lips of the poor, better than any a queen could bestow. (294)

Here, as elsewhere, Alcott asserts the importance of real work and real accomplishment for women, and the names of English writers Jo gives are meant to serve as a challenge to young American women to learn, to act, and to work. Writing, she suggests, is a viable route to independence. But as her most well-received writing implies, women authors are contained by the kinds of cultural practices they are supposed to be literate in: teaching, nursing, homemaking, mothering, and writing about good "little women."

Nowhere perhaps does Alcott demonstrate the connection between action and belief and investigate those traditionally female literate practices more clearly than in her novel *Work*, where her heroine, Christie Devon, hungers for work to make herself independent and self sufficient and leaves her uncle's farm to fulfill what she calls a new "declaration of independence." Subtitled "A Story of Experience," *Work* is the clearest example of how Alcott tied women's agency to the accomplishment of work, to paid labor. Published in 1873, *Work* was popular during its day, although criticized for its "cant on the subject of Negro rights" and for its not being a novel at all but instead a "serious, didactic essay on the subject of woman's work" (qtd. in Elbert xxxix).

Christie learns through experience the difficulties and constraints placed on women who are paid laborers. Longing for a larger life in the world of work and experience, Christie moves to the city, and the novel traces her growing understanding of her position as woman and worker through a series of female jobs, including seamstress, servant, governess, factory worker, actress, and nurse. Alcott demonstrates the position of both single and married women who have limited skill and experience and are therefore taken advantage of or who fail and are cast aside. The book is both a kind of *bildungsroman* and an indictment of sexual inequality. Christie, who eventually marries a progressive intellectual man but loses him quickly when he dies in the Civil War, becomes an advocate for working women at novel's end. Invited to speak at a gathering for work reform, Christie stands on the lowest step of the platform to speak: "I am better here, thank you; for I have been and mean to be a working-woman all my life" (428).

Alcott's writing is populated with women like Christie, who make their way in a world where their skills and needs are seldom recognized, where they need to become literate in both the world of work and the world of men in order to succeed. In these novels, Alcott embodies pragmatic ideals of action, experience, contingency and use in the lives of the characters she creates. Still, unlike her heroine in *Work*, Alcott's own experience as a writer suggests that women succeed through subversion, that part of their literacy education is to mask power and skill with a surface compliance to accepted norms.

In her recently recovered anonymous and pseudonymous stories and novels, however, Alcott's beliefs about women's independence, selfhood, and power are demonstrated explicitly and dramatically. In her anonymous novels, most attributed to her only in the last twenty years, Alcott's rhetoric is neither masked nor qualified but overt concerning women's rights and needs in a profoundly sexist culture. In all these stories, women become active agents in their own destinies, and in most of them, women learn hard lessons about the methods they must employ in order to acquire that agency.

In these stories, which follow the plot of popular thrillers, women characters may begin as naïve or powerless, but locate strength through their sexuality, intelligence, and wit. Sometimes wrongheaded or even evil, they are nonetheless active agents in their own lives. The characters in these narratives allowed Alcott to give full expression to her understanding of the relationship between action and consequence, in the role of contingency and circumstance, and in her notion that actions should follow from beliefs. All the thrillers portray different, more equal (though it is a hard fought equality) relationships between the sexes, where sex roles change and traditional behavior is challenged.

A case in point is the novel *A Long Fatal Love Chase*, the first stalker novel in American literature. The main character Rosamund, like Jo and Christie, desires experience and the chance to leave her constrained domestic environment. She meets a dark, handsome stranger, Philip Tempest, and travels with him to Europe, insisting that he marry her first. She soon discovers he is both evil and already married, and the rest of the novel is a story of Rosamund's constant attempts to escape Philip's clutches. Rosamund changes her beliefs about relationships and her agency as a woman throughout the novel. She takes on many of the same employments as Christie in *Work*—governess, actress, and seamstress—in an attempt to hide her identity from Tempest, becoming stronger and smarter with every consecutive occupation. She succeeds, becomes literate in the ways of the world, because she changes, even though her success is qualified by her death. Alcott demonstrates that the characters who cannot change to meet changing circumstance, usually male, fail or are evil. Tempest fails in his quest when he accidentally kills Rosamund at the end of the novel. Stabbing himself, he cries impotently, "Mine first—mine last—mine even in the grave!" (346). She has escaped him and won.

Women in Alcott's thrillers achieve prominence on the stage, get rich, and most of all, conquer men through all manner of deception, superior reasoning, and stronger will. Females stand up to males, arguing and sometimes physically assaulting them. In "Taming a Tartar" (1868), for example, Alcott demonstrates women's power for good through a feminist struggle for control in a relationship with a potentially abusive, powerful Russian estate lord. The woman tames him in verbal and physical battles, and finally has her way as well as her man, as she promises to love, honor and "*Not* obey you" (246).

In *Behind a Mask,* the heroine Jean Muir is a poor governess with a shady past, a strong will, and skill in language and action that allow her to succeed in a world that "had no pity for poverty" (191). Literate in all the ways a woman must be if she is poor and wants to change her lot, Jean uses her considerable skill to teach the young daughter in the family French and geography. But she also ingratiates herself with the invalid mother with her humility and ability to pour tea, charms the young sons with her maidenly gentleness and weakness, and wins the affections of the elder uncle who holds title and money with her talent for reading aloud. After *Behind a Mask* was republished as Alcott's, a reviewer wrote in 1995, "If they ever make a movie of 'Behind the Mask' forget Winona Ryder. This Alcott heroine calls for Leona Helmsley" (Elbert xvi).

In all the thrillers, Alcott shows women who learn to become literate in the ways of a world they have little control over or ability to change. They are thrust into experience or choose it, like Christie Devon or Jo March, and they work hard to achieve money and security. They learn the lessons of paid work, both the freedom it affords and the humiliation it often includes. The rhetoric in these stories is not apologetic or ameliorative, not compromising as it might seem in the novels like *Little Women.* Instead, it is straightforward, often striking a triumphant tone, as at the end of *Behind a Mask,* when Jean marries the uncle despite the discovery of her treachery. She laughs at the outraged nephew as she admits to her acting talent throughout, "Is not the last scene better than the first?" (202).

In her more famous works, especially in *Little Women,* the rhetoric Alcott chooses is, unsurprisingly, less overt than in *Work* with regard to women's work and women's roles in a sexist culture. Jo March is a young woman who wants to be a boy, who rails against the constraints of petticoat, hair ties, and careful talk that young women had to comply with if they were to be ladies, if they were to be the dear "little women" Mr. March called upon them to be in his letters home from the war front. "I can't get over my disappointment in not being a boy," Jo cries, "and it's worse than ever now, for I'm dying to go and fight with Papa, and I can only stay at home and knit, like a poky old woman!" (5). Jo accomplishes boyish feats, not only running and whistling and climbing out attic windows, but also working outside the home and writing to make money. Although she ends married to the fatherly Professor Bhaer, her continual questioning of her role and her limitations continue to strike chords among her many generations of readers. As Sarah Elbert points out, women readers continue to find some part of their own questions about their lives and their own aspirations in Jo's character: "Women reading her work found that she said something about their lives—she made them visible to themselves" (xiviii).

In *Little Women*, as in Alcott's other work, there is the suggestion of the importance of work and of action for women. Like Alcott herself, Jo is a pragmatist. She understands that inquiry is the way to understanding, that actions demonstrate belief rather than assertions of belief, as she cuts her hair, her "one beauty," to support the war effort and her father. She experiments and takes risks, writing romances, moving to the city, and trying for independence. Jo bravely refuses the given, fundamental things in her culture and struggles against the limitations these "givens" imposed. Yet Jo's story is also about loss. In the end, she is contained by traditionally proper literary practices despite her desire to write decidedly improper stories, as she becomes the wife of the professor who has taught her to renounce that desire. Readers often cry at the end of the novel, perhaps in recognition of the loss of Jo, the untamable girl who at last becomes a tamed woman.[2]

ALCOTT'S PRAGMATIC INFLUENCE

In writing both her named and her hidden novels and stories, Alcott created a new working space that allowed her both freedom and control. Her influence becomes in many ways as strong as that of the members of the Metaphysical Club, for her characters and their strivings have become deeply a part of American culture. Jo has been an icon for thousands and thousands of girls and young women—and not for her submissiveness to Marmee or Professor Bhaer, but for her courage, her insistence, and her desire for action and work in the world. She always questions herself and she always operates with beliefs she holds contingently. Through Jo and her many other women characters, Alcott encourages her women readers to act too. She specifically urges women to find work of their own, as in her essay "Happy Women," which touts the virtues of spinsterhood:

> It is not necessary to be a sour, spiteful spinster, with nothing to do but brew tea, talk scandal and tend a pocket-handkerchief. No, the world is full of work, needing all the heads, hearts and hands we can bring to do it. Never was there so splendid an opportunity for women to enjoy their liberty and prove that they deserve it by using it wisely. (205–06)

Alcott asserts directly and by example that work, and becoming literate in the language of work, is women's freedom, their path to self-determination and self-respect. Alcott uses the pragmatic concept of contingency to exhort women to find work wherever they are, to learn how to succeed in the circumstances they find themselves in, and to be impatient with received ideas that would prevent their entering the world of work and of experience.

Now that we have Louisa May Alcott's more complete body of work, we can look more fully not only at her pragmatism but also at her rhetoric—including her use of gothic situations to demonstrate contemporary problems and her use of a wide range of female characters who feel the same desires that men do. Alcott uses sentimental and traditional trappings—marriage, courtship, motherhood, and role-bound behaviors in general—in ways that undercut those cultural practices, surreptitiously and directly. She provides alternatives for women by creating characters who yearn for experience and find it, who need work and are hired to do it, and who learn the lessons of a culture to become more successful, more literate, within it.

Readers of Alcott must question the certainties about the idyllic domestic fiction we may have read as children. It seems clear that Alcott worked to undermine some of the traditional scenes she painted, and her hidden writing as well as her life suggest how far from traditionally domestic she was. Like other recently popular alternative stories that re-imagine the original—*Ahab's Wife* and *The Wind Done Gone* for example—Alcott's story makes readers think in new ways about the stories we thought we knew. Putting her writing in conversation with the Metaphysical Club and with Menand's story of the Club's influence, readers hear Alcott's voice as part of a philosophical movement as well as a critical commentary on that movement. Alcott's work enriches and extends the Metaphysical Club's pragmatic idea by suggesting how women, who could anticipate independence through literacy but hardly philosophical influence, might employ a pragmatism of their own at work, in the home, and in their imaginations.

NOTES

1. See, for example, Paul Boghossian's review in *The New Republic*, which worries that Menand chose "what to pursue and for how long to pursue it ... on purely narrative grounds: would it make for a good yarn?" (35).
2. The casting of Gabriel Byrne in the latest file adaptation of the novel suggests the filmmaker's understanding that Jo's marriage to the professor involves painful loss. Film audiences feel comforted by Jo's marrying the dashing, handsome Byrne, who is portrayed in the novel as much more bumbling, and much more didactic.

WORKS CITED

Alcott, Louisa May. *Aunt Jo's Scrap-bag*. Boston: Little, Brown, 1929.

——. *Behind a Mask*. Showalter 97–202.

——. "Happy Women." Showalter 203–06.

——. *Jo's Boys and How They Turned Out*. Boston: Little Brown, 1920.

——. *The Journals of Louisa May Alcott*. Ed. Joel Myerson, Daniel Shealy, and Madeleine B. Stern. Boston: Little, Brown, 1989.

——. *Little Men: Life at Plumfield with Jo's Boys*. Boston: Little, Brown, 1910.

——. *Little Women*. New York: Signet, 2004.

——. *A Long Fatal Love Chase*. New York: Dell, 1997.

——. *Rose in Bloom*. Chicago: Winston, 1933.

——. "Taming a Tartar." *A Double Life: Newly Discovered Thrillers of Louisa May Alcott*. Ed. Madeleine B. Stern. Boston: Little, Brown, 1988.

——. *Under the Lilacs*. Chicago: Winston, 1934.

——. *Work: A Story of Experience*. Ed. Sarah Elbert. New York: Schocken Books, 1977.

Boghossian, Paul. "The Gospel of Relaxation." Rev. of *The Metaphysical Club*, by Louis Menand. *New Republic* 10 Sept. 2001: 35–39.

Elbert, Sarah. Introduction. *Work: A Story of Experience*. By Louisa May Alcott. New York: Schocken Books, 1977. ix–xliv.

Lewis, R. W. B. *The Jameses: A Family Narrative*. New York: Farrar, Straus and Giroux, 1991.

Menand, Louis. *The Metaphysical Club: A Story of Ideas in America*. New York: Farrar, Straus and Giroux, 2001.

Peirce, Charles Sanders. "How to Make Our Ideas Clear." *The Essential Peirce: Selected Philosophical Writings*. Vol. 1. Ed. Nathan Hauser and Christian Kloeser. Bloomington: Indiana UP, 1992.

Showalter, Elaine, ed. *Alternative Alcott*. New Brunswick, NJ: Rutgers UP, 1988.

West, Cornel. *The American Evasion of Philosophy*. Madison: U of Wisconsin P, 1989.

"Diverse in Sentiment and Form": Feminist Poetry as Radical Literate Practice, 1968–1975

Kathryn T. Flannery

> The decline in adult literacy means not merely a decline in the capacity to read and write, but a decline in the impulse to puzzle out, brood upon, look up in the dictionary, mutter over, argue about, turn inside-out in verbal euphoria, the "incomparable medium" of language—Tillie Olsen's term. And this decline comes, ironically, at a moment in history when women, the majority of the world's people, have become most aware of our need for real literacy ....
> —Adrienne Rich, *On Lies, Secrets, and Silence*

In 1978, when she was writing these words, Adrienne Rich was acutely aware of the forces arrayed against feminism, not least of which was a "culture of manipulated passivity, nourishing violence at its core" (Foreword 14). Rich also knew it could be otherwise: five years earlier, she had observed a remarkable renaissance evident in "women reading and writing with a new purposefulness" outside the classroom door ("Toward" 126). Ordinary women, outside traditional educational institutions, were not only actively rediscovering "lost sources of knowledge" but looking more critically at familiar texts ("Toward" 126). Further, women were writing: "With the help of the duplicating machine," Rich observes, "documents, essays, poems, statistical tables are moving from hand to hand, passing through the mails" ("Toward" 126). Against the "essentially passive-voiced dominant culture," Rich posed a recent history of women's activist literacy to draw encouragement from the remarkable proliferation of print that defined and refined what feminism could mean (Foreword 13).

A commonplace understanding of mid-century feminism has it that especially the younger radical participants in the Women's Liberation movement turned away from books to indulge in an ecstasy of discussion in the process of consciousness raising (see Sarachild; Echols). An echo of this commonplace can be found in composition studies that locate one origin for collaborative learning in women's "rap groups" (see Bruffee; Faigley) or that seek to distance current feminist practice from earlier navel-gazing. Rich's invocation of what she calls the women's university-without-walls is a reminder that women were in fact engaged not just in talk but in multiple acts of literacy on a remarkable scale. While consciousness raising was indeed an important element in mid-century feminist activism, as it was in the civil rights, student's rights, and anti-war movements, an emphasis on an iconoclastic orality obscures the extent to which women's liberation was enabled by and enabled a proliferation of populist, counter-culture forms of writing and reading. Consciousness raising itself was not simply "talk," but would be better understood as a literacy event, in the sense that Shirley Brice Heath has defined it: that interaction of the oral and the written as human beings engage in meaning making (350–51).

My interest in returning to this moment in our relatively recent past is to understand how women taught themselves to extend their literacies to transform the world around them. As Donna Haraway has argued, struggles over literacy, over the "meanings of writing," have been a "major form of contemporary political struggle" (175). But surprisingly few studies have looked at the material forms through which second-wave women engaged in print. And yet it is precisely through such forms that we can begin to reconstruct something of how women seized the tools, as Haraway puts it, "to mark the world that marked them as other" (175). The ephemera produced out of activism—are never fully readable outside the complex contexts of women interacting with women with revolutionary intent. Nonetheless, making visible the material traces of feminist literacy begins to complicate our understanding of the role of literacy in a movement that is quickly receding from living memory.

Feminist publications from the late sixties and early seventies make clear that women were writing (and reading) across a range of genres: they published diaries, "herstories," coming-out stories, cultural analyses, reportage, manifestoes, fiction, drama, how-to instructions (for everything from changing a tire to starting a health clinic), children's literature, parodies, cartoons, and most strikingly, poetry. One of the more surprising discoveries for me in rereading feminist newspapers, journals, newsletters, and small press publications from across the country is the remarkable number and diversity of ordinary women—young, old, working-class and poor, women of color and white, lesbian and straight—who were going public with their poems. A full account of the development of feminist periodicals and presses is beyond the scope of this essay. Suffice it to say that these were largely voluntarist, grassroots activities, run on a shoestring, with materials distributed through the loose network of women's liberation groups across the country (see McDermott; Flannery). Periodicals and presses depended on ordinary women submitting their work with no monetary reward and with only the glory of furthering the cause. Occasionally, an established poet would appear, as well as early poems by poets whose work would appear in establishment publications. But most often, ordinary women submitted poems, sometimes under pseudonyms, sometimes anonymously, and then disappeared from view.

Traditionally understood to be an elite form, poetry was recast through feminism as radically populist—not simply in the sense that the "content" was intended to appeal to a broad audience, but that ordinary people were expected to write poems, read poems, have something to say about them, and then to act on them. Like other movements of the sixties and seventies, feminism found poetry to be a powerful means of truth-telling that depended on taking poems "out from between closed covers resting on shelves, out from the armchair under the reading lamp, out from those quiet moments of private contemplation that have become the canonical setting for poetry, and into public places" (Sullivan 1). But perhaps more than other movements, feminists expected poetry to do a kind of political and pedagogical work that was more or other than polemic or propaganda. If feminist polemic had an obligation to make the case for particular versions of feminism, to posit an ideological common ground for a new movement, feminist poems from the period evidence no such burden. Rather, as Jan Clausen suggests, feminists seemed to have treated poetry as a "clean slate, an open field" (21). Poetry thus held out the promise of "real literacy" requiring writer and reader to "puzzle out, ... mutter over, argue about, ... the 'incomparable medium' of language" (Rich, Foreword 12). This is not to say that women were inventing out of nothing, but it is to say that they felt free to borrow widely from the larger cultural forms and contents that establishment, elite, or school poetry had seemed to ignore or put off-limits. Words alone would not be enough to radically transform a culture that seemed to depend on collective passivity, but poetry served as one way women who might not otherwise think of themselves as writers could resist such passivity by pushing against the confines of language, by using language to probe realms of experience and ideas that had seemed unspeakable.

Clausen has argued that to understand the resurgence of feminism in the latter half of the twentieth century, one has to "take into account the catalytic role of poets and poetry": "It is not too great an exaggeration to say that poets … made possible the movement" (5). While feminists rediscovered neglected women poets, enabling a "tremendous release of poetic energy," they also saw in poetry the power to galvanize women in the movement by engaging them across a spectrum of difference as critical users of language (Clausen 5). The women's movement nurtured poetry not only by providing venues for work that might not otherwise see the light of day, but also by developing writing workshops for women, many of whom had been excluded from the poetry establishment or were seeking alternatives to that establishment. Of course the poems themselves, diverse in content and form, serve as the most important trace of what women were producing and what women had available to them as models for writing. The poems are often the only evidence of a remarkable level of anonymous feminist literate practice. But one can also find evidence in scattered records from the poetry workshops that suggests something about the work feminists thought poetry should do and the sorts of pedagogies they developed to teach themselves how to enter into print.

In order to understand how poetry functioned as a form of radical literacy, I focus on a brief moment of political volatility from the first flush of independent, radical feminist newspapers in 1968 to what one might call the "mainstreaming" of feminism in the mid-seventies. In the Fall 1970 issue of Baltimore's *Women: A Journal of Liberation*, the opening editorial considers what is required to create an "artistically free community," one in which art plays a part in "the everyday life of every person" ("Editorial" 1). Readers are urged to join in a "radical questioning of old meanings" not only about "what constitutes art" but also about what is required to be an artist. Art is rendered meaningless for most people, the editorial asserts, to the extent that the artist is defined in terms of "special 'genius,' as someone set apart from 'the rest of us,'" or as a "prophet" who has a "new vision of the world for us" (1). They grant that "the artist creates an original work, but that original work is paradoxically the product of the age … not independent from the society that the artist lives in" (1). To be revolutionary, "art must be part of the everyday life of every person, placed where everyone can enjoy it—in the streets, on buses, in factories and in schools and offices" (1). But how to make such art possible? While the editorial offers a utopian vision of the necessary prerequisites—"a socialist economy, … an egalitarian community where the need to be superior to other people doesn't exist, but is replaced by a genuine respect for all people, as equals, capable of accomplishing anything collectively" —the journal itself, and other feminist publications like it, can be read as offering something more immediate and material (1). By creating space for poetry as a form of activist literacy, feminist publications quite literally provided incentive for women to participate in the creation and spread of revolutionary art.

In her early survey of feminist periodicals, Ann Mather noted the unusual emphasis given to poetry, suggesting that it was "rapidly emerging as a favorite form of expression for women" (19). Not only did periodicals publish poems in surprising numbers, but they included reviews and critical essays about earlier women poets who were newly rediscovered or in need of critical reevaluation. These critical essays functioned not only to compensate for omissions in traditional literary histories, to reconstruct a women's literary heritage, but also to model a feminist critical practice and to provide encouragement and inspiration for emerging poets. Many of these essays give testimony to the difficulty women in the past faced when they attempted to go public with their verse, suggesting that poetry itself is a radical and courageous act. Alix Shulman's essay on the forgotten American poet, Voltairine de Cleyre, for example, introduces readers to a poet and anarchist who argued for expanding the definition of literature to include "the entire body of people's expressed thought" (6). Cleyre is represented as a "free spirit ... owing no allegiance to rulers, heavenly or earthly," who asked only that she be remembered through the printing of her poems (7). While such acts of recovery are, of course, a recognized part of second-wave feminist literary criticism, it is important to read such essays not as academic performance, but—in the context of feminist periodicals—as political work that was not merely recuperative but could function to rally new poets by modeling reading and at the same time modeling writing. Feminist publications conveyed the message that brave women in the past had understood poetry as a necessary part of their intellectual—and in the case of someone like Cleyre, revolutionary—effort. To write poetry as part of the women's movement would thus be to continue in the line of such courageous women.

Critical essays lent greater force to the calls for poetry sent out by feminist publications. Most periodicals actively solicited poems from readers as part of their effort to extend ownership of the publications beyond editorial collectives and to make the publications more representative of the larger feminist community. The *off our backs* editorial group announced in its second issue that they wanted "at all times ... news stories, pictures, analytical articles, poetry, drawings and cartoons" ("Wanted" 11). In the undated first issue of Detroit's *Womankind*, the inaugural editorial invites readers to participate in the making of the paper by contributing "well-written reportage, essays, fiction, and poetry" (1). Women did in fact take up these invitations in great numbers. While some periodicals included only a single poem an issue, most provided more space, often designing a full page of poems and graphics. Periodicals included poems as part of the informational mix: a single newsprint page of *Womankind*, for example, includes poetry, graphics, a boxed item on Title VII of the 1964 Civil Rights Act, and an advertisement for men's slacks and jeans, suggesting that reading poetry could be as useful as understanding the provisions of federal statute or finding wearable clothing.

Importantly, the very proliferation of feminist poetry, produced outside what James Sullivan calls the "hierarchies of proper access"—that is the traditional paths toward recognition as a poet through universities, established poetry workshops, salons, retreats, and mainline publishers—mitigated against aesthetic or political uniformity (3–4). In part because the women's movement was not a univocal force but a decentralized network of loosely affiliated groups and the publications reflected that coalitional diversity, no subject matter dominates, no particular party line prevails, and no set of formal elements distinguishes the feminist poems from poems appearing in the larger culture (see Felski 166). At least in the volatile early years of the movement, feminist periodicals and small press publications seem to have been more interested in creating space for women to exercise creative freedom than in furthering a single-minded aesthetic or political agenda. Women borrowed forms from popular culture, from protest songs, from children's verse, rock and roll, and blues, as well as a range of traditional poetic forms. Prose poems, free-verse, poems that combine narrative and lyric elements, formal sonnets, sing-song rhymes, parodies of familiar verse are all in evidence. Feminist poems could be about anything from the serious to the silly, from the celebratory to the scathingly critical, from the austere to the boisterously raunchy. Although there are plenty of poems that outline the workings of patriarchy and some that imagine sweet revenge against masculinist power, there are many others that convey the complexity of what it means to be female, what it means to be black and lesbian in America (Gray 36), to grow old (Marsden 11), to give birth to oneself (Schaeffer 74), to lose a child (O'Donnell n.pag.), to wear a mini-skirt (Brower 14), to dance (Glixon 25), to fear madness (Burton 48), to attempt suicide (als 50), to imagine oneself a paramecium (Oleszek 35), "to lie langerously [*sic*] / side by side" another woman (Claytor-Becker 41).

But, it was not only variety in form and content that shaped the reader's experience of feminist poetry. Women were reading poetry from a number of sources, attending readings at women's bookstores and centers, and sharing their own mimeographed poems in group meetings. Because women were often multiply affiliated, they drew on writings not only from other contemporary movements—anti-war, civil rights, black power, and increasingly the gay rights movement—but from mainstream literary traditions as well. Any single publication, then, or any poem within a publication, was most likely to be read in the context of that larger circulation of both radical counter-culture and mainstream poetry. Thus, in turning to a single publication to suggest how poetry functioned in its material context, I want to keep in the foreground this web of interactions that helped to shape literacy practices among movement women.

CELL 16 JOURNAL: NO MORE FUN AND GAMES

In one of the first independently feminist periodicals published in 1968, an untitled journal produced by Boston's Cell 16 (later to become *No More Fun and Games*), thirty out of the eighty pages are devoted to poetry. No editorial introduction, dates, or prefatory apparatus situate for the reader the contents of this small folio typescript pamphlet in relation to a particular group or ideological position. Toward the end of the pamphlet, an address and phone number are given "for further information on female liberations," but no contact person or group is named. Like much early movement publication, this pamphlet is designed to circulate among women who share a context, as if a preface already exists in the interrelationships among the women who wrote and printed this simple booklet, and between them and the larger circle of local women and men active in the movement. There is thus an intimacy, or insider quality, to these poems, suggesting that the poets wrote at least initially for one another, and thus could presume on some level a sympathetic reception.

The poems suggest a range of possibilities. Some serve as angry punctuation to the prose polemics also included in the pamphlet, referencing directly the outer world of politics and confrontation; others put that outer world in tension with what traditionally has been figured as private. Some poems are all hard surfaces, opaque codes resisting reading, and others are startlingly childlike valentines. Few come close to raw confessional of the sort that has come to stand reductively for women's verse in this period, and thus the omnipresent first-person operates less like an autobiographical "I" than an abstracted first-person female. The pamphlet opens with Ellen O'Donnell's poem, "The Anniversary." The two numbered stanzas offer spare images without direct reference to current events or an identifiably feminist understanding. Reference to the outer world is oblique, with the language of love poetry interrupted only by one allusion to the New Testament Book of Revelation: "Pale blue sheets / your heart beating, / loudly under my ear. / If we can steal / moments from Armageddon / We have won" (n.pag.). A reader in 1968 might well recognize in "Armageddon" a contemporary reference: this was a year in which repressive forces seemed to be closing off revolutionary possibilities, and the battle of the last days did not seem so far off. Martin Luther King, Jr.

was assassinated and urban riots followed in the wake of his murder; television coverage of demonstrations outside the Democratic National Convention in Chicago brought into everyone's living room images of police brutality; Robert Kennedy's assassination; the fear that the FBI was infiltrating radical groups; and the election of Richard Nixon to the White House all defined a climate in which radicals felt embattled. The poem references none of this directly, but stays in the bedroom: "I have been / shined and polished / rubbed with oil, / pummeled and perfumed. / Now you want me to tint my tears / to match the pillowslips." The poem ends there.

As an outsider to Cell 16, I cannot know who the "you" is or how exactly I am to put the reference to Armageddon together with tinting tears. But in the course of reading the pamphlet, I can begin to build an understanding. A poem that comes several pages later in the pamphlet, Roxanne Dunbar's "On Revolution," suggests that the common view, especially among male radicals, was that because (presumably white) women were not "dying in Ghettos" they had "no right" to revolution. To yoke tears on the pillowslips with Armageddon would thus seem out of proportion, unseemly, hyperbolic. And yet, at least one lesson to be learned from the poems assembled here is that women in fact needed to make the "unseemly" connection, to recognize that, as another Dunbar poem concludes, "there is an enemy in your house tonight / If you choose Mastery to Being" ("The Politicians" n.pag.). Still, it would be difficult to understand fully as an outsider the full force of O'Donnell's "The Anniversary" or how (or if) it could be expected to serve as a radical feminist introduction to the eighty pages of the pamphlet that follow. I am struck instead by how it provides only the barest warning through that word "Armageddon" and that the rest of the pamphlet is required to make that word resonate.

In the pamphlet, poems do not stand on their own, they do not signify independent of context, but need the reader to make them mean, as we would expect if we presumed that any text is the barest trace of the more complex literacy event that produced it or that evolved out of it. The material form of the pamphlet serves as a footprint to direct us to the larger interactional context. Each piece within the pamphlet can stand for a contribution to an ongoing conversation or debate among the members of the collective that produced the pamphlet. The pamphlet in the aggregate does not represent a unified distillation of that debate, but rather the ragged, unresolved, volatile nature of the literacy event(s) of which the pamphlet is the only trace. Immediately following the first poem is a harsh polemic on slavery that hinges on an analogy between the enforced inferiority of Africans brought as slaves to the New World and that of women, concluding with an untitled poem by Roxanne Dunbar that extends the analogy of the polemic and echoes the hint of warning from "The Anniversary": "God let it not end in masculine / Amalgamation / So much blood / and fear / and loneliness / wasted / and hope gone / The culprit left clean / Always clean / Never daunted." Amalgamation can be heard as an off-echo of Armageddon, especially with its more direct image of the final battle, full of blood and fear and wasted hope. Another Ellen O'Donnell poem follows a few pages later that asks who would want to be "sovereign / of such a barren country?" ("The Tarnished Camelot" n.pag.). The speaker of the poem is about ready to flee, "knapsack ready," but she hears her "sisters crying" and she has to risk her hard-won freedom to turn back. She is needed, and some sense of the ugly force that calls her back is contained in the final stanza with its possible reference to Sylvia Plath's poem "Ariel": "There's a child of ten / numb within her Ariel's mind / fresh from sweaty fingered cretins / posturing as men / friends of the families, neighbors / custodians." Who will be there, the poem asks, to restore her?

While Roxanne Dunbar's poem, "Essay on a Week in New York 3 July, 1968," exposes the inadequacy of any simple "personal solution" to the kind of violence alluded to in O'Donnell's poem, Dunbar also rejects the "retreat immoral" represented by Yippies—figured as counter- cultural drop-outs—as well as the inadequacy of "Black Liberation turned to Black / Patriarchy" that only works to save half of humankind—because "Half is not enough." Dunbar is reflecting a growing worry, one expressed more forcefully later by writers anthologized in Toni Cade Bambara's *Black Woman,* that prominent men in the Black Power movement were telling black women that unless they subordinated themselves to men they would be "part of the problem" (Chalmers 162; see also Anderson-Bricker 57–58). The poem reinforces the prose arguments made elsewhere in the pamphlet (and elsewhere in the movement literature) that women needed to attend to their own needs. Maureen Davidica's polemic, "Women and the Radical Movement," for example, asserts that "women must unite in liberation groups … [and] it is up to the women to stand up independently, to demand a society not based on an enslaving family unit with its male/ female dependency" (n.pag.). "Liberation," she concludes, "is an irreversible process and there can be no stopping at the half-way mark" (n.pag.).

If the solutions to social, political, and economic inequity cannot be simply "personal" or individual, but have to entail collective action, many of the poems nonetheless register the extent to which such inequity is registered first as very personal, at the very intimate level of the female body. Gail King's "boston—1776," for example, associates hair straightening and skin bleach with racist and sexist understandings of what it means to be American, when the default position is always white and male: "wrapped round a process / is your flag and that / process is Dr. Pepper's / hair straightener, / Skin bleach … / O brutha beware" (n.pag.). The poem seems to ask what sort of revolution was it in 1776 (or by implication, is it in 1968) that requires such erasure, and requires the complicity of the oppressed. If King's poem underscores the way racism and sexism together doubly mark the female body, O'Donnell's "There are Five Senses" seeks to dramatize the female body as consumable goods (and again, there is the recognition of necessary complicity on the part of the woman). Here the relationship between women and consumerism is literalized through an image of the female body as food. O'Donnell's language is oddly old-fashioned as if to underscore the imbalance in the relationship. The speaker fears the sound of the man's footstep, knowing that while he seeks to consume her through sex, he "savors nothing": "I clothe myself in disarray / rather than be importuned / to disrobe. / No feast possible for / the eye alone. / He must touch / fingering to shreds. / Beauty to him / is only a prelude. / He is full / and I am hungry" (n.pag.).

In the context of the pamphlet, the final line carries greater weight, especially following two prose pieces that work to expose the relationship between power and sex. O'Donnell's prose reflection, "Thoughts on Celibacy," suggests that "graceful loving" is possible only when neither partner seeks to "mold the other person's energy." Another polemic, one that circulated beyond the confines of this pamphlet through the extensive movement reprint network, Dana Densmore's "On Celibacy," argues that men and women are "programmed to crave sex" as part of consumer culture, and thus sex is not intended to ever actually satisfy but to leave women (and men) hungry. While such an argument may now seem reflexively familiar, the repetition of the idea in these polemics and in the poetry suggests that it was an idea that was still new and needed repeating.

For all the hard-edged, anti-romanticism of such prose and some of the poetry, a number of the poems seem to hearken back to another more innocent time. O'Donnell's "My Autumn" is organized in three proper stanzas, each a rhyming quatrain. The poem echoes elements of the Petrarchan tradition with its sense of longing: "I've watched the starling / wend on home / and wished him love / though I have none." This longing expresses potential more than it does desperation. "Although my soul / is single still," and "never filled," the speaker says·in the second stanza, she nonetheless has love to offer others. The poem concludes with the speaker wishing "love / to every living thing, / while I await / my season's pleasure." In a pamphlet with poems that address "male Judases" who "dish out daily betrayal" (Anonymous, untitled) or that confront the "one lost poet / who turned his cock to a sword" (King, "Mr Jones") and polemics on the "Sexual Castration of the Female," O'Donnell's "My Autumn" seems almost quaint, out of place. And yet, more of the poems in this publication are about love or longing than anything else. It is as if the pamphlet as a whole keeps in tension visions of Armageddon with visions of the pillowslip. The "personal is the political" is not yet a catch phrase in this early publication, but rather the poems in the aggregate suggest the pressing need for articulating the relationship between those domains.

Across publications, one could find not only a range of forms and contents, but also something of the sifting of language Rich has argued is necessary for real literacy—"for many women, the commonest words are having to be sifted through, rejected, laid aside for a long time, or turned to the light for new colors and flashes of meaning: *power, love, control, violence, political, personal, private, friendship, community, sexual, work, pain, pleasure, self, integrity*" ("Power and Danger" 247). One can find poems of greater complexity in other feminist publications, and as the movement spread, more publications appeared (including some specifically devoted to the arts), making more room for women's work. But to read the Cell 16 pamphlet as a primer for emerging poets is to understand how poems were expected to turn over the "commonest of words" in order to push against the limitations of language, to make visible ways of understanding that were available neither in mainstream nor male-dominated radical verse. In this sense, the poems did not simply repeat the arguments of the polemics but served as another form of literate action, another way for women to engage in revolutionary work.

While feminist publications provided a venue for women's poetry and offered models of flexible, revolutionary literacy practices, some women also sought more structured, communal opportunities to learn how to write poetry. To address the growing demand, poetry workshops began appearing across the country, and their scattered traces provide another perspective for considering feminist poetry as a form of radical literacy.

WOMEN'S POETRY WORKSHOPS

Women's poetry workshops were organized around the country, some as part of women's liberation schools or free schools, others as free-standing operations. Inspired in part by the freedom or liberation schools associated with the civil rights movement and borrowing elements from the open schools movement, women's liberation schools were among the counter-institutions that emerged in this period to "provide services which meet the needs of women now"; to "raise the expectations … as to what is possible"; and "to demonstrate that the problems addressed are social [rather than personal] in nature and in solution" (CWLU-Hyde Park 11). As the Hyde Park Chapter of the

Chicago Women's Liberation Union put it, "in contrast to consciousness raising, such programs dispel the specter of endless problems without apparent solutions" (11). Counter-institutions, at their best, provided a vision of alternative organizational structures and practices that could serve as a critical measure for judging the distance between a feminist ideal and a dominant reality (CWLU-Hyde Park 12; see also Felski 168).

Organizers of women's liberation schools wanted to take learning into their own hands on the principle that "what we don't know, we must learn; what we do know, we should teach each other" (Grimstad and Rennie 123). This shared learning was more than "just talk," but involved exercising and extending the range of literacy practices available to women. Thus, the Sojourner Truth School for Women in Washington D.C. advertised itself as a place for women who "have long been denied recognition of the importance of what they are capable of doing" where they could learn how to cast off dependence "on authority figures from car mechanics and plumbers to professors and realtors" (Grimstad and Rennie 125). Most of the women who founded Breakaway, a Free School for East Bay Women (San Francisco), had experienced "the oppressive environment of male-dominated schools or colleges," and they had chosen to "avoid getting entangled in a women's studies program in a conventional campus setting" (Grimstad and Rennie 123). Believing that they would have greater freedom to develop innovative approaches outside established institutions, they decided "not only to break away from sexist education, but to break away from orthodox modes of learning which have alienated so many women from conventional institutions—intellectual one-upping, ego-tripping, teacher/pupil dichotomies, smart/dumb labels" (Grimstad and Rennie 123). Within the context of such counter-cultural critiques of establishment institutions and practices, poetry workshops were cast as utopian women's spaces whose purpose was to further revolutionary art.

Cambridge Women's School, for example, offered courses in black history, socialist feminism, labor history, women and literature, lesbianism, dialectical materialism, Marxism, painting, welfare awareness, auto mechanics, women's health, and "Voices of Women (Poetry)." This longest running, independent women's school in the United States (it was closed finally in 1992) was founded as a collective in the fall of 1971 by twenty women active in women's liberation. Intended as "an alternative source of feminist education," with a socialist-feminist orientation, the classes were taught, often in teams, by volunteers. Fees were kept low to insure that "all women would be able to participate" (Women's School [Cambridge, MA] Records 1). By 1973, the Women's School was offering both a Writing Workshop for those interested in both poetry and fiction (or "other forms") and a separate Poetry Workshop. The blurb for the Writing Workshop promises: "We will empha-size mutual criticism and support within the group; students [are] expected to bring one piece of work every week, preferably with cop-ies." Participants could expect to focus on "the writing of poetry as an expression of the female experience," however that might be defined (Grimstad and Rennie 126). Similar hints can be found in course de-scriptions from the Everywoman's Center in Amherst (now an official part of the University of Massachusetts). The center offered a poetry workshop in the Fall of 1973, entitled "Where Would You Go If You Were Going?" and intended "for all of us: to support and encourage both be-ginners (even if you've never shared your poems before) and more prac-ticed writers." The co-conveners of the workshop expressed their interest in a "discussion of women poets ... dealing particularly with the issues of women's experience, Third World women, and a new lan-guage/culture" at the same time they expected the workshop to ad-dress the "specific needs/desires" of participants "with possible focuses on writing, reading, or analysis" (Grimstad and Rennie 128).

Like other courses offered through the women's liberation schools, poetry workshops were intended to make learning opportunities widely available to women, to break down the traditional barriers be-tween teacher and learner, expert and novice, to tie the creation of new work to an understanding of a longer tradition of women's writing, and to create a balance between criticism and support. As such, they were intended as alternatives to established creative writing workshops, that were understood to have been founded by (elite) men for (elite) men and structured to revolve around the Great Writer at whose feet the nov-ices were expected to sit. The earliest mainstream workshops gathered together a relatively homogenous group of people who could read one another's work and critique that work on some level as social equals—even as the structure was a reminder that the workshop leader was clearly more equal than anyone else.

The pedagogical assumptions of the establishment workshops were implicit for the most part rather than explicit, revolving around an es-tablished or at least recognizable aesthetic. Rather than a pedagogy that emphasized the chasm that divided the great writer from the lowly nov-ice (even as it could presume social equality), the women's poetry work-shop attempted to create approaches to literacy learning that would allow all women to soar. If the feminist periodicals were intent on pub-lishing the work of ordinary women (on the egalitarian principle that ordinary women can produce extraordinary work), the feminist writing workshop was intent on insuring that ordinary women could recognize what they already know (and know how to do), and to push further in order to learn in concert with others what they still need to know. Many women in the movement recognized the paradoxical tension at the heart of such pedagogical aims: how could they encourage all women to develop themselves as writers—a kind of creative egalitarianism—at the same time that they wanted to celebrate the unusual accomplishments of some women; how, in other words, to nurture a non-elitist art that would not prevent some women from soaring?

Some sense of the difficulty in achieving such goals is evident in a remarkable retrospective account of a women's writing workshop begun in 1975 in Oneonta, New York. As a "document of community and a primer for establishing creative writing workshops," Beverly Tanenhaus' *To Know Each Other and Be Known: Women's Workshops* is a rich account of an evolving and reflective pedagogy (vii). Taking as her starting point Toni Morrison's assertion that "Women don't know what they know, don't use what they know, don't respect what they know," Tanenhaus recalls that she had seen too many women "try to sabotage their writing by trivializing their efforts through apology or boast …. Either response," she asserts, "dilutes the intense confrontation demanded between the writer and her words" (2, 13). On more than one occasion, she heard "strong writers describe themselves as scribblers or dabblers, terms that are belittling and inaccurate" (13). How then to develop a creative writing pedagogy that would enable women to respect their work and the work of other women, to insure that intense confrontation between the writer and her words that would, in Adrienne Rich's terms, define "real literacy"? Part of what was at stake was the complex question of authority: women would have to learn to claim their own authority to go public with their words, but to do so they would have to negotiate authority with one another, with the prominent writers who came as guests (who in some sense stood for recognized poets in the larger culture), with Tanenhaus in her role as teacher, and with literary tradition. Writerly authority, in other words, would not come automatically; it would not be simply granted as a superficial gesture in the name of either egalitarianism or feminism.

In addition to interacting with established writers—Adrienne Rich and Toni Morrison in the first year—participants attended workshops and worked individually with Tanenhaus. Her aim was to establish an atmosphere that was both friendly and professional. While she was clearly identified as discussion leader in the workshops, she also recognized that in the personal conferences it was necessary to "break down the hierarchical distances between teacher and student, inevitable in a structured classroom" (12). As discussion leader, Tanenhaus "assum[ed] that burden of careful listening, of keeping track of comments, of making sure that everyone had a chance to speak and that feedback was consistently constructive" (7). She could not presume, in the way that established writing workshops of the time might have, that participants were homogeneous in experience or background. She thus established working guidelines to insure a mutual valuing of "our writing and our time." This meant that "anyone who sauntered in late" was viewed "as breaking our contract and disrupting the class" (6). Pride in one's work and respect for others was registered in the most basic of ways: "if a workshop leader allows a woman to present ... a poem with numerous scrawled revisions toppling into the margins, she is reinforcing the writer's lack of respect for her work and for her audience" (6). Copies were expected to be legible, accurately typed; participants were expected to come to the workshop having read the work beforehand. However personal a piece of writing might be, readers were expected to refer to the speaker of a piece as "the narrator" because this "provided a distance that honored the individual's privacy and encouraged objectivity among readers intimate with the writer." Writers were to remain silent until after the work was discussed. Tanenhaus realized that a writer could nonetheless manipulate response by bringing only work considered safe or through using "hostile body language or intrusive charm," but she found that for the most part silence allowed multiple perspectives to be aired without "being short-circuited by the author's explanation" (6). Thus, the writer could see how the writing worked on its own terms, unaided by explanation or apology: "this rule of silence ... provided a safe space for the writer to listen" and only after listening could the writer respond to the groups' comments and ask questions for further clarification (7).

The "rules" alone, however, could not ensure that the workshops would function productively. Tanenhaus needed a way to enable women at different stages and with different kinds of preparation to take part, and in this, she projected a particular vision of feminist pedagogy:

> A workshop leader must be attuned to people who are just beginning to sail into the discussion and make space for their comments. At the same time, the more self-confident, verbal women must not be made to feel that they are crowding the shyer types by their eloquence and perceptiveness. In the classroom, we still battle sexist stereotypes that praise an inhibited, insecure woman as beguilingly demure, and condemn a self-assured, articulate woman as overpowering. Ideally, each woman in the room is thoughtfully, comfortably contributing her comments. Then, each of us will feel her individual importance in articulating her insight, not only for the benefit of the writer but for the creation of community among us where people respond from generosity as well as shrewd, critical judgement. (8)

While Tanenhaus acknowledges that this sense of community will not develop if the workshop leader dominates the discussion, she does not construct the feminist teacher as abnegating her authority (Emig and

Butler 132). Rather, teacherly authority is redefined in terms of respecting work and time, attentive listening, making room for both the shy and the verbal women to be heard, and modeling generous and critical judgment. Establishing such teacherly authority is thus also a way to model writerly/readerly authority.

Because workshop participants sometimes hesitated to point out weaknesses in one another's work, "fearing that their negative feedback would be taken as lack of support," Tanenhaus needed to show the ways in which critic and writer are necessary to one another, to make clear the extent to which each has to take risks to go public with her words: "It is crucial," she asserts, "that the writer trust the critic's good will and that the critic understand that shrewd negative comment is at the very least constructive and often exhilarating." To do otherwise, "to censor one's criticism" would be "a lack of generosity and a gesture of contempt that will keep a writer from developing her finest potential" (11). But to get to that point, participants had to "feel free to disagree with each other's analyses, including statements by the teacher" (11). Tanenhaus developed several strategies to encourage generous and critical working relationships. In terms that will no doubt seem familiar to composition teachers, she explains how she learned that it was better if she did not tell a writer everything she could about the work, but instead tried "to figure out what I know about her work that she can use" (9). She did not want to overwhelm the piece of writing with her own impressions but tried to offer "focused critical feedback." As a way to fracture the univocal force of her teacherly voice, on occasion she offered a response to a piece of writing "along with a careful presentation of contradictory points of view," and then asked workshop participants to weigh the different perspectives (9).

Initially she did not give assignments because she assumed that women would come with a "backlog of writing," but she found that assignments or writing prompts if treated as invitations were necessary to unblock the writer. She discouraged unfocused discussion of craft in favor of illustrating technique through examples at hand, and most importantly, "no one was allowed to state a one-dimensional pejorative reaction to work, since 'I hate it,' or even 'I love it,' would leave the writer helpless to evaluate the response" (11). Instead, each reader was expected to support her critical comments with specific reasons, and thus to risk putting into words her thinking. In this way, as Tanenhaus observes, "the critic shares the writer's vulnerability since she puts herself on the line when she analyzes" (11).

In reflecting on the women's writing workshop process, Tanenhaus makes clear the reciprocal relationship between how women interact with one another and the art they are capable of producing. It may seem to go without saying that writing and reading are not isolated from human interaction but necessarily enmeshed in it, but the notion of the writer as a brave, even heroic, isolate was certainly dominant, with the conjoined idea that to write well, one had to separate onself from the herd. In the women's workshop, women had to recognize how the dominant culture constrains them, even as they were learning to trust one another, to find support in the collective. Tanenhaus observes that when they are too fearful of expressing ideas that prove threatening to the status quo, women are handicapped as writers: "The means by which a woman is sabotaged vary, although the reasons for sabotage are culturally consistent—under patriarchy, all women pay a price for challenging the company line, whether it's specific retaliation in a personal relationship, trivialization or ridicule by male audiences ('You're too political / angry / narrow-minded / sensitive / paranoid'), or simply the loneliness of being an outsider" (16). Her observation echoes feminist publications of the time in suggesting both how much courage it would take for feminist/outsiders to come into print, and how important it was for them to do so. One reaction to such acts of sabotage might be to create a nurturing women's world where criticism is outlawed, but Tanenhaus did not believe that would produce revolutionary art in the sense of art that would challenge the patriarchy or make it yield.

The confrontation between a writer and her words necessary to produce art was not going to happen until women learned to really hear one another, to offer generous as well as negative commentary, to disagree with each other's readings of a given work, and to seek out constructive exchanges. Such opportunities could not protect women completely from negative forces in the larger culture, but such experiences would better arm them to work to defeat those forces when they returned to their daily lives. The implication in Tanenhaus's pedagogy is that if women could engage with one another this way, they were more likely to produce poetry that could do real work in the world, and such poetry would necessarily be opposed to propaganda as the antithesis of vigorous exchange. Tanenhaus recalls that while workshop participants "reveled in their emerging insights" about feminism, they also worked to "to avoid the forced ideology that can swamp the best-intentioned efforts" (30). In this sense, workshop participants "were unwilling to confuse politically correct rhetoric with eloquence or to record as awesome events mere bandwagon miracles" (30).

As both the Cell 16 journal and the poetry workshops suggest, avoiding propaganda did not mean that feminist poetry ought not be forceful. Tanenhaus quotes Audre Lorde's poem, "Power," to underscore the distinction: "I have not been able to touch the destruction / within me. / But unless I learn to use / the difference between poetry and rhetoric/ my power will run corrupt as poisonous mold / or lie limp and useless as an unconnected wire" (qtd. in Tanenhaus 32). "No true political poetry can be written with propaganda as an aim," Adrienne Rich argues, if by that one means to "persuade others 'out there' of some atrocity or injustice" ("Power and Danger" 251). As is evident in such publications as the Cell 16 journal, feminist poetry was expected to be neither an object to be contemplated in tranquility, nor a form of sloganeering, but a way to make sensuously present one's "relationship to everything in the universe" (Rich, "Power and Danger" 248). Feminist poetry thus was to be an enactment of real literacy, requiring writer and reader to brood over, argue about, hammer through the limits and possibilities of language in order to resist a culturally mandated passivity that allowed for the perpetuation of violence against the historically disenfranchised. Indeed, what is most striking to me as I read the tremendous outpouring of poetry in the periodicals and pamphlets is that women understood their acts of literacy at once as acts of rebellion and re-creation. Marking the world that marked them as other required creating counter-institutions that would make room for women to teach one another not just "basic literacy" but "critical literacy" (see hooks; Bunch). In this sense it is not merely that ordinary women wrote in such numbers—a remarkable fact in itself—but that they built structures and developed processes to ensure that such radical acts of literacy would seed more and more radical acts that would transform the world.

WORKS CITED

als. "suicide/to pearl." *Moving Out* 2.1 (1972): 74.

Anderson-Bricker, Kristen. "'Triple Jeopardy': Black Women and the Growth of Feminist Consciousness in SNCC, 1964–1975." *Still Lifting, Still Climbing: Contemporary African American Women's Activism.* Ed. Kimberly Springer. New York: New York UP, 1999. 46–69.

Bambara, Toni Cade. *The Black Woman: An Anthology.* New York: Signet, 1970.

Brower, Millicent. "Midi/Mini." *The New Broadside* 1.1 [1971]: 14.

Bruffee, Kenneth. "Collaborative Learning: Some Practical Models." *College English* 34 (1973): 634–43.

Bunch, Charlotte. "Feminism and Education: Not by Degrees." *Quest: A Feminist Quarterly* 5.1 (1979): 7–18.

Burton, Gabrielle. "People Who Listen to Voices End Up in the Loony Bin (Written before WL)." *Women: A Journal of Liberation* 2.2 (1971): 48.

Cell 16. Untitled. [later, *No More Fun and Games: A Journal of Female Liberation.*] Boston: Cell 16, 1968.

Chalmers, David. *And the Crooked Place Made Straight: The Struggle for Social Change in the 1960s.* Baltimore: Johns Hopkins UP, 1991.

Clausen, Jan. *A Movement of Poets: Thoughts on Poetry and Feminism.* Brooklyn: Long Haul P, 1982.

Claytor-Becker, Catherine. "They lie langerously [sic] …" *Moving Out* 2.1 (1972): 41.

CWLU–Hyde Park. *Socialist Feminism: A Strategy for the Women's Movement.* 1972. Women's Liberation Movement On-Line Archival Collection. Special Collections Library. Duke University, Durham, NC. 6 Mar. 2006 <http://scriptorium. lib.duke.edu/wlm/socialist/>.

Davidica, Maureen. "Women and the Radical Movement." Untitled. [later, *No More Fun and Games: A Journal of Female Liberation*]. Boston: Cell 16, 1968, n.pag.

Densmore, Dana. "On Celibacy." Untitled. [later, *No More Fun and Games: A Journal of Female Liberation*]. Boston: Cell 16, 1968, n.pag.

Dunbar, Roxanne. "Essay on a Week in New York 3 July, 1968." Untitled. [later, *No More Fun and Games: A Journal of Female Liberation*]. Boston: Cell 16, 1968, n.pag.

——. "On Revolution." Untitled. [later, *No More Fun and Games: A Journal of Female Liberation*]. Boston: Cell 16, 1968, n.pag.

——. "The Politicians." Untitled. [later, *No More Fun and Games: A Journal of Female Liberation*]. Boston: Cell 16, 1968, n.pag.

——. Untitled. [later, *No More Fun and Games: A Journal of Female Liberation*]. Boston: Cell 16, 1968, n.pag.

Echols, Alice. *Daring to Be Bad: Radical Feminism in America, 1967–1975.* Minneapolis: U of Minnesota P, 1989.

Editorial. *Women: A Journal of Liberation* 2.1 (1970): 1 [back page].

Emig, Janet, and Maureen Butler. Prefatory Interview. *The Web of Meaning.* Ed. Dixie Goswami and Maureen Butler. Upper Montclair, NJ: Boynton/Cook, 1983. 132–34.

Faigley, Lester. *Fragments of Rationality: Postmodernity and the Subject of Composition.* Pittsburgh: University of Pittsburgh P, 1992.

Felski, Rita. *Beyond Feminist Aesthetics: Feminist Literature and Social Change.* Cambridge: Harvard UP, 1989.

Flannery, Kathryn T. *Feminist Literacies, 1968–1975.* Urbana: U of Illinois P, 2004.

Glixon, Lynn. "To Earth Onion." *off our backs* 2.2 (1971): 25.

Gray, Vernita M. "Letter to the Editor." *Are We There Yet? A Continuing History of* Lavender Woman, *a Chicago Lesbian Newspaper, 1971–1976.* Ed. Michal Brody. Iowa City: Aunt Lute, 1985.

Grimstad, Kirsten, and Susan Rennie. *The New Woman's Survival Catalog: A Woman-Made Book.* New York: Coward, 1973.

Haraway, Donna. "A Cyborg Manifesto: Science, Technology, and Socialist-Feminism in the Late Twentieth Century." *Simians, Cyborgs, and Women: The Reinvention of Nature.* New York: Routledge, 1991. 149–81.

Heath, Shirley Brice. "Protean Shapes in Literacy Events: Ever Shifting Oral and Literate Traditions." *Perspectives on Literacy.* Ed. Eugene Kintgen, Barry Kroll, and Mike Rose. Carbondale: Southern Illinois UP, 1988. 348–70.

hooks, bell. "Educating Women: A Feminist Agenda." *Feminist Theory: From Margin to Center.* Boston: South End, 1984. 107–15.

King, Gail. "boston-1776." Cell 16, n.pag.

——. "Mr Jones." Cell 16, n.pag.

Marsden, Karen. "Plastic Wrinkle War." *Woman Becoming* 2.1 (1974): 11–12.

Mather, Ann. "A History of Feminist Periodicals, Part III." *Journalism History* 2.1 (1975): 19–23.

McDermott, Patrice. *Politics and Scholarship: Feminist Academic Journals and the Production of Knowledge.* Urbana: University of Illinois Press, 1994.

O'Donnell, Ellen. "The Anniversary." Cell 16. n.pag.

——. "Empty Crib." Untitled pamphlet. Boston: Cell 16, 1968. n.pag.

——. "My Autumn." Cell 16. n.pag.

——. "The Tarnished Camelot." Cell 16. n.pag.

——. "There are Five Senses." Cell 16. n.pag.

——. "Thoughts on Celibacy." Cell 16. n.pag.

Oleszek, Mary Jo. "The Science in Me." *Moving Out* 2.1 (1972): 35.

Rich, Adrienne. Foreword. "On History, Illiteracy, Passivity, Violence, and Women's Culture." *On Lies, Secrets, and Silence*. New York: Norton, 1979. 9–18.

——. "Power and Danger: Works of a Common Woman." *On Lies, Secrets, and Silence*. New York: Norton, 1979. 247–58.

——. "Toward a Woman-Centered University." *On Lies, Secrets, and Silence*. New York: Norton, 1979. 125–55.

Sarachild, Kathie. "A Program for Feminist Consciousness Raising." *Notes from the Second Year: Women's Liberation*. Ed. Shulamith Firestone and Anne Koedt. New York: Notes, 1970. 78–80.

Schaeffer, Susan Fromberg. "Womb Song." *Moving Out* 2.1 (1972): 74.

Shulman, Alix. "Viewing Voltairine de Cleyre." *Women: A Journal of Liberation* 2.1 (1970): 5–7.

Sullivan, James. *On the Walls and in the Streets: American Poetry Broadsides from the 1960s*. Urbana: U of Illinois P, 1997.

Tanenhaus, Beverly. *To Know Each Other and Be Known: Women's Writing Workshops*. Pittsburgh: Motheroot Publications, 1978.

"Wanted: Copy." *off our backs* 1.2 (1970): 11.

"Women for a Better Society." *Womankind: A Newspaper for Women* 1.1 (n.d.): 1.

Women's School (Cambridge, Mass.) Records. 1971–1992. Archives—Special Collections Dept. Northeastern U. Libraries, Boston. 5 Mar. 2006 <http://www.lib.neu.edu/archives/collect/findaids/m23find.htm>.

8

Branded Literacy: The Entrepreneurship of Oprah's Book Club

Bonnie Kathryn Smith

In October of 2001, the twenty-first century saw its first literacy scandal, and that scandal was ultimately about the message sent by a brand. The scandal occurred when novelist Jonathan Franzen complained publicly about the possibility that his novel, *The Corrections*, would be relegated both to corporate and middlebrow realms when it was selected as an Oprah's Book Club pick. Franzen's comments were at once controversial enough to earn him criticism from both the popular press and from the elite literary authors in whose company he presumed himself to be. One of Franzen's public statements about readers was broadcast on October 15, 2001, part of an interview on National Public Radio's *Fresh Air.* Host Terry Gross asked Franzen whether he was surprised that *The Corrections* was chosen as an Oprah pick, and Franzen replied that "it literally had never once crossed my mind" that *The Corrections* might be an Oprah's Book Club selection. For one thing, Franzen continued, Oprah's choices were mainly paperbacks written by females, while his own book was "too edgy to ever be an Oprah pick." (As of January 2006, Oprah has chosen 59 books for the Book Club; 38 were written by women, and 21 were written by men.) When Gross went on to ask Franzen if his novel, because it was entered into the canon of Oprah's Book Club, could reach many readers who might not have otherwise found his book, he insisted that *The Corrections* "is—first and foremost—it's a *literary* book .... It's an open question how big the audience is, to which it will be accessible and beyond the limits of that audience, I think there's going to be a lot of, 'What was Oprah thinking?'" In print, the emphasis on the word "literary" is mine, although in the interview, Franzen emphasized the word "literary" in his speech so as to push the idea that Oprah's readers would be befuddled by the "literariness" of

157

The Corrections and would wonder why she had not chosen a more accessible book.

Franzen's insinuation that the "edginess" and "male-ness" of *The Corrections* would confound and alienate those he imagined as Oprah's readers was a way of cueing in Gross's listeners on the "literariness" of his novel. That there are indeed such cues to the realm of "high culture" is an established fact both in and out of literacy studies. Pierre Bourdieu, for example, has thoroughly documented such cues and passwords in his milestone ethnography of French culture, *Distinction: A Social Critique of the Judgment of Taste*. By naming and accounting for the ways that "experts" gain a monopoly on intellectual and cultural capital, Bourdieu found that obtaining passwords of the "high" aesthetic world helps maintain a system in which the aesthetically elite dominate. Bourdieu's discussion of knowledge versus recognition of works or practices especially relates to the way readers have been imagined and constructed; for example, Bourdieu notes that many who have not read literary prize-winning books will nonetheless state opinions about those books. Thus, many acknowledge a hierarchy of books and readers based on prize or acclaim as a way of aligning themselves with those they believe seem most knowledgeable (318).

Franzen's book is such an intriguing case because of the author's overt comments about audience, because of the fact that *The Corrections* did obtain prize and acclaim as the 2001 National Book Award Winner, and because it literally became part of a brand when it was chosen by Oprah's Book Club. Brands generate consumer choice and corporate revenue, and brands contribute to what Bourdieu identified in "The Forms of Capital" as cultural capital, that is the mechanism by which individuals and groups grab onto and maintain class status through *habitus,* credentials, or display of goods (245). In short, an individual selects (or rejects) goods based on brand identification because doing so limits seemingly endless choices provided by the market, inspires trust, and contributes to one's identity construction. Branding is a practice that has especially created vast wealth and influence since the mid-1980s, when, as Naomi Klein recounts in *No Logo*, management theorists began to suggest that "corporations must primarily produce brands, as opposed to products" (3). Brands have come to symbolize the movement away from an industrialized economy, which manufactured products, toward a knowledge economy that sells ideas and goods; these ideas and goods have been personalized by brands. Just as Martha Stewart's brand is "personalized" by the person and reputation of Martha Stewart, Oprah Winfrey's brand is personalized by her *habitus* and credentials. Given the persistence of branding in the twenty-first century and given Deborah Brandt's definition of literacy as "illuminat[ing] the ways that individual acts of writing [and reading] are connected to larger cultural, historical, social, and political systems," it's important to acknowledge that Oprah's Book Club brand signals ways readers are connected to larger cultural and economic systems ("Literacy" 392).

How that "O" logo cues readers is also memorably articulated by columnist and critic Eric Alterman in an article he pointedly titled "Literature of the Masses: Why I Never Chose to Read a Book Recommended by Oprah." Alterman writes, "I never chose to read an Oprah-approved book and I am snobbish enough to feel a little queasy about carrying around one with that tacky sticker on it." (Some Oprah's Book Club picks actually have a silver-dollar-sized seal embossed on the cover, not a "tacky" sticker, as Alterman claims.) So with the seal, Oprah's picks have received a literal and figurative branding, and in Alterman's eyes, Oprah's acclaim brands these texts as *certain kinds of books for certain kinds of readers*. Like Bourdieu's readers, Alterman states an opinion about a text that has received acclaim but that he has not read, but unlike Bourdieu's readers, Alterman does not view that "acclaimed text" with high regard. Alterman admits without shame that he considers himself in the upper echelons of readers. He is not an Oprah reader; therefore, he does not, to use Bourdieu's terms, have *knowledge* of the novels Oprah picks. But Alterman does *recognize* an Oprah pick on the surface by the seal on its cover, and he certainly recognizes that Oprah books are not for self-proclaimed "snobbish" readers like himself.

And so it seems that what Oprah's brand signifies ultimately bothered Jonathan Franzen more than the idea that he might lose male or elite readers. Right after *The Corrections* became the forty-third pick of Oprah's Book Club—and just before Franzen's invitation to be on the show was politely rescinded by Oprah following his public statements about the Book Club—Franzen told *The Oregonian*, "I see this as my book, my creation, and I didn't want that logo of corporate ownership on it … I know it says Oprah's Book Club, but it's an implied endorsement, both for me and for her" (Baker). Franzen didn't bother to mention that when Farrar, Straus, and Giroux initially released *The Corrections* in September 2001, they printed a generous 90,000 copies, but later that month, after Oprah picked *The Corrections* for the Book Club, the publisher ran more that 600,000 copies emblazoned with the "O" moniker (Farr 76). An implied endorsement, indeed!

Shortly after Franzen made these and other comments about how *The Corrections* didn't belong in Oprah's Book Club, a colleague of mine told me she purchased Franzen's novel, but—she recounted with pride—had insisted on going through the shelves at Barnes & Noble to find a copy that bore the brand of Oprah's Book Club. Bearing Oprah's seal in the midst of controversy about just who "literary" readers were was important to my colleague; for her, making sure she was seen reading a copy of *The Corrections* emblazoned with the Oprah's Book Club logo was like wearing a T-shirt declaring she was for the home team. On the other hand, in her study *Reading Oprah: How Oprah's Book Club Changed the Way America Reads*, Cecilia Konchar Farr notes that reporter Monica Corcoran followed up on Franzen's remarks by publishing a piece in the *New York Times* describing how readers on the East and West coasts "were requesting copies of *The Corrections* sans O" (Farr 76). So, even though my colleague was a doctoral student in literature, she was going against those perceived "elite" readers on the East and West coasts by looking for copies of *The Corrections* that did not bear Oprah's seal. What's going on here? What are the signifiers behind the sign of this corporate logo? And what does this hubbub about a brand mean for women and literacy in the twenty-first century?

BEHIND THAT "O" LOGO: OPRAH, THE GLOBAL GIDEON

Oprah Winfrey has built a brand based on personality and ethos, and Oprah's brand is shaped in part by her own well-known stories. To understand what Oprah's brand and logo represent, we must understand how Oprah has used her own literacy narrative to sell her beliefs about reading. Her multiple roles and her own literacy narrative help us grasp how she successfully blends public and private realms. Because she ardently believes that reading can "change your life," because her Book Club picks have changed the economics of American book publishing (and some might argue, the craft of American fiction writing as well), and because the individuals who make up her readership often mirror her interpretative strategies, Winfrey inhabits two powerful roles. As an editorial in the *New York Times* pointed out, Winfrey serves as a critic-advisor to the contemporary "common" reader à la Samuel Johnson ("Think Tank"). But, based on her readers' testimonies about how reading her particular picks has changed their lives, I maintain we should also regard Winfrey as a kind of therapeutic evangelical who prescribes reading to the public, believing that reading is a salve that can improve one's life and heal one's soul. Investigating Winfrey's roles as critic and evangelist deepens our understanding of how Oprah's brand influences literacy at the turn-of-the-millennium.

Winfrey draws from her own literacy narrative to argue for the life-changing powers of reading. Her lifelong zeal for reading and initiating conversations about reading is particularly evident in the following anecdote she tells about her life as a reader: in the A&E Biography *The Heart of the Matter,* Winfrey discusses reading Alice Walker's National Book Award-winning novel *The Color Purple* in the early 1980s, and deciding it was so important that it needed to be read by everybody. So she took whatever extra money she had, bought as many copies of

The Color Purple as she could afford, put them in a backpack she carried around Chicago, and handed them out to people she met on the streets ("Oprah Winfrey"). Like an evangelist handing out pamphlets, Winfrey distributed copies of Walker's novel to any passerby who would take one ("Oprah on *The Color Purple*"). Handing out *The Color Purple*, just as the Gideons give out copies of the New Testament, foreshadows Winfrey's successful entrepreneurship and evangelism. But the Gideon-like Winfrey operates globally; she is the first woman to own and produce her own television talk show, and her material empire goes far beyond the daily talk show that made her a household name. Winfrey's company Harpo includes her internationally syndicated daily program, *O* (the Oprah magazine), a production company that makes films and television shows, and Oxygen Media, Inc., a television/Internet conglomerate meant especially "for women."

Each of these endeavors illustrates ways that, for Winfrey, matters of the spirit and soul congregate alongside innovative entrepreneurship. Winfrey spreads her message by blending public and private worlds. Specifically, Winfrey's evangelical brand of reading takes place on a particular stage—the television. In a profile of Winfrey, linguist Deborah Tannen holds that one of Winfrey's most notable contributions is her ability to use television's unique power to unite public and private realms. Television, Tannen notes, "is most often viewed in the privacy of our homes. Like a family member, it sits down to meals with us and talks to us in the lonely afternoons. Grasping this paradox, Oprah exhorts viewers to improve their lives and the world."

In addition to television, Winfrey uses the web as a tool for blending public and private realms. Along with information, news, and advice, her website includes message boards and posts letters that readers have written about novels chosen for Oprah's Book Club. Some of these readers appear on the television show because they have written interesting letters in response to Oprah's prompt, "Tell us how this book affected you." These writers appear in a book discussion with Oprah, the book's author, and occasionally with some celebrity. The letters were (and remain at this writing) publicly posted on Oprah's official website, http://www.oprah.com. The letters posted on the website are chosen by the staff of Oprah's Book Club. According to the site's invitation to post responses to the books, "Guests are chosen based on their reaction to the book, but they don't even have to like the book to be chosen! A personal connection to the book helps, but isn't mandatory" ("Oprah's Book Club Facts"). The letters are discrete testimonies written in a particular context (just after reading the book), for a particular situation (explaining how one responded to the book, and, perhaps in some cases, trying to get chosen as a participant in the discussion with the author).

By showcasing the letter-writers and the letters on her television show and on the website, Oprah's enterprise further erases old lines between public and private and helps to promote her own beliefs about literacy.

Oprah's and her readers' beliefs about literacy have a rich history. Though ancient, the idea that reading can change (and save) your life remains durable. In medieval Europe, readers who read scripture silently were said to have a more direct pathway to God and therefore to salvation; this pathway minimized the importance of the church and, some claim, led to the Protestant reformation (Cavallo and Chartier 15–20). Paolo Freire linked his method of teaching literacy as contextualized practice to mental, spiritual, political, and economic liberation. Janet Duitsman Cornelius has traced the ways in which becoming literate was an act of resistance for slaves in the antebellum American South because reading and writing led to a liberated consciousness. Beth Daniell's *A Communion of Friendship: Literacy, Spiritual Practice and Women in Recovery* illustrates ways contemporary women use literacy practices to nurture their communal and spiritual lives. And the idea that reading can change your life is certainly alive and well in popular and political discourse. In a 2001 interview with Jim Lehrer on *NewsHour* regarding the current state of education in the United States, First Lady Laura Bush, former teacher, librarian, and literacy advocate, asserted that reading "doesn't just let your child know that reading's important, but it lets your child know that they're [sic] important." Such an entrenched conviction—that reading engages self-esteem, attitude, personality, even vision of one's place in the world—suggests that the populace believes the activity of reading edifies and thereby changes life for the better, thus clearly connecting literacy to identity.

So, if most people believe reading edifies, how has the inheritance of this belief affected the reading and testimonies of actual contemporary readers? Jonathan Franzen could only *imagine* responses Oprah's readers might have when they read his book. Certainly, recovering responses made by the "anonymous" masses of cultural consumers has proven difficult, but not impossible (see, for example, Radway; Rose). Oprah's own way of combining her beliefs about the life-changing power of literacy with her entrepreneurial methods provides a vivid illustration. On her website, Oprah implores readers to "tell us how this book affected you," to write and speak about how reading can be a life-changing activity. In turn, Oprah's website and her television show promote readers' actual responses to her prompts about life changes attributed to reading. Unlike the romance readers in Radway's ethnographic study, whose responses were immediate and often dialogic, website response to Oprah's Book Club titles are not put in service of dialogue. Instead, such responses are inextricably yoked to her brand, thereby combining old ideas about how reading can change lives with contemporary methods of promoting growth of a brand.

BUILDING THE BRAND THROUGH READER RESPONSE

Reader response is not privileged in the models of textual criticism most often taught in the schools, models that typically focus on literary texts' formal features. But in Oprah's brand of reading, readers are given agency because their responses are *the primary means* of textual interpretation. Such response-as-interpretation is formalized by the letter-writers who are invited on air because, in the view of Oprah and her staff, they have effectively responded to Oprah's "tell us how this book affected you" prompt. Specifically, readers chosen by the show often report that they feel empowered because they identify with a character who has—or acquires—agency over the course of the book.

Several letters written for the Oprah's Book Club's pick for February 2000 will be sampled here as a mini-illustration of these "empowerment" reports. Letter-writers Guadalupe "Lupe" Pfaff, Carol Maillard, and Halley Suitt wrote to Oprah in response to Isabel Allende's *Daughter of Fortune*, which was announced as an Oprah's Book Club pick on February 17, 2000 ("Daughter of Fortune Discussion Group Members"). Following Oprah's directions to report how the book has affected them, these letter-writers identified with characters, and in some cases, Oprah Winfrey herself, because most letters begin with "Dear Oprah" and some readers invoke incidents in Oprah's life or quote what they consider to be her "wise sayings."

Letter-writer Lupe reflects on how her experience as a child raised in two cultures—her mother's "Latin, aristocratic and oligarchical one" and her father's "impoverished, southern American roots"—mirrored the experiences of Allende's heroine Eliza. Lupe reported that it was "surreal" to read *Daughter of Fortune* because its setting in nineteenth-century Chile closely resembled her maternal family's life in 1960s Panama. Lupe reports that her mother's family, once aristocratic, clung to their family name and lineage when their monetary assets were threatened by "the new wealth" in mid-century Panama, recounting a time when Lupe and her brothers made friends with "the 'wrong' people"—the "waiters, pool, and bathroom attendants"—at the aristocratic Union Club her grandfather helped found. Lupe's full-blooded Panamanian relations blamed her and her brother's behavior on the fact that they had "all that American blood surging" through them. Lupe identifies her own social rebellion as an analogue to the ways in which *Daughter of Fortune*'s heroine Eliza rebelled: "Anyhow," Lupe writes, "Eliza rebelled and *forged* her own path and destiny and I loved every minute of her adventures while at they same time seeing some of myself in her and in her story" (emphasis mine). Lupe's use of the word "forge" is noteworthy given the plot of *Daughter of Fortune* because Eliza not only "forges" a path as a female immigrant-entrepreneur in nineteenth-century California, but also disguises herself as a boy in order to survive, thereby committing an altogether different sort of "forgery" by counterfeiting her own identity ("*Daughter of Fortune* Discussion Group Members").

Such examples of counterfeited identify are common in the novels that comprise the Oprah-canon and in readers' responses; Oprah's readers themselves often have both the moxie to place themselves in the novel's rhetorical situation and the willingness to stretch the reality of their own circumstances for the purposes of identifying with a character or situation. Such a willingness illustrates how Oprah values alliance building. To compete globally and maximize the potential for reaping ideas and information from human capital, businesses and entrepreneurs in the twenty-first century must rely more heavily on alliances than ever before. Alliance building in Oprah's brand of reading works in the following ways: Readers do (and should) carefully look and listen for ways in which the text's plot, characters, and sometimes the author's biography link up with the reader's own life; reading is a way to change your own life through the example of a character or plot you might not normally have consulted for guidance or as an exemplar. The benefits of reading are most effectively harvested when explored in public discussions during which readers articulate the changes reading has made in their own lives and respond to changes reported by others.

This practice of alliance building can also be seen at work in the written testimony of letter-writer Carol, who composed a litany detailing how she related to many of *Daughter of Fortune*'s characters ("*Daughter of Fortune* Discussion Group Members"). Carol eventually turns her focus to the women in the novel, noting that their behavior was outside the comfortable realms that make up our usual images of nineteenth-century women. These women were instead women who, according to Carol, "found their way to their true selves as best they could." Carol's description of the characters then shifts into a deconstruction of the American cliché of the melting pot; Carol appreciates that books like *Daughter of Fortune* dissuade Americans from romanticizing history. But Carol is not immune to romanticizing; she writes, "I immediately connected with Eliza because of the circumstances of her being found and cared for and because her birth date was close to mine so I felt I understood her motivations." Carol goes beyond material and physical circumstances to find a way to testify about how she was able to ally herself with the character Eliza. This letter-writer, who decries the ways in which Americans romanticize their own histories, forces the close birthday connection between herself and Eliza as a way to build an alliance. Carol's act of allying herself with the character Eliza is not simply an exercise in romantically looking for an astrological connection, though; rather, Carol looks to astrological circumstances to explain how she understood her heart was "right next to Eliza's." Carol's reading of *Daughter of Fortune* is overtly political in content, yet always concerned with the sentiments of her own soul and the soul of the novel's characters.

Carol's way of explaining how her own heart is "right next to" Eliza's forges an alliance with the character, but Carol's alliance with the character Eliza is tied up in brand promotion and the economics of selling books. Such a report of empowerment should be treated with a healthy dose of skepticism because presumably, after Oprah's viewers watch the episode of the Book Club in which Carol discusses how her heart was "right next to Eliza's," they will head to the nearest Barnes and Noble or log on to Amazon.com to purchase a copy of Allende's novel with an "Oprah's Book Club" seal emblazoned on the cover. Or, they might log on to the "boutique" section of Oprah's own website and purchase some of Oprah's special edition Book Club totes and T-shirts.

Like Lupe and Carol, letter-writer Halley is concerned with explaining how she forged an alliance with a character, and Halley's report of empowerment seems less of a stretch. Halley reports that upon reading *Daughter of Fortune,* she became energized by the novel's themes, which she interpreted as an amalgamation of American entrepreneurship and multiculturalism. Halley crystallized her vision of this amalgamation by reporting that she herself was inspired to reorient her professional life following her reading of Allende's novel; in her reading Halley realizes she needs to act upon her own potential for creating monetary capital. A California businesswoman like Allende's character Eliza, Halley reports that desire for financial and professional success in the global economy is closely tied to themes of multiculturalism and what she terms "a new humanism." "Like Eliza and Paulina, the gutsy girls of the 'new' economy of the 1850's," Halley writes, "I'm also trying to start my own business in the new network economy of the 1990's and the '00's.' This book gave me a 'go girl' kick in the butt I really needed." But reading *Daughter of Fortune* gave Halley more than just the call to action she said she needed: Halley goes on to remind herself and her audience that "[w]e can really succeed if we remember we are all ONE-TRIBE" ("*Daughter of Fortune* Discussion Group Members"). According to Halley's report, seeing that characters Eliza and Paulina succeeded with obstacles similar to hers encouraged her to become Oprah-like by embarking on her own adventure as a humanist-spiritualist-capitalist in the global economy of her own time.

A REVAMPED BRAND: MAKING THE "CLASSIC WORKS ACCESSIBLE TO EVERY WOMAN AND MAN"

In sum, Oprah's brand of reading is supported by the inherited idea that reading can change lives and by reader testimonials in support of that idea. Oprah's reader-consumers have built up this brand because they trust Winfrey as a book critic. Ever the savvy businesswoman-galpal, Oprah uses her credibility and her sincere belief in literacy's life-changing powers to market reading. The following four literacy lessons summarize Oprah's strategies and her brand.

1. *Oprah teaches readers how to read.* Readers read privately, but, under Oprah's direction, readers do (and should) carefully tune their eyes and ears to look and listen for ways in which the text's plot, characters and sometimes author's biography link up with the reader's own life. This reading for alliance is evidenced in Oprah readers' testimonies.

2. *Oprah teaches readers what reading does.* Reading, and especially reading fiction, is a way to change your life in profoundly meaningful ways. In particular, Oprah suggests that change can happen when readers read about a character who is in a plot analogous to their own life situations. Through characters' examples, readers can learn more about themselves and they can learn what actions they should (or should not) take. Associations between the character's life and the reader's life need not be overt or obvious.

3. *Oprah teaches readers how and why to make reading public, civic, and shared.* Discussing the profound ways reading changes one's life is best shared aloud with a community in public spaces (such as the Oprah show or even a book group that gathers together in real life or in virtual space). Such "public reading" is a fruitful way to converse about writing. Making reading public is a way to articulate the changes reading has made in one's own life and further, to respond to changes others report.

4. *Oprah teaches readers why to read.* Overall, Oprah teaches that reading makes a difference. As enthusiastically exclaimed on the Book Club section of Oprah's website, books can "make us laugh [and] make us cry, but most importantly, they change our lives!" ·

Oprah's brand is sustained by these literacy lessons, but just as Apple retooled its brand with the wildly successful iPod, Oprah has been retooling her brand since she renamed the Book Club "Traveling with the Classics" in February 2003. In Oprah's own words to the Association of American Publishers (which was documented in a speech promoted on her website), "Traveling with the Classics" states the following as its mission:

> I cannot imagine a world where the great works of literature are not read.
> My hope is *The Oprah Winfrey Show* will make classic works of literature
> accessible to every woman and man who reads. I hope to invite readers
> throughout the world to visit or revisit a universe of books of enduring
> usefulness, because I believe that the sublimity of this experience, this gift
> to ourselves, is something that we owe to ourselves. ("Oprah's Book Club
> Is Coming Back")

So for Oprah, the televised reading evangelist, literacy is democratic,
utilitarian, and sublime. "The great works of literature" are "gifts we
owe to ourselves," and gifts she says she wants to give Everyman and
Everywoman. Reading lifts us up, reading is for everyone, and Oprah
rightly understands that there's power in her pulpit.

As of September 2006, Oprah's "traveling with the classics" picks included John Steinbeck's *East of Eden*, Alan Paton's *Cry, the Beloved Country*, Gabriel García Márquez's *One Hundred Years of Solitude*, Carson
McCullers' *The Heart Is a Lonely Hunter*, Leo Tolstoy's *Anna Karenina*,
three novels by William Faulkner (*As I Lay Dying*, *The Sound and the Fury*,
and *Light in August*), James Frey's *A Million Little Pieces*, and Elie
Wiesel's *Night*. I suspect that this revamping of the brand is partly a reaction to the Franzen flap over "literariness." By naming the Book Club
"Traveling with the Classics" and by overtly proclaiming that the mission of the show is to make the classics "accessible," Oprah wants to
grab literature with a capital L for her flock. Additionally, in the tradition of Mortimer Adler and Charles Van Doren, E. D. Hirsch, and Harold Bloom, Oprah wants to seize the very idea of "classics"—and
therefore the very idea of a canon—as a pointed way of defining what's
"literature" for those who look to her as their primary book critic.

Despite this attention to "literariness," *Reading at Risk*, a National Endowment for the Arts study released in 2004, lamented that at the beginning of the twenty-first century, we are experiencing a nationwide
decline in literary reading. In contrast to Jonathan Franzen's gendered
"literary vs. paperback" dichotomy, literary reading is defined by the
NEA report as reading novels, short stories, plays, or poetry. Given that
broad definition, reading for Oprah's Book Club would certainly count
as "literary reading," and were it not for Oprah's efforts from 1996 forward to "get the country reading again," the numbers in the *Reading at
Risk* report would likely be lower. The *Reading at Risk* report rightly worries that a decline in literary reading could signal a decline in civic participation. Yet, since it began in 1996, Oprah's Book Club has had
far-flung consequences upon the practice of reading in civic life.

Already, Oprah's Book Club-like scenes of communal reading have
emerged on television and in communities. The *Today* show and *Good
Morning America* have sponsored books as their picks, inviting members of already-existing Book Clubs to come on their respective shows

and talk about how they read those particular novels. Community-wide reading programs have sprung up in large and small American cities. Such programs recommend a novel for all of that city's citizenry to read and discuss. In Oprah's hometown of Nashville, for example, the city-wide Book Club called "Big, Big Book Club" features volumes selected by individuals like the city's most well known waitress and a Tennessee Titans football player. Publishers, booksellers, and writers now work in a world in which readers go on television to explain how a particular book has affected them intellectually and, more often than not, spiritually. As such forms of branding continue, public readers will find themselves wedged in a rhetorical realm that is a hybrid of a tent revival, a therapy session, and a stockholder's meeting; public readers will be invited to write about how novels like *One Hundred Years of Solitude* "affected them" *and* they will be invited to read their next classic while lounging in special edition Oprah's Book Club pajamas they purchased from www.oprah.com.

If we are to characterize reading in contemporary America, we must acknowledge that readers and sponsors of reading like Oprah Winfrey merge matters of the spirit and soul alongside economic, technological, and informational complexities. This union is complicated; in the Oprah model, readers' interpretations often depend on ephemeral spiritual or emotional alliances forged with plots, characters, and authors; readers often zero-in on ways in which reading has changed their lives. But because these readers' interpretations are public, they are yoked as well to publishers, booksellers, and even authors who stand to profit from Oprah's brand, which features readers' often charismatic, public interpretations. And yet, Oprah's role as teacher and preacher of literacy should not be overshadowed by unease about the money publishers, authors, and booksellers reap from her enterprise.

Although Oprah and her Book Club are literal brands, I do not believe we should wrinkle our noses at her logo or regard her or her enterprise solely with suspicion or cynicism. Time and time again, her readers report in letters, in uncensored chat rooms, on the television show, and in the context of their own book groups that the assignments she gives them provide opportunities for them to think critically about themselves and the world. Like her letter-writer Halley, Oprah's project is *both* about tapping into entrepreneurship *and* about the way literacy can sometimes "kick [us] in the butt," thereby making us think critically about the conditions of our lives. Consistent with her own pioneering history, Oprah effectively encourages contemporary readers to revamp their definitions of profit. And ultimately, her zealous conviction that the profits of literacy are personal, empathetic, spiritual, and life-changing outshines all other features of her brand.

WORKS CITED

Adler, Mortimer J., and Charles Van Doren. *How to Read a Book*. New York: Touchstone, 1940.

Allende, Isabel. *Daughter of Fortune*. Trans. Margaret Sayers Peden. New York: Perennial, 2000.

Alterman, Eric. "Literature of the Masses: Why I Never Choose to Read a Novel Chosen by Oprah." *MSNBC.com*. 18 Apr. 2002 <http://www.msnbc.msn.com/>.

Baker, Jeff. "Oprah's Stamp of Approval Rubs Writer in Conflicted Ways." *Oregonian* 12 Oct. 2001: Arts and Living 5.

Bloom, Harold. *The Western Canon: The Books and the School of the Ages*. New York: Riverhead, 1994.

Bourdieu, Pierre. *Distinction: A Social Critique of the Judgment of Taste*. Cambridge: Harvard UP, 1984.

———. "The Forms of Capital." *Handbook of Theory and Research for the Sociology of Education*. Ed. John Richardson. New York: Greenwood. 241–58.

Brandt, Deborah. "Literacy." *Encyclopedia of Composition and Rhetoric*. Ed. Theresa Enos. New York: Garland, 1996. 392–93.

Bush, Laura. Interview. *NewsHour with Jim Lehrer*. PBS. 11 May 2001. 15 Nov. 2005 <http://www.pbs.org/newshour/bb/white_house/jan–june01/laurabush.html>.

Cavallo, Gugliemlo, and Roger Chartier. *A History of Reading in the West*. Cambridge, UK: Polity, 1999.

Cornelius, Janet Duitsman. *Slave Missions and the Black Church in the Antebellum South*. Columbia: U of South Carolina P, 1999.

Daniell, Beth. *A Communion of Friendship: Literacy, Spiritual Practice, and Women in Recovery*. Carbondale: Southern Illinois UP, 2003.

"*Daughter of Fortune* Discussion Group Members." *Oprah.com*. 21 Nov. 2003 <http://www.oprah.com/obc/pastbooks/isabel_allende/obc_letters_daughter.jhtml>.

Farr, Cecilia Konchar. *Reading Oprah: How Oprah's Book Club Changed the Way America Reads*. Albany: State U of New York P, 2005.

Franzen, Jonathan. *The Corrections*. New York: Farrar, Straus and Giroux, 2001.

———. Interview. *Fresh Air*. 15 Oct. 2001. 21 Nov. 2005 <http://www.npr.org/templates/story/story.php?storyId=1149495>.

Freire, Paolo. *Pedagogy of the Oppressed*. Trans. Myra Bergman Ramos. 1970. New York: Continuum, 2000.

Hirsch, E. D., Jr. *Cultural Literacy: What Every American Needs to Know*. New York: Vintage, 1988.

Klein, Naomi. *No Logo*. New York: Picador, 2002.

"Oprah's Book Club Facts." *Oprah.com*. 21 Nov. 2005 <http://www.oprah.com/obc/facts/obc_facts_2000003.jhtml>.

"Oprah's Book Club Is Coming Back." *Oprah.com*. 11 Oct. 2006 <http://www.oprah.com/books/classics/books_classics_news.jhtml>.

"Oprah on *The Color Purple*." Videoclip. *Oprah.com*. 21 Nov. 2005 <http://www.oprah.com/tows/after/200211/tows_after_20021122.jhtml>.

"Oprah Winfrey: The Heart of the Matter." *Biography*. A&E Cable Network. Madison, WI. 26 November 2002.

Radway, Janice A. *A Feeling for Books: The Book of the Month Club, Literary Taste, and Middle-Class Desire*. Chapel Hill: U of North Carolina P, 1997.

——. *Reading the Romance: Women, Patriarchy, and Popular Literature.* Chapel Hill: U of North Carolina P, 1984.

Rose, Jonathan. *The Intellectual Life of the British Working Classes.* New Haven: Yale UP, 2001.

Tannen, Deborah. "Oprah Winfrey." *Time* 8 June 1998: 196–98.

"Think Tank: If It's Goodbye Books, Then Hello ... What?" *New York Times* 23 Sept. 2000: B11.

United States. National Endowment for the Arts. *Reading at Risk: A Survey of Literary Reading in America.* Research Division Report No. 46. June 2004. 6 Mar. 2006 <http://www.arts.gov/pub/ReadingAtRisk.pdf>.

PART II

Women's Literacies in a Globally
Interdependent World

Professing "Western" Literacy: Globalization and Women's Education at the Western College for Women

Shevaun Watson
Morris Young

The Western College for Women, one of the oldest sites of female education in America and a forerunner in international studies, provides a
unique case for inquiry into issues of women, literacy, and globalization. Founded in 1853 as the Western Female Seminary in Oxford, Ohio,
as a "daughter" school of Mount Holyoke, Western had a long history of
developing women into "world citizens" (Jenkins, "How" 21). With its
original missionary goal of preparing women to devote themselves to
Christian service throughout the world, and its well-established commitment to admitting and funding foreign students, the college was
perfectly poised to transform its central mission in 1954 to international
studies. In the post-World War II atmosphere of increased exchange between schools across the world, and recognizing the need to "justify its
existence in the American scene in the mid-twentieth century," Western
College aimed to be a leader in international education ("Plan"). As one
of the first U.S. colleges to "emphasize the non-Western world," Western trustees globalized the curriculum in recognition of the fact that
their graduates lived in a world community (Brickman).

Our discussion of women's education at Western is organized along
two strands of observation: first, we examine Western's long-standing
interest in global concerns and its mission "to encourage through the
shared experiences of international life on the campus general attitudes
of goodwill toward all men [sic] and appreciation of all civilizations";
second, we discuss how women at Western negotiated the "cultural exchange" between the "domestic" and the "global" as they used their

education to find "an appreciation of their capabilities, potentialities, and responsibilities, and to prepare them for their role in today's world" ("Preliminary Statement" 3). To focus our discussion, we trace the role of international students and international education through the history and curriculum of Western College. We then examine a collaboratively written essay by Western students in response to the major curricular shift toward international education that emerged in the 1950s. We use this essay as a lens through which to view how the global had an impact on women's education; and conversely, how Western's women used the global to imagine new modes of action. Underlying these issues is the role of literacy at Western. Literacy operates on two levels here: on one, literacy is the "basic" content and curricular knowledge acquired within the institutional space of the college; on another, women's literacy is, we suggest, the development of practices and knowledge to negotiate—perhaps even to "translate"—between the rhetorical and political spaces of the domestic, civic, and global. Our analysis is influenced by Brian Street's conception of "social literacy," as well as Anne Ruggles Gere's and Jacqueline Jones Royster's discussions of the role of literacy as cultural work that allowed women to insert themselves into civil society. We also turn to the work of Amy Kaplan who reimagines domesticity, and Carla Freeman and Kristin Hoganson who theorize connections between gender, domesticity, and globalization.

CURRICULAR HISTORIES AND CULTURAL LITERACIES

Oxford, Ohio, has been primarily a place of education since the chartering of Miami University in 1809. To name a small town in Southwestern Ohio, then an outpost in the American "West," after the English university certainly indicates a grand educational vision. But unlike the English Oxford, which was long an all-male bastion of antiquarianism and Anglicanism (Miller 62–63), the Ohio town became an important site of progressive women's education in the nineteenth and twentieth centuries. Alongside the Oxford Female Institute (1849) and Oxford Female College (1856), both finishing schools for affluent young women, the Western Female Seminary was founded to provide an alternative, affordable education to white women. Western was established in 1853 by Reverend Daniel Tenney, who having studied under Lyman Beecher at the staunchly Calvinist Presbyterian Lane Seminary, sought to meld evangelism with practicality in a woman's education. Western was strongly supported by the Oxford Presbyterian Church, but the school was never explicitly denominational (see Nelson 279).[1] Tenney looked to Mount Holyoke Female Seminary, which had developed a successful model of women's education by "combin[ing] advanced academic work with evangelical Christianity" for students of "limited financial means" (Nash 171). Mount Holyoke sanctioned Western Female Seminary as a "daughter" school in 1855. Tenney actively recruited faculty and graduates from Mount Holyoke, even traveling there several times to acquire the best and the brightest for Western. The school's first principal, Helen Peabody, and all the original teachers hailed from the "mother" school, bringing "all the details of Mount Holyoke with them" (Nash 173). Most notably, Western adopted Holyoke's "domestic system" of education wherein faculty and students lived, cooked, and cleaned together.[2] The students at Western would be prepared to do God's work first and foremost, but these women of the middling classes would also be self-sufficient and well educated.

As an alternative to women's education in Oxford, Western provided academic rigor instead of ornamental instruction. Western's scholarly emphasis for women was unparalleled, certainly in that part of the country. Speaking at Western's first anniversary, Rev. Samuel Fisher from Lane Seminary hailed the women's school as "unique in the extent it combines the intellectual with the practical" (qtd. in Nash 173). Unlike Oxford Female Institute and Oxford Female College, which taught needlework, piano, guitar, wax flower work, and other superficial necessities of a lady's training, Western offered a wide range of courses in mathematics, sciences, and humanities, providing students with the opportunity to accumulate valuable educational and cultural capital. Instruction in music, drawing, painting, and French was available only to those students who could "attend to them without serious detriment to their standing in the regular studies" (Catalogue, 1856). The first, or "junior," year included ancient and European history, natural history, ecclesiastical history, algebra, botany, and the principles of Euclid. The middle year studies consisted of physiology, chemistry, natural philosophy, astronomy, advanced botany, and "Evidences of Christianity." As seniors, students learned geology, natural theology, mental and moral philosophy, analogy, and Milton's *Paradise Lost*.

The three-year curriculum required classes in composition and reading each year, in addition to instruction in English and Latin grammar, elocution, and rhetoric throughout the curriculum. Newman's *Rhetoric* and Whately's *Logic* were key texts. The course catalogues reveal a belletristic orientation to English language studies until the early 1900s. As the 1889 English course descriptions illustrate, advanced literacy was conceived as the ability "to speak and write the English language as used by the best writers of the day" (16). Rhetoric was subsumed under the "Essay," involving skills such as literary criticism, philosophy of style, and "Reproduction of Masterpieces" (16). The 1904 Catalogue demonstrates the typical shift in late nineteenth- and early twentieth-century rhetoric studies from belletrism to current-traditional instruction in punctuation, diction, sentence structure, paragraphing, and out-lines.[3] The word "rhetoric" dropped out of the curriculum by 1920, but students were by this time both required and invited to study a wider range of rhetorical skills in an expanding English curriculum, which included courses in public speaking, debate, basic and advanced composition, the modes of discourse, news writing, creative writing, play production, and composition pedagogy (38–41). Western pursued this comprehensive approach to developing students' literacy through the 1950s and 1960s.

Western's literacy education for women was firmly grounded in the evangelical ethos of nineteenth-century Protestantism. Literacy in early America was long tied to the Reformation doctrine of *sola scriptura*, making lifelong Bible reading the central objective of any education, formal or informal. By the nineteenth century, the American ideology of literacy encompassed a three-fold quest: material improvement, individual growth, and Christian salvation. These goals are clearly illustrated in Tenney's desire to offer women an intellectual experience that was at once fundamentally practical and evangelistic. Academic work was imbued with the spiritual directives of individual conversion and social activism. Just as mass conversion experiences created a sense of cohesion among disparate peoples during the Second Great Awakening, conversion offered Western women a sense of purpose and belonging within the unique Oxford community. "Western faculty were deeply concerned with the salvation of their students" because conversion functioned as a mode of entry into a responsible society characterized by individual concern for the general welfare (Nash 175). At Western, as in many voluntary societies of the nineteenth century, social reform was perceived as a spiritual obligation. Tenney perceived in women an untapped potential that could be realized by broadening their knowledge and experience, while deepening their relationship with God. The strong evangelical underpinnings of the curriculum encouraged women to apply their literacy to the social good. Western's approach to literacy education is a compelling example of Street's definition of "social literacy" as "both behaviour and the social and cultural conceptualizations that give meaning to the uses of reading and/or writing" (2). Literacy at Western was not merely a functional tool of gainful employment but, as Royster would describe it, a "subjective tool in generating action" (43). The tradition of social activism that came to define Western grew out of a conception of literacy instruction that harmonized democratic and Christian ideals. Western aimed to develop in women what Royster understands as a "sociocognitive ability … to gain access to information and to use this information variously to articulate lives and experiences and also to identify, think through, refine, and solve problems"—the ability, in other words, to act in the world (45).

From its inception, Western's educational mission was always global in perspective, configuring literacy in a way that accounted for "both text and context," as Royster puts it (ix). Western employed a distinctly global context for the teaching of texts from the beginning to develop a type of cultural literacy that expanded students' intellectual frontiers so they could appreciate the ideas they encountered in their courses more broadly. In the early days, text and context came together in monthly "concerts," which featured the reading and discussion of letters from missionaries around the world. Sometimes missionaries would visit campus to share their experiences abroad with students (Nash 175). The connection between literacy practices and action in the world was made manifest at these important events. By 1875, 36 Western graduates were missionaries themselves in countries around the globe, a vocational trend that continued into the early twentieth century (Jenkins, "Western" 2). Western paid special tribute to the women who undertook global work. Between 1911 and 1953, the college conferred honorary degrees upon 11 women who served in international affairs and awarded five alumnae for their distinguished work in foreign countries (Nelson 231). As educational historian Margaret A. Nash sums up, "Combining the value of hard work with an evangelical mandate, Western sent young women out into the world invested with the spirit to be active and useful" (176).

CULTURAL EXCHANGES, DOMESTIC CONSUMPTION, AND GENDERED NARRATIVES OF GLOBALIZATION

While the intercultural ethos of Western led women to explore the globe and participate in missionary projects, the college itself provided its own sphere where cultural exchanges between American and international students occurred through a common educational experience. While an interest in global issues became more integral in curricular matters as Western modernized itself, a tension emerged between the deep-rooted tradition of Christian evangelism and a growing secularism associated with advancing the academic reputation of the institution. In 1886, the Board of Trustees noted that the principal, Helen Peabody, felt that "any effort to advance the standard of scholarship would impair the religious tone of the school" (qtd. in Nelson 84). Earlier in 1883, the Board had worried that "an undue prominence is given to the subject of foreign missions in the annual catalogue" by listing the names of teachers and students who served as foreign missionaries (qtd. in Nelson 84). Even after Western had become an accredited college, adopted a rigorous curriculum, and remained "undenominational by charter," it continued its tradition of emphasizing Christian principles, even continuing to require three years of courses in the Bible, as well as maintaining a Y.W.C.A., a missionary society, and a student volunteer group on campus (Nelson 129).

Western's dedication to developing women into "world citizens" was redoubled in the post-World War II atmosphere of increased cultural exchange (Jenkins, "How" 21). Foreign students studying at American colleges increased nearly 400 percent in the decades following the war, and "while many institutions adjusted to accommodate the demand for [these] admissions, few incorporated any changes into their educational programs" (21; see also Nelson 228). Western was a remarkable exception. International students had been part of the student body since 1902 (Nelson 107), a tradition that allowed Western to boast of one of the highest percentages of foreign students—fourteen percent—before World War II, and more than 10% in the mid-1960s representing forty countries (Brickman).

Furthermore, in its centennial year the school inaugurated one of the country's first International Programs and identified itself specifically as an international college. Western saw this shift to an explicit global focus for its second century as a natural and necessary extension of its founding mission to create world citizens. In addition to its original goals as a small Christian liberal arts women's college, Western would now also be defined by an international emphasis, offering "through the formal academic program a systematic presentation of the world's major systems of culture ... [and] encouraging through the shared experiences of international life on campus general attitudes of goodwill toward all men [sic] and appreciation of the values of all civilizations" (Catalogue, 1953). The explicit international component to a Western education "[did] not in any sense represent a radical change" from the school's original mission, but it did seek to formalize the advancement of "one world awareness" and the recognition that Western graduates lived in a world community ("Plan"). However, support was not unanimous in the Western community of alumnae, students, and faculty. A growing fear about the purpose and future of women's colleges raised concern about Western's transformation. Alumnae waited to be convinced this new direction was in the best interest of the college, while some students resisted the shift away from evangelical missionizing (Nelson 236). Despite these concerns, one hundred years after its founding, Western recommitted itself to a global vision of women's education, though in a more secular guise.

According to historian Kristin Hoganson, globalization "can be understood broadly as the economic, cultural, technological, political, social, environmental, and other developments that have connected people, nations, and regions in distant parts of the world" (56). Through its curriculum and extracurricular activities, Western attempted to create the opportunity for globalization on its own campus. The entire curriculum was infused with "global data." At the center of the International Program was a four-year cycle of geographical areas of emphasis: Latin America, the Middle East, Asia, and Africa. Each year an area specialist came to campus from the region being studied to serve as a residential visiting scholar. She or he would offer special courses, lectures, and programs relating to the area. Each spring, this scholar was joined by other experts for an "area conference" to inaugurate a summer travel seminar to the region, a noncredit course open to juniors and seniors. Maintaining its commitment to social action within a global context, Western created a major in intercultural studies, which prepared students for foreign assignments in government, business, journalism, education, or religion. This global perspective reached beyond courses to many aspects of campus life. More international students were admitted to the college, and they contributed to a wide array of globalized campus activities, including art exhibits, talks, dinners, dances, festivals, and clubs.

On the whole, it seems students responded positively to the new program, seeing the international focus as an opportunity to create a productive new world view and meaningful relationships across cultural and national boundaries. To illustrate student reaction to Western's newly defined curricular mission, we turn here to a collaboratively written essay by students in Ruth Limmer's English 201 exposition class. Limmer, the primary instructor in creative and expository writing, was a faculty member at Western from 1954 through 1973, and was herself well-traveled, having spent time in the Middle East, Asia, and various parts of Europe (*Focus* 7). The essay, "International Education At Western," is a complex narrative that addresses the gendered dimension of globalization, constructions of domestic, civic, and global spheres, and the consumption and production of knowledge. We also turn to this piece as an example of the literacy practices of a group of young college women using writing as a means for participating in both their immediate intimate community of friends and classmates and in an imagined global community that they sought to join. These students, to use Gere's framework in understanding clubwomen's literacy practices, were employing literacy "to imagine themselves as participants in a widespread activity that connected them with multiple but invisible others," and "through writing and reading, they established new and intimate relationships that extended across the open spaces of the expanding nation" (21).

"International Education At Western" begins with a collective expression of support for the new International Program and argues for the "greatness" of the program while also articulating practical goals to be accomplished:

> Western College has recently initiated a program of international educa-
> tion. As we, a group of foreign and American students, envision the fu-
> ture greatness of such a program, we would like to state what we now see
> as our goal. For us, it is an understanding between peoples of different na-
> tions.

As this prelude suggests and as the following passages clearly demonstrate, an idealistic, even a romantic, vision is at work here: better understanding between different peoples is alone enough to create a
better world. And while this idealized view itself is not necessarily
gendered female, the construction of globalization and how these students may participate in this dynamic does take on a distinctly
gendered dimension. As Carla Freeman suggests, discourses about
globalization have generally constructed an "implicit, but powerful,
dichotomous model in which the gender of globalization is mapped in
such a way that the global : masculine as local : feminine" (1008). Thus,
Western students entering a discourse of globalization might require
adopting a masculinist rhetoric or reimagining globalization within
local terms.

As part of their strategy to create intercultural understanding, the
students turn to the personal as a way to draw connections between
what seem to be abstract global concerns and the local, immediate experiences of "real" people:

> Personal relationships are the basis of this understanding. As Sumie Ito
> has said, it is necessary for every individual to feel the need for this un-
> derstanding "from the bottom of his heart." Why does she and all of us
> stress this? Because we recognize the attainment of peace as the ultimate
> aim of international education, and peace can be attained only through
> understanding .... It must begin with the individual—through friend-
> ship, exchange of ideas, subsequent appreciation of these ideas—the re-
> alization that certain plants may be grown in only certain kinds of soil
> .... Diana Haynes has told us that before she knew any of our Oriental
> students she imagined a Chinese lady as having a flat nose, slanted eyes,
> and bound feet; and Jessie Preston had the idea that the Chinese woman
> was very backward and uneducated. Yong Choy thought every Ameri-
> can housewife was lazy because her husband helped to wash her dishes
> and she had an "electric mop." Ellen Toeke had the idea that Latin Amer-
> ican parties were heavily chaperoned, ending very early in the evening
> .... Topaz Lee was worried that she could not follow the table manners of
> the American girls. She thought the Americans were so undisciplined
> that they would drape their legs all over the table if they wished. These
> are the simple misconceptions and they have been eliminated, but the
> larger ones take time and require more effort. If we overlook the great
> importance of taking this time and effort, a thing which many of us do,
> we are contributing nothing to international education.

The goal described here is quite lofty: world peace. But it is recognized as a complex issue that the students acknowledge is not easily achieved, comprehending that even they cannot escape conflict among themselves in a small idealistic setting. While these students believe that change can begin with personal understanding, working as individuals to overcome personal prejudices based on assumptions about cultural—even biological or physiognomic—difference, there is also an understanding that larger structural forces at work which will "take time and require more effort." As Freeman argues,

> A gendered understanding of globalization is not one in which women's stories or feminist movements can be tacked onto or even "stirred into" the macropicture; rather, it challenges the very constitution of that macropicture such that producers, consumers, and bystanders of globalization are not generic bodies or invisible practitioners of labor and desire but are situated within social and economic processes and cultural meanings that are central to globalization itself. (1010)

Although the turn to the personal might suggest that these women students are simply "stirring" themselves into an existing discourse of globalization, presenting distilled and simplistic understandings of complex processes, we also see a desire to unpack the naturalized and masculine discourse of globalization by moving beyond a purely economic analysis of global and transnational market forces and geopolitical dynamics. That is, in this narrative, we begin to see a gendering of globalization as female where existing binaries of power are dismantled, and the possibilities of international education make such a large concept as world peace seem achievable.

While these students appear to imagine themselves in three public spheres—the domestic, the civic, and the global—in fact, we see these students transgressing the boundaries of these spheres, challenging the limits of gender and nationalities in order to imagine a different kind of citizenship. While the gendering of Western as a women's college might suggest a particular construction of domesticity—remember that the college employed a "domestic system"—we see what Amy Kaplan describes as a "more mobile and less stabilizing" domesticity that "travels in contradictory circuits both to expand and contract the boundaries of home and nation and to produce shifting conceptions of the foreign" (583). Students' awareness of the effects and limits of nationalism allows them to question the imagined difference between domestic and foreign subjects:

> Strong nationalist feelings dominate and narrow our thinking…. The realization that there are other nations, other cultures equal to ours, may even come as a shock. It may come as still more of a shock that the aim of

international education is not to Americanize the foreigner—would we as exchange students to Turkey desire to be made into real Turks? Hardly .... Because of this strong nationalist feeling, because of our misconceptions and prejudices, the foreign student has a great awareness that she is from another country. You know this feeling. It is comparable to being in a room with people who have no interest in common with you. Somehow, you have the feeling that they dislike you. Imagine how terrible it must be!

While a particular U.S. nationalism is foregrounded here, the acknowledgment of other nations, cultures, and peoples allows for these differences to become resources rather than barriers to creating understanding. In particular, the explicit statement that "the aim of international education is not to Americanize the foreigner" is significant when contrasted to the Americanization movement of the early twentieth century and to a generally hostile environment for immigrants and non-Americans as illustrated by various U.S. immigration policies, naturalization laws, and legal decisions about eligibility for citizenship, as well as the emergence of the United States as a world superpower.

In arguing that domesticity is "more mobile and less stabilizing," Kaplan suggests that one reconfiguration of domesticity is to move from an understanding of "men and women inhabit[ing] a divided social terrain" to "oppos[ing] the domestic to the foreign," where "men and women become national allies against the alien, and the determining division is not gender but racial demarcations of otherness" (582). In this reconceptualization, Kaplan argues, "the cultural work of domesticity might be to unite men and women in a national domain and to generate notions of the foreign against which the nation can be imagined as home" (582). In the case of Western, we see the domestic sphere is reordered in such as way to imagine the foreign, but not as a means to reinforce U.S. nationalism. Rather, the domestic sphere is reconfigured so that American and non-American women have a public sphere where they can engage each other not to overcome individual prejudice alone but to generate cultural meaning together. Though the alignment of Western's women appears to work against the domestic/foreign binary suggested by Kaplan, the imagining of the nation as home still has resonance as these women do not eschew their citizenship but hope to welcome others to their "home." As Kaplan points out, "If domesticity plays a key role in imagining the nation as home, then women, positioned at the center of the home, play a major role in defining the contours of the nation and its shifting borders with the foreign" (582). Western women then not only become key actors in moving toward international education and global understanding, but also imagine themselves as critical participants in the world as they simultaneously operate within the domestic, civic, and global spheres. A domesticity that is "more mobile and less stabilizing," then, reimagines both the ideological and material conditions of women who work across nationalist and gendered boundaries as well as against binaries that continue to organize knowledge in specific ways. In fact, domesticity in this sphere begins to function as a pragmatic and experiential act, providing opportunities for these women to engage, practice, and question their ideas rather than to reinforce and reify beliefs based on the knowledge of others.

These students also consider other markers of cultural difference that have often worked to exclude others from participation in American culture: language and religion. Instead of arguing for assimilation as a means for transgressing difference, the students recognize the chauvinism of assuming English and Christianity as the goals and desires of all:

> The language handicap is also a barrier toward understanding. Many foreign students have a certain fear when they begin to speak English. It is difficult to express yourself fully in another language. You know this feeling too—it is like trying to pull your first-year French on Francoise Puech for the sheer novelty of it. It really frightens you .... Western College and Western girls find a great strength in the Christian religion .... Somehow we forget that every student is not a Christian. Abida Sultana reminds us that some foreign students and some Americans are not. It may be difficult for us to understand the value of other religions, but to achieve understanding we must do this .... Again the students seek to take responsibility for their own learning, to place themselves in the position of others in order to understand cultural difference and to see difference as a resource to draw upon rather than merely a matter of taste.

In the minds of these students, they have already accomplished some form of global understanding because of the friendships they have formed. Yet they also realize that there remain some barriers, and perhaps it is the Americans who have a less compelling reason for becoming "literate" in the culture of others:

> Foreign students feel very grateful for their opportunity to learn about America. They are thrilled by every new American custom and expression they learn. But Americans lack this enthusiasm. International education becomes a one-sided experience. Foreign students realize that they are deriving more benefits from this program than American students. But the true goal, we think, is sharing. It is not enough that just one group learns. Why don't the American student absorb more? Because frequently there is an actual lack of interest. Some of us have thought about the importance of international education. The only thing we know about the program is that we have girls from different nations in our classes. So what? Is the only purpose of this program to have people on our campus

to stand around and look picturesque in their native costumes, to help in the language department? So, do we have international education? Yes, of course we do, but there are still many difficulties to overcome before we realize the ideal international education that will eventually make a contribution to the world.

The students clearly appreciate what has already been achieved, but it is their acknowledgment of the work that still needs to be done that is key here. Their criticism of the "lack of interest" by Americans and the almost cynical remark about people looking "picturesque in their native costumes" suggests that these students are seeking real material and political change from international education, not merely ornamental representations of global peace and understanding.

Despite their critique of what they see as the danger of these superficial engagements with culture, we still see a type of cultural consumption by these students as they continue to describe their processes for developing greater intercultural understanding. The appropriation and consumption of the foreign is seen as an opportunity for understanding:

> Perhaps a deeper interest may be stimulated by the wearing of native costumes on the campus and the eating of foreign food—having foreign dishes prepared for dinner, and etc. The foreign student is a potential storehouse of information once we are motivated to learn. Did you see Yong Choy's birthday dinner last month when American girls squeezed into Oriental costumes? "They could hardly breathe," commented one Chinese student. Interest was stimulated. We wanted to know about the costumes and the country they represented. This is a great idea; this is international education.

We see here what Hoganson has termed "cosmopolitan domesticity": "bourgeois householders' enthusiasm for imported goods and styles perceived to be foreign, in large part because of their very foreignness" (57). Though we do not argue that international students who attended Western College were viewed solely as exotic objects for consumption, we do want to suggest that a type of cultural consumption took place on the part of both American and non-American students who sought to learn about each other through an exchange of cultural productions and practices. Thus, while an element of consumption did occur, the production of new knowledge emerged from the interaction between these students.

The final section of the students' essay returns to the theme of friendship and further develops what friendship should be in the service of creating deeper global understanding. There is a critique of superficial relationships and the difficulty of creating meaningful interactions between people.

Equally important is the necessity for friendship between foreign and American students. We are not looking for the "Hello, how are you?" type of friendship, but are seeking a more lasting and satisfying relationship, which will be the foundation for the exchange of ideas, for understanding, for the general perfection of international education. With a truly deep friendship, the other advantages of international education will be discovered by a natural process.

How do we make friends? Through social activities which might well include more get-togethers where we may enjoy foreign food, have time to talk, and be casual and informal .... Rooming together is another aid to understanding. Since a roommate has the privilege of knowing one's real self, sharing one's true feelings and aspirations, rooming together may prove to be a satisfying relationship and a basis for friendship .... But as Rosalind Chu said, we cannot make friends with foreign students by starting a conversation over foreign food. Let's talk about what we have in common: history homework, chapel talks, the production of Alice in Wonderland. These are the things which, as a start, provide many good opportunities for friendship if we have the time, that is, if we realize the importance of taking the time.

While the students have been careful to describe their appreciation of cultural difference up to this point, they turn to a strategy of identifying commonalities to create the basis for relationships. In a sense they are seeking *topoi* they can use to generate new meanings. The essay ends with a statement of their goals and an assessment of their progress toward these goals:

International education—the ideal. Understanding, friendship, participation in social activities—the first steps. "We are here together to create a new world," says Yong Choy. Western College has provided the opportunity—a glorious challenge—yet we know this is just the beginning. We are only on our way.

What is remarkable about this essay by these Western students is both the idealism and practicality they identify and seek to achieve. On one hand, they imagine a process of international education that can become the basis for new relationships, cultural understanding, and world peace. On the other, they find analogies for these lofty ideals within their own personal lives and in the setting provided by Western College. While it may seem naïve on their part to draw such an easy connection between friendship among a group of individuals and the larger structural dynamics of globalization, their belief in the possibility created a unique context for education.

Despite the innovation of international education and long-standing loyalties by Western alumnae which continue to this day, the Western College for Women closed its doors as an independent institution of higher education in 1974 and was absorbed by Oxford's other school, Miami University. Growing fiscal concerns, including a meager endowment, dwindling resources, and competition from state-supported universities like Miami, contributed to the financial demise of Western (Hoyt 113). However, it may have ultimately been the public sphere that Western imagined for itself that caused or hastened its decline. As Phyllis Hoyt, long-time dean of students at Western, writes in her memoir: "If Western had been two hundred miles south or east, closer to a sympathetic environment in which such an institution would be understood, it may have flourished" (113). While Western was able to create an environment within its campus borders to encourage global thinking—to provide women with the opportunities to imagine themselves as global citizens—the environment beyond campus within the larger context of a changing U.S. sociopolitical landscape of the 1970s made this a difficult prospect. Feminist movements during this period also redirected attention to the U.S. domestic sphere, as American women began to focus more intensely on their own material and political conditions. Ironically, while American women worked to insert themselves into a public sphere where they had long been underrepresented or excluded, a public sphere such as that created by Western College was lost.

In the case of the Western College for Women, the professing of "Western" literacy is complicated by an unusual and progressive interest (for its time) in the global exchange of ideas. Women at Western constructed and located themselves beyond domestic and civic rhetorical/political spaces, and in global spaces where they imagined themselves as world citizens. The uses and cultural work of literacy, in this instance, resulted not in the pervasive globalization of "Western" literacy alone, but in engaging the global to transform Western women.

NOTES

We would like to thank Diane Kaufman and the staff at the Western College Memorial Archives for their assistance and expertise on this project. Archival materials that appear in this essay are used with the permission of the Western College Memorial Archive.

1. In 1893, Western became an accredited college offering Bachelor of Arts degrees, and the following year, changed its name to Western Female Seminary and College. A decade later, the name was changed again to Western College for Women.
2. The "domestic" system continued until 1916 when the college offered students the option of paying higher tuition in exchange for not working.
3. See Berlin, Connors, and Johnson for useful overviews of this trend. See Miller for an elaboration of the trend's roots in Scotland and Ireland. See

Brereton for an array of primary sources documenting these curricular changes.

WORKS CITED

Berlin, James A. *Rhetoric and Reality: Writing Instruction in American Colleges, 1900–1985.* Carbondale: Southern Illinois UP, 1987.

Brereton, John C., ed. *The Origins of Composition Studies in the American College, 1875–1925: A Documentary History.* Pittsburgh: U of Pittsburgh P, 1995.

Brickman, Dorothy. Letter to Hugh Jenkins. 5 Apr. 1990. Western College Memorial Archives. Miami University, Oxford, OH.

Catalogue of the Western Female Seminary. Annual publication, 1856–1973. Western College Memorial Archives. Miami University, Oxford, OH.

Connors, Robert J. *Composition-Rhetoric: Backgrounds, Theory, and Pedagogy.* Pittsburgh: U of Pittsburgh P, 1997.

Focus on Western Faculty. Western College Memorial Archives. Miami University, Oxford, OH. n.d.

Freeman, Carla. "Is Local: Global as Feminine : Masculine? Rethinking the Gender of Globalization. *Signs* 26 (2001): 1007–37.

Gere, Anne Ruggles. *Intimate Practices: Literacy and Cultural Work in U.S. Women's Clubs, 1880–1920.* Urbana: U of Illinois P, 1997.

Hoganson, Kristin. "Cosmopolitan Domesticity: Importing the American Dream, 1865–1920." *American Historical Review* 107 (2002): 55–83.

Hoyt, Phyllis. *Where the Peonies Bloomed: A Memoir of My Year at Western College.* Oxford, OH: Western College Alumnae Association, 2000.

Jenkins, Hugh. "How the Non-West Was Won: Western College for Women, Forerunners of Internationalization." *National Association of International Educators Newsletter* 43.8 (1992): 21.

——. "Western College for Women: An International College." Unpublished manuscript. Western College Memorial Archives. Miami University, Oxford, OH. n.d.

Johnson, Nan. *Nineteenth-Century Rhetoric in North America.* Carbondale: Southern Illinois UP, 1991.

Kaplan, Amy. "Manifest Domesticity." *American Literature* 70 (1998): 581–606.

Limmer, Ruth, et al. "International Education at Western." *Scope* 14.1 (1954). Western College Memorial Archives. Miami University, Oxford, OH.

Miller, Thomas P. *The Formation of College English: Rhetoric and Belles Lettres in the British Cultural Provinces.* Pittsburgh: U of Pittsburgh P, 1997.

Nash, Margaret. "'A Salutary Rivalry': The Growth of Higher Education for Women in Oxford, Ohio, 1855–1867." *The American College in the Nineteenth Century.* Ed. Roger L. Geiger. Nashville: Vanderbilt UP, 169–82.

Nelson, Narka. *The Western College for Women.* Dayton: Otterbein P, 1967.

"A Plan for Western College for Women." Faculty Memorandum, 1952. Western College Memorial Archives. Miami University, Oxford, OH.

"A Preliminary Statement for Western: An Action Program for the 60s." Western College Memorial Archives. Miami University, Oxford, OH.

Royster, Jacqueline Jones. *Traces of a Stream: Literacy and Social Change Among African American Women.* Pittsburgh: U of Pittsburgh P, 2000.

Street, Brian V. *Social Literacies: Critical Approaches to Literacy in Development, Ethnography, and Education.* London: Longman, 1995.

Considering the Meanings of Literacy in a Postcolonial Setting: The Case of Tunisia

Keith Walters

The black-and-white photograph was among the most arresting I'd seen during the twenty-odd years I'd been going to Tunisia, where I served as a Peace Corps volunteer from 1975–77. I had found it in a recently published book, *La femme tunisienne à travers les âges* ("Tunisian Women across the Ages"), during my last stay there in 1997–98. Published by the Institut National du Patrimoine, an agency of the Tunisian government, the book contained essays that lived up to its title, documenting aspects of the lives of women since Phoenician times in what is today Tunisia. As happy as I was to see such a volume, its existence stood as additional evidence of the Tunisian government's efforts to appropriate women's issues and capitalize upon them: by setting itself up as the protector of women's rights, the government sought simultaneously to create itself abroad as a liberal, tolerant, moderate, and modern state with Islam as its official religion even as it hoped to discredit further the aspirations of political Islam's followers within its borders.

The image appeared in Selwa Zangar's article devoted to the *École de la rue du Pacha*, the Pacha Street School, the name older Tunisians use even today for the *École des jeunes filles musulmanes de Tunis*, the Muslim Girls' School of Tunis. This school, the most prestigious early school in Tunisia built uniquely for Muslim girls as part of the French colonial education system, began elsewhere in 1900 as the *École Louise-René Millet*, named for the wife of the French *Résident Générale*, but was moved to Pacha Street and renamed in 1911.

The photograph shows the entrance to a large white two-story building along a cobblestone street; surely, the doors and windows were

Figure 10.1. *La sortie de classe, à l'école des jeunes filles musulmanes de Tunis*
[Going home from the Muslim Girls' School of Tunis]. Chercuitte,
L'Illustration, 1907; rpt. in Zangar 177.

painted a particular shade of light blue, as they are across Tunisia even
today. One of the two large wooden doors forming the arched doorway
was open. Out of the door came a row of six or so young Muslim girls,
veiled in a way I have seen only in pictures from early last century. Their
faces were covered by a transparent black fabric, while their bodies
were engulfed by a large piece of white cloth, perhaps silk, falling to the
ground. When walking, girls or women held the white fabric out in
front of them so that it would not touch the front of their body, revealing
its contour. Closer to the foreground of the picture are two European
women, likely French and no doubt the teachers at the school, wearing

fitted, dark bustled dresses and large hats. Off to the right, a man happens to be walking along the street. The style of his cloak gives him away as almost certainly not of high status. Above the door is what Tunisians call a *barmaqli* window, an enclosed balcony extending out a foot or so over the street. As wide as the large doorway below—perhaps eight feet, it has windows on three sides; behind these windows are latticed wooden screens, *mashrabiyya,* that permit the breeze to come in. The screens also enable females to see out without being seen. The windows visible on the first and second floors of the building likewise have panels of latticed screens. Visible in the distant upstairs window are the faces of two female domestics, looking out over rugs or linen airing in the window, their modesty or honor an issue of comparatively less concern than that of the women they serve.

This image (Fig. 10.1), entitled *"La sortie de classe, à l'école des jeunes filles musulmanes de Tunis,* "Going home from the Muslim Girls' School of Tunis," and dated 1907, captures many aspects of female Tunisians' access to literacy. It points to ways in which literacy in Tunisia, as elsewhere, has been and remains classed and urbanized, even as it is gendered. Published where it was, it indicates the ways in which literacy, especially literacy for females, is always part of larger social structures and ideologies, a multivalent signifier in the policies of governments, whether colonial or postcolonial, and in the preaching of religious zealots or social reformers in Tunisia and around the world. From a different perspective, the photograph likewise reminds us of the ways in which Tunisian Muslim girls and women have often walked "under Western eyes" (Mohanty) even as they have been scrutinized by the eyes of men, Arab and European. In other words, it offers us the opportunity of reflecting on the nature of literacy in colonial and postcolonial settings.

As historians Frances Gouda and Julia Clancey-Smith note in their introduction to the volume *Domesticating the Empire: Race, Gender, and Family Life in French and Dutch Colonialism, postcolonial* and related terms have come to be used in a number of ways; "particularly in literary studies, ... the word *colonial* is employed as a metaphor for any form of elite or cultural domination" (273, n. 5). I use the term *postcolonial* in a much narrower sense, one that focuses on the aftermath, beginning around or during the second half the twentieth century, of European imperialism in countries outside Europe that had been directly controlled by one or more European powers. (Tunisia gained independence from France in 1956.) As Gouda and Clancey-Smith demonstrate, although largely ignored until recently, colonial practices, whether those set in motion by institutions or the contact of daily life, gendered both the colonizer and colonized in complex ways. Schooling was such an institution. As noted, the first school specifically for Muslim Tunisian girls was named for the wife of the highest French colonial administrator, partly because of her concern with the education of "indigenous" girls. Sex-segregated education, whether provided by Catholic religious orders, Europeanized Jews, the colonial government, or the newly independent Tunisian government, gendered administrators, teachers, and students. ("Mixed" education, which was required by Tunisian law after 1968, gendered its participants in other ways, of course.)

By now, scholars of literacy are all too aware of the ways in which literacy and literate practices are profoundly local, profoundly historicized, and surely profoundly gendered. Thus, while there are significant generalizations to be made about the nature of literacy or its meanings, there are likely far more interesting stories to be told about its local character and meaning in any given time and space. In this essay, I seek to offer some of those stories, as I understand them, about the access of Tunisian girls and women to literacy and about the meanings of literacy in their lives. To achieve this goal, I first present data from the most recent Tunisian census (1994) to offer an overview of the demographics of literacy in contemporary Tunisia. I then provide additional information about the history of female Tunisians' access to literacy and schooling, seeking to explicate the social meanings of these events. To render these facts and this history human, I likewise offer vignettes from the lives of three Tunisian women and a Tunisian man that yield insight by demonstrating how literacy or the lack of it is experienced by differently positioned social actors. In so doing, I hope to make clear how and why the meanings of literacy in any social context are necessarily multivalent and contested, simultaneously intensely personal and public, exceedingly local and universal.

THE DEMOGRAPHICS OF GENDERED LITERACY IN TUNISIA

According to data from the 1994 census, 78.1% of Tunisian males aged 10 and older were literate at that time while only 57.7% of Tunisian females were, figures fairly comparable to those from Algeria while considerably higher than the ones from Morocco.

As Figure 10.2 demonstrates, however, literacy is by no means spread equally across generations. (Simple inspection of other census data shows that, predictably, literacy is more likely to be found in urban than rural areas, in more prosperous regions of the country than in less prosperous ones, and in more affluent neighborhoods than in less affluent ones.) In fact, to the extent that we can take these data as apparent-time evidence of literacy rates in the past and projections for the future, we can claim that in just over a century, Tunisia has gone from being overwhelmingly illiterate in 1994—nearly 84% of males 80 and over were illiterate

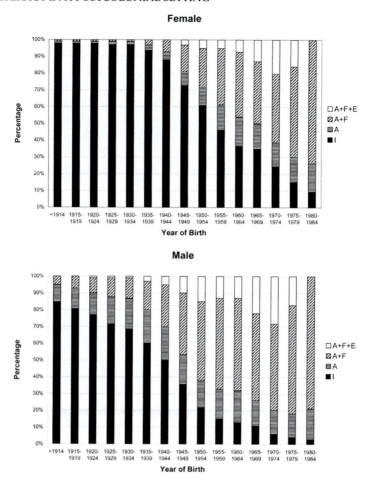

Figure 10.2.   The demographics of literacy in Tunisia by sex and age (1994). I
= illiterate; A = literacy in Arabic only; A + F = literacy in Arabic and French; A
+ F + E = literacy in Arabic, French, and English. The study of English begins
late in secondary school, which accounts for the 1980–84 data. (Data derived
from various charts in *République Tunisienne*.)

and 98% of women were illiterate—to one that will, within a few decades
be almost completely literate—less than 4% of boys and 10% of girls aged
10 to 14 were illiterate. This age-graded distribution of access to literacy
is linked in complex ways to Tunisia's past as a colony of France
(1881–1956) and then independent nation. Both Tunisia's first president,
Habib Bourguiba, who served from 1956–1987, and its second president,
Zine Abedine Ben Ali (1987–), have made education and hence literacy

priorities in their efforts to create a citizenry ready to participate in the modern world. As the data show, while education began to become more readily available to Tunisian males late in the colonial period, it became available to Tunisian females, in any real sense, only after independence. Although Tunisian females have come a long way in catching up with their male counterparts, they still lag behind. Further, in contrast to early last century, when females and males had an almost equal chance of being illiterate, young girls in the 1990s were three times more likely than young boys to be illiterate.

Yet these simple comparisons fail to reveal much of what makes understanding literacy in Tunisia such a challenging task. As I have described elsewhere ("Language, Gender, and the Political Economy of Language"), the linguistic situation there is quite complex, characterized by Arabic diglossia and Arabic/French bilingualism, as well as the presence of other languages of quite different statuses—English, Italian, and Berber. The consequences of diglossia for literacy are immediate and quite salient (Ferguson; Walters, "Fergy's Prescience"). Because diglossic languages are characterized by the existence of two varieties of the same language—one spoken, unstandardized, and associated with daily life and the other more grammatically complex, highly codified, traditionally written and associated with education and formality—the linguistic distance between the spoken and written varieties of the language is far greater than, say, the distance between any variety of spoken English and the standardized variety of English that is normally written. (Practically speaking, an Arab illiterate has limited comprehension of the televised nightly news read aloud in the written variety of the language.) Thus, native speakers of any national dialect of Arabic face an especially complex task in learning the written variety of their own language, a task made more challenging by the nature of the Arabic writing system, which, like that of Hebrew, indicates long vowels and consonants but not short vowels. (Because of the written variety's fit with the morphological basis of the language's structure and, more importantly, because of its symbolic importance as unifier of Arabs and its links to the Arab and Muslim past, efforts to reform the script, whether by simplification or the substitution of the Latin script, as Atatürk did with Turkish in 1928, have met with total failure.)

The second language of Tunisia and Tunisians is French, a Roman-script language, whose social meanings cannot be separated from the colonial past and France's place as part of Europe and the West. Nor can they be separated from the sorts of information available in French (and other Roman-script languages like English) and the values represented in them. Whereas publications in Arabic continue to be overwhelmingly religious or educational in topic, French and other Roman-script literacies offer a much wider range of genres and topics, whether one considers science and technology (with little or no lag time for translations) or the romance novel and even pornography. (While pornography is understandably illegal in Tunisia, used second-hand French-language romance novels, thrillers, and mysteries are readily available in bookstalls of the capital city.) In contrast, aside from textbooks, the majority of books available in Arabic treat religious topics.

As explained in the following discussion, once formal education became available to Muslim Tunisian girls in the late nineteenth century, a European language, most often French, was the language of instruction, and the status of the language, especially in education, has continued to evolve. I know Tunisian women in their 60s who graduated from high school before independence and who have French *baccalauréats,* or high school diplomas, guaranteeing entry to university. They studied the same curriculum and took the same exams their age-mates in France did. As small children, they had recited the poem known to all French children of that generation, "Nos ancêtres, les Gaulois," "Our Ancestors, the Gauls." Some among them earned a *bac classique*, requiring several years' study of Latin and Greek in high school. They studied precious little of the written variety of Arabic, however, and it was often taught by someone who was French, using the grammar/translation method. (Hence, we might ask whether the "additive" model of language learning—first Modern Standard Arabic, then French, and finally English—assumed by the 1994 census does not in fact project, without justification, the present situation into a far more complex past.)

Because Arabic-language texts appropriate for the Tunisian context and for teachers sufficiently qualified to teach in Arabic were simply not available, French remained the language of instruction in many disciplines for many years after Tunisian independence. By the time I taught English in a high school in a poor region of Tunisia in the mid-1970s, twenty years after Tunisians had gained independence, French was still the language of instruction for everything except religion, Tunisian history, and, of course, English. Thus, success in science or math was predicated on mastery of French, and many of the teachers with whom I taught were natives of France, completing their military service or doing contract work for the French government as part of a foreign-aid program. Tunisian education was completely Tunisified by the late seventies, and the foreign teachers were gone. Arabic has become the language of instruction for primary and secondary education and for several departments at the university level and at the law school. Today, French is taught as a language, not used as a medium of instruction, beginning in elementary school. The census data and these facts about the changing role of French in education help us appreciate why Tunisian men and women of each generation have and have had such different relationships with each of their languages and why literacy means literacy in French for some Tunisians, literacy in Arabic for others, and literacy in both languages (and English) for yet others.

SOME MILESTONES IN TUNISIAN GIRLS' AND WOMEN'S ACCESS TO LITERACY

For well over the last century, education, especially education for girls and women, has been a much-debated topic in Tunisia. Indeed, it is even today. In this section, I offer some of the most basic facts about the history of education in Tunisia, especially for females.

Before doing so, I wish to offer a bit of history of the debates about education for girls and women. According to Souad Bakalti, as early as 1897, Cheikh Mohamed Essoussi,[2] a Tunisian, published a book entitled *The Blossoming of the Flower, or A Study about Women in Islam*, which "timidly" called for education for girls without calling into question any of the traditional interpretations of Qur'anic teachings. The Arab world was shocked just a few years later when Qasim Amin, an Egyptian influenced by Western thinking, published *The Liberation of Woman* in 1899, arguing for formal education for females. In the 1920s, a group of Tunisians called *Jeunes Tunisiens*, ("Young Tunisians," patterned after the Young Turks, who had sought to modernize the Ottoman Empire at the end of the nineteenth century), began arguing that females should be educated lest the Muslim world fall further behind the West. Best known among Tunisians, however, is Tahar Haddad's 1930 *Our Women in Islamic Law and Society*, which argued against traditional interpretations of Qur'anic passages dealing with women and argued strongly for education for girls as part of his vision for a radical reform of Islam. Haddad was himself a product of a traditional Qur'anic education. As Mounira Charrad notes, "[t]he point [of his argument] was not primarily to educate women for their own sake, but to make them better able to contribute to the stability of the family and better able to educate future generations of Tunisians" (216). In fact, Bakalti points out that Haddad argued that if Muslims did not design a system of education for their daughters, the French or the Catholic Church would be all too glad to do so. Haddad's book caused such controversy that he was stripped of his degree from the Zitouna Mosque and denied the right to practice law. In many regards, Haddad's method of argumentation was that later used by the newly independent Tunisian government when it changed the Personal Status Code in 1957, giving Tunisian women greater legal rights than any of their Arab Muslim sisters (Charrad 2001).

Yet, 1930 also marked the year when the first Tunisian Muslim woman, Tewhida Ben Cheikh, a graduate of the École de la rue du Pacha, enrolled in the Université de Paris; upon finishing there in 1937, she became the first female Muslim doctor in Tunisia. In a narrative of her experiences, Ben Cheikh recounts how her mother silenced an uncle, a sheikh (or Islamic teacher), who opposed the daughter's traveling to France for an education by citing the Islamic directive to educate oneself (Blili 25). That these events—the furor caused by Tahar's treatise and Ben Cheikh's enrolling in university abroad—could have occurred during the same year, and only 26 years before independence, reminds us how complex literacy is at the local level. While a very few daughters of the Tunisian Muslim elite became well educated and were able to study abroad, a Tunisian man associated with the religious elite who dared call for education for females, even with the goal of making them better Muslims and better mothers, lost his reputation only to die a few years later a broken man.

Before the 1830s, the only schools in Tunisia were Qur'anic schools for boys, which taught the Qur'an by rote and literacy skills in the written variety of Arabic, and schools for educating the very small number of Jewish boys in Hebrew and Judeo-Arabic, the dialect of Tunisian Arabic spoken by Jews and written in the Hebrew script. (For many centuries, Jews were prohibited from using the Arabic script because of its association with Islam.) Once a Muslim boy had memorized the entire Qur'an, if he wished to continue his studies, he went to the Great Mosque (*Ez-zitouna*, "The Olive Mosque") in Tunis as Haddad had done, where he studied the Islamic sciences: Arabic grammar, rhetoric (focusing on the correct interpretation of the Qur'an), theology, and jurisprudence. Muslim girls were permitted to attend Qur'anic schools only in 1944. By 1952, one in 100 students in Qur'anic schools across the country was female, and a secondary level for girls was added at the Zitouna Mosque. A very small number of girls—a handful out of over 2,500—were training to be teachers of Arabic there. Even at that time, however, they complained that their Arabic-only education did not prepare them adequately for modern life.

In 1831, a brother and sister who were Tunisian Jews[3] opened the first "modern" school, offering an alternative to traditional religious education: instruction in a European language in subjects that included math and science. In 1838, in response to France's take-over of Algeria in 1830, the Ottoman government in Tunis opened a military academy to prepare (male) soldiers by teaching them French and modern subjects (math and sciences) as well as offering military instruction. Worth noting is the fact that the Ottoman government, not the French, brought the French language to Tunisia.

By the 1840s, the foreign Christian communities—Italian, British, Maltese, and French—in Tunis and in several other large towns began schools for the children of their communities and often accepted Tunisian children, Muslims and Jews, generally with the hope, it seems, of converting them. In 1875, The *Collège Sadiki* was opened and offered young

Muslim men an education that included modern sciences and foreign languages (Turkish, French, and Italian) as well as Arabic and the Islamic sciences. This school trained the bilingual and bicultural men who would later lead the country to independence from the French.

Traditionally, girls from families of means, whether Muslim or Jewish, were trained by a (female) teacher who taught them such skills as weaving, embroidery, sewing, and lace-making; Muslim girls were also taught some suras of the Qur'an, which they memorized, and in some cases basic literacy and numeracy skills in written Arabic. (Neither Paul Sebag nor Bakalti comments on the religious education of Jewish girls during this period.) Daughters of the elite were sometimes taught by European governesses. By 1883, when the French colonial government established its *Direction de l'Enseignement,* there were twenty-three private schools in Tunisia, ten of which were for girls and had been established by various French Catholic religious orders (Dornier). There were three Jewish schools, established by the Tunisian Jewish community, which accepted girls.

As Bakalti notes, a report from the colonial government in the 1890s states that during the 1880s, the number of Tunisian Muslims receiving "a French education," which included no instruction in Arabic, grew considerably. In 1895, of the 474 Muslims students in French schools, 6 were girls; by 1905, of 3,145 Muslim students, 54 were girls. By 1945, Muslim girls made up 89% of the Muslim students receiving a French education and by 1954, two years before independence, 97% of the Muslim students. During the last few decades of the French protectorate, yet another possibility for schooling for Tunisian Muslims, *les écoles franco-arabes,* had been developed, and for several reasons, Muslim families preferred sending their sons to these schools while providing their daughters with a French education. Hence, far more Muslim boys than girls during this period were educated; however, of the Muslim girls receiving educations, many received educations emphasizing the French language and a French curriculum.

On the basis of information from the sources cited here, one can argue that during the first quarter or so of the 20th century, a major impetus for Tunisian Muslims of the professional class to educate their daughters (and educate them in French schools) was the presence of that part of the Jewish community that was assimilating to a way of life much influenced by the French colonizers. Both of these groups chose initially to educate their daughters as a way of demonstrating their "modernity" and improving the daughter's status on the marriage market (and hence the status of the family as a whole), a point I investigate further in "Gendering French in Tunisia," in which I examine the historical roots of Tunisian language ideologies of language and gender.

As just noted, independent Tunisia has invested a great deal in providing its youth "universal" education and has succeeded to a high degree in many ways. Among the achievements of the country has been providing access to literacy for Tunisian girls and women.

VIGNETTES OF LITERACY

Among others, I have argued ("Opening the Door") that issues surrounding women and women's rights are foundational to questions of national identity in the countries of the Arab Muslim world.[4] Indeed, any issue related to this topic, including the right of girls and women to be educated, becomes a trope of sorts. In this section, I offer four short vignettes about women's and girls' access to literacy—three involving women and one involving a man. My goal is to complement the account offered of census data, languages of literacy in Tunisia, and the history of education for women in Tunisia with human stories because, in the end, the meanings of literacy are tied to individuals' embodied experience of it.

"I'd have died to learn to read and write," she said during an interview in 1986 for my dissertation on language variation and change in Korba, a small Tunisian town of perhaps 8,000, an hour or so Northeast of Tunis, in an especially prosperous agricultural region of the country. Later during the interview, a woman I'll call Mabrouka, who was in her early sixties at the time, expressed disappointment with her children—a daughter and two sons, now adult, who once had a chance to "read," as we say in Tunisian Arabic, but had managed to make it no further than the sixth grade, failing the competitive entrance exam to secondary school.

In the mid-eighties, almost no one in Korba could name a woman over 50 who could read or write, though the vast majority of young girls "read" as long as they could stay in the system or as long as their families permitted them to. As in many places in the world and sometimes even in the United States, the education of sons continues to be more highly valued than that of daughters, who will most likely marry and become part of other families. At the same time, a growing number of younger women in Korba had received or were receiving post-secondary educations in a range of fields, an opportunity that forced them to leave Korba and live in larger cities affording them exposure to not only what they might learn from books and laboratories but also new ways of being in the world, ways of being Tunisian *and* educated *and* a woman, not available to them in their hometown.

Not everyone in Korba saw education for young women as a positive thing. During another of the interviews for my dissertation, a young man in his late twenties who had not been able to pass the high school exit exam but had a stable job working in the public transportation system explained that girls needed only to learn to read and write and to use silverware in the European fashion (instead of eating with their hands, as Tunisians traditionally did and as older, rural, and poorer Tunisians continue to) so that they would not embarrass their husbands should they have to eat in public places like restaurants. As he saw it, additional education was wasted on females. His views, not uncommon among many Tunisian men, represent a complex mixture of ideologies: a longing for an imagined patriarchal model of Arab family life in the past, where fathers ruled with absolute power, on the one hand, as well as a deep conviction, bolstered by the tenets of political Islam, that a society based on what its followers would term "Islamic values" could counter the insidious influences of globalization, while contributing to some version of Arab nationalism, on the other. Those holding such attitudes, including some women, contend that were women to stop working outside the home, men could find jobs more easily, gaining their proper place in society, and, morality in society in general would improve as women returned to their true sphere and stayed home. (See Malika Zmiti-Horchani's article on Tunisian women's rights and my discussion of it in "Opening the Door.")

Yet while some Tunisian men do not support education for women and many Tunisian women, especially older ones, mourn the literacy they never had the chance to receive, other Tunisian women have managed, despite the patriarchy, to become literate to varying degrees. During 1997–98, when I lived in Carthage, a suburb of Tunis, a woman I will call Aziza cleaned for me weekly. At the time, she was in her early forties. She'd grown up in a town thirty minutes or so South of Tunis, and her father had prevented her from going to school as a child. Indeed, he forbade her brother from teaching her what he had learned at school. After she married, she faithfully followed early educational TV programs aimed at teaching literacy skills in written Arabic to adults. Because of Arabic diglossia, Aziza was learning not only a script but also a variety of Arabic quite different from her native dialect. As she reported it, her efforts empowered her to sign her name, to understand much of the national news (always read aloud in the written variety of Arabic), to make lists of things to help her remember them, to read street names and building signs and hence to find addresses, and to support her children in their homework when they were small in ways she otherwise couldn't have.

She made a point of working for foreign families: the work was less arduous than it would have been had she worked for Tunisians, the employer-employee relationships were quite different from those she experienced when working for Tunisians, the pay was better than it would have been with Tunisians, and the families generally spoke French whereas Tunisians would have spoken Arabic—at least to her.

(I do not necessarily take these claims as criticism of the Tunisians for whom Aziza might have worked; rather, she was simply exploiting one salient and essential aspect of local-expatriate relations at all levels and profiting from it in multiple ways.) By working for foreign families, she picked up some French and very rudimentary Roman-script literacy skills.

Quite aware of the little that I, as a researcher, can do for Tunisia or Tunisians, I offered to teach her English while she worked for me. Each week, I'd write out a simple functional dialogue about going to the market or washing clothes or needing to change her work schedule because of a sick child—topics she suggested—record it on a cassette tape, copy it in English into a notebook she'd bring, and then write it out across the page in transliterated Arabic, which she could read with some difficulty. Finally, I'd provide a line-by-line translation of the dialogue into Tunisian Arabic using the Arabic script. (Although the spoken dialect is not usually written, those who speak the dialect and know the script can read texts written in dialectal Arabic with little effort. Certainly, reading the dialect was easier for Aziza than reading [and translating] the written variety of Arabic would have been. It was also easier for me.) After the floor was mopped and the laundry hung out to dry, she and I would sit down and practice a bit. From a note she once left me in Arabic and French, I can attest that her literacy skills were very, very basic; yet I am sure she is counted, with pride, among those claiming literacy in the figures above for Arabic and French. Perhaps she will claim English next time. What Aziza understood is that literacy is power of several sorts. It has to do with self-worth. It is enabling. It is practical. It can bring better wages and better working conditions. It can on occasion be translated into material advantage for oneself and those one loves.

Yet, at the same time that we admit that literacy has brought Tunisian women like Aziza and the daughters and granddaughters of women like Mabrouka opportunities they could not otherwise have had, it would be too simple to imply that these opportunities necessarily come without pain. I think here of Fatiha, as I'll call a Tunisian friend, a woman now in her sixties, who was from a small town but educated in the colonial school system in French because of her father's commitment to education for his daughters and sons. Like many women from newly independent developing countries who were in college in the 1960s, she had initially been passed over for opportunities for study abroad because she was a woman at a time when early Western development programs favored men. As she grew older and international funding priorities became more gender neutral, even favoring women, younger women were chosen. Finally, she managed to realize her dream of coming to study in the United States. Thanks to luck, pluck, and a great deal of hard work, she turned a one-year fellowship into a chance to complete a doctorate. As she struggled to finish her dissertation, dealing with the insecurities we've all wrestled with, she one day broke down while we were having a conversation. Sobbing, she said that her biggest fear was that all possibilities for funding would run out before she finished and that she would have to return home with no degree. A single woman who had endured a great deal of hardship because she'd never married—itself a fact tied in complex ways to her literacy and educational background—she noted that she had no husband and no children, only her career, and that she could not bear the possible loss of face were she to return home to Tunisia, where marriage and family remain so important to women, without a degree. Although she went on to complete her doctorate, return to her post as a university teacher back home, and receive the promotion her degree had earned her, I have never forgotten this conversation. I do not wish to. It reminds me of the complex ways in which access to literacy of various sorts in specific languages or the lack of it creates certain options while closing off others. It cannot help but become a significant kind of symbolic capital (Bourdieu) whose meanings are always ultimately local even as they can give rise to generalizations extending beyond the local.

SOME TENTATIVE CONCLUSIONS

In this chapter, I have tried to examine Tunisian females' access to literacy and the languages of literacy from several perspectives: by examining census data to provide an overview of the demographics of literacy, by considering historic milestones in girls' access to literacy in the country, and by providing a few short narratives showing how literacy or its absence becomes woven into the fabric of individuals' lives at the most profound of levels. Several generalizations emerge from these data; some likely apply more broadly to postcolonial settings or so-called developing nations in general.

First, Tunisian females have far more access to education and hence the languages of literacy now than at any time in the past. Nearly all of these gains have come since Tunisia's independence in 1956. At the same time, these changes result in the feminizing of illiteracy in new ways; certainly the stigma of illiteracy grows greater, especially for younger girls and women, than it has been at any time in the past.

Second, closely related to the first observation is a fact of which Tunisians are very aware: while literacy in the abstract represents a generalized (and to some extent generalizeable) set of cognitive abilities and social practices, *in situ*, literacy always means literacy in a specific language or in specific languages. Seen from this perspective, literacy necessarily grants one access to some texts and fosters participation in certain social contexts and groups but not others. Further, the value and meanings of literacy in such situations are inseparably linked to personal and societal attitudes toward specific language(s), the texts available in that language or those languages, and the social capital that knowledge of that language or those languages, including the written variety, represents. At one level, these claims are the most obvious of truisms: Because I do not speak or read German, I have no access to German-language texts that have not been translated into a language I am able to read. Yet, the consequences of these claims are palpably salient for Tunisians because they live in a multilingual country, where the value of one's literacy, however calculated, is related to the language(s) one can or cannot read.

Third, the further one moves from the colonial period, the more one sees greater uniformity of education among all Tunisians, including Tunisian females. Tunisians educated before independence, which included a significant number of girls and young women, might have been educated in Qur'anic schools; schools run by European religious orders; schools set up by the French colonial government primarily for the purpose of educating the children of the colonizers and the children of the elite among those Tunisians they employed; or colonial schools designed for the purpose of educating a larger number of Tunisian children, especially boys. Today, Tunisian children are, with rarest exception, educated in schools taught in Modern Standard Arabic and requiring several years' study of French and English. Significantly, the demographics of Tunisia have shifted from an exceedingly complex mixture of Muslims, Jews, and Christians with origins around the Mediterranean to something far more homogeneous: over 98% of Tunisians today are Arab Muslims. Such a process of homogenization has occurred across the Arab world in the past half century and has consequences of many sorts for these societies, including literacy there. In all these countries, the literacy associated with "universal education" has come to mean literacy in Arabic while Roman-script literacy associated with a Western language is associated with elite status, the meaning of which continues to change. In colonial Tunisia, such literacy indexed social position as well as an openness to participating in at least some of the goals of the colonial *mission civilisatrice*; today, such literacy is seen in terms of the processes and necessities of globalization.

Especially when one remembers that the mean age in Tunisia is less than 21, a greater percentage of the Tunisian population has had extended exposure to Modern Standard Arabic and, to lesser degrees, French and English than any time in the past. These shared resources often play complex roles in public debate about national identity, and hence women's issues including literacy and education, and in the symbolic construction of the nation-state within the Arab Muslim world and on the larger world stage.

Scholars (e.g., Bakalti, Charrad, Marzouki) agree that Tunisian women—and women in Arab Muslim countries more generally—have been granted the right to literacy or access to it and the languages through which access comes because men in power were convinced that doing so was good for the nation-state imagined in some way: for improving the quality of child-rearing of the next generation, for making the country modern, and for creating a particular image of the country abroad. Further, as is currently the case in Tunisia, women's issues, including literacy, have been an exploitable resource that governments or political groups can seek to appropriate for any number of causes.

Yet, despite these facts, Tunisian girls and woman have fought for access to literacy individually and collectively; thus far, at least, they do not take it for granted. They have likewise used the literacy and the knowledge of the varieties of language associated with literacy in ways not foreseen by male decision makers (cf. "Opening the Doors"). At the same time, literacy has not translated automatically into "simpler" or "easier" or "better" lives, as earlier research on literacy sometimes claimed would be the case. As symbolic capital whose value and meanings continue to shift, literacy has, however, resulted in different sorts of options for those who become literate and those who do not, complicating their lives and societies in ways assuredly unimagined by the Muslim girls who attended school on the *rue du Pacha* less than a century ago.

NOTES

1. As I was revising this chapter, I discovered Julia Clancey-Smith's very important essay on education for Muslim women in colonial North Africa. The essay is significant not only for the information it provides on the École Louise-René Millet but also for its particularly insightful discussion of the complexity of doing research on education for girls in colonial settings like Tunisia.
2. Throughout, I transliterate Arabic or Hebrew names as conventionalized in the individual's country of origin, literate practices reminding us of one consequence of colonialism: a name often has several spellings, depending most importantly on whether the individual is from a country where French or English is the primary second language and more generally part of the colonial heritage. In the bibliography, titles are transliterated using the system most widely used by Anglophone scholars.
3. This pair were *livournais* that is, of Jewish families that had come to what is today Tunisia from Italy beginning in the sixteenth century, fleeing persecution there even as their parents and grandparents had fled Spain and Portugal in the 1490s. The Livournais became part of already socially complex Jewish communities across Tunisia, where Jews had lived since

the time of the Phoenicians according to some accounts, with later groups arriving after the destruction of the first and second temple in Jerusalem. Indigenous Berbers became part of this community in a subsequent era. Jews later came to Tunisia directly from Spain during the Inquisition, and Jews continued to immigrate to Tunisia from Italy well into the colonial period. See Sebag and Simon & Tapia. On education for Jewish girls in colonial Tunis, see Walters ("Education for Jewish Girls"); for insights into how the colonial project gendered the teachers of these girls, whether European or Tunisian, see Land.

4. Similar arguments can, of course, be made about Western nations. To participate in specific (though changing) debates are women's reproductive rights and abortion, for example, and to have particular vested interests in them as we construct these issues and arguments are among the constitutive features of being American.

WORKS CITED

Amin, Qasim. *The Liberation of Women: A Document in the History of Egyptian Feminism.* Trans. of *Tahriir al-mar'a.* 1899. Trans. Samiha Sidhom Peterson. Cairo: American U of Cairo P, 1992.

Bakalti, Souad. *La femme tunisienne au temps de la colonization, 1881–1956.* Paris: L'Harmattan, 1996.

Blili, Leïla. "Tawhida Ben Cheikh: La médecine au feminin." *Mémoire de femmes: Tunisiennes dans la vie publique, 1920–1960/Nisaa' wa Thaakara: Tuunisiyyaat fii al-Hayyat al-'Aama.* Ed. Habib Kazdaghli. Tunis: Édition Média Com, 1993. 21–30.

Bourdieu, Pierre. *Language and Symbolic Power.* Ed. John B. Thompson. Trans. Gino Raymond and Matthew Adamson. Cambridge: Harvard UP, 1991.

Charrad, Mounira. *States and Women's Rights: The Making of Postcolonial Tunisia, Algeria, and Morocco.* Berkeley: U of California P, 2001.

Chercuitte. *La sortie de classe, à l'école des jeunes filles musulmanes de Tunis.* "Les Houris a L'École." By Albérie Cahuet. *L'Illustration* 130 (5 Oct. 1907): 226–27.

Clancey-Smith, Julia. "Envisioning Knowledge: Educating the Muslim Woman in Colonial North Africa, c. 1850–1918." *Iran and Beyond: Essays in Middle Eastern History in Honor of Nikki R. Keddie.* Ed. Rudi Matthee and Beth Baron. Costa Mesa, CA: Mazda Publishers, 2000. 99–118.

Dornier, François. *Les Catholiques en Tunisie au fils des ans.* Tunis: Imprimerie Finzi, 2000.

Essnousi, Mohammed. *Épanouissement de la fleur ou etude sur la femme dans l'Islam.* Trans. Mohammed Mohéddine Essnousi and Abdel Kader Kébaili. Tunis: n.pag., 1897.

Ferguson, Charles. "Diglossia." *Word* 15 (1959): 329–40.

Gouda, Frances and Julia Clancey-Smith. Introduction. *Domesticating the Empire: Race, Gender, and Family Life in French and Dutch Colonialism.* Ed. Julia Clancey-Smith and Frances Gouda. Charlottesville: U of Virginia P, 1998. 1–20.

Haddad, Tahar. *Notre femme: La legislation islamique et la société.* Trans. of *Imra'atuna fii al-shari'a wa al-mujtama'a,* 1930. Tunis: M.T.E., 1978.

Land, Joy A. "Corresponding Lives: Women Educators of the Alliance Israélite Universelle School for Girls in the City of Tunis, 1882." May 2006. G. E. von Grunebaum Center for Near Eastern Studies. Paper 5. 24 November 2006 <http://repositories.cdlib.org/international/cnes/5>.

Marzouki, Ilhem. *Le mouvement des femmes en Tunisie.* Tunis: Cérès Productions, 1993.

Mohanty, Chandra. "Under Western Eyes: Feminist Scholarship and Colonial Discourses." *Feminist Review* 30 (1988): 61–88.

Sebag, Paul. *Histoire des Juifs de Tunisie: Des origines à nos jours.* Paris: L'Harmattan, 1992.

Simon, Patrick, and Claude Tapia. *Le Belleville des Juifs tunisiens.* Paris: Éditions Autrement, 1998.

République Tunisienne. Ministère du Developpement Economique. Institut National de la Statistique. *Recensement général de la population et de l'habitat de 1994: Caracteristiques d'éducation, tableaux statistiques* [Preliminary internal report]. Mimeo. 1997.

Walters, Keith. "Education for Jewish Girls in Nineteenth- and Early Twentieth-Century Tunis and the Spread of French in Tunisia." *Rethinking Jewish Culture and Society in North Africa: Papers from the 2004 American Institute of Maghrib Studies Conference.* Ed. Emily Gottreich and Daniel Schroeter. Bloomington: Indiana UP, in press.

——. "Fergy's Prescience." *International Journal of the Sociology of Language* 163 (2004): 77–109.

——. "Language, Gender, and the Political Economy of Language: Anglophone Wives in Tunisia." *Language in Society* 26 (1996): 515–56.

——. " 'Opening the Door of Paradise a Cubit': Educated Tunisian Women, Embodied Linguistic Practice, and Theories of Language and Gender." *Reinventing Identities: The Gendered Self in Discourse.* Ed. Mary Bucholtz et al. Oxford: Oxford UP, 1999. 200–17.

——. "Gendering French in Tunisia: Historicizing Language Ideologies." In preparation.

Zangar, Selwa Khaddar. "Une école pionnière, l'école de la rue du Pacha." *La femme tunisienne à travers les âges.* Tunis: Ministère de la Culture, Institut National du Patrimoine, 1997. 176–80.

Zmita-Horchani, Malika. "Tunisian Women, Their Rights, and Their Ideas about Their Rights." *Women of the Mediterranean.* Ed. Monique Gadant. Trans. A. M. Berrett. London: Zed, 1986. 110–19.

11

Women and the Global Ecology of Digital Literacies

Gail E. Hawisher
Cynthia L. Selfe
with Kate Coffield *and* Safia El-Wakil

For the past several years, we have been collecting stories of how people born in the United States during the twentieth century have acquired the literacies associated with technology. Our goal has been to gather information about digital literacy practices as they have occurred in the lives of U.S. citizens and, then, to analyze the stories within the larger contexts of the historical, political, economic, and ideological forces that have shaped these same people's lived experiences. The United States, however, is not the world; and, as recent events have demonstrated, increasing our understanding of people from other nations, cultures, and sites of literate practice may prove an essential element for productive global citizenship. Thus, with this chapter, we begin a new international phase of our larger digital literacy project, collaborating with two women, one a U.S. citizen, the other a citizen of Egypt, both of whom currently make their homes in Cairo, Egypt.[1]

The literacy narratives that follow illustrate for us the many rich and varied meanings that attach themselves to literacy here and abroad, today as well as in the past. In writing of nineteenth-century women in the United States, Catherine Hobbs observes that questions of how literacy affects women and how women affect literacy remain neglected in current histories of education and the teaching of writing. In her words, "women's participation in transforming [nineteenth-century] literacy has not yet been thoroughly explored" (4). Hobbs also asks whether the contemporary meaning of literacy has shifted to include "types of literacy bearing more cultural capital ... leaving women again with less

effective, lower-valued print literacy" (2). Writing in Australia of twentieth-century women, Dale Spender makes a corresponding argument
about information technologies. She notes that new information technologies—writing, print, and now electronic—tend to exclude women
from positions of influence. When writing became part of Western culture, few women were scribes and fewer yet authors. When print was in
its ascendancy as a primary communication medium, few women
played a major role in publishing companies. As electronic media have
taken center stage in the contemporary world, women occupying various social, cultural, and economic positions have arguably less access—or, more accurately, different access—to today's literacies than
their male counterparts. To overcome these recurring conditions,
Hobbs would have women work for "effective literacy"—and we
would add "effective electronic literacy"—that is, "a level of literacy
that enables one to effect change in her own life and society" (1), thus se-
curing power to enact change in the world. In this chapter, we present
the literacy narratives of two women who grew up before the entrance
of computers as writing technologies but who nevertheless persisted as
adults in their efforts to acquire what we are calling the literacies of
technology.

In collecting the literacy narratives of Kate Coffield, a U.S. citizen
born on 16 August 1947 in Cuyahoga Falls, Ohio, and Safia El-Wakil,
born on 19 February 1942 in Cairo, Egypt, we came to a more global understanding of digital literacy and the complex contexts within which it
develops. The importance of technology gateways that provide people
local and global access for digital literacy development and the value of
international collaborations for extending digital literacy practices and
enhancing cross-cultural understandings also took on greater meaning.
Three key themes emerged from the narratives of these two women and
are discussed more fully in later sections of the chapter:

- *Women's digital literacy—and their literacy in general—exists and
  develops within a cultural ecology,* a complex set of related factors that
  shape, and are shaped by, people's use of computers as tools and environments for reading and composing: social and educational practices, values, and expectations; cultural and ideological formations
  like gender; class, age, and race; political and economic trends and
  events; family practices and experiences; and historical and material
  conditions—among many other factors.

- *Women exert their own powerful agency in, around, and through digital literacies and can change the cultural ecology within which they acquire
  such literacies.* Personal motivations, interests, actions, resources, and
  personalities shape the practice of digital literacy as well as the value
  that individual women place on digital literacy. In some cases, these

factors allow women to pursue digital literacy despite gender, age, or cultural expectations that might otherwise prevent or hinder their actions.

   • *Specific conditions of access to technological systems—at both local and global levels—can have a substantial effect on women's acquisition and development of digital literacy.* Access to computers—and to the literacies of technology—cannot be accurately represented as an isolated or monodimensional formation. Rather, access is best understood as part of a multidimensional cultural ecology. Simple physical access to computers is necessary but insufficient for the acquisition and development of digital literacies.

We have chosen the stories of these women to relate *not* because we want to suggest they are representative in any way, but rather because their lives span cultures and literacies in interesting and, we think, informative ways. Both women have had the experience of living in, and benefiting from, different cultures; both grew up in the world of print and only later entered the world of digital communication; both have used their ability to establish cross-cultural relationships and their interest in digital literacies to enhance their own lives and the lives of people with whom they collaborate.

NOTES ON METHOD

Before we begin, a few important remarks are in order about the approaches and assumptions that have shaped this project. First, we note that our research seeks not only to study how people acquire and develop the literacies of technology but also to work with participants as co-authors, and to learn from them. Further, we hope not only to tell people's stories accurately and in context, but also to hold ourselves accountable (Britzman) for the narratives we convey. Following the lead, then, of scholars such as Caroline Brettell, Patti Lather, Shulamit Reinharz, and Kamala Visweswaran, we have attempted to develop a research methodology that works toward an ethical understanding of agency and involves participants directly, not only in the data gathering but also in the data-reporting stages of our project. Part of this methodology involves asking the participants to co-author the chapters with us in the hope that we can write with and about them in a manner that suits all parties.

   Second, we acknowledge our adherence to life-history methodology, an approach used by Deborah Brandt and grounded in oral-history and life-history research (Bertaux; Thompson). With this methodology, we have attempted to probe people's technological literacy experiences through a standard set of interview questions that ask for demographic data and for information about family history, stories about literacy practices and values, memories of schooling environments and workplace experiences, and descriptions of technology use or avoidance. We then analyze the information from these literacy narratives within the larger contexts of historic, political, economic, and ideological movements, attempting to reconcile and to register, micro-, medial-, and macrolevel perspectives in the interest of obtaining a more robust, multidimensional image of technological literacy acquisition and development.

Brandt's oral-history and life-history methodology, we should add, is congruent with the ecological model of electronic literacy studies outlined by Bertram Bruce and Maureen Hogan. As these researchers point out, electronic literacy practices and values can be understood only as

> constituent parts of life, elements of an ecological system...that give us a basis for understanding the interpenetration between machines, humans, and the natural world .... [L]iteracies, and the technologies of literacy, can only be understood in relation to larger systems of practice. Most technologies become so enmeshed in daily experience that they disappear. (272)

The life history interviews we present in this chapter are *not* meant to be representative of a larger population. These two narratives constitute only a minute portion of the story of how individual women have adapted their literacy values and practices to computer-supported environments during the late twentieth and early twenty-first century in the United States and in Egypt. This acknowledgment, however, is not meant to diminish the values of these richly textured stories. We believe they offer key insights into women's literate lives and that they may, as well, offer direction for further study and exploration.

Finally, we note our own positioning and limited vision as researchers. We are both middle-class, middle-aged, white academics whose professional careers have been essentially coincidental with the invention of personal computers in the late 1970s and the diffusion of these machines into college classrooms in the early 1980s. We are U.S. citizens whose lives have been limited primarily to the United States although we have made professional visits to Zimbabwe, Japan, Norway, Australia, Greece, Germany, New Zealand, the Netherlands, Hong Kong, the United Kingdom, and Egypt where we have worked in what we consider to be productive ways with colleagues interested in technology use in educational environments. We consider our worldview limited by our own culture and enhanced by an exposure to other cultures and viewpoints.

In what follows, we turn to the United States, Egypt, and the literacy narratives of Kate and Safia. When we first met our co-authors, they were both writing instructors in the First-Year Writing Program at the American University of Cairo, or AUC, as it is commonly called.

KATE COFFIELD'S STORY: GROWING UP IN THE UNITED STATES, 1950s–1980s

To establish perspective on the cultural ecology for women's digital literacy development in the United States, we relate the story of Kate Coffield, born into a large, Catholic, mostly Scots-Irish family on 16 August 1947 in Cuyahoga Falls, Ohio, where her father was a sales manager in a men's clothing store and her mother a homemaker and, before she married, a secretary. Growing up, Kate classifies her family as lower-middle class with her parents holding high expectations for their four children's education, but only Kate and her much older half-sister went straight through their schooling and completed undergraduate degrees. Like many of the participants in our larger study, Kate could not remember a time when she was unable to read—or write, for that matter. After attending public schools in Cuyahoga Falls, Ohio, she graduated from high school in 1965. She then entered Ohio University in Athens, Ohio, where her only school memory of computers occurred during her senior year when Ohio University moved to computerized registration. Although she had signed up as an English major for "The Bible as Literature," she was placed in a graduate engineering course, suggesting perhaps the technological contexts into which the future would take her. She graduated from the university in 1969 but then felt at loose ends and took off for Boston. As she puts it,

> In 1971, after two years of the postcollege disillusionment typical among '60s English grads, I set off for Boston in my '59 VW bug. It was a long drive, but I was sure it would be more like college there than in Akron, Ohio. After about three weeks of job-hunting, I was down to my last $50, and my prospects seemed pretty grim. In that realm of the educated, with PhDs driving cabs and tending bar, nobody wanted to hire a female English BA, overqualified for secretarial work, underqualified for everything else, and too clumsy and temperamental to wait tables. One day, my employment agent phoned, saying, "Get on over to MIT right away—they *want* a college grad!" I flew across the bridge to Cambridge on my ratty bicycle, looking equally ratty myself (Janis Joplin hair, kangaroo-print hot pants outfit) and reached the upper floors of 545 Technology Square, home of the Artificial Intelligence Laboratory. I still remember details about that day 25 years ago, including everybody's names, but this is just a summary of events that set the stage for my future with computers.

Kate thrived in the MIT "techie" environment. Although classified as a "group secretary," this was 1971, she says, and she was treated with respect, "as a colleague, not an 'office girl.'" Working on projects such as ELIZA, SpaceWar, and LOGO with those whom Steven Levy in his 1984 *Hackers* would term in his subtitle "Heroes of the Computer Revolution," Kate learned much about the intricacies of mainframe computing. Despite immersing herself in this environment for only a year and a half, Kate is certain that Marvin Minsky, Terry Winograd, Seymour Papert, and her work in the Artificial Intelligence Lab "permanently immunized [her] against computer phobia."

Kate did little with computers during the next 10 years in which she worked as a water sports instructor at Club Med and as an advertising copywriter for a time, but—at age 37 as a graduate student specializing in teaching English as a Foreign Language—she again took up computers, still working with mainframes. This time, however, she completed a project for a graduate class while earning a master's degree in teaching English as a Foreign Language in Cairo, Egypt. Today Kate serves as University Web Manager for AUC, a position she assumed in 2001 after teaching in the university's writing program since 1982.

SAFIA EL-WAKIL: GROWING UP IN EGYPT, 1950s–1980s

When we examine the cultural ecology for women's digital literacy in Egypt during this same general period and consider the life history narrative of Safia El-Wakil, a different story emerges, but one that today, nonetheless, is intimately tied to literacy and the new information technologies. Born on 19 February 1942, Safia was brought up in a well-to-do, educated, Muslim Egyptian family in a spacious house with a beautiful garden, where her parents, grandparents, brother, aunts, uncles, and cousins made their home. Divided into several apartments, it was a traditional Egyptian home where Safia's extended family all lived together. She has fond memories of spending many hours in the gardens, playing with her brother, one year her junior, and her many cousins. In 1947, when Safia was five—the year Kate was born—she moved with her mother, father, and brother into a smaller apartment because her mother wanted to enter the modern world, so to speak—that is, she wanted her husband, herself, and their children to live as a nuclear family. When asked about the values her family placed on literacy, Safia explains:

> My grandparents and parents gave great value to reading both at home and at school but not enough to writing. My paternal grandfather graduated from the oldest university in the world (the prestigious "Al Azhar" in Cairo), but both my grandmothers did not complete their school education because of early marriages expected from girls at the time. While some girls were encouraged to continue their education at home once they reached the age of puberty, other women from my mother's genera-

tion were strongly motivated and managed to pursue their studies at the university level despite social disapproval. My mother was married at the age of 17, straight after leaving school, and was quite happy to be the housewife she always wanted to be. Education at the university, graduate and postgraduate level, became very common during the years I grew up in, and although I was encouraged to get married at an early age I was expected to pursue serious studies at the same time. It is quite interesting to note here how the men in my family, my father and my husband (rather than my mother), were those who offered me the greatest support in pursuing higher levels of education.

Safia further explained that she often heard her grandparents say that although higher education was a must for boys, it was prestigious for girls. She learned to read when she was three years old, and at five was sent off to an excellent, experimental British school in Alexandria, Egypt, where she studied English along with French, history, literature, Arabic, music, science, and religious studies in elementary and secondary school. While there, she also participated actively in sports—swimming, field hockey, horseback riding and tennis—and in 1960 she earned the privilege of playing on the Egyptian National Hockey team. She also attended a year of school in Switzerland; earned a BA from Cairo University; continued her education at the American University of Beirut in Lebanon from which she received an MA; and finally earned a MLitt. from St. Hugh's College of Oxford University in the United Kingdom, which took her beyond her master's work. Microcomputers, however, didn't become a fact of life in Egypt—or in the United States for that matter—until Safia had been married, had two sons, was widowed, and then returned to Cairo from Great Britain, where her immediate family had moved in 1975 when civil war broke out in Lebanon. When asked how she came to teach in the writing program at AUC, in 1987, Safia explains:

> After being widowed I wanted to return back to Egypt finding it easier to live as a single woman in a country where a women's identity and freedom is much respected and to take care of my parents who were growing older and in need of care and attention. Soon after enjoying a couple of years as chief administrator in a teacher training program at the Fulbright commission in Cairo, I accepted a position offered to me at AUC, where I spent fifteen years teaching in the Writing Program (in the English and Comparative Literature department). I also taught in the Core Seminar courses (a cultural study course).

Safia encountered her first computer in 1982 when she was visiting the United States, which, coincidentally, was the same year that Kate began her work in Cairo. But except for the brief time in which Kate used mainframe computers for a master's project and except for word-processing workshops in which each participated in the late 1980s, neither came to rely on computers for teaching or writing until the 1990s when these machines became a staple at the AUC campus. It was at this time that Kate and Safia began to see how they might use information technologies to abet their students' writing and learning.

THE CULTURAL ECOLOGY FOR WOMEN'S DIGITAL LITERACY IN THE MIDDLE EAST AND THE WEST

In looking at what we have defined as the cultural ecology for women's digital literacy—that is, the complex web of social forces, historical events, economic patterns, material conditions, and cultural expectations within which both women and computer technologies co-exist—we need to focus on both Egypt and the United States. Many of us in the United States, of course, are familiar with the turbulent 1960s and the years following, the historical context in which Kate came of age. Here's how she describes her undergraduate experience from 1965–1969:

> College at Ohio University was entirely different [from my high school], with a larger and more diverse population and a lot more freedom. In and out of class, we were awakened to the civil rights movement, the anti-Vietnam war protests, Indian philosophies, conspiracy theories, sex, drugs, and music music music ... which surrounded and encompassed all. We sang, we marched, we loved, we got stoned, we drove for hours in doorless trucks to rock concerts, we nursed friends through scary illegal abortions. Some drowned in all this and disappeared from school, either temporarily or permanently. I was among the lucky ones who managed to live the life but still hang in and graduate with honors.

Thus, in many respects, the social movements afoot in the United States—the civil rights movement, Vietnam War protests, second-wave feminism, the rise of a counterculture—all paved the way for Kate first to take off to Boston as a single woman in 1971 and then to embark in 1982 on a journey across the world that resulted in her teaching writing in Cairo, Egypt.

During this same period, social unrest was also characteristic of Egypt and the Middle East. As a colony of Great Britain from the late nineteenth century until 1936 when it gained its independence, Egypt was influenced tremendously by Great Britain even as it struggled to be free. Internal politics played a significant role after independence, and in 1952, when Safia was ten years old, King Farouk was overthrown by a military junta, and Gamal Abdel Nasser was officially elected president in 1956, the same year in which Egyptian women were granted equal voting rights (Botman).

In 1967, while Kate was in college and Safia was married and attending the American University of Beirut, Egypt lost to Israel in the Six-Day War and turned increasingly to help from the Soviet Union (Kjeilen). But Anwar al-Sadat, who succeeded Nasser in the presidency after Nasser died in 1970, became increasingly unhappy with unkept promises from the Soviets, and in the years following expelled them from Egypt (Sullivan). During this time, the economy in Egypt continued to deteriorate, with a growing disparity between rich and poor. Sadat became convinced that peace with Israel was essential for any kind of Middle East stability, and, finally, in 1979, signed a peace treaty with Israel. On October 6, 1981, two years after he received the Nobel Peace Prize, Muslim fundamentalists assassinated Sadat. As Kate prepared to move to Cairo, Muhammed Hosni Said Mubarak was elected president. According to some sources, Mubarak has not only reinvigorated the Egyptian economy but also has played a major role in working to develop the entire Middle East ("Mubarak"). Today, with about 70 million people, Egypt is the largest of the Arab nations.

Social and political upheavals obviously influenced Safia's life, first in Egypt and then in Lebanon where she moved with her husband in the 1960s. There they raised their sons until the 1975 Civil War, and, as Safia alludes to earlier, moved to Great Britain where her husband could continue his business career. Interestingly, Kate arrived in Cairo and Safia returned to Cairo in the early 1980s just as personal computers were making their appearance on the global scene and just as Mubarak was attempting to revitalize the Egyptian economy.

These accounts of two women writing instructors hint at some of the political turmoil that has occurred during their lifetimes but would be incomplete without some mention of the opportunities that became available to women in Egypt and the United States during these years. There were a great many women's movements throughout the Middle East, but Egypt especially has had a proud feminist history. As far back as 1923, the decade in which Safia's mother was born, the Egyptian Feminist Union was founded, calling for "political rights for women ... equal secondary and university education, and expanded professional opportunities for women" (Al-Ali 6). Some, however, argue that the women's movement did not come of age until the period from 1945 to 1959. During these years, Bint El-Nil (Daughter of the Nile) was formed and campaigned for women's full political rights, along with establishing literacy programs and social services for women.[2] Into the present, however, tensions continue to exist between what counts as public rights for women and what counts as rights for women within the home. In an attempt to rectify this situation, Jehan Sadat, spouse of Anwar, worked to reform the Personal Status Law, which governs marriage, divorce, custody of children, and so on, and in 1979 a law—Jehan's Law, as it came to be called—was instituted by presidential decree. Nonetheless, conflict remains between Islamists who perceive such reforms as anti-Islamic and activists in the Egyptian feminist movement who understand such reforms as just and fair. Today, despite ongoing pressures exerted on Egyptian women activists accused of betraying "authentic culture" in favor of "Western thought," many persist in efforts to create and maintain a feminist platform promoting grassroots change for the benefit of all women (Al-Ali 9).

KATE AND SAFIA: MAKING CHANGE IN DIGITAL LITERACY ENVIRONMENTS, 1980s AND 1990s

The complex cultural ecology which affected Egypt and the United States both shaped and was shaped by Kate's and Safia's work with technology as these two women became faculty members at AUC in the 1980s and sought ways to improve teaching with technology when computers became available to them. By this time, the opportunities for change in digital computing environments had begun to accelerate rapidly given the production and marketing of cheaper, rugged microcomputers starting in the late 1970s. By the 1980s, AUC's writing program, too, had begun experimenting with computers and, in 1986, Kate remembers spending hours in a workshop to learn WordStar, the preferred program in U.S. universities and at AUC at the time. By 1987, Safia had joined a three-day tutorial on how to use computers for word processing and remembers fearing, as she puts it, "the mysterious behavior of the machine."

Although both Kate and Safia now had access to computers, the specific conditions of their access did not provide sufficient opportunities to integrate these machines fully into their teaching and to transform the literacy experiences they offered students in their classrooms. It wasn't until 1993, for instance, that a new writing program director, an avid Macintosh user, obtained a grant for computers at AUC. He formed a computer committee for which Kate volunteered. As a member of this committee, she helped lay out the plans for the writing program's new lab. Kate tells stories of trying to set up the facility with eighteen Macintosh computers and four Stylewriter II dot-matrix printers in one of the university's older rooms, which featured a working fireplace and a balcony but only two electrical outlets. By mid-March of 1994, Kate had managed to do most of the everyday labor in setting up a computer lab that she, Safia, and a few other colleagues and their students took up immediately but that received little attention from most of the other faculty.

It was also during this time, 1994 and 1995, that the Internet came to AUC: Kate tells of the memo the faculty received from Dr. Mona Kaddah, Director of the Academic Computing Center.[3] It began:

> It is with utmost pleasure that I announce that full Internet connectivity has been achieved at AUC! The connection became operational at precisely 12:30 p.m. today. We have managed to overcome many problems and delays, going to great lengths to introduce the Internet to AUC in as short a time as possible. In doing so, we become the third Internet node in Egypt, and that includes FRCU, the Foreign Relations Coordination Unit, which is the national node in Egypt. (Kaddah, Memo, 5 Apr. 1994)

At this time, AUC also began to make travel grants available for faculty interested in learning more about the new technologies, and in 1994 Kate took advantage of a grant to attend the Computers and Writing Conference at the University of Missouri. The following year, both she and Safia won another grant to attend the two-week Computers in Writing-Intensive Classes Workshop at Michigan Technological University (CIWIC), an experience Safia attributes to making a great deal of difference to her computing expertise.

Kate and Safia also invited us to visit AUC in 1999 to give lectures at a technology symposium. Our visit changed not only our own understanding of digital literacy practices but also the digital literacy values we brought back to the United States. Kate and Safia's efforts allowed us to meet faculty members interested in technological literacies from a wide variety of disciplines and to immerse ourselves in a small part of Egypt's ancient and contemporary culture. As a result, we both came to understand more fully one of the global patches within which digital literacies were being developed.[4] For us, Cairo's markets, the Nile, the Pyramids, the mosques and minarets, the calls to prayer, its people, 14,000,000 of them, provided a rich historical, social, and political context for the noisy, everyday life of a rapidly growing society replete with Internet cafés. We also learned a great deal about women's lives in this patch of the global, cultural ecology. In this same year, Suzanne Mubarak, spouse of the president, gave an address to recognize the 100th anniversary of the book, *Tahrir al-Maraa* (*The Emancipation of Women*), written by Qasim Amin, in 1899. Our visit coincided, as well, with Technosphere '99, a conference attended by people from over 20 Arab countries and organized to discuss how science and technology intersects with the world of Arab women ("Global Connections"). More than anything, however, our stay allowed us to see firsthand the changes Safia and Kate were making in the digital literacy environments for teaching and learning in their department, at the AUC, and for the 5,000 students that attended that institution. We took this understanding of women's abilities to forge change back with us to the United States.

We also returned with an understanding of the strategies that Kate and Safia deployed as agents of change. We noticed, for instance, how they made use of transnational collaborations to shape the conditions of access for changes they wanted to make in their own digital literacies and those practiced at their home institution. In the middle 1990s, for instance, Safia became a regular attendee at the annual Computers and Writing Conferences in the United States and in 2001 returned to Michigan Tech's CIWIC to develop her multimedia literacies—manipulating digital video and still photography to present visual essays, using Flash animations to convey movement and emphasis, and presenting narratives composed on the virtual stage of Macromedia Director. Importantly, Safia was not following the lead of most other women at her home institution. Rather, she was responsible for many of the "firsts" that altered the shape of the digital literacy environment at AUC. In 1999, for instance, she produced the first interactive course web pages and was the first faculty member at AUC to require that students construct web pages to complement their course projects. Safia also entered into an online collaboration between her classes at AUC and those of Daniel Martin, a faculty member at Rockhurst University, a Jesuit school in Kansas City, Missouri. The two writing instructors conducted an online discussion forum for three semesters with students from Cairo and Kansas City, a collaboration Safia found especially productive following the events of September 11, 2001. In 2002, an article recounting these discussions and her collaboration with Dan was published in *Kairos*.[5]

EMERGING THEMES

It is a daunting task to do justice to Kate's and Safia's many stories and to the remarkable changes they made at a microlevel to their own digital literacies and the digital literacy environments of their classrooms; at a medial-level to the digital literacy practices and values of AUC and the many students they taught; and at a macrolevel to our own practice, valuing, and understanding of digital literacy. In this final section, we try to highlight a few tentative themes that have emerged from their case studies.

Cultural Ecologies and Literacies of Technology

We can understand literacy as a set of practices and values only when we properly situate these elements in a particular historical period and cultural milieu, and within a cluster of material conditions. These contexts constitute an ecology of digital literacy that functions both locally and globally, that shapes micro-, medial-, and macrolevels of experience for individuals. The work of contemporary literacy scholars—Brian Street, John Gee, Harvey Graff, and Deborah Brandt—reminds us that we cannot hope to understand any literacy until we understand the complex social and cultural systems, both local and global, within which literacy practices and values are situated.

As these two literacy narratives indicate, the ways in which women from various nations acquire and develop literacies of technology—or are prevented from doing so—depends on a constellation of factors: among just a few of them, income, education, access and the specific conditions of access, geographical location, and support systems. Within any given nation, many of these factors depend, as well, on technological infrastructure, a critical mass of skilled engineers and scientists, investment in education and educational technology, political stability, and technology policy (*Spanning*).

Because many factors contribute to the complex ecology within which literacy practices and values exist, individual case studies of digital literacy are valuable—these personal narratives are capable of demonstrating the highly textured ways in which micro-, medial, and macrolevel factors shape the lived experiences of real people. The cases of Safia and Kate, for instance, indicate that Egypt's macrolevel attempts to provide spaces for women to contribute to many areas of its society supported Kate's and Safia's medial- and microlevel efforts to acquire the literacies of technology. That AUC itself is peopled by many women administrators—Kate's dean and director of academic computing are women, as are all but two members of her web team—indicates some of the medial-level opportunities that women made for themselves at AUC.

Although both Egypt and the United States are part of a *global* ecology for literacy that was shaped by the general development and distribution of information technologies—especially the inventions of the microcomputer in the late 1970s—these cases also make clear that *national* patches also shape digital literacy practices and values. At AUC, for instance, informed by the historical and contemporary values of Egyptian feminism, women were encouraged to occupy positions as university administrators. Both Kate and Safia took part in, and strategically used this context to influence the digital literacy practices, values, and environments of the AUC. This observation is not meant to suggest that women in Egypt are exempt from the challenges common to women in other parts of the world. As in the United States, for instance, poverty in Egypt is feminized, and Cairo has extensive urban squatter sections occupied by large numbers of families headed by women. As heads of their own households, however, Kate and Safia managed to leverage their personal resources—their education, their economic positions, their interests, their backgrounds—strategically and in ways that allowed them to have a greater influence over their life's choices. In part, Safia and Kate were able to do so because they managed their own affairs and their own financial resources. Their travel in the United States to develop digital literacies and to change the digital literacy environment at AUC, for instance, may have been more difficult had they had less freedom to allocate their own finances and time in the ways that they did.

WOMEN'S AGENCY, CHANGE, AND DIGITAL LITERACY ENVIRONMENTS

As we have tried to suggest, although macro- and medial-level formations shape the opportunities people have to acquire digital literacies in cultural ecologies, it is also true that individuals' own motivations, interests, actions, and personalities shape the acquisition and development of these same literacies at the microlevel, and, in turn, also shape macro- and medial-level formations in a duality of structuration. The literacy narratives of Safia and Kate illustrate what Giddens would call the "duality of structure" (5). This concept explains how the actions of people are not only influenced by the society within which they live and the technological systems they inhabit, but also help actively constitute—and change—these environments. As we have conducted these interviews, and many others in our larger study, we have become convinced that individual women's personal motivations, resources, and talents, under certain conditions, can influence their use of technology and their development of digital literacies at a microlevel. Such motivations and strategic actions further, under certain conditions, can shape the larger cultural ecology at medial-and macrolevels. Macrolevel social movements of the 1960s paved the way for Kate's medial-level experiences with mainframe computing technology at MIT, her travel to Boston and Cairo, her confidence in experimenting with computing during her tenure at AUC, but the ways in which she explored her own individual interests and leveraged her resources also shaped her digital literacies at the microlevel. Kate, for example, thrives on immersing herself in the intricacies of computing technology. As she explains it:

> I suspect I'm part of a minority in academia who are attracted to computer systems and networks per se rather than just using them to accomplish tasks. I love problem solving, troubleshooting, and the challenge of helping friends and colleagues with their computers. Sometimes I feel that this cuts too much into my personal time, but in all honesty, I enjoy this

aspect of my work more than I do teaching writing, and if I could make a living as a technical support person, I would probably do so.

Kate's personal beliefs and interests feed back into the larger cultural ecology—in this case, contributing to an increasingly apt fit for digital literacy and changing the larger digital environments of which she is a part. Kate made this statement in 2000, for example, one year before she accepted her new administrative position as University Web Manager, a position in which she continues to make her mark on the medial-level of the university environment for practice and valuing of digital literacies and, in turn, the macrolevel national environment for such literacies within Egypt and around the world.

Although Safia, unlike Kate, would not characterize herself as a computing aficionado, her personal interests in digital literacies have also shaped the cultural ecology within which she lives, not only at the microlevels, but also at the medial- and macrolevels. While most of Safia's friends believe "that you could only be computer literate if you started at a young age," her acquisition of such literacies and at what she calls "a ripe age," has, nevertheless, had a key impact on her own life as well as on the lives of the many students with whom she has worked. A specific example can illustrate how this dynamic operates. Safia, for instance, has always had a deep love of language and literature, a passion that led her in the late 1980s to become an artist of Arabic calligraphy. Here's how her art is described at a recent exhibition of her work:

> El-Wakil's love of calligraphy came about while reading the Quran. She referred to her calligraphy in this exhibition as "words that lighten the heart"—words, she said, that are taken from the Quran. One work, however, was adapted from the text of a poem. Some of El-Wakil's works reflect a new experience involving digital artwork. She designed the pen she used on the computer and produced her calligraphic works with the use of art programs. Strongly believing that by adopting the new you do not shed tradition, El-Wakil emphasized that novelty in artwork "brings back tradition in a new form." ("Calligraphy Exhibition": See Figs. 11.1 and 11.2, and the cover of this collection, for recent examples of her art.)

In producing digital pieces, Safia explains:

> I used Photoshop and an electronic tablet for the calligraphy. I was investigating the possibility of using a computer to write artistically without losing the symmetry and discipline of letters much revered in the art of calligraphy. It was fun to sharpen the reed nib of my electronic pen on screen and use the different effects of a computer program to bring about

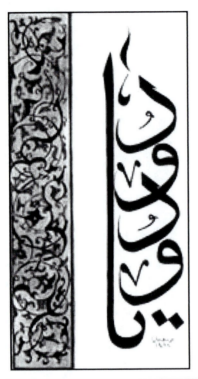

Figure 11.1.   Safia El-Wakil, from "Calligraphy Exhibition," American University in Cairo, 2001.

Figure 11.2.   Safia El-Wakil, from "Calligraphy Exhibition," American University in Cairo, 2001.

varied perspectives to my compositions. It was also revealing to be able to observe the different ways we envision letters to take shape.

Safia's personal enthusiasm for such literacy practices in electronic environments has not only affected her own microlevel practice of calligraphy but also flavors her medial-level work at the American University of Cairo, where she has helped students develop their own digital literacy values by involving them in creating web sites and composing the content for these sites in the classes they took with her. The effects of this work, further, are multiplied by the numbers of students Safia has taught and magnified by their participation in important sectors within Egyptian culture. These students have learned not only to use computers, and to enjoy this use, but also to rely on them as environments within which to practice their own literacies. Safia's commitment to, and understanding of, digital literacies have also shaped and changed the ways in which we both now understand reading and composing in computer environments, the ways in which we introduce and talk about such subjects to other teachers with whom we work, and the ways in which we teach students—and learn—about digital literacies in the United States. Thus, Safia's personal interests and motivations have also influenced Egypt's digital literacy, the practice and value of digital literacy in the United States, and the global cultural ecology for digital literacy.

THE COMPLICATIONS OF ACCESS

Although universities and workplaces have provided women important physical access to computers, these particular technology gateways do not always provide the specific conditions under which this access becomes most useful. Kate and Safia, for example, actively shaped the specific conditions under which they could develop digital literacy by establishing collaborations that reached across geographical locations, and, at the same time, productively enriched cross-cultural understandings. In today's difficult times, we want to underscore with these two case studies the continued importance of global connections and collaborations among institutions, organizations, and individuals in making such collaborative projects possible. Both Kate and Safia, for instance, gained access to computers in Egypt through the American University of Cairo, an institution founded by Americans in 1919, which admitted women as early as 1928. This institution, which today serves over 5,000 students on its campus in Cairo, has a mission "to provide high quality educational opportunities to students from all segments of Egyptian society as well as from other countries, and to contribute to Egypt's cultural and intellectual life" ("Mission Statement"). In recent years, AUC has come to serve as an important gateway to new information technologies not only for faculty such as Safia and Kate, but also for many Egyptian and U.S. students as well.

Although AUC provided an initial local gateway to technology for both Kate and Safia, however, the conditions of this access in the early 1990s could offer only a limited environment for their development of digital literacies. In seeking other conditions under which they could more easily expand their technological literacies, Kate and Safia began collaborations with colleagues in the United States—both interacted with colleagues during workshops at Michigan Tech, both attended the Computers and Writing Conferences in the United States, and both communicated across geopolitical borders in virtual environments to exchange information on classes and pedagogical approaches.

In each case, while Safia and Kate succeeded in expanding their own digital literacies, they also contributed richly textured cultural perspectives, personal insights, and expertise to their U.S. colleagues. Their visits to the United States added international depth to the professional discussions at the Computers and Writing Conferences and taught colleagues a great deal about the international diffusion of computer technologies, the challenges faced by colleagues teaching in other countries, and the nature of literacy practices in Egyptian universities. In addition, these visits resulted in an opportunity for Gail and Cindy to visit AUC, where they engaged in similar kinds of exchanges, and extended their own digital literacy skills and understandings.

IN SUM

For us, this investigation of digital literacies has provided a valuable venue for the study of, and exchanges with, other cultures, individuals, and nations, and a clearer understanding of a larger global ecology for digital literacies. In sharing their stories, Safia and Kate have taught us not only about the national patches of the complex global ecology within which they acquired and developed digital literacies, but also about the ways in which their own literacy interests, values, and practices, in turn, have affected both the national patches and global ecology these two women continue to inhabit. Moreover, their stories have provided graphic demonstrations of how adaptable these two women have been in acquiring and exploiting new literacies, and how creatively and generously they have used cross-cultural collaborations—among cultures, institutions, organizations, and people—to enrich their own and others' digital literacies and understandings.

Our work with Kate and Safia has convinced us that women, here and abroad, should continue to be part of these collaborations if the larger goals of literacy are to be served. If we define literacy as the power to enact change in the world, we cannot—indeed must not—ignore people and their use of information technologies in all parts of the world. Our field, as well as our culture, has much to learn from our international colleagues.

NOTES

1. The research project from which these studies are drawn consists of over 350 literacy narratives from people who participated in life history interviews or completed online a technological literacy questionnaire. For a more complete description of this larger project, see Selfe and Hawisher, *Literate Lives*.

2. There are others, however, who chart a long history of women's active involvement in politics, government, and commerce in Egypt going back as far as Queen Hatshepsut in ancient Egypt. As Safia explains, "Queen Hatshepsut (in Ancient Egypt) must have been the first woman in the world to rule a country, women in early Islam seemed to be the first in the world to join an army as medical nurses, and seventeenth century Egyptian women must have been among the few in the world allowed to retain their maiden name after marriage." Safia also points to Egyptian women's roles in the late eighteenth century: "An interesting book is *Women and Men in Late Eighteenth Century Egypt* by Afaf Lutfi al-Sayyid Marsot. Here al-Sayyid Marsot (who taught at UCLA) discovers through her research that Egyptian women in the eighteenth century were able to conduct their own commercial businesses with their own finances, and what ensues is quite interesting. She narrates how such activities came to an end as a consequence of Western men, who trading with Egypt, could not come to terms with businesses being held by women at the time, whereby the Ottoman leader had to prohibit women from such activities as a means to encourage the economic growth of the country."

3. Interestingly, as Kate points out, academic computing at AUC is administered by a high proportion of women. Kate tells us:

    > At AUC we have a good number of women in both administrative and IT positions. The dean to whom I report is a woman, as are all but two members of the web team (most of whom are AUC alumnae) and the director of academic computing. I believe I'm the only American woman IT administrator—others are Egyptian. Having been at AUC for twenty-plus years, I'm known to top administrators as well as to faculty, staff, and many students and alumni. Also, through computing work in the English department (1993–2000) I got to know most key people in various IT units. Several were either members of the search committee or had other input (as references, for example) into the search process when I was selected for the job. I suspect all this makes my work life much easier than it would be if I were a "stranger" American, new to Cairo or to the university.

4. In using the term *patch*, we are indebted to the work of Jay L. Lemke. In *Textual Politics*, he writes:

> ... activities in human communities are interrelated both in terms of exchanges of matter and energy and in terms of relationships of meaning. The fundamental unit of analysis will turn out to be a 'patch,' a mini-ecosystem containing human organisms in interaction with their social and material environments according to both cultural and ecological-physical principles. The patch is part of a mosaic of other patches each with its own unique history, all interacting and forming a larger scale patch in a larger scale ecosocial system .... underlying them are the interconnected doings, the ecological and social processes that link organism to organism, organism to environments, and which at smaller scales operate to constitute organisms, artifacts, landscapes, dialects, communities, cultures, and social individuals as self-organizing systems. (94)

When we use the term *patch*, we refer to the smaller eco-units of families, peer groups, institutions, professions, and so on.

5. See El-Wakil and Martin's "Armchair Cyber Travelers: A Kansas City-Cairo Discussion Group" at <http://english.ttu.edu/kairos/7.3/binder2.html?coverweb/martin/index.htm>.

We've included here an excerpt from their article to underscore the importance of these kinds of collaborations and online discussion groups. El-Wakil and Martin write:

> We did not realize once the discussion was launched that we would be so cautious on treading on sensitivities whether religious, political, or otherwise, nor did we know the extent of our responsibilities in monitoring those discussion threads. At one point in our discussion an anonymous writer sent a hate mail to our American students (leaving instructors and Egyptians out of the distribution). One Rockhurst student, who had already sent back a response, forwarded the message to Dan, and he forwarded it to Safia right away. Thanks to the different time zones, we were able to deal with the anonymous e-mail before potentially angry responses fueled themselves into a flaming thread of misunderstanding.
>
> Dan's suggestion was for his students not to respond, especially considering the complete uncertainty of the source. Anyone in the world could have sent it. In no way did Safia wish to ignore the situation, but saw it as a great *learning opportunity* for our students. While America was asleep, Safia had the chance to meet her students in class and reflect on what had happened. After a fruitful class discussion, the AUC students (who were disturbed by the hate mail) decided to send warm apologetic messages to their Rockhurst classmates before the next sunrise in the Kansas City. Upon waking up all the Rockhurst classmates responded by friendly exchanges of good feelings and a consensus on how no one is ever spared the madness that exists in our world today. After the hate mail,

Rockhurst students seemed to understand more poignantly the intensity of feeling regarding Israeli/Palestinian issues, and the Cairo students demonstrated in their responses that reasonable and calm voices can prevail over those of hatred.

WORKS CITED

Al-Ali, Nadje S. "The Women's Movement in Egypt with Selected References to Turkey." United Nations Research Institute for Social Development (UNRISD) Programme Papers on Civil Society and Social Movements. 1 April 2002. UNRISD, Geneva. 15 Mar. 2003 <http://www.unrisd.org/unrisd/ website/ document.nsf/(httpPapersForProgrammeArea)/9969203536F64607C1256 C08004BB140?OpenDocument>.

Amin, Qasim. *Tahrir al-Maraa* (The Liberation of Women: A Document in the History of Egyptian Feminism). Trans. Samiha Sidhom Peterson. Cairo, Egypt: American U in Cairo P, 1992.

Bertaux, Daniel. *Biography and Society: The Life History Approach in the Social Sciences.* Beverly Hills, CA: Sage, 1981.

Botman, Selma. *Engendering Citizenship in Egypt: The History and Society of the Modern Middle East.* New York: Columbia UP, 1999.

Brandt, Deborah. *Literacy in American Lives.* Cambridge, UK: Cambridge UP, 2001.

Brettell, Caroline B., ed. *When They Read What We Write: The Politics of Ethnography.* Westport, CT: Bergin and Garvey, 1993.

Britzman, Deborah P. "'The Question of Belief': Writing Poststructural Ethnography." *Working the Ruins: Feminist Poststructural Theory and Methods in Education.* Ed. Elizabeth A. St. Pierre and Wanda S. Pillow. New York: Routledge, 2000. 27–40.

Bruce, Bertram C., and Maureen P. Hogan. "The Disappearance of Technology: Toward an Ecological Model of Literacy." Ed. David Reinking, et al. *Handbook of Literacy and Technology: Transformations in a Post-Typographic World.* Mahwah, NJ: Lawrence Erlbaum Associates, 1998. 269–81.

"Calligraphy Exhibition." *Gateway.* The American University in Cairo. 2001. 16 Mar. 2003 <http://www.aucegypt.edu/publications/gateway/november2001/ calligraphy_exhibition.htm>.

El-Wakil, Safia, and Daniel J. Martin. "Armchair Cyber Travelers: A Kansas City-Cairo Discussion Group." *Kairos* 7.3 (2002). 24 Mar. 2003 <http://english.ttu.edu/ kairos/7.3/binder2.html?coverweb/martin/index.htm>.

Gee, James Paul. *Social Linguistics and Literacies: Ideology in Discourses.* 2nd ed. London: Taylor and Francis, 1996.

Giddens, Anthony. *Central Problems in Social Theory: Action, Structure and Contradiction in Social Analysis.* Berkeley: U of California P, 1979.

"Global Connections: the Middle East Timeline." *Global Connections: The Middle East.* PBS. 2002. 25 Mar. 2003 <http://www.pbs.org/wgbh/globalconnections/ mideast/timeline/text/qwomen.html>.

"Global Network: Cairo, Egypt." *Mega-Cities: Innovations for Urban Life.* 5 Dec. 2001. 26 Mar. 2003 <http://www.megacitiesproject.org/network/cairo.asp>.

Graff, Harvey J. *The Legacies of Literacy: Continuities and Contradictions in Western Culture and Society.* Bloomington: Indiana UP, 1987.

Hawisher, Gail E., and Cynthia L. Selfe. "Collaborative Configurations: Researching the Literacies of Technology." *Kairos* 7.3 (2002). 24 Mar. 2003 <http://eng­lish.ttu.edu/kairos/7.3/binder2.html?coverweb/hawisher/index.htm>.

Hobbs, Catherine. Introduction. "Cultures and Practices of U.S. Women's Literacy." *Nineteenth-Century Women Learn to Write*. Ed. Catherine Hobbs. Charlottesville: UP of Virginia, 1995, 1–33.

Kaddah, Mona. Memo to faculty at the American University of Cairo. 5 April 1994.

Kjeilen, Tore. "Gamal Abdu l-Nasser." *Encyclopedia of the Orient*. Lexicorient. 1996–2003. 14 Mar. 2003 <http://i-cias.com/e.o/nasser.htm>.

Lather, Patti. "Drawing the Line at Angels: Working the Ruins of Feminist Ethnography." *Working the Ruins: Feminist Poststructural Theory and Methods in Education*. Ed. Elizabeth A. St. Pierre and Wanda S. Pillow. New York: Routledge, 2000. 284–311.

Lemke, Jay L. *Textual Politics: Discourse and Social Dynamics*. London: Taylor and Francis, 1995.

Levy, Steven. *Hackers: Heroes of the Computer Revolution*. Garden City, NY: Anchor, 1984.

Marsot, al-Sayyid and Afaf Lutfi. *Women and Men in Late Eighteenth Century Egypt*. Austin: U of Texas P, 1995.

"Mission Statement." American University of Cairo. 26 Nov. 2003 <http:// www.aucegypt.edu/>.

"Mubarak, Muhammad Hosni Said." *ABCNews.com*. 2001. 14 Mar. 2003 <http:// abcnews.go.com/reference/bios/mubarak.html>.

Reinharz, Shulamit. *Feminist Methods in Social Research*. New York: Oxford UP, 1992.

Selfe, Cynthia L., and Gail E. Hawisher. *Literate Lives in the Information Age: Narratives of Literacy from the United States*. Mahwah, NJ: Erlbaum, 2004.

Spanning the Digital Divide: Understanding and Tackling the Issues. Bridges.org. May 2001. 4 March 2003 <http://www.bridges.org/spanning>.

Spender, Dale. *Nattering on the Net: Women, Power, and Cyberspace*. Melbourne: Spinifex, 1995.

Street, Brian V. *Social Literacies: Critical Approaches to Literacy in Development, Ethnography, and Education*. London: Longman, 1995.

Sullivan, Terry. "Anwar al-Sadat." *Camp David Accords: Framework for Peace*. 14 Mar. 2003 <http://www.ibiblio.org/sullivan/bios/Sadat-bio.html>.

Thomson, Paul. *The Voice of the Past: Oral History*. Oxford: Oxford UP, 1988.

Visweswaran, Kamala. *Fictions of Feminist Ethnography*. Minneapolis: U of Minnesota P, 1994.

The Emotional Effects of Literacy: Vietnamese Women Negotiating the Shift to a Market Economy

Ilene Whitney Crawford

In July 2002, I spent two weeks researching women's foreign language literacy practices in Vietnam, inspired by Deborah Brandt's encouragement to investigate how economies granting unequal access to opportunity and advancement impact different people's literacy practices over time (8). In her study of twentieth-century American literacy practices, *Literacy in American Lives*, Brandt shows that the evolution of capitalism powerfully informed the literacies Americans acquire and practice. I wanted to better understand how capitalism informs the acquisition and practice of literacies in contexts outside of the United States, and I specifically wanted to understand how the acquisition and practice of English literacies is related to capitalism's expansion. My friend and colleague Thuan Vu wanted to return to Vietnam to collect images to use in a series of paintings that examined his identity as a Vietnamese American. I saw a unique opportunity to collect literacy narratives from women that I would have no means of making contact with otherwise. Vietnam's 1986 *doi moi* reforms are transforming Vietnam from a socialist economy to a socialist market economy (Thi 93). In addition to liberalized laws allowing access to foreign trade and investment, this shift has prompted the growth of knowledge-based economies that require people who are highly literate in English (Summerfield 203; Wright 242). I wanted to meet women who, in Brandt's terms, felt compelled to acquire English literacies in this changing economy; I wanted to see whether or not these women were being granted equal access to new economic opportunities. Thuan and I felt that we could both better achieve our objectives by traveling together, so we co-authored a

Connecticut State University Research Grant, which funded our research. Because I am essentially monolingual, my ability to meet people while traveling abroad required a partner who spoke the language and knew the culture. Although my monolingualism served Thuan no purpose whatsoever, we found that our shared knowledge of critical race and postcolonial theories helped him to examine his experience of returning to Vietnam for the first time since his family left in 1975, as much as it helped me examine how I traveled and conducted research.

Thuan and members of his extended family served as translators, informants, and contacts, and were thus instrumental to my research. I owe a considerable debt to Thuan and other members of the Vu family who encouraged and supported my research, including Trieu Vu, Mr. and Mrs. Chuong Vu, and Khanh and Ngoc Vu. I conducted a dozen interviews during my two weeks in Vietnam. I met women through Thuan and Khan Vu's extended family and through my own canvassing of shops and markets in Ho Chi Minh City. The women I interviewed all lived in Ho Chi Minh City and ranged in age from their late teens to their seventies, with most women in their teens and twenties. Their level of education ranged from ninth grade to master's degree level. I interviewed each woman one or two times. Interviews ranged from twenty minutes to two hours. The longer interviews were conducted in English. Several shorter interviews were conducted in Vietnamese with Thuan Vu or Khan Vu serving as translators. I have continued a series of e-mail interviews with four women since I returned; the interviews with Thuy Nga and Hoang Thi Kieu Trang in particular have been extensive. In addition, I conducted six interviews with Vietnamese immigrants living in Vietnamese communities in California and Connecticut in the weeks immediately preceding and following my trip to Vietnam. One of these, Hoang Thi Kieu Trang, has been especially helpful reading early versions of this chapter and correcting my many overgeneralizations.

In my small research sample, I found that different literacy sponsors are granting different Vietnamese women very different access to Vietnam's changing economy. Brandt defines literacy sponsors as "any agents, local or distant, concrete or abstract, who enable, support, teach, and model, as well as recruit, regulate, suppress, or withhold literacy—and gain advantage by it in some way" (19). In short, the kinds of reading and writing we do are always in the interest of someone or something, be it employers, nations, or economies. I found that material constraints rendered some institutional literacy sponsors ineffective in Vietnam. Some women with whom I spoke were able to supplement these less effective sponsors with more effective sponsors they secured for themselves. Those who were able to secure more effective literacy sponsors were better able to participate in these new economies. The women with whom

I spoke also provided evidence that the shift to capitalism is in part an emotional shift, but in some ways the new emotional stances required to "buy into" capitalism complement the emotional stances and investments Vietnamese citizens are already encouraged to have.

FINDING LITERACY SPONSORS

In Vietnam, the state is an ambivalent sponsor of its citizens' foreign language literacies. Although hardly a story unique to Vietnam, written language has functioned as a Trojan horse, serving as a conduit for colonization and cultural transformation. Alexandre de Rhodes, a Jesuit priest in the 1600s, invented *quoc-ngu*, a roman alphabet with diacritical marks to signify the tonal features of spoken Vietnamese, an invention that facilitated the Church's efforts to convert people to Christianity (SarDesai). Religious conquest was followed by political, as *quoc-ngu* enabled the French to open Vietnam to new cultural influences, which eventually led to its colonization. Historically, the French education system was a similar conduit for the values and economic interests of French colonizers. While curricula in schools established for Vietnamese students had a "heavy emphasis on teaching the French language," Gail Kelly argues that these schools "oriented students not to the European world but rather to a redefined Vietnamese culture and society" (9). Students spent most of their time studying French and Vietnamese speaking, reading, listening, and writing. Textbooks, however, featured French-authored descriptions of Vietnamese culture, including the benefits of the French colonial presence (Kelly 11–14).

The colonial schools also spent significant time recommending traditional farming and village crafts as suitable occupations (Kelly 18). "Colonial educators agreed with politicians on the need to keep Vietnamese dependent on French rule," Kelly argues, which required a steady supply of unskilled manual labor to harvest rubber, coal, and other raw materials (19). Today, the state is anxious about the access Vietnamese citizens have to foreign news, opinion, and cultural influences, and its sponsorship of foreign language literacies is marked by its attempts to regulate the content of the languages studied. Access to satellite TV is heavily restricted, and Vietnam's two state-run channels feature Vietnamese sports, traditional arts, inspirational programs, and news with a pro-government perspective. The English textbooks and magazines I surveyed consistently featured readings about politically neutral news events and cultural phenomena (Kirn and Hartmann; Richards, Tran, and Nguyen; Rogerson, Gilbert, and Le; Oshima, Hogue, and Le; *Sunflower*).

Schools provide foreign language instruction but their effectiveness is constrained by challenging material conditions. Vietnamese students rarely work with native-speaking teachers. Foreign language instruction consists of small amounts of reading, writing, and translation. Students often recite vocabulary or sentences written on the board during class and translate sentences for homework. There is very little, if any, conversation practice (Thuy and Hoang, 12 July 2002 interviews; Nguyen Uyen; Kim). The material constraints of Vietnam's education system make alternative pedagogies unlikely. Vietnam's schools are underfunded, crowded, lacking basic materials. Large classes without enough books or native-speaking teachers can do little more than translation exercises. Adult education classes face similar constraints; in addition, they cost around $20 a month, which is an enormous expense (Huynh; Thuy, 12 July 2002; Nguyen Thoi; Kim).

The few women who go on to university can make foreign language study a significant part of their work, but do not find it much easier to get access to native speakers or better materials. At the Natural Science University of Ho Chi Minh City, for example, Hoang Thi Kieu Trang says her university suffers from the same lack of access to texts. While she has access to Internet sites that publish current research in high energy physics and nuclear physics, she does not have access to current issues of the most well-known journals, saying "it's ... difficult to find and collect completely and continuously papers on a subject that I am researching. In this case I usually use the online databases of the university libraries or borrow from professors" (Hoang, 26 Nov. 2002 e-mail). But, she says, "a problem happening with the Internet is it takes so much money and time (because of the low download rate here)" (21 Oct. 2002 e-mail).

Thuy Nga, a translator and secretary for a telecommunications company in Ho Chi Minh City, says her university experience was also marked by a lack of access to materials. An economics major who also studied Japanese for four years, Thuy found it difficult to practice reading and writing Japanese because Japanese–Vietnamese dictionaries with Japanese kanji are very rare. Japanese–Vietnamese dictionaries render Japanese in the kana alphabets, which show the pronunciation, but not the meaning that the kanji characters show. She had a photocopied Japanese–English dictionary she used as a university student like her fellow students did, and a Vietnamese–English dictionary. As she read and practiced her Japanese, it was a two-step relay to do any translation (Thuy 14 Aug. 2002 e-mail). Like her experiences in English, her studies focused on reading, writing, and translation exercises, with minimal conversation and no opportunities to work with a native Japanese speaker.

The difficulty institutional sponsors like schools have had in delivering access to native speakers of foreign languages has prompted all of the women with whom I spoke to attempt to find their own sponsors by devising strategies to gain better access to native speakers. For these women, live and recorded models for conversation and pronunciation, such as tourists and DVDs, and access to computers and the Internet functioned as more effective literacy sponsors than their access to public schools did.

For women living in Ho Chi Minh City, Ben Thanh market represents an opportunity to make contact with native speakers of English. The market, located within walking district of the major tourist hotels, is a popular site for tourists. Several women told me that they visited the market with the express purpose of finding people with whom to practice English conversation (Nguyen Uyen; Huynh; Le). I visited the market several times myself while I was in Ho Chi Minh City, both to shop and to meet merchants interested in being interviewed about their literacy practices. On each occasion, in addition to merchants using English to encourage me to buy their products, women approached me to exchange basic greetings and questions in English, or to show me short messages they had written.

Many of the women with whom I spoke owned a few English books and magazines, although they said that it was difficult to find time to read and that books and magazines were very expensive (Hoang; Thuy; Cong; Le). Pirated American movies, however, are readily available and relatively cheap compared to books or magazines; these were cited over and over by the women with whom I spoke as their primary means of practicing English comprehension and pronunciation and idioms (Thuy and Hoang 12 July interviews; Le; Kim). Each household's television is the center of family and nightlife; other entertainment options are too expensive (Thuy and Hoang 12 July interviews). Women cited action (*The Matrix, Gladiator*) and romance (*Titanic, Moulin Rouge*) as examples of their preferred genres and current favorites.

E-mail communication is also an important way for women to gain access to native speakers. Brandt reminds us that "access to computer technology" represents a "new ground of literacy development" that can be read to "bring deeper insight into configurations of inequity and class stratification" (181). None of the women with whom I spoke owned a personal computer, but Thuy and Hoang, unlike most women, have access to computers through work and school. Major cities like Ho Chi Minh City and Hanoi have hundreds of Internet cafes that charge around $0.40 an hour for access. I have been able to continue my interviews and correspondence with Hoang and Thuy over e-mail, and this has been instrumental to my own work on this project. In turn, they both believe that communicating in English with a native speaker helps them improve their written English. Women do not have widespread access to computers, though. Thuy tutors a high school girl whom I have attempted to correspond with by letter; the very slow pace of the mail and the expense of postage, however, have proven to be insurmountable constraints. Without access to a computer, it is all the more difficult for women to make and sustain contact with English speakers.

STRUCTURES OF FEELING

How do Vietnamese women entering this emerging knowledge-based economy feel about acquiring English literacies? Emotions, as Donna Strickland argues in this volume, serve as powerful sponsors of literacy. The "supposedly 'private' instances of our feelings," Megan Boler reminds us, *pace* Foucault, "[are] experiences in which economic power and dominant culture are deeply invested" (21). I began this project already interested in the connections between emotion and literacy, specifically in the similar ways in which our emotional performances and our literacy practices are means by which we take our place in the world as gendered, raced, and classed subjects. As I have argued elsewhere, the ways in which we read and write are in essence ontological actions—expressions of the feelings we have been taught to have about which kinds of human subjectivity are valuable (Crawford; Strickland and Crawford). Since our emotions are schooled performances, they can often serve to align us with a dominant culture's values and beliefs (Jaggar 152, Worsham 216). Raymond Williams describes these "meanings and values … actively lived and felt" by a generation as "structures of feeling" (132). My e-mail conversations with Hoang Thi Kieu Trang and Thuy Nga after I returned and my research in Vietnamese history have shown me that in some instances acquiring English literacies requires structures of feeling that indeed complement dominant Vietnamese cultural literacies. Cultural literacies include the ways individuals are taught to read and write themselves in relation to the group. In postcolonial Vietnam, for example, schools teach cultural literacies that create a world in which "national time, collective space, the notion of a big family of nation, patriotism, and work ethics [are] of prime importance" (Vasavakul 243). Hoang, for example, believes that her English literacies complement her efforts to be a good Vietnamese citizen, and her feelings about doing work in English are very positive. Thuy also feels that her English literacies complement her efforts to be a good Vietnamese citizen, but overall, she feels more ambivalent about her English literacies because they compete with the Japanese literacies she is more personally invested in acquiring.

A PhD student in physics at the Natural Science University of Ho Chi Minh City, Hoang Thi Kieu Trang needs highly specialized English literacies to read textbooks and journals, attend conferences, lecture to her advanced students, and produce her own scholarship (21 Oct. 2002 e-mail). Hoang also teaches at the Institute of Physics of Ho

Chi Minh City, where she expects her junior and senior students to read some course materials and receive some lectures in English. Seniors do frequent reading skills exercises to prepare them to write their undergraduate theses. "In my point of view," she says, "they should get ready for further studying and research encircled by English" (21 Oct. 2002 e-mail). Hoang believes that Vietnam is still in the process of making up for the isolation and intellectual losses it suffered from 1975–1980 when many South Vietnamese were expelled from their university posts. She feels strongly that she has a responsibility to use English to better herself as a person, her chosen field of Physics, and the nation of Vietnam.

Thuy Nga does not derive the same sense of satisfaction or identity from her foreign language literacy practices. Thuy's story illustrates Brandt's argument that "literacy takes its shape from the interests of its sponsors .... Obligations toward one's sponsors run deep, affecting what, when, why, and how people write and read" (20). Consequently, "the literacy that people practice is not the literacy they necessarily wish to practice" (8). Thuy is frustrated by the fact that although she majored in economics and studied Japanese for four years at university, she works for a company that sells telecommunications services, such as mobile phone access. She says it is a common problem for university graduates to end up with jobs outside of their fields, since many people get their jobs through family connections, as she got hers. Her parents advised her to pursue Japanese and economics to improve her "marketability" and she followed their advice (Thuy 12 July 2002 interview). A degree in these subjects gave her the currency to compete in the white collar job market, but no guarantee that she would actually use the literacies and knowledge the degree certifies.

The literacies Thuy Nga is acquiring in her workplace represent what Brandt would call a "literacy opportunity" (7) for her, but are in great conflict with the foreign language literacies she wants to practice, since she remains interested in improving her Japanese. Her literacy is an economic resource, one she is acquiring for the "opportunities and protections it potentially grants its seekers" (Brandt 5). However, she feels a great deal of "regret" about the erosion of her Japanese literacies and ambivalence about the kind of specialized English literacies in the field of telecommunications she is now compelled to acquire (12 July 2002 interview).

Nonetheless producing correct English and teaching others to produce correct English is something she takes great pride in. Thuy also tutors three high school students in English. She has been hired by the students' families to help them prepare for the university entrance exam, which emphasizes grammar and usage (8 Oct. 2002 e-mail). "So," she says,

I often focus on the basic grammar points in their text books and after that I explain more, relating knowledge outside their textbooks. For example, when they learn 'relative clause' in their text books, they just know that 'which' can replace a ... noun, that's all. I will teach them the sentences in which 'which' can be used for replacing a [noun] .... Sometime[s] I teach them new reading texts so that they can learn more vocabularies. Generally, it takes me a lot of time to prepare for teaching. (8 Oct. 2002 e-mail)

She feels that the two boys she tutors are "lazy," while she praises Vy, who wrote to me, as a hard worker (25 Oct. 2002 e-mail). While it is time-consuming, Thuy feels that it benefits her work life because "it is also the way I review and consolidate my English grammar" (22 Sept. 2002 e-mail). Reading, writing, and the process of translation are her comfort zones in both English and Japanese.

Listening and speaking, on the other hand, are practices that frustrate Thuy a great deal (12 July 2002 interview). In the fall of 2002, Thuy was asked to attend the Vietnam Information and Telecommunications Exhibition as her company's representative. In preparation for the exhibition, she enrolled in the evening English classes but felt frustrated by the lack of emphasis on conversation when, she believed, she would need to speak in English about her company's services. The highly specialized language of the telecommunications industry is also something she must learn, and she resents the amount of free time it takes to read material she takes home from work. Not invested in the industry, Thuy would rather have a job related to economics, or at least in international business, where she can resurrect her Japanese (12 July 2002 interview). In later e-mails, she qualified her ambivalence about the English literacies she feels compelled to perform, saying that while from elementary school to her adult working life English has been compulsory, English "has been a useful and necessary skill for me" (28 Aug. 2002 e-mail).

The women with whom I spoke are quite aware that they are working to acquire foreign language literacies in far less than ideal conditions. They realize that their lack of access to native speaking teachers puts them at a severe disadvantage. However, they all express the sentiment that this simply means that in order to achieve their goals, they will have to work harder than those with more advantages (Hoang; Thuy; Le). In addition, they all believe that studying English will result in economic advancement (Nguyen Thoi; Hyunh; Thuy). Whether these ideas were expressed for my benefit or because they "really" believe them seems almost beside the point. Their consistent expression of these beliefs indicates to me that these women have been encouraged to take these ideas as axiomatic.

I am struck by the emotional stances embedded in these women's literacy practices because those emotions seemed so familiar: by doing the kind of reading and writing that they do, Hoang and Thuy feel they are independent subjects, able to determine their place in the world, undeterred by material constraints, qualified to teach others, becoming better people—not because education makes one a better person (although they believe this, too), but because they show themselves to be hardworking, and not lazy.

Such sentiment in the face of overwhelming material constraints raises questions about the emotional schooling required to engender and support such beliefs. Describing the history of literacy instruction in the United States, J. Elspeth Stuckey argues that the lie of literacy is that all literacy instruction is equal, when mechanisms such as standardized school tests and the literacy program curricula put economically disadvantaged people through endless "grinding" steps of reading and writing that amount to "social exploitation" without any chance of success (102). Stuckey's descriptions bear a striking resemblance to the foreign language pedagogies most of the women with whom I spoke experienced. Yet these women also expressed feelings of faith in their ultimate success. Stuckey would argue that this faith is evidence of the "lie" of literacy—that these foreign language literacies can provide equal access to an information economy, when in fact the poor, among others, are not taught the specific literacy practices that give access to that economy (118, 122). Donaldo Macedo and Henry Giroux similarly problematize literacy initiatives in poor and immigrant communities in the United States as well as in the Third World on the grounds that such literacy programs "reduce the concept of literacy and the pedagogy in which it is situated to the pragmatic requirements of capital" thus preventing literacy's role in creating critical consciousness (Giroux qtd. in Macedo 18).

What can the emotions embedded in the Vietnamese women's literacy practices reveal, then, about the consequences of their country's shift to a market economy? These women's accounts of their attempts to acquire foreign language literacies are poignant because it is the exception, rather than the rule, for the reading and writing rituals that they practice in schools, in the universities, in adult education classes, and in private to add up to high levels of literacy in foreign languages. But regardless of whether they were likely to achieve a high level of foreign language literacy, the women with whom I spoke consistently said they believed that their hard work would result in economic advancement. They were all using a similar emotion to negotiate their changing economic context: faith. Faith underwrites the schoolwork, the money invested in night classes, the viewing of pirated copies of American movies, and the individual efforts to practice reading and writing for a few minutes in between customers, on break, or in the evenings. Their faith makes them sure that their hard work will result in economic advancement despite the many material constraints they encounter. Their literacy practices might be collectively treated as structures of feeling, the way in which they live and feel their faith in themselves as hard-working, not lazy, individuals and therefore worthy of material rewards. This is the promise of literacy instruction in a late capitalist context, a promise which may elicit the faith of Vietnamese women because it already complements beliefs they hold about the value of hard work and national advancement.

I regard this faith with mixed feelings. It is easy for me to think that many of the women with whom I spoke are naïve, that they face far too many obstacles to realistically think that they will become literate enough in English or Japanese or Chinese to operate their own international business profitably, or secure a well-paying office job. It is also easy for me, firmly ensconced in a full-blown consumerist economy, to warn of the crippling "waning of affect" that accompanies late capitalist life (Jameson 10). But their faith is also familiar to me, because it is so similar to the faith for which I have been rewarded. Who am I to discourage this faith in women who live in a country of grinding poverty and few options? Wasn't I born late enough in the twentieth century to receive and benefit from literacy instruction that gave me significantly more options than, say, women in my grandmother's generation? Can I really claim that disaffectation and alienation are the sum total of my late capitalist existence? Of course not.

Thuy's feelings of frustration, regret, and irritation are evidence that capitalism cannot completely deliver on its promises. But Thuy and Hoang's experiences are also evidence of the fact that it is possible for women with some access to technology and education to assemble reasonably effective literacy sponsors for certain highly specialized academic or professional literacies. This is no small feat in a country still decimated by histories of colonialism and war and a country where gendered expectations of women constrain their working lives. Literacy does, in fact, truly function as resource, raw material, and currency for Hoang and Thuy (Brandt 188). Their role as knowledge workers in their economy confers material and symbolic benefits upon them. I am convinced that the structures of feeling their literacy practices represent provide a useful barometer for gauging the effects of advanced capitalism, in that the subjectivity that results is taking on the shape required of a successful consumerist subject. I am not sure, however, that I can read their stories only as evidence that capitalism's expansion has proved harmful. Terry Eagleton cautions us against making the "'culturalist' error of taking television, supermarket, 'life style,' and advertising as *definitive* of the late capitalist experience" (39). To make the case that "advanced capitalism expunges all traces of 'deep' subjectivity ... is not so much false as drastically partial" (38). Eagleton is posing a direct challenge to Jameson's version of late capitalism, arguing that in many ways subjects inhabiting these economies seek out and make meaning in their lives, rather than caving in to a "waning of affect": the same people who "watch television and shop in supermarkets," Eagleton argues, also participate in activities such as "studying the bible, running a rape crisis centre, joining the territorial army and teaching one's children to speak Welsh" (39). In short, he argues, "advanced capitalism ... oscillates between meaning and non-meaning, pitched from moralism to cynicism and plagued by the embarrassing discrepancy between the two" (Eagleton 39).

Without embarrassment, I want to retain two ways of looking at the structures of feeling I saw in the Vietnamese women with whom I spoke, then. First, looking more cynically at these structures of feeling, I want to keep in mind Brandt's discovery that in the case of the twentieth-century United States, the increasing alignment of literacy practices with capitalist expansion left an increasing number of people behind (189). This is a very real danger in Vietnam as well—even the small sample of women with whom I spoke suggests that, despite Vietnam's recent socialist history, a growing gulf between haves and have nots is developing. Their literacy practices, and the emotional stances embedded in them, can serve to deepen this gulf. But second, reading these structures of feeling morally, I want to look to Hoang's and Thuy's roles as literacy sponsors themselves as evidence of how those same emotional stances can enable women to "lift as they climb." They are practicing an ethic of care similar to that practiced by members of the National Association of Colored Women, who felt bound to sponsor other African American women's literacy acquisition. Hoang's and Thuy's lives reflect what Eagleton calls "deep" subjectivity because they in fact lift as they climb—Hoang in her work as a university instructor of Physics, and Thuy in her work as an English tutor for high school students. As teachers, they work to sponsor other students' literacies and make economic advancement possible for them. Thuy's and Hoang's faith in themselves and their nation, which we see both motivating and supporting their literacy practices, cannot easily be categorized as naïve or transgressive, but as "both-and" efforts to negotiate their shifting economic contexts.

WORKS CITED

Boler, Megan. *Feeling Power: Emotions and Education.* New York: Routledge, 1999.

Brandt, Deborah. *Literacy in American Lives.* New York: Cambridge UP, 2001.

Crawford, Ilene. "Building a Theory of Affect in Cultural Studies Composition Pedagogy." *JAC* 22 (2002): 678–83.

Cong, Thanh Diep. Personal Interview. 14 July 2002.

Dung, Kim. Personal interview. 10 July 2002. Thuan Vu, interpreter.

Eagleton, Terry. *Ideology: An Introduction*. London: Verso, 1991.

Hoa, Tran Thi. "Worker's Education: Vocational and Technical Education for Women in Vietnam." *Negotiating and Creating Spaces of Power: Women's Education Practices Amidst Crisis*. UIE Studies 7. Ed. Carolyn Medel-Anonuevo. Hamburg: UNESCO Institute for Education, 1997. 61–64.

Hoang, Trang Thi Kieu. Personal interview. 10 July 2002.

——. Personal interview. 12 July 2002.

——. E-mail. 21 Oct. 2002.

——. E-mail. 26 Nov. 2002.

Huynh, Kim Phung. Personal interview. Khanh Vu, interpreter. 10 July 2002.

Jaggar, Alison M. "Love and Knowledge: Emotion in Feminist Epistemology." *Gender/Body/Knowledge: Feminist Reconstructions of Being and Knowing*. Ed. Alison M. Jaggar and Susan R. Bordo. New Brunswick: Rutgers UP, 1989. 145–71.

Jameson, Fredric. *Postmodernism, or, The Cultural Logic of Late Capitalism*. Durham, NC: Duke UP, 1991.

Kelly, Gail Paradise. *French Colonial Education: Essays on Vietnam and West Africa*. Ed. David H. Kelly. New York: AMS P, 2000.

Kirn, Elaine, and Pamela Hartmann. *Interactions Two: A Reading Skills Book*. 3rd ed. Ho Chi Minh City: Nha Xuat Ban Thong Ke, 2000.

Le, Yen Pham Hoang. Personal interview. 14 July 2002.

Macedo, Donaldo. *Literacies of Power: What Americans are Not Allowed to Know*. Boulder: Westview, 1994.

Nguyen Huu Thoi. Personal interview. 9 July 2002.

Nguyen Uyen. Personal Interview. 20 Dec. 2002.

Oshima, Alice, Ann Hogue, and Le Huy Lam. *Writing Academic English*. 3rd ed. Ho Chi Minh City: Nha Xuat Ban Thanh Pho Ho Chi Minh, 2002.

Richards, Jack C., Tran Van Anh, and Nguyen Thanh Yen. *Listen Carefully*. Ho Chi Minh City: Nha Xuat Ban Tre, 1997.

Rogerson, Pamela, Judy B. Gilbert, and Le Huy Lam. *Speaking Clearly: Pronunciation and Listening Comprehension for Learners of English*. Ho Chi Minh City: Nha Xuat Ban Thanh Pho Ho Chi Minh, 1997.

SarDesai, D. R. *Vietnam: Past and Present*. 3rd ed. Boulder: Westview, 1998.

Strickland, Donna, and Ilene Crawford. "Error and Racialized Performances of Emotion in the Teaching of Writing." *A Way to Move: Rhetorics of Emotion and Composition Studies*. Ed. Dale Jacobs and Laura R. Micciche. Portsmouth, NH: Boynton/Cook-Heinemann, 2003. 67–79.

Stuckey, J. Eslpeth. *The Violence of Literacy*. Portsmouth, NH: Boynton/Cook, 1991.

Sunflower 106. Ho Chi Minh City: Nha Xuat Ban Dong Nai, 2002.

Thi Le. "Rural Women and National Renovation Process in Vietnam." *Asia-Pacific Journal of Rural Development* 5.1 (1995): 93–102.

Thuy Nga. Personal interview. 12 July 2002.

——. E-mail. 14 Aug. 2002.

——. E-mail. 28 Aug. 2002.

——. E-mail. 22 Sept. 2002.

——. E-mail. 8 Oct. 2002.

——. E-mail. 25 Oct. 2002.

——. E-mail. 9 Dec. 2002.

Vasavaskul, Thaveeporn. "Managing the Young Anarchists: Kindergartens and National Culture in Postcolonial Vietnam." *Kindergartens and Cultures: The Global Diffusion of an Idea.* Ed. Roberta Wollons. New Haven: Yale UP, 2000. 214–50.

Williams, Raymond. *Marxism and Literature.* New York: Oxford UP, 1977.

Worsham, Lynn. "Going Postal: Pedagogic Violence and the Schooling of Emotion." *JAC* 18 (1998): 213–41.

Wright, Sue. "Language Education and Foreign Relations in Vietnam." *Language Policies in Education: Critical Issues.* Ed. James W. Tollefson. Mahwah, NJ: Erlbaum, 2002. 225–44.

13

Post-Apartheid Literacies: South African Women's Poetry of Orality, Franchise, and Reconciliation

Mary K. DeShazer

Political poetry provided an important form of communal and aesthetic resistance during the apartheid era in South Africa (1948–1994) by challenging the racist domination of indigenous African people, who comprised 87% of the population, by European colonial settlers, who comprised 13%. Motivated by the belief that "culture is a weapon of struggle," anti-apartheid poets of the 1950s–1980s often addressed in polemical terms such themes as colonization, land rights, geographic and cultural dislocation, and state-sponsored violence (Sachs 19). During the 1990s, however, many politically engaged poets and critics interrogated certain apartheid-era poems for their "ungainly platitudes" and "sloganizing," even as they critiqued the sterile aestheticism of a rigidly Eurocentric poetic tradition (Stent 74). In her essay "Standing in the Doorway," the poet Ingrid de Kok explores the viability of a "post-apartheid imagination" that would offer "resistance to cultural amnesia." This new imaginary must "unwrite, retell, and organize the nature of the record," she argues; writers and artists who chart "the contours of the post-apartheid literary enterprise" should enter fiercely into debates over competing cultural genealogies (5–6). In addition, de Kok joins Dorothy Driver, Mazisi Kunene, Isabel Hofmeyr and other literary scholars in urging consideration of how issues of gender, race, class, and postcoloniality intersect in South Africa's multilingual poetry.

Gender figures prominently in any post-apartheid imaginary, because women's voices, especially those of black women, have emerged in contemporary South Africa as an important source of postcolonial agency. Analyzing new discursive formations in black women's writing, Driver has claimed that they "represent the act of writing as a place of thinking, sometimes also dreaming, a realm in which they might locate or create new selves away from the 'camouflage of coherence,' the political order which stereotypes them in another's eyes" (47). Certainly, black and white women's poems contributed significantly to the anti-apartheid movement; as I argued in my 1994 study of dissident poetry by South African women, many writers of the 1980s and early 1990s, from domestic workers to academics to comrades-in-arms, developed a distinctive "poetics of resistance" to challenge the pernicious racism of the apartheid state (DeShazer 133–231). Many poets continue to address poverty, violence, land reform, health care, and the right to literacy—a particularly vexed topic in a country in which 65 percent of rural women cannot read or write (Cock and Bernstein 168).

As a U.S. feminist scholar of South African poetry, I am interested in charting the contributions of women poets to the shifting terrain of the post-apartheid imagination through what I have termed "post-apartheid literacy narratives." To develop this concept I have drawn upon definitions of literacy offered by Paolo Freire and Ann Berthoff. In *Pedagogy of the Oppressed* and in *Literacy*, Freire establishes that the acquisition of literacy can contribute to the initiation of a "critical consciousness" through which an act of "reading the word" simultaneously involves "reading the world"; widespread illiteracy is thus a political challenge that "education as a pedagogy of knowing" can help to address (*Pedagogy* 66–67). As Berthoff explains, "authentic literacy" necessitates not only "the mastery of a code" but also "the making of meaning"; thus she usefully defines literacy as "the realized capacity to construct and construe in graphic form representations of our recognitions" (140–41). Freire and Berthoff agree, then, that "naming the world becomes a model for changing the world" (Berthoff 121). For many South Africans struggling to inaugurate a fully democratic post-apartheid nation—and especially for black women, once doubly disenfranchised—the representation of emergent political recognitions in graphic form becomes a vital act of literate agency. When women inscribe their experiences of life in the new South Africa through the lenses of race, gender, and transformed national identities, they engage in post-apartheid literacy narratives. For many women, these literate inscriptions have taken poetic form—for as the African American political poet Audre Lorde reminds us, "poetry is not a luxury. It is a vital necessity of our existence. It forms the quality of light within which we predicate our hopes and dreams toward survival and change, first made into language, then into idea, then into more tangible action" (37).

From interviews that I conducted with more than fifty South African poets in 1992, 1996, and 2003, and from close analysis of their writing, I have identified three key types of poems in which contemporary women inscribe their post-apartheid literacies: *oral poetry, franchise poetry,* and *poetry of reconciliation.* Each category of post-apartheid literacy narratives serves as a vibrant postcolonial act of aesthetic intervention. Taken together, these poems offer what Jacqueline Jones Royster has called a "thick description" of women's literate practices by providing rhetorical, historical, and ideological perspectives on gendered subjectivities in the new South Africa (9). Indeed, their writing reveals that the poets and essayists considered in this chapter engage in literate practices as acts of survival and cultural affirmation. What Royster has claimed for African American women rhetors also holds true for South African women: They "write kaleidoscopically," revealing the historical contexts of their literacy production, the complex formation of a postcolonial ethos (both situated and invented), and the power of rhetorical action to inform and persuade their listeners that change is possible (62–70). In this context, then, literacy indicates word-making, composing, and performing, not just writing in a European sense.

In the first category are oral poems, which have been composed and performed for centuries by black women and men across South Africa and in a variety of indigenous languages. Understanding the role of oral literatures is vital, for as Kunene explains, to most indigenous Africans the advent of written literature "violated one of the most important literary tenets by privatizing literature," whose value accrued by "being disseminated in communally organized contexts" (16). South African critics debate whether oral poetry represents a pre-colonial, "pure" African genre or whether this form has become today a cultural hybrid. In examining Zulu women's *izibongo,* or praise poetry, and Sotho women's *kiba,* or songs of migrancy, I emphasize their hybridity. Unlike men's *izibongo,* sung at public gatherings, women's *izibongo* are performed in private circle ceremonies. These poems use highly figurative language and naming rituals to celebrate authors' accomplishments, and they work collaboratively in that poets invite audience members to add lines, thus introducing "metacommentaries" on the texts. While performances of *izibongo* occur in rural areas, *kiba* are performed in cities as a way for performers and audiences to reconnect with their homelands. Originally danced by pipe-playing male industrial workers during recreational competitions, *kiba* by migrant women today feature lyrics and dance but no musical instruments; their compositions typically chronicle geographic dislocation, critique oppressive authority, and assert female solidarity. Like *izibongo, kiba* are highly improvisational; composers revise the words of traditional songs to comment on current sociopolitical issues. Ultimately women's *izibongo* and *kiba* resist privatization and redefine conventional notions of *literacy* and *literature.*

The second category, *franchise poetry,* marks the pivotal year of 1994 as a moment of negotiated revolution, when blacks received the right to vote for the first time and a once-banned political organization, the African National Congress (ANC), became South Africa's governing party. Several women writers document this historic moment by celebrating the franchise, including Nadine Gordimer, Joan Baker, and Gcina Mhlophe. In her commentary on the 1994 election Gordimer muses that "until this day there was always the unseen difference between us, far more decisive than the different colours of our skins: some of us had ... the mark of citizenship, and others did not. But today we stood on new ground" (51). In her poem "Home," Baker explores racial difference via her location as a visitor to Cape Town's landmark Paarl Rock, whose "white side" she infiltrates (Congress 177). Mhlophe code-switches from English to Zulu in her franchise poems, thereby celebrating an indigenous "song of Africa" while honoring her country's multilingualism (the new Constitution recognizes eleven official languages) (86). These writers claim a post-apartheid space of representation that interweaves oral and written literacies.

The third category, *poetry of reconciliation,* has emerged from the broadcast hearings of South Africa's Truth and Reconciliation Commission (TRC), convened from 1996 to 1998 to hear testimonies from thousands of citizens, mostly black, whose rights were violated and loved ones killed during the apartheid era. These proceedings had an enormous impact on the psyche and the art of two prominent white women poets, Ingrid de Kok and Antjie Krog. In her poems about the Commission, de Kok explores the moral ambivalence as well as the emotional power of the hearings. The murkiness of competing truths and multiple accounts also provides subject matter for Krog, who as an Afrikaner, a poet, and a journalist covering the proceedings struggles with an ethical dilemma. "No poetry should come forth from this," she initially declares in her memoir, *Country of My Skull,* yet finally she deems it essential to seek forgiveness in poetry (364–65). Black women have also chronicled the TRC hearings, most recently Pumla Gobodo-Madikizela, whose memoir *A Human Being Died That Night* recounts the emotional and political fallout of the testimonies from her perspective as a psychologist who was raised in the townships and as a commissioner at the hearings. Ultimately, these writers inscribe a postcolonial poetics of redemption and inaugurate new forms of post-apartheid literacy narratives.

POETRY OF ORALITY: "THE PEPPER IS WORDS THAT STAB"

Oral literatures are being revalued in the new South Africa, as cultural critics examine the intersections and hybrid nature of indigenous and postcolonial literary forms. As de Kok has noted, in the "connective tissue" of South African literature, "exile speaks to home, margins to centre, local indigenized forms to international discourses" (5). In other contexts and eras, indigenization has been viewed in binary terms; Ngugi wa Thiong'o, for example, claimed in 1973 that African people should "create their own songs, poems, dances, literature, which embody a structure of values dialectically opposed to those of the ruling classes of the oppressing race and nation" (27). As Karen Press has argued, however, indigenous cultural production has rarely remained intact; rather, it has been both mobile and capable of mobilization during times of crisis (28–30). Hofmeyr concurs that oral literatures should not be consigned to "a monolithic and undifferentiated time and space" but rather seen as circulating beside, transforming, and being transformed by other literary forms at varied historical moments (91). Both South African women's praise poems, or *izibongo,* and their songs of migration, or *kiba,* illustrate well the fluid and elliptical qualities of contemporary orature.

For readers who do not speak or understand indigenous African languages, myself included, issues of translation arise in any analysis of women's oral poems. Two cultural anthropologists, Elizabeth Gunner and Deborah James, have watched the performances of women's *izibongo* and *kiba* and then collected and translated those poems, Gunner in KwaZulu-Natal and James in the Northern Transvaal. In my analysis I draw upon their insights and translations. Zulu and Sotho poetry is available to most U.S. literary critics through the studies of such scholars; we, in turn, place our trust in a mediator's interpretations. On another level, however, all of South African literary production and distribution involves complex acts of translation. As Stephen Gray has noted, disseminating writing in South Africa has long required linguistic and racial boundary crossings, acts of "carrying information across one or another socioeconomic barrier, literally of 'trading'" (20–21). Leon de Kock agrees that South African literature "has seldom been regarded in its totality as an integrated field," yet he rightly acknowledges that written texts, especially those in English or Afrikaans, have held center stage; for centuries, colonial policies "relegated African-language literature to a lesser status and deprived it of primacy in the cultural and educational domains" (267). Moreover, while many South African critics have devalued indigenous literature by men, some have ignored women's orature altogether. These historical realities underscore the value of Gunner's and James' scholarship, with its emphases on oral poetry, gendered hybridities, and black women's cultural production.

Gunner's analyses of *izibongo* identify various approaches to homage and complaint that women have devised. Traditionally performed by Zulu male *izimbongo* (bards) as a ritualized homage to war, *izibongo* have been adapted as celebrations of female subjectivity. In addition to their praising capacity, these poems sometimes lodge complaints and help to resolve conflicts between the poet and her husband, his parents, or other women. This poetry resists appropriation by Zulu men, who as public bards determine the stylized, formal nature of their own *izibongo* but who lack access to women's recitations. However, women's *izibongo* invite appropriation by female members of the audience, who may revise passages in serious, ironic, or bawdy ways during recitation.

Izibongo often begin with an opening formula or question; the poems then rely on a series of linking progressions. Consider, for example, this poem attributed to MaCele of Zenzele:

> What is it smelling at Zenzele?
> The pepper is smelling.
> The pepper is words that stab.
> They carry spears and arrows,
> They stab the husband's heart.
> And they stab at the in-laws' home as well. (Gunner 18)

As Gunner points out, lines 1–2 are linked by the motif of unpleasant smell, lines 2–3 by the metaphor of pepper, and lines 3–6 by the image of stabbing, directed first at the husband's heart and then at the dwelling of his intrusive parents. She also asserts that during performance such a complaint would be viewed not as an insult but as an invitation to restore healthy relationships (18). Considering the poem as a literacy narrative, we see that the *izimbongi* addresses not only family politics but also her politics of location as a wordsmith. Indeed, she valorizes her literate practice as a promulgator of words that wound as intensely as do the presumed offenses of her husband and his parents. This poetic agency intersects with her domestic identity: she is a wronged wife and daughter-in-law and an experienced cook who recognizes bitter pepper when she smells it. By flinging pepper/words in retaliation, she becomes an agent of familial change. Furthermore, the poet assumes a traditionally male-defined role as a warrior who brandishes weapons/ words effectively; she speaks not only for herself but also for other abused women.

Migrant Sotho women's *kiba* likewise reveal how literate practices can contribute to social critique. Like *izibongo, kiba* revise a traditionally male idiom, adapting it to challenge sexist behavior and claim women's rights. Most migrant women poets are domestic workers; in search of paid employment, they typically move from the countryside, where they earned a scant living farming or brewing beer. Unlike *izibongo*, however, *kiba* are performed in public spaces for audiences of men as well as women; these performances thus raise community awareness of migrants' travails. *Kiba* also invite audience participation: "as with other 'emergent' genres, the audience interprets the lyrics' significance, and even constructs the song anew at different performances through their differing interpretations" (James 99). As a fluid genre, therefore, *kiba* foreground the literacies and economic issues of rural women in search of urban identities.

An example of *kiba* by Paulina Mphoka revises the lyrics of popular Sotho composer Johannes Mokgwadi, whose original song addressed police surveillance of a prisoner named Tsodio, who killed his uncle in a fit of rage and was subsequently haunted by the uncle's ghost. Although Mphoka's poem retains Mokgwadi's words in its five central lines, it also emphasizes the problem of police harassment of women:

> Woman who wears a skin, woman of beer
> She sells beer
> The police of Lebowa are looking for her.
> Tsodio is thin, he does not sleep
> He is troubled by [the ghost of] his uncle
> Who is called Matšhabataga
> Tsodio has killed Matšhabataga
> He is also troubled by police.
> Women have now joined the soldiers
> They are getting passes just like the men. (James 98)

As James points out, the enigmatic references to Lebowa (regional) police activity are clarified and intensified in the final two lines, which recall South African police brutality during the apartheid era, when black workers were forced to carry identification books that limited their movement; officers often beat and/or imprisoned those who failed to produce their passes upon request (98–99). By linking one woman's narrative of unfair scrutiny by police (lines 1–3)—scrutiny that occurs because she has sold home-brewed beer without a license—to that of the violent but repentant Tsodio (lines 4–8), Mphoka might be signaling her empathy toward a fellow transgressor. Or, as James suggests, Mphoka could wish to imply that beer-brewing women's "crimes" pale in comparison to those of murderous men (99). By linking the woman of beer's narrative to the experience of earlier black women who resisted apartheid (lines 9–10), Mphoka connects historical exigencies to contemporary migrant experience, recontextualizes the economic perils of African workers, and asserts female solidarity across generations.

Both *izibongo* and *kiba* reveal subversive potential as they hybridize traditional poetic forms and engage in literate practices for sociopolitical ends. In their capacity for recirculation in the post-apartheid era, these oral texts, now published in translation, are central to an emerging South African feminism that highlights black women's cultural production. As Cock and Bernstein have noted, during the anti-apartheid struggle feminism was often viewed as an elitist ideology that threatened to disrupt the solidarity of activist women and men and deny real differences between black and white women (138). Between 1993 and 1994, however, the Women's National Coalition—comprised of members from all major political parties—successfully canvassed more than seventy women's organizations to research what South African women identified as their most pressing needs and addressed them in a National Women's Charter. Feminism in the new South Africa thus embraces rural and migrant women as sources of counterhegemonic knowledge—knowledge to which the composers of *izibongo* and *kiba* contribute greatly.

POETRY OF FRANCHISE: "BUT NOW, WE HAVE CAST OUR VOTES"

For the past decade South Africans have witnessed a remarkable political transformation in which the multiracial ANC has twice been elected to govern and democratic values have prevailed. In their essays and poems about Election Day 1994 and the months preceding it, black and white women explore linguistic access and franchise as forms of empowerment. Their writings thus link African women's speech acts to cultural transformation.

Joan Baker's "Home" interrogates the oppressive insignia of Afrikaner nationalism and affirms her own identity as a racially mixed analyst of colonial history. "The shadows of the Paarl Rock / and the language monument" dominate the landscape of the Hawerquas mountains toward which she turns, perusing these landmarks to the Voortrekkers and the Afrikaans language from a perspective that the laws of apartheid long denied her: the "long forbidden white side," which "defies pen and paper imagery." As she transgresses boundaries, the speaker asserts her own resistant subjectivity. "I am the alien / stalking virgin paths / garnished with fallen petals," she insists, drawing strength from her status as "Other"; "I am a trespasser," a woman climbing trees "no child has climbed." Yet surely the "rich Cape soil" belongs to her, as it belonged to her ancestors. Baker ultimately unveils illicit words carved on walls in once segregated public places, words crying out to be heard as apartheid wanes:

> In the literature on the walls
> words come out of hiding
> tripping in their haste
> to spill on this page
> to tell of realities
> I am home.   (Congress 177)

A "pre-franchise" poem set during the time of transition to democratic rule, "Home" constitutes both an anti-apartheid treatise and a political literacy narrative. Indeed, Baker here transforms "the arias of our oral couplings / violence and death"—the disturbing music that blacks were forced to sing during the apartheid era—into her own stumbling, tumbling post-apartheid lyrics.

Other South African women have ruminated upon the significance of their country's first free election. In her commentary on the franchise Nadine Gordimer observes "a sense of silent bonding," as people of all races queue up to vote, many standing in line for hours. She finds especially moving the commitment to franchise by the nonliterate, who signed with an X: "The day has been captured for me by the men and women who couldn't read or write, but underwrote it, at last, with their kind of signature. May it be the seal on the end of illiteracy, of the pain of imposed ignorance, of the deprivation of the fullness of life" (51–52). Although Gordimer's concern for improving her country's literacy rates is valid, like many white writers of English, the global hegemonic language, she assumes that illiteracy equals ignorance (albeit it imposed). This assumption discounts the linguistic and rhetorical power of oral poets, who may lack writing skills but are hardly ignorant. Nonetheless, by celebrating the new democracy Gordimer, a Nobel laureate, brought international visibility to this historical moment. As she further notes, although desegregation of public places began several years before the election, until this day racial inequality remained enshrined. By making universal "the right that is the basis of all rights, the symbolic X, the sign of a touch on the controls of polity," South Africans "changed the base on which ... society was so long built" (52).

The emotional intensity that universal franchise evokes is apparent in Gcina Mhlophe's poems about the vote, in which she code-switches from a colonial language to an indigenous one that many "superliterate" South Africans cannot read. She thus reminds them, subversively, that they have much to learn. As O'Brien notes, Mhlophe "breaks out of English altogether" in her franchise poems (20). Her counterhegemonic practice is most evident in "A Vote for Unity," in which the speaker's excitement on election day is palpable: "But now, we have cast our votes / Looks like the waiting is over ... / If it were not for the song of Africa / That keeps blowing at the embers, / Reviving the flame of survival, where would we be?" Having posed this question in English, the poet pays homage in Xhosa to the leaders of her country's liberation:

O Sontonga, owaqhamuka entabeni ehlabelela
Ecela kuThixo uMdali
Nkosi sikelel' iAfrika ...
O Stephen Bantu Biko, iinto zoSobukwe
O Victoria Mxenge noDorah Damana ...

Iqhawe lamaqhawe uNelson Mandela
(O Sontonga, appearing on the mountain singing
begging the Lord
God bless Africa …
O Stephen Bantu Biko, child of Sobukwe
O Victoria Mxenge and Dora Damana …
Hero of heroes, Nelson Mandela).
                    (86–87, trans. O'Brien 20)

The men to whom Mhlophe alludes might well appear in any praise-
song: Sontonga, the black teacher in a Methodist mission school who
composed the new South Africa's national anthem, "Nkosi sikelel'
iAfrika," in 1897; Biko, the Black Consciousness advocate who was
murdered in prison in the 1980s by police agents; Mandela, the ANC
leader who after thirty years of political imprisonment became South
Africa's first black president and remains its international voice of con-
science. The women Mhlophe honors, however, have often disappeared
from historical annals. Mxenge was a lawyer and Black Consciousness
activist murdered by government forces during the anti-apartheid
struggle. Damana co-founded South Africa's Federation of Black
Women in the 1960s and was herself an oral poet of resistance (DeShazer
241–42). Mhlophe's litany offers a feminist perspective on the franchise,
as she claims rhetorical and historical space for black female activists.
Their legacies serve as literate touchstones in the new South Africa.

POETRY OF RECONCILIATION: "THIS COUNTRY … BREATHES BECALMED"

The hearings of South Africa's Truth and Reconciliation Commission
inaugurated a new epoch in the country's history, as victims and per-
petrators of crimes committed under apartheid came forward to seek
and offer explanation. Certainly the TRC hearings, broadcast by radio and television throughout the land, called forth complex emotional responses in all who listened or observed. In a memoir about
her experience at the TRC, Pumla Gobodo-Madikizela claims that the
language of testimony both *connects* listeners to trauma and allows
them to *detach*:

> Language communicates. At the same time it distances us from the trau-
> matic event as it was experienced, limiting our participation in the act of
> remembering. We cannot fully understand what victims went through, in
> part because the impact of the traumatic event cannot be adequately cap-
> tured in words. So what function does a victim's testimony serve if it only
> creates a gulf between language and experience? Is its function to force us
> to see the real story of a violent political past? (85–86)

Gobodo-Madikizela raises important questions about both the unreliable nature and the stark validity of traumatic memory. Her observations also shed light on how and why the TRC testimonies functioned as post-apartheid literacy narratives that awakened many South Africans to new expressions of outrage, grief, and remorse.

White South African poets have documented the TRC hearings in literacy narratives of their own; their poems agonize over contested truths and personal accountability even as they inscribe the possibilities of cultural and individual healing. For Ingrid de Kok the anguished narratives presented at the TRC raise the epistemological issue of whether "truth" is ever knowable. When witnesses' recollections conflict and victims' voices cannot be recovered, she muses in "At the Commission," what purpose can the evocation of past atrocities serve? "In the retelling / no one remembers / whether he was carrying a grenade / or if his pent-up body / exploded on contact with / horrors to come." Traumatic memories often defy factual analysis, de Kok suggests; she agrees with Gobodo-Madikizela that trauma narratives "are not simply about facts. They are primarily about the impact of those facts on victims' lives and about the painful continuities created by the violence in their lives" (86). In the testimony to which de Kok responds, however, the line between victim and perpetrator has blurred, since the man might have been planning to launch a grenade or might have had one thrown at him. "Would it matter to know / the detail called truth," the poet wonders, "since, fast forwarded, / the ending is the same, / over and over?" The imagery of videography intensifies this eerie scene, which can be sped up or replayed endlessly. Frustrated that answers remain elusive, the poet focuses her lens on the trauma of the dying man: "The questions, however intended, / all lead away from him / alone there, running for his life" (49). Elsewhere de Kok has claimed that "the TRC presents itself as the grand political elegy for the country" and, as such, demands new literary initiatives, "investigating the relationships between stories and history, staging the drama of individual and collective experiences and perspectives; examining discontinuities and lacunae" (7). As "At the Commission" illustrates, her own poetry probes the hearings' many ramifications and contributes to filling these gaps.

For Antjie Krog, a poet and a reporter assigned to cover the proceedings, the TRC experience initially evoked a conflict over the morality of transforming human suffering into art. "May my hand fall off if I write this," she declares in her memoir, stricken after the first days of testimony. Yet she felt compelled to bear witness despite her ethical qualms: "If I write this, I exploit and betray. If I don't, I die" (65–66). As a white woman and a writer of Afrikaans, the language employed by the apartheid state, Krog inhabits intermediate ground at the hearings. Neither

criminal nor victim, she is nonetheless implicated in her country's hor-
ror, in part because "all the words used to humiliate, all the orders given
to kill, belonged to the language of my heart" (313). This sense of complicity leads her, in "long white shadow," to confront the legacy of colonial misrule:

> set me set me from revenge and loss
> from ruins set me from the long white scar the lichen and ash set me free
> into remorse oh my hand my hand grabs the sheet like a throat   (Krog 345)

Employing a fragmented discourse of purgation, Krog imagines herself
strangling the ghostly shadow of the apartheid regime in a cathartic act
of closure.

Once she has acknowledged culpability, Krog can evoke the possibility of societal and personal transformation. Inspired by the Commission hearings, she dedicates "for us all; all voices, all victims" to the
speakers of the testimonies. As South Africans eschew racial hatred, the
wounded country and the shattered poet can be reborn. Today her country "breathes becalmed," Krog claims:

> it sings, it ignites
> my tongue, my inner ear, the cavity of heart
> shudders toward the outline
>   new in soft intimate clicks and gutturals
>
> of my soul the retina learns to expand
> daily because by a thousand stories
> I was scorched
>
> a new skin.

Her reborn country inspires Krog to embrace a new, embodied language,
a hybrid of her native Afrikaans, with its unique guttural sounds, and
those indigenous languages whose dynamic clicks punctuate the African
air with song. A chastened petitioner, she seeks redemption:

> You whom I have wronged, please
> take me
> with you   (364–65)

Gobodo-Madikizela employs equally vivid tropes throughout her
memoir to recount the tension between the empathy she experiences
and the detachment she finds essential to facilitate the testimonies.
Time after time she describes herself as "picking up pieces of narrative,"
treasuring "crumbs" of "sacred memory" (88–90). As a black woman,
she devises certain rhetorical gestures to protect herself from fusing her

own memories of racist abuse with those of the testifiers. For example, she explains that in her role as a commissioner she used strategic restatement to affirm a testimony, recover from shock, and comfort the grieving. To a Mrs. Khutwane, for instance, sexually violated by a soldier she brokenly describes as having been her son's age, Gobodo-Madikizela replies softly, "The soldier could have been your child" (92). In addition, she acknowledges the impossibility of being a neutral observer, a "blank screen," even as she strives to be objective (94). Ultimately Gobodo-Madikizela narrates the new dimensions of post-apartheid literacy that she developed at the hearings and inscribes a poetics of redemption:

> South Africans face the challenge of how to embrace the past without being swallowed by the tide of vengeful thinking. The Truth and Reconciliation Commission was a strategy not only for breaking the cycle of politically motivated violence but also for teaching important lessons about how the human spirit can prevail even as victims remember the cruelty visited upon them in the past. If memory is kept alive in order to cultivate old hatreds and resentments, it is likely to culminate in vengeance, and in a repetition of violence. But if memory is kept alive in order to transcend hateful emotions, then remembering can be healing. (103)

CONCLUSION: "UNSETTLING THE DIVIDES"

South African women's poetry of orality, franchise, and reconciliation illuminates in new ways the metaphorical representations of literacy that Sylvia Scribner identifies in "Literacy in Three Metaphors" (11–21). Oral poems such as black women's *izibongo* and *kiba* reveal the complex negotiations of *literacy as adaptation:* they reflect the economic, social, and political imperatives that have converged in the new South Africa to relocate this indigenous form from a position on the cultural margins to a position near the international "centers" of literary valuation and production. Franchise poems such as Joan Baker's "Home" and Gcina Mhlophe's "A Vote for Unity" complicate the metaphor of *literacy as power,* which denotes for Scribner the ways in which "expansion of literacy skills is often viewed as a means for poor and politically powerless groups to claim their place in the world" (11–12). In Baker's and Mhlophe's poems, the representation of expanded literacy skills, as demonstrated through the act of enfranchisement, constitutes a way for once disempowered black women to claim political agency. By employing such strategies as code-switching, poetry of franchise affirms not the false binary of literacy versus illiteracy but the cultural reality of multiple literacies. Finally, white women's poems of reconciliation such as de Kok's "At The Commission" and Krog's "for us all; all voices, all

victims" advance the concept of *literacy as state of grace,* a perspective
motivated by the (somewhat utopian) desire to imagine equitable relationships across racial, gender, and class differences in South Africa and
contribute to a spiritual as well as a sociopolitical transformation.

Women's post-apartheid poems thus contribute to a feminist postcolonial praxis that is vital to our understanding of gender and literacy
in a globally interdependent world. As U.S. academics who teach an increasingly diverse student population, we need to develop "transnational critical consciousness" (Wiegman 73–74). This consciousness
will help, in Robyn Wiegman's words, to "unsettle the faulty and dam-
aging divides within contemporary feminist theory around First World
and Third World, theory and practice, and activism and academy" (7).
Scholars of women and literacy bear particular responsibility for making literacy studies transnational, since 565 million women around the
world lack literacy, but few of them lack agency or voice. I share
Wiegman's concern that feminist professors too often rely on comparative international models when we "globalize" our fields of inquiry,
thus inadvertently reifying a Eurocentric approach to women's knowledge production. In using poetry and testimonies by South African
women to investigate not only racism and colonialism but also the formation of post-apartheid literacies, feminist scholars can gesture toward new modes of transnational practice.

WORKS CITED

Berthoff, Ann E. *The Sense of Learning.* Portsmouth, NH: Boynton/Cook, 1990.

Cock, Jacklyn, and Alison Bernstein. "Gender Differences: Struggles Around
'Needs' and 'Rights' in South Africa." *NWSA Journal* 13 (2001): 138–52.

Congress of South African Writers Women's Collective, ed. *Like a House on Fire: Contemporary Women's Writing, Art and Photography from South Africa.* Johannesburg,
South Africa: COSAW Publishing, 1994.

de Kok, Ingrid. "At the Commission." *Running Towards Us: New Writing from South
Africa.* Ed. Isabel Balseiro. Portsmouth, NH: Heinemann. 49, 2000.

de Kock, Leon. "South Africa in the Global Imaginary: An Introduction." *Poetics Today* 22.2 (2001): 263–98.

____. "Standing in the Doorway: A Preface." *World Literature Today* 70 (1996): 5–8.

DeShazer, Mary K. *A Poetics of Resistance: Women Writing in El Salvador, South Africa,
and the United States.* Ann Arbor: U of Michigan P, 1994.

Driver, Dorothy. "Transformation through Art: Writing, Representation, and Subjectivity in Recent South African Fiction." *World Literature Today* 70.1 (1996):
45–52.

Freire, Paolo, with Donaldo Macedo. *Literacy: Reading the Word and the World.* London: Bergin and Garvey, 1987.

Freire, Paolo. *Pedagogy of the Oppressed* 1970. Trans. Myra Bergman Ramos. New
York: Continuum, 1990.

Gobodo-Madikizela, Pumla. *A Human Being Died That Night: A South African Story of
Forgiveness.* Boston: Houghton Mifflin, 2003.

Gordimer, Nadine. "April 27: The First Time." *S.A. 27 April 1994: An Authors' Diary.* Comp. André Brink. Pretoria, South Africa: Queillerie, 1994. 51–52.

Gray, Stephen. "Some Problems of Writing Historiography in Southern Africa." *Literator* 10.2 (1989): 16–24.

Gunner, Elizabeth. "Songs of Innocence and Experience: Women as Composers and Performers of Izibongo, Zulu Praise Poetry." *Women and Writing in Southern Africa: A Critical Anthology.* Ed. Cherry Clayton. London: Heinemann, 1989: 11–39.

Hofmeyr, Isabel. " 'Not the Magic Talisman': Rethinking Oral Literature in South Africa." *World Literature Today* 70.1 (1996): 88–92.

James, Deborah. "Basadi ba baeng / Visiting Women: Female Migrant Performance from the Northern Transvaal." *Politics and Performance: Theatre, Poetry and Song in Southern Africa.* Ed. Liz Gunner. Johannesburg, South Africa: Witwatersrand UP, 1994. 81–110.

Krog, Antjie. *Country of My Skull: Guilt, Sorrow, and the Limits of Forgiveness in the New South Africa.* New York: Random House, 1998.

Kunene, Mazisi. "Some Aspects of South African Literature." *World Literature Today* 70.1 (1996): 13–16.

Lorde, Audre. *Sister Outsider: Essays and Speeches.* Trumansburg, NY: Crossing, 1984.

Mhlophe, Gcina. " A Vote for Unity." *S.A. 27 April 1994: An Authors' Diary.* Comp. André Brink. Pretoria, South Africa: Queillerie, 1994. 86–87.

Ngugi wa Thiong'o. *Writers in Politics: Essays.* London: Heinemann, 1981.

O'Brien, Anthony. *Against Normalization: Writing Radical Democracy in South Africa.* Durham, NC: Duke UP, 2001.

Press, Karen. "Building a National Culture in South Africa." *Rendering Things Visible: Essays on South African Literary Culture.* Ed. Martin Trump. Athens: Ohio UP, 1990. 22–40.

Royster, Jacqueline Jones. *Traces of a Stream: Literacy and Social Change among African American Women.* Pittsburgh: U. of Pittsburg P., 2000.

Sachs, Albie. "Preparing Ourselves for Freedom." *Spring Is Rebellious: Arguments about Cultural Freedom by Albie Sachs and Respondents.* Ed. Ingrid de Kok and Karen Press. Cape Town, South Africa: Buchu Books, 1990. 19–29.

Scribner, Sylvia. "Literacy in Three Metaphors." *American Journal of Education* 93.1 (1984): 6–21.

Stent, Stacey. "The Wrong Ripple." *Spring Is Rebellious: Arguments about Cultural Freedom by Albie Sachs and Respondents.* Ed. Ingrid de Kok and Karen Press. Cape Town, South Africa: Buchu Books, 1990. 74–79.

Wiegman, Robyn, ed. *Women's Studies on Its Own: A Next Wave Reader in Institutional Change.* Durham, NC: Duke UP, 2002.

Gender and Literacies: The Korean "Comfort Women's" Testimonies

Gwendolyn Gong

"Wartime exploitation of women for sexual service is part of a long and inglorious tradition," writes historian George Hicks in *The Comfort Women: Sex Slaves of the Japanese Imperial Forces* (1). In the 1930s and throughout World War II, Korean schoolgirls and young women were duped, coerced, or abducted by the Japanese military to become "comfort women," a euphemism for those females who "serviced" officers and soldiers in "comfort stations," that is to say, brothels situated alongside Japanese military camps.[1] While women from other countries such as the Philippines, Malaysia, and Indonesia were also forced to become "comfort women," over 80%, or up to 200,000, are estimated to have been Korean.

Given this figure, it is amazing that the existence of the Korean "comfort women" remained an unspoken matter for fifty years. The silence was broken in 1991, when 74-year-old Kim Hak-soon identified herself as having been a Japanese military sex slave and agreed to testify in a Tokyo District Court. Upon learning that Kim had agreed to tell her story, more women came forward, with local and international support, to speak the unspeakable for all the world to hear. For many of these women, the postwar era had been a time of self-censorship and self-imposed silence. Their denial or concealment enabled them to hide their shame and protect their families from the suspected truth and certain embarrassment.

As the women began to tell their stories, the oral versions were also being transformed into written versions that could circulate in broader contexts. The purpose of this chapter is to explore the relationship between gender and literacy by considering the different forms of literacy the Korean "comfort women's" testimonies reflect. Doing so

259

will enable us to explore what the testimonies actually reveal about how the various literacies affected these women before, during, and after their captivity. Moreover, it will show how the literate version of the testimonies produced in English have informed the international community of these events and served subsequently as a call for redress.

ASPECTS OF LITERACY AND LITERACIES

Several key notions about literacy influence my discussion of the Korean "comfort women's" testimonies. The first flows from the ideological model of literacy, which views literacy as a form of social practice embedded in socially constructed realities. According to Street in both *Literacy in Theory and Practice* and *Social Literacies*, this model contrasts with the autonomous model of literacy, wherein literacy is viewed primarily as a set of schooled skills (i.e., simply learning to decode written texts) that are largely invariant from culture to culture. In contrast, the ideological model acknowledges that literacy develops from the complex interplay among culture, shared knowledge, personal and social identity, and the various speech communities in which one participates. The forms of literacy involved in the Korean "comfort women's" stories are a distinctive amalgam of personal and cultural dimensions that will be explored below.

The second aspect of literacy theory that has influenced my interpretation is the idea that literacy can empower the powerless, which Paolo Freire identifies as liberatory literacy, especially as articulated in *Pedagogy of the Oppressed* and *The Politics of Education: Culture, Power and Liberation*. While Freire makes us aware that literacy can both oppress and liberate, he advocates the positive and enabling power of literacy that can lead to critical consciousness, that is, to the ability to perceive social, political, and economic contradictions in order to act against oppressive forces (*Pedagogy* 27–56). As the interpretations in this chapter will make evident, the telling of the stories, especially as they have been transformed into various written forms, have given voice to the women and have prevented the stories from fading into historical footnotes.[2]

The third element of my interpretation rests on the notion that literacy is not a singular or unitary phenomenon; that is, multiple literacies exist. In the case of the Korean "comfort women," at least four major types of literacy were involved in their stories: (a) the schooled literacy of their childhood; (b) the orality of their stories as informed by their previously acquired literacy (i.e., Walter Ong's idea of secondary orality); (c) the transformation of their stories into written texts using the Korean script; and (d) the subsequent translation of the stories into an international language such as English. By literacies, then, I mean the various social forms that language takes when used by members of speech communities in context. These literacies are multiple and enabled: they include oral and written language, schooled and vernacular literacies, mother tongue language and second language, dominant and nondominant languages that develop from *literacy practices* or literacy "events" (Heath; see Barton; Daniell). As Pat Herbert and Clinton Robinson explain, "In a literacy event, people communicate in everyday life using a mixture of oral and literate features, but the notion of literacy practices refers not only to the literacy event, but also to the ideas and constructions that people have of what is happening when they are involved in it" (122; see also Baynham; Street, *Social Literacies*). People develop and employ different literacies for different political, social, economic, and personal situations.

In the case of the Korean "comfort women," I refer to the diverse forms of dominant or schooled literacies (i.e., courtroom transcripts) as well as vernacular literacies (e.g., anecdotes, confessions, informal oral histories) that their testimonies evolved into—literacies that have become agents of social, political, and personal change (see Fairclough; Gee). The conventions of various social and political literacies shaped the testimonies in ways that enabled their use in the Korean and Japanese governments' gradual efforts to recover the missing history of the Korean "comfort women." As we shall see in the Korean "comfort women's" testimonies, political and personal circumstances not only forced them to use new forms of literacy events to survive, but it also required them to abandon their native language. The women were forced to speak in Japanese, the language of their captors.

In sum, then, I approach the testimonies of the Korean "comfort women" in light of an ideological view of literacy and the dynamic aspects it implies. The Korean "comfort women's" testimonies provide insights about the relationship between gender and literacies that developed from three social contexts and time frames: Japanese-occupied Korea prior to World War II, "comfort stations" in Asia during World War II, and Korea after liberation. To examine these insights, the following analysis considers how the testimonies evolved as literacies, yielding the narrators' public voice and resulting in international recognition.

TESTIMONIES AS EVOLVING LITERACIES

In this chapter, I focus on a representative collection of nineteen narratives that appear in Sangmie Choi Schellstede's edited volume, *Comfort Women Speak*, published in 2000. The testimonies were taped from 1994–1996 in Seoul and Oryu-dong, Kyunggi-do Province, in South Korea, in Pyongyang, North Korea, in New York City, and in Washington, D.C. The work of transcribing and translating the narratives into

English was begun in 1996 by the Washington Coalition for Comfort Women Issues (WCCW), and, as Schellstede notes, represents "the first [project] of its kind in the United States" (ix).

The women featured in the volume were aged 65 to 77 when they told their stories. By the time the book was published in 2000, two of the women had died. I imagine more have passed away since. These women were taken from their homes as schoolgirls and young women, ranging in ages from 12 and 21. The length of their captivity in military "comfort stations" was reportedly between one to nine years, and they were stationed in various camps in China, Russia, Japan, Taiwan, the Philippines, New Guinea, and Burma.

In line with Freire's observations, the narratives in Schellstede's book represent examples of the power of *literacies* to liberate. The testimonies began as oral histories told in Korean. They were archived on videotape, transcribed into Korean script, and finally translated from Korean to English in written texts. As oral testimonies, the stories were difficult even for speakers of Korean to understand, largely because the "comfort women" spoke in different Korean dialects. Once the dialects were fully interpreted, the narratives were transcribed into written Korean. Ultimately, the written Korean texts were translated into English, which allowed these stories to circulate throughout the English speaking world. Having the Korean "comfort women's" stories translated and published in English has placed on a world stage the issue of what happened to these women when they were young.

Schellstede's collection of testimonies provides glimpses of these women and the various ways their literacies influenced them before, during, and after their captivity. In Japanese-occupied Korea prior to World War II, young women possessed schooled literacy in their native Korean language and acquired colonial literacy (Japanese). Ordinarily, possessing multiple literacies should have opened up educational and economic possibilities for these young women; ironically, this acquired literacy or knowledge of Japanese may instead have made the women more likely targets by "recruiters." During World War II, the women's multiple literacies made them vulnerable again. In the "comfort stations," the women's knowledge of Korean was used against them by their captors. Forced to speak only in Japanese, the women's native literacy (Korean) was suppressed to strip them of their personal and national identities, as well as to dehumanize them through verbal, physical, and psychological abuse. After liberation in Korea, getting the women's stories was difficult because of self-censorship. However, the women's silence eventually was followed by whispers of their stories (secondary orality), ultimately resulting in the transcription of their narratives in their Korean dialects to their translation and publication in English (multiple and enabled literacies). By tracing the evolving literacies associated with the Korean "comfort women" testimonies, we can learn much about how power shapes literacy, as well as how literacy can become a form power.

I begin by looking at the role that literacy played in these women's lives during the Japanese colonial period during which they were first recruited. (Quotations of testimonies come from *Comfort Women Speak* and thus are followed by page references only.)

Colonial Literacy and Recruitment

Through the testimonies, it is clear that both Japanese officials and local Koreans used trickery, deception, and force to "enlist" thousands of young females as "comfort women." In many instances, the promise of educational opportunities, the prospect of well-paying jobs that would enable them to earn financial assistance for their families, or the obligation to participate in government-related service in order to demonstrate their "required" support for the Japanese Emperor were attractive lures, resulting in "willing volunteers." In the narratives, however, are also contrasting scenarios. Unsuspecting "recruits" recount being taken unwillingly, typically abducted by uniformed Japanese police from their yards or nearby fields, presumed by families to have disappeared without a trace. Several reports even describe how girls were coerced into "volunteering" to leave home when officers threatened to take their mothers or older sisters.

Ironically, however, education played a role in the "recruitment" of a number of "comfort women." In all but two narratives, the speakers suggest or explicitly mention the importance of education and their ability to read and write in Korean, their native language. In Japanese-occupied Korea, they had also learned the Japanese language in school, usually taught by Japanese teachers. Possessing literacies in both Korean and Japanese, Korean schoolgirls and women may have been considered especially good "candidates" as future "comfort women" by the Japanese military.

In the following passages, note how the schoolgirls' academic success and desire for further study were used for recruitment purposes. Kang Duk-kyung was only 13 years old:

> One day my school teacher, who was Japanese, visited my home and asked me if I wanted to go to Japan to further my education and do something "good" for the Emperor. I was flattered, but was too shy to question his motives. So I said yes. When I showed up at the school ground for the appointment, at least 50 other girls had gathered there. My school was coeducational, so I thought many of my classmates including boys would be there. However, the only person I recognized was Lim Sook-ja, the smartest girl in my class. (15–16)

Moon Pil-gi's story reveals how education was used to lure her into service:

> I was 15 years old. One day a man in our village visited me when my parents were not around and asked me if I was interested in going to a good school. I told him that I was always interested in schooling and that I would even go to a night school if I had to work during the day. He then told me not to mention this talk with him to my parents. At that time there were rumors of drafting young Korean girls for work in Japan, China, or in the far away places. (63–64)

While the "recruiting" means were varied, the recruits' fate was the same: military sexual slavery. Throughout their testimonies there are scenes depicting masses of young girls and women being transported to military bases all over Asia in buses, in trucks, in trains, and by boats and ships. Initially herded together from their small towns, they would later be divided and sent to different camps with military brothels.

Language Use and Identity

Language was also used to undermine the Korean identities of the women, especially since the use of their primary spoken and written language was forbidden. For example, upon arrival at "comfort stations," the new recruits were given Japanese names and numbers; they were instructed not to speak Korean. Hwang Kuem-ju recalls, "The Japanese had made all Koreans change their names. So instead of 'Hwang,' I was called 'Hurko Nagaki'" (5). Kim Sang-hi's experience echoes that of Hwang: "The soldiers gave out numbers to us. I was #4. My own name was replaced with a Japanese name 'Takeda Sanai'" (31). Kim Dae-il describes her first day when a lieutenant said, "This is Japan. From now on, you must not speak Korean. Your new and only name is 'Shizue.'" She continues, "[I] was assigned a number for identification, and a small space of four feet by six with one *tatami*, a Japanese straw mattress, for the floor" (25).

The relationship between language and identity was made even more explicit when intimidation was added in the mix. Threats and punishment for using their mother tongue were severe. Recollects Kim Young-shil,

> A soldier came up to me and put a name tag on my chest. It had a Japanese name "Eiko" written on it. He then told me, "From now on, you must not speak Korean. If you do, we will kill you. Now, your name is Eiko." ...
>
> There was a girl next to my cubicle .... One day an officer overheard her speaking to me and accused her of speaking Korean. He dragged her out to a field and ordered all of us to come out there. We all obeyed. He said,

"This girl spoke Korean. So she must die. You will be killed if you do too. Now, watch how she dies." He drew his sword. Horrified, I closed my eyes and turned my face away. When I opened my eyes, I saw her severed head on the ground. (49–50)

The language that people use signals their identity, power, status, and role in society (Barton; Barton and Hamilton). What the testimonies make clear is that prohibiting the Korean "comfort women" the right to their own language was a important step for subsequent violations. Their Korean identities were stripped from them, replaced by Japanese names, dehumanizing numbers, and sexual slavery.

The loss of Korean identity was supplanted by a new one: that of "comfort woman." The soldiers reinforced this new identity through a combination of racist verbal abuse, punishment, intimidation, poor living conditions, and poor health care.

Stories of Racist Language

Japanese soldiers hurled racial slurs and insults at the "comfort women" to intimidate and further dehumanize them; this hate talk extended the assaults waged against their Korean identity. Kim Yoon-shim, only 12 years old when she was abducted, describes the prejudice she withstood from the soldiers she "serviced": "Verbal abuse from the soldiers was constant and unbearable. They told me 'Chosun' (a traditional name for Korea) people are liars, distrustful, subhumans and have no ancestors. No one cares; no one can trace if Chosun people are killed, the soldiers said" (45). According to Moon Pil-gi, "[A soldier] said that our Korean race should be eradicated from the earth" (66). The language of prejudice was wielded like a weapon against the "comfort women." While the physical imprisonment and violations were painful, the cultural and psychological damage caused by hate talk was also harmful.

Stories of Rape, Intimidation, and Punishment

The nineteen narratives in *Comfort Women Speak* reveal what life as a military prostitute was like; these stories, now in written form, serve as World War II crime histories that contain vivid and disturbing descriptions of all-too-common events. Kim Dae-il's story depicts the physical abuse and verbal taunting that were part of the daily life of a "comfort woman":

So we were made sex slaves and were forced to service 40 to 50 soldiers each day. One time a soldier sat on top of the stomach of a pregnant "comfort woman" who was almost full term. Apparently this act induced labor. As a baby started to appear, he stabbed both the infant and the mother and exclaimed, "Hey, these *senjing* (dirty Koreans) are dead. Come and see." (26)

Elsewhere, in Kim Yoon-shim's testimony, she indicates that soldiers often did use a *saku*, translated as a *sack* or *condom*; however, the men usually "washed, dried, and reused" (45) them, resulting in women contracting infections and sexually transmitted diseases as well as becoming pregnant. Japanese military doctors were sent in to "comfort stations" to conduct physical examinations on the "comfort women" at least once a month (and sometimes more often), but the health care provided was far from adequate or competent.

Stories of Disease and Psychological Trauma

According to human rights scholar Karen Parker and legal researcher Jennifer Chew, only one out of four "comfort women" survived their ordeal as military sex slaves, and of those, only a small fraction, now ages 65 to 85 are still alive. Hicks adds, "Those who did survive were often left barren and scarred by physical and psychological problems. 'Comfort women' continue to die from conditions attributable to their sexual enslavement" ("What Form Redress?" 88).

In the "Foreword" of *Comfort Women Speak,* Dongwoo Lee Hahm writes, "Today, these former 'comfort women' … live with the terrifying memories of their captivity and sexual enslavement. Many suffer from irreparable psychological and physical wounds" (vii). In every testimony, vivid images of disease and psychological disorders are presented. For example, Kim Soon-duk tells of her traumatic ordeal:

> I became ill soon after I became a sex slave and started to bleed severely through my vagina. The treatment at the hospital could not stop it. One day our manager gave me packets of black powder to take once a day. After several days of taking [the powder] the bleeding was reduced. He then told me the powder was made from the leg of a Chinese soldier's corpse. From that day on I started to dream of human legs rolling around. I even dream of [them] to this day. The place I stayed was very close to the battlefront. I saw many corpses. (39)

Madness and suicide are implicit and explicit themes in the testimonies. The stories show young women in situations where they could not cope, physically, mentally, or culturally. Yi Yong-nyo offers insight into how hopeless and helpless these women felt:

> This life as a "comfort woman" continued for three years. There was no hope of returning home. Some girls became very ill. Some lost their minds. In three years our original group of 25 girls was slowly reduced to about 10. I remember one committed suicide. She was 21. When they cre-

mated her, they told us to come and watch the process. We had no choice but to watch it. We did just about everything they told us to. (97)

In the testimonies, women talk about the medical and psychological problems they endure even now because of their treatment in the "comfort stations." Most survivors express feelings of isolation and loneliness that result from estrangement from family members and their unwillingness to marry or inability to bear children. Images of isolation and loneliness pervade the narratives, complementing another key metaphor throughout their volume: silence.

PSEUDO-LIBERATION: SOUNDS OF SILENCE

The recollections of liberation in the testimonies present snapshots of the "comfort women's" continued struggle as they searched for their homeland, families, and dignity. While joyful images of liberation may have been true for some wartime victims, such was not the case for these Korean women. For example, Hwang Keum-ju remembers:

On the day of liberation, I did not know what was going on. Suddenly, there were no sounds of horses, motor vehicles or soldiers. I was hungry so I went out to the kitchen to drink some water. There I saw clothes that the Japanese soldiers had abandoned. One last Japanese soldier stood in the kitchen. He asked me, "Why haven't you left? Your country is liberated, and my country is sitting on a fire." Because of the atomic bomb his country was burning like hell, he told me, and I'd better leave quickly ....

So I left the barracks on the evening of the 15th of August. I walked. On the road I picked up abandoned clothes and shoes to wear. I begged for food. I was alone and walked all the way to the 38th parallel. At the 38th parallel, American soldiers sprayed me with so much DDT, all the lice fell off me.

It was December 2nd when I finally reached Seoul. (8)

Unlike Hwang Keum-ju, Kim Yoon-shim travelled by fishing boat to get back to Korea from China. To earn her passage, she cooked, cleaned, washed clothes, and "serviced" fishermen. After about a month, the Captain dropped her off, saying she was in Korea. She recalls:

It was an island. I found out later that it was a leper colony. I knocked on a gate. The lepers came out with welcome and gave me some rice. I made up stories about my past because I simply couldn't tell them the truth. They helped me send a letter to my parents .... I couldn't go home .... [Once] a girl leaves home, she is not supposed to return to her parents' home, according to our custom. (47)

Whatever the details of their individual stories about the return home after the war may be, all of the testimonies echo Kim Yoon-shim's admission that liberation at the end of World War II was not liberating for the Korean "comfort women." These women were physically set free; however, their voices were muted by fear and shame.

After liberation, their silence continued, only this time it was self-imposed. It is interesting to note that, in their testimonies, the dominant metaphor associated with liberation is silence. Ironically, these women possessed schooled and vernacular literacies in both Korean and Japanese; nevertheless, they were unable to use their literacy to effect change: they could not lift their voices to liberate themselves.

Silence is not uncommon especially for women who, for cultural or economic reasons, may be afforded less status or power in their communities (Yang). In "Literacies, Gender and Power in Rural Pakistan," Shirin Zubair reports a case in which Pakistani women referred to themselves as *"caged"* and *"silent birds"* (198). *Silence* is a metaphor for invisibility and suggests that agency is external—that those in power decide who will be silent or silenced (Kramsch). In her analysis, Zubair makes use of a Freirean perspective to further understand the significance of metaphor of silence: "[I]n the culture of silence the masses are *mute*, they are prohibited from creatively taking part in the transformations of their society and therefore prohibited from being .... These birds are not wilfully silent—their voices have been silenced" (199). The "comfort women's" situation is more complex, however. While in captivity, the "comfort women" were forcibly silenced by their captors; after they were free, they continued their silence.

For fifty years, these women existed as powerless, silent survivors who despite various literacies could not write their own stories. As a consequence, there was no conversion of their self-image, no belief in their own rights, no call for apologies and reparations from the Korean and Japanese governments; no demand for full and accurate accounts to be included in government documents and history texts (see edited collections by Kim and Choi; and Hein and Selden).

Why did these women remain silent for so long? Here, the cultural norms and dynamics mentioned earlier come to the fore. In "Re-membering the Korean Military Comfort Women: Nationalism, Sexuality, and Silencing," Yang summarizes the reasons proposed by cultural historian Chin Sung Chung:

> First of all, the [postwar] Japanese government had "classified" documents that pertained to the colonial government and the military. Second, the United States punished Japan only lightly for its World War II crimes, because [they] wanted to use Japan as a base from which to expand capitalism in Asia. This in turn permitted the [postwar] Japanese government to officially ignore the damages ... to its colonies in Asia. Third, due to shame and guilt, the victims, offenders, and witnesses remained silent about the military Comfort Women issue. The paucity of research about

the atrocities committed under the Japanese colonialism, especially those related to gender, further contributed to the "darkness" surrounding the Military Comfort Women issue. (126–27)

Yang emphasizes that not only the Japanese but also the Koreans attempted to conceal the "comfort women" issue. The social atmosphere in postwar Korea contributed as well to the "non-issue" of the "comfort women." Although Korean educators had assisted the Japanese in "recruiting" young girls, the Korean government kept silent about their involvement. And accordingly, the Korean government turned a blind eye, failing to recognize the plight of these women and refusing to seek reparations for them after the war. Given these conditions, the women understandably continued their silence. They had no venue, no social and rhetorical situation, and no discourse community that made speaking out worth the risks. With no opportunities to bear witness, there was no reason to expose their past; with no exigence calling them to speak, the women remained silent. But the opportunities for literacy practices would eventually present themselves half a century after liberation had occurred in 1945.

LITERACIES AS LIBERATORS

In the 1990s, the "comfort women" issue came into public view in Korea and abroad, beginning with Kim Hak-soon's lawsuit against the Japanese government, held in a Tokyo District Court, and continuing with an official international investigation, which resulted in the publication of the *Report of the Special Rapporteur on Violence against Women* by the United Nations Commission on Human Rights in 1996 (Coomeraswamy). Also of major importance to the Korean "comfort women" movement were local and international support groups, such as the Washington Coalition for Comfort Women Issues (WCCW) in the United States and The House of Sharing in Seoul, South Korea. These investigations and support groups helped to encourage the Korean "comfort women" to tell their stories. The work of the WCCW in publishing the narratives in *Comfort Women Speak* illustrates the notion of *enabled* literacy practices: that is, the women's stories are now part of the public historical record because of the literacies of many people.

For the Korean "comfort women," true postwar liberation became possible through their testimonies, the result of *practiced multiple literacies*. As oral narratives told in different Korean dialects, the women's testimonies were inaccessible and thus had minimal influence in local, regional, or international circles. However, when the experiences were transformed from *vernacular literacies* (i.e., anecdotes, confessions, oral histories, and videotaped testimonies in the Korean women's native dialects) to *dominant or schooled literacies* (i.e., witnesses' accounts transcribed in standard Korean and translated into formal written English text), the women's words gained currency, significance, and power at home and abroad.

Did these women lose power because they did not pen their testimonies in Korean themselves? Did their failure to write reduce their narratives or truths? The answer to both of these questions is no. Granted, had these women spoken and written of their experiences in their own dialects, their stories would have been archived, with a greater chance of being acknowledged in Korea and Japan sooner. However, to achieve greater world impact, their testimonies would still have required translation into an international language such as English; intermediaries would still have been needed to convert these women's "evolving literacies" from vernacular literacies to dominant or schooled literacies, from oral to literate forms. The permutations involved in the Korean "comfort women" narratives challenge us to expand our definition of literacy, embracing the broader notions of multiple literacies and enabled literacies—different forms of expression that language takes when it is socially, politically, linguistically resituated.

CONCLUSION

As this case reveals, the evolution of the Korean women's testimonies through a succession of literacies was necessary so that the narratives could serve as means to free these women from silence: restoring their dignity and peace of mind, "writing" their existence into being, narrating the war crimes against them into history, and calling for redress from Japan.

What do the narratives tell us about gender and literacies? The women's testimonies have exposed how these women became the "collateral damage" of war, suffering human rights violations in the form of rape, abuse, neglect, and estrangement. Through the narratives, we have observed how education and the women's literacy abilities in their native language and in the colonial Japanese language increased their vulnerability to be recruited as military sex slaves. In addition, we have noted how language and literacies can be used to strip away these women's cultural and linguistic identity and humanity, reducing them to sex objects answering to foreign names and numbers. Through the testimonies, we've witnessed the physical and psychological trauma endured by these women during and after the war.

Yet in these narratives we've also seen how the testimonies such as those published in *Comfort Women Speak* are important literacies that hold the promise of empowerment; of cultural, social, historical, and political change; of human rights; and of dignity and justice for these women. With the existence of a literate English language version of these testimonies, the international community has bona fide documentation of these women's exploitation as military sex slaves; the personal accounts preserved in the written word are now part of the literate record. Given the Korean "comfort women's" ages and frailty, these texts serve as "surrogate" voices—their enduring pleas for international action and justice. Multiple literacies have enabled these stories to come out of the silence.

NOTES

1. The term *comfort women* is a translation of the Japanese, *jugun ianfu,* that refers to women of various ethnicities, nationalities, and social backgrounds who became sexual laborers for the Japanese military before and during World War II. The use of the term *comfort women* is controversial. Some critics contend that *comfort women* is the "oppressor's" term and should refer only to paid professional prostitutes. As these testimonies make clear, this is not the case, especially for the nineteen narrators who refer to themselves by this name and whose stories are featured in this chapter. Consequently, I have chosen to use the euphemism, joining a host of historians, ethics and legal scholars, human rights advocates, and participants in international courts who have used it, despite its awkwardness and inaccuracy. To indicate the euphemism's sense of irony and to raise readers' consciousness that the term should not be used naively (i.e., to cover up atrocities), I put it in quotation marks.

2. For many people, the events and issues of World War II have largely been resolved in the sixty years since it ended. So it might be wondered whether the subject of this chapter has any contemporary resonance. As one who has lived in Asia since 1993, it is clear to me that Japanese colonial behavior through the end of World War II remains a vivid source of irritation for most of Japan's neighbors. For example, whenever a Japanese Prime Minister makes his annual pilgrimage to the shrine that commemorates Japan's war dead, including convicted war criminals, editorials in East Asian newspapers roundly criticize the act. Another measure of the residual enmity felt occurred during the 2004 Asian Soccer World Cup hosted by China. Every time the Japanese team played, the Chinese fans were raucously hostile. Some pundits wondered if Beijing will be able to control its anti-Japanese crowds during the 2008 Summer Olympics. One final example of the deep mistrust Asian neighbors still harbor against the Japanese concerns their close scrutiny of each new edition of Japanese history textbooks, which are treated as an indicator of how willing the Japanese are to accept the consequences of their military conquests and colonial deeds. Accordingly, the recognition given to the "comfort women" issue in the last decade can hardly be dismissed as "ancient history."

WORKS CITED

Barton, David. *Literacy: An Introduction to the Ecology of Written Language*. Oxford: Blackwell, 1994.

Barton, David, and Mary Hamilton, eds. *Local Literacies: Reading and Writing in One Community*. London: Routledge, 1998.

Baynham, Mike. *Literacy Practices: Investigating Literacy in Social Contexts*. London: Longman, 1995.

Coomeraswamy, Radhika. *Report of the Special Rapporteur on Violence against Women*. Geneva: United Nations, 1996.

Daniell, Beth. "Narratives of Literacy: Connecting Composition to Culture." *College Composition and Communication* 50 (1999): 393–410.

Fairclough, Norman. *Language and Power*. London: Longman, 1989.

Freire, Paulo. *Pedagogy of the Oppressed*. Trans. Myra Bergman Ramos. New York: Seabury, 1970.

———. *The Politics of Education: Culture, Power, and Liberation*. Cambridge, MA: Bergin and Garvey, 1985.

Gee, James Paul. *Social Linguistics and Literacies: Ideology in Discourses*. 2nd ed. London: Taylor & Francis, 1996.

Hahm, Dongwoo Lee. Foreword. *Comfort Women Speak: Testimony by Sex Slaves of the Japanese Military*. Ed. Sangmie Choi Schellstede. New York: Holmes and Meier, 2000. vii.

Heath, Shirley Brice. *Ways With Words*. New York: Cambridge UP, 1983.

Hein, Laura, and Mark Selden, eds. *Censoring History: Citizenship and Memory in Japan, Germany, and the United States*. Armonk, NY: M. E. Sharpe, 2000.

Herbert, Pat, and Clinton Robinson. "Another Language, Another Literacy? Practices in Northern Ghana." *Literacy and Development: Ethnographic Perspectives*. Ed. Brian V. Street. London: Routledge, 2001. 121–36.

Hicks, George. *The Comfort Women: Sex Slaves of the Japanese Imperial Forces*. St. Leonards, NSW, Australia: Allen and Unwin, 1995.

———. "What Form Redress?" *When Sorry Isn't Enough: The Controversy over Apologies and Reparations for Human Injustice*. Ed. Roy L. Brooks. New York: New York UP, 1999. 87–91.

Kim, Elaine H., and Chungmoo Choi, eds. *Dangerous Women: Gender and Korean Nationalism*. New York: Routledge, 1998.

Kramsch, Claire. *Language and Culture*. Oxford: Oxford UP, 1998.

Ong, Walter J. *The Presence of the Word*. New Haven: Yale UP, 1967.

Parker, Karen, and Jennifer F. Chew. "Reparations: A Legal Analysis." *When Sorry Isn't Enough: The Controversy over Apologies and Reparations for Human Injustice*. Ed. Roy L. Brooks. New York: New York UP, 1999. 141–45.

Schellstede, Sangmie Choi, ed. *Comfort Women Speak: Testimony by Sex Slaves of the Japanese Military*. New York: Holmes and Meier, 2000.

Street, Brian V. *Literacy in Theory and Practice*. New York: Cambridge UP, 1984.

———. *Social Literacies: Critical Approaches to Literacy in Development, Ethnography and Education*. New York: Longman, 1995.

Yang, Hyunah. "Re-membering the Korean Military Comfort Women: Nationalism, Sexuality, and Silencing." *Dangerous Women: Gender and Korean Nationalism*. Ed. Elaine H. Kim and Chungmoo Choi. New York: Routledge, 1998. 123–39.

Zubair, Shirin. "Literacies, Gender and Power in Rural Pakistan." *Literacy and Development: Ethnographic Perspectives.* Ed. Brian V. Street. London: Routledge, 2001. 188–204.

15

The Outlook for Global Women's Literacy

Catherine L. Hobbs

Basic literacy rates for men and women in the United States generally equalized in the nineteenth century—concurrently with the rise of the common school and the entrance of women into the teaching profession. But in the developing world today, gender remains a factor in the achievement of literacy, although boys and girls are beginning to make progress in achieving equal access to primary education. Nevertheless, it remains true that nearly two-thirds of the world's illiterates are women, and 60% of the eligible children out of school are girls (UNESCO, *Statistical Yearbook*, 2003). Meanwhile, development studies show that educating women can be beneficial in a number of ways. Not only can education improve the quality of their lives, but women teach and inspire others. Yet despite this, girls and women in the poorest, least developed areas, especially Southern Asia and sub-Saharan Africa, face steep barriers to obtaining either formal schooling or alternative literacy education. The good news is that combined efforts on many fronts are helping to narrow the literacy gap between the world's men and women.

We know that race, ethnicity, social class, and other factors including age and geography cause inequities in literacy and other cultural capital. Some argue that gender becomes less important than other factors or recedes in importance when other factors are taken into account. Yet although other factors do exist, and indeed interrelate, the world's critical gender inequities should not be overlooked in literacy studies. Although reliable statistics are hard to come by, the widespread impact of gender inequality reveals itself clearly in literacy outcomes in the least developed countries, where the adult literacy rate falls as low as 60 literate women for every 100 men or even lower, compared to the worldwide rate of 88 women to 100 literate men (UNESCO, *Statistical Yearbook*, 2006).

In the introduction to my 1995 edited collection, *Nineteenth-Century Women Learn to Write*, I explored the history of U.S. women's literacy. Later, in reading on global women's literacy, I was struck by the parallels and contrasts between women's learning to read and write in our own industrializing, urbanizing nation and in developing nations today. Literacy rates for women in many of the least developed countries have run about 45–50%, the same as in our own period of colonial development. Literacy rates can rise quickly when conditions are ripe, as they earlier did for Soviet, Cuban, or Nicaraguan women; or they can stagnate when women must spend so much time trying to feed their families that there is neither time, resources, nor energy to go to school.[1] As in U.S. literacy patterns, rural women, the displaced, immigrants, minority, and older women have lower levels of literacy and are often left out of literacy planning. As Soltow and Stevens show us, at home, the rise of the common school (along with mass print culture and Protestant revivalism) was a major factor in boosting U.S. women's literacy, leading to the entrance of women into the teaching profession. It is not yet clear what forces in Southern Asia or sub-Saharan Africa will work to encourage literacy for girls and women. Economic globalization includes forces that can increase literacy rates, such as jobs that can demand higher levels of literacy. But in the past, other forces such as IMF and World Bank policies and programs have also worked against literacy for women.

Those organizations have now joined forces to improve the literacy levels of girls and women. New local, small-scale economic programs such as those in microcredit lending produce new literacy and numeracy needs and promise. New opportunities to be teachers can also provide jobs for women and help motivate women to study. Increases in access to interesting and appropriate reading material also boosts women's literacy as it did in our own developmental period.

Much of my work in composition and literacy uses the term "literacy" in a broad sense quite closely related to rhetoric, as in "computer literacy" or "civic literacy." I have previously used the term "effective literacy" to mean a level and type of literacy that enables someone to act effectively in the world and achieve active citizenship as well as her own personal and economic goals (Hobbs 1). In its use of the UN's and others' definitions of literacy, this chapter may seem to return to a more technical view of literacy as basic reading and writing, but I mean to retain the broader sense of "effective literacy." The UN definition of illiteracy has been the inability to "read and write and understand simple written messages in any language." What "simple" or "understanding" means is not spelled out, as Stromquist notes (*Increasing Girls*). According to UNESCO's *Education for All Global Monitoring Report of 2002*, a person over 15 is considered literate "who can both read and write with understanding a short simple statement on their everyday life" (45).

This modification clarifies issues somewhat by making the literacy relevant to particular lives. What these definitions do not say speaks loudly. Both development and literacy studies show us that the very alphabet and language chosen for literacy and learning bring in issues of power and rhetoric. As a recent report notes:

> Considerable evolution has occurred within United Nations agencies in recent years in thinking about literacy. Whereas illiteracy was once thought of as a social pathology, it is now viewed as a structural phenomenon and a social responsibility. Likewise, whereas literacy used to be viewed as a panacea for social development, it is now seen in the context of broader educational and socio-economic interventions. The task is no longer to "eradicate" illiteracy but rather to create literate environments and societies. (UNESCO, *Education for All* 31)

Progress in thinking about literacy is also being made at home. In 1992, the U.S. National Adult Literacy Survey measured only literacy in English, despite the presence of multiple language groups in our own country. Repeated in 2002, literacy in Spanish was taken into account. Still, measurements of literacy are tricky. A statement may be "simple" in a familiar context (e.g., familiar family stories or at the market), but may not be simple in another (e.g., instructions for taking a prescription or reading a weather report warning of drought). Literacy experts such as Deborah Brandt and Brian Street agree that literacy is best studied in particular social contexts or rhetorical situations. Literacy is no doubt best learned that way as well, although globalization efforts often imply unwarranted commonalities, as if Western school education could be homogenized, modularized, and transported universally while still remaining relevant to diverse peoples' lives.

According to UNESCO's *World Education Report 2000*, nearly two-thirds of the world's illiterate adults were women. Forty to fifty percent of women in the least developed countries are illiterate. The literacy gap exists mostly because of inequities in schooling: about 100 million children are out of school, and 60% of them are girls. As for adults, today about 559 million adult females are illiterate, while 316 adult males are illiterate (UNESCO, *World Education Report 2000* 38, Table 2.4). Bangladesh, India, and Pakistan have nearly half the world's illiterate adults, while they had only a third two decades ago. But there is also good news, as programs in China, India, and Zambia are making rapid progress in reducing illiteracy (UNESCO, *Education for All* 7).

Statistics such as these are difficult to gather and cover a wide range of situations in various countries, so are indicative only of trends. Literacy statistics primarily are derived from census data, frequently based on self-reports. "Illiteracy" is a concept that has confounded researchers for many reasons. The decision to divide people into literates and illiterates is itself one that needs to be questioned. Literacy is a complex phenomenon that becomes even more complex outside a Western context. Numbers of years in school rather than self-reports are often used as indicators of ability (this definition was adopted by UNESCO in 1962). Although years of school are often substituted, as Stromquist notes, a woman with only two or three years of schooling can sometimes read, while one with eight or nine years of schooling has trouble with basic reading material. Researchers point out that number of years attending school can be deceptive if the student drops out and reenters or repeats grades repeatedly. Nevertheless, if the extent of women's global illiteracy is fuzzy, the negative social and economic correlatives are clear: illiteracy is related to family health—especially fertility and infant mortality—crime and unrest, poverty, long-term dependence on welfare programs, and the success of sustainable development programs. Meanwhile, limited educational opportunities tend to restrict women to menial roles in most industries and occupations, which also increase prejudice against women with better skills. Wage gaps exist, with women making 60–70% of what men make, according to the World Bank. Illiterate women face increased discrimination and are more vulnerable to abuse in employment.

To summarize a few trends on the positive side, educated women are more likely to be employed and to earn more than less-educated women. Countries that educate women are more likely to have higher GNPs. Educated women have healthier families. They are more likely to delay marriage and to have fewer children. One study links higher women's education levels with lower levels of government corruption. There is even a positive association between women's education and men's life expectancy (Stromquist, *Increasing Girls'* 17–18). When women are educated, they improve their own lives as well as those of adults and children around them.

WOMEN'S LITERACY AND DEMOCRACY IN IRAQ

In light of these putative benefits of women's literacy, we should be concerned about women in Iraq, a special case because of the recent decline in their levels of literacy and U.S. responsibility for their long-term outcomes. At present, women there suffer from poverty and illiteracy that was not typical of their recent history. Literacy plummeted in the final years of the Saddam Hussein regime after the first Gulf War because of declining prospects for girls. Prior to the first war, Iraqi women's literacy was the highest in the region, except for Israel. Under the secular regime, women had many rights and they participated in many professions.

Today, rising fundamentalist movements, often populated by young family men, are leading a backlash against women, especially those who dare to educate themselves or expect their daughters to have the same education as their sons. This and a rising level of violence compound the issues from the final days of the Hussein regime. By the end of the Hussein period, there was a large gap between men's and women's literacies. "Despite the Baathist regime's egalitarian rhetoric and a widespread misperception in the West that women had it relatively good in Saddam Hussein's secularist Iraq, the gap in literacy rates in favor of men is an extraordinary 32 percentage points," write political scientists M. Steven Fish and Matthew Kroenig. "No country with such a literacy gap is a democracy." Indeed, although the figure is not certain, according to UN statistics, only about a quarter of Iraqi women today can read and write. Moreover, Isobel Coleman shows that:

> [R]obust democracy is exceedingly rare in societies that display a large gender gap in literacy rates and a skewed gender ratio (usually a marker of inferior nutrition and health care for girls and infanticide or sex-selective abortion). He [Fish] argues that societies that marginalize women generally count both fewer anti-authoritarian voices in politics and more men who join fanatical religious and political brotherhoods—two factors that stifle democracy.

The United States is currently in danger of compromising Iraqi women's future by giving in to fundamentalists. There were only six women ministers and three women on the governing council. Now girls are being pressured to cover themselves before going out to school, and pressures similar to what we saw in Iran (see Azar Nafisi's *Reading Lolita in Tehran*) are taking place, further discouraging equality in educational life. The mixing of sexes in schools is becoming more unacceptable, and women and girls are finding that the streets are not safe for travel to schools. Parents often choose to keep their daughters at home rather than attend school for fear of kidnappings.

Meanwhile, satellite TV has suddenly opened a new world to many rural women who seldom leave their homes or villages. One woman told NPR's Anne Garrels in 2004 that she and her household and village seldom miss an episode of "Oprah," although they had no notion of such things just a short time ago. Surprisingly, the emphasis on relationships and solving human problems on "Oprah" seemed to bridge the cultural divide. Despite these superficial appearances of opportunity for Iraqi women, with deteriorating circumstances there today, women's literacy in Iraq is likely to suffer further decline.

MEASURING LITERACY AT HOME

Measures of literacy are more stable and easier to make in industrialized countries that have done individualized testing than those reported in this chapter (primarily using UN statistics). Although UN statistics show that only about 1% of the population in Western countries like the United States is illiterate, Western literacy experts have generalized that perhaps about 10% in industrialized countries cannot read or write adequately (Ballara 9). The United States is one of few countries that have used scientific surveys and testing to measure the population. The 1992 National Adult Literacy Survey did not measure the dichotomy between literate and illiterate people, but looked at three areas: prose literacy, document literacy and quantitative literacy. Results showed that well over 10% of U.S. citizens seem to have serious problems reading and writing, scoring in the lowest category of ability (see Kirsch, Jungeblut, and Kolstad). Comparatively, the survey showed that men and women had roughly the same levels of prose reading. However, on the reading of documents and on math, women scored slightly lower than men. The 2002–03 results show rising levels for women.

Nonetheless, such a general survey tells us little about how these literacies are relevant to particular women's lives.[2] Any English-only survey measuring whether a rural Cherokee woman from Northeastern Oklahoma can read an urban bus schedule teaches us very little about relevant literacy levels in one sector of my own state. (I am, in the first place, assuming that a Native American woman would participate in such a survey, whereas persons in such an oversurveyed population likely would not.) Traditional women's literacies such as reading and manipulating recipes or following craft instructions are in any case missing from these surveys.

In the United States, the National Center for Educational Statistics is currently analyzing data from the 2003 National Assessment of Adult Literacy. What will it and other recent census reports tell us about the progress or lack of progress we have made in particular places in our own country?[3] My point is that even in the developed world, measurements of literacy are not easy to make or interpret. It takes something like Deborah Brandt's study of literacy around Madison, Wisconsin, to provide real insight into the meaning of "literacy in American lives." Brandt interviewed 80 people around Madison, in a rich historical and analytical study of literacy in the United States. We have few similar studies of the developing world.[4]

It is impossible to say at this moment whether in my locale our diverse Oklahoma women are ahead, equal to, or beyond men in literacy in general, if there is any such thing.[5] Because we know relatively little about our own literacies, we should be modest in making pronouncements about other parts of the globe. In our own history, women learned to read and write and then became teachers. In the developing world, there is a great need for women teachers. Often families don't want their daughters to be taught by males. "The strategic importance of the teaching profession for the advancement of women has probably been underestimated up to now by national policy-makers," the 1995 *World Education Report* states (45). Teaching can also provide one of few "modern" wage-paying occupations for women that has some status and governmental protection.

WOMEN'S LITERACY IN THE DEVELOPING WORLD

To delve further into literacy in other parts of the world, in 66 countries—a third of the membership of the UN (191 countries)—the literacy gap has been estimated to be larger than 10 percentage points. "Few other indicators capture as decisively the imbalance in the status of men and of women in society as does this simple measure" (UNESCO, *World Education Report 1995* 24).[6] Perhaps this is because literacy correlates with fertility, family health, employment possibilities and other positive factors previously mentioned.

As the 1995 *World Education Report* notes, the worldwide literacy gap is tied to a cycle of poverty and early marriages, where illiterate mothers rear illiterate daughters who are then married off early, continuing the cycle (44). Although education is important, more than education is needed to break these cycles. Basic needs must be met and infrastructure built—these women need water wells, fuel, energy supplies, health services, and employment or other income-earning possibilities. So issues of literacy, education, and development have become inseparable. Horsman has identified barriers to women's participation in literacy programs even in developed countries, including unemployment, poor housing, poor food, difficulty of traveling to the program and lack of childcare (her studies are primarily Canadian). She and Rockhill (who works with U.S. Latina/os) also note problems with increased domestic violence faced by women whose husbands are threatened by or otherwise disapprove of their educational endeavors (Horsman, *Too Scared to Learn*).

Fortunately, the global literacy gap between men and women has been closing slowly. However, this is not true everywhere. While absolute numbers of illiterates in the world are leveling off, they are still increasing in certain regions—sub-Saharan Africa, the Arab states, and Southern Asia—with women forming the majority in each case. Absolute numbers of illiterates increased in 50 of 63 countries of these regions from 1980–1995 (UNESCO, *World Education Report 1995*).

The 1995 *World Education Report* summarizes: "While literacy rates are rising in all major regions of the world, and male-female literacy gaps ... are slowly closing at the global and regional levels, there still are many individual countries—for example, those in the Sahel—[Niger, Mali, Senegal, Mauritania, Gambia, Burkina Faso, Chad, Guinea-Bissau, Cape Verde]—where the male-female literacy gap is not closing despite increases in both their male and female literacy rates" (29–30). A complex network of problems including drought, civil strife, and AIDS plague many of these countries. Of 32 countries failing to meet UNESCO goals on education and literacy, 11 are experiencing wars and civil unrest.

SCHOOLING AND GENDER

There has been a narrowing of male-female gaps in participation in formal education in most regions. The Dakar Framework for Action supporting universal primary education and working to end gender disparity reports progress, if uneven. In the Latin America and Caribbean region, the male-female disparity in enrollment ratios has effectively disappeared at all levels. More than 1 billion young people, 20% of the world population, are enrolled in formal education today, while only 10% were enrolled in 1953, the earliest year UNESCO measured enrollment (*World Education Report 1995* 19).

However, girls remain less likely to be enrolled in school. For the age group 6–11, when students receive primary or first-level education, nearly a quarter of the world's girls are out of school (85 million) as compared to one sixth, or 60 million boys. As the 1995 *World Education Report* notes, it is primarily because of this longstanding imbalance that the literacy rate of world's women is significantly lower than that of men.

Over the past two decades, newer statistical measures have helped to clarify issues related to school attendance, offering new insights into the attendance of both boys and girls, in particular the relative importance of school access and leaving (UNESCO, *World Education Report 1995* 39.) These measures include "school life expectancies"—"the number of years of formal education that a person of a given age can expect to receive in the future," defined in 1993, and also "school survival expectancy," or school life expectancy just *for those persons who get into school*. These measures clarify the school attendance gap and show that when girls get into school, they tend to survive as well or better than boys. School life expectancies of girls in developed countries actually tend to be higher than those of boys, while school life expectancies of girls are lower than those of boys in developing countries, where higher proportions of girls never get into school. Girls in the Latin America/ Caribbean region have slightly higher school life expectancies than boys, but in more than 100 countries, participation in schooling is lower for girls than for boys.

In most of the world's countries, if a child has not entered first grade by age 11, he or she is unlikely to ever do so. In sub-Saharan Africa today less than half of 6–11 year-old girls are estimated to be in school, so they are unlikely ever to receive formal education (UNESCO, *World Education Report 1995* 36, Table 2.1). In Southern Asia, just over one-third are in school; in the Arab states, just over a quarter. Southern Asia, with its large population, has the same number of out-of-school girls in 6–11 age group as the Arab countries, with about 30 million out of school in each area expected by 2000. For the 12–17 age group, many more are out of school (see *World Education Report 1995* charts). Since the 1995 report, gender disparity in education has reduced dramatically, yet these poorest areas have improved the least.

Family poverty is apparently the factor most important to keeping girls out of school whether in rural or urban areas. This is often reinforced by cultural norms and traditional conceptions of the division of labor in the household for tasks ranging from the care of younger siblings to fetching water and collecting firewood that are less favorable to girls' than to boys' participation (UNESCO, *World Education Report 1995* 44).

Both schooling and literacy programs for those who miss schooling will be important for the future. Large-scale literacy programs have shown great success—for example, in Nicaragua and Brazil and currently in India, China, and Zambia. But small-scale programs sponsored by NGOs or Grass Roots Groups (GRGs) show great promise for those who miss school by providing instruction fine-tuned to the needs of their participants. This is crucial in teaching young women, who are usually responsible for child tending and family needs, and can participate only if their needs are acknowledged.

Quality of curriculum is a problem in most of these countries. Just what girls and women should read and write has recently become more of an issue than it has been in the past. Programs have been criticized for reinforcing women's subservient position, thus making it difficult for them to reform their condition. Stromquist critiques textbooks in industrialized and developing countries for universalizing unequal Western notions of passive womanhood (*Increasing Girls'* 41). In those texts, language sets out important human actions as always performed by men, who are notably absent from significant domestic scenes. Sexual stereotypes of women as potential victims or fearful and submissive are present in arguments, examples, and illustrations. Stromquist makes numerous suggestions, including that in reading materials women be represented as acting in a wide range of settings and possibilities and that classroom climates and pedagogies be made friendly to girls (41).

Statistics show, however, that the educational system may be "less 'unfair'" to girls than the economic, social, and cultural conditions are in limiting their entrance into school. This suggests that the real challenge for national policymakers in many of the poorest countries is less one of ensuring that girls are retained once they get into school than of devising ways of encouraging parents to send their girls to school at all (UNESCO, *World Education Report 1995*). Unfortunately, in some countries, notably Iraq, parents who want to do well for their daughters and would send them to school cannot because of rising street violence.

The UN has been active in bringing women's rights to the forefront of national policy over two decades. Complex relations between the education of men and women and the development process have resulted. Four World Conferences on Women have been held, in Mexico City in 1975, Copenhagen in 1980, Nairobi in 1985, and Beijing, in 1995. The UN Decade for Women, with the theme "Equality, Development and Peace," was held from 1976–85. The Education for All Declaration agreed upon in 1990 in Jomtien, Thailand, set up specific activities to be implemented in order to educate all. This policy emphasizing primary school education for all, and education for girls remains the major statement at present.[7] Building on this emphasis, a meeting in Dakar, Senegal, in 2000 set out the Dakar Framework for Action, calling for Education for All by 2015 and eliminating gender disparities in schooling and literacy. These meetings all work to implement educational statements in the Universal Declaration of Human Rights.

Most national governments and development agencies now support activities centering on primary education, which some fear will impact adult literacy programs negatively. In the long run this emphasis does seem like the most efficient way of boosting literacy rates in general, but it could have tragic consequences for the many women who miss schooling early on. Thus recognizing education as more than formal schooling and utilizing NGOs, the media, and diverse local resources are crucial steps, many believe, in supporting women's literacy. "Literacy from below" supports the program of those who would like to see "globalization from below" (Brecher, Costello, and Smith). To counter homogenizing globalization, "decentralization" programs have been proposed and are being enacted (see Rideout).

Working in Africa, Birgit Brock-Utne also takes a decentralized approach. She has criticized the emphasis on primary education (as well as on girls' education) as not serving Africa well for the future. She notes that over the decades of the sixties and seventies, primary enrollments doubled in Asia and Latin America and tripled in Africa (2). However, over the eighties, in part because of an economic recession, two-thirds of the countries of sub-Saharan Africa had educational expenditures cut in real terms (3). The bad economic conditions were then exacerbated by economic structural adjustment programs (SAPs) implemented by the World Bank and IMF. Further declines in education led to the Jomtien, Thailand, Education for All conference in March 1990, funded in large part by the World Bank and IMF. Sponsors included the United Nations Development Program (UNDP), UNICEF, UNESCO, 155 governments, almost as many nongovernmental organizations (NGOs) and intergovernmental groups. Brock-Utne asks how much the Southern hemisphere was able to influence the declaration that came out of the conference. Although the conference claimed to focus on Education for All, in reality, she claims, the target was the Third World, and the agents of change were the North.[8]

ECONOMIC STRUCTURAL ADJUSTMENT AND OTHER FACTORS

Structural adjustment programs (SAPs) of the eighties made attaining literacy more difficult for both sexes because they mandated educational and health fees and brought about changes that often forced women to work more hours to find food, fuel, and water. Women farmers produce most of the food in sub-Saharan Africa because the men often go to work in cities, leaving women to scratch out a bare agricultural existence. Land allocated for corporate farming or industrialization can cause women to have to walk farther to gather fuel or water. When food is tight, children must be kept home to help with the work. If one child goes to school, it is likely to be a boy (UNESCO, *World Education Report 1995*; see also Scully). If SAPs have raised GNP of these countries, they haven't ensured higher wages. The difficulties often fall to women to bear.

Women's bodies also bear the weight of illiteracy. When conditions are at their worst, as in rural India and Thailand, young girls can be sold into the global sex trade, missing the opportunity for an education that might give them power over their lives. NGOs sponsor programs to purchase young girls or otherwise place them in safe houses and ensure they are educated. Destabilized countries are more likely to have problems with what is essentially female slavery.

Microcredit lending programs that help women become small entrepreneurs usually entail education and basic literacy programs. These currently expanding programs began with Women's World Banking and the Grameen Bank in Bangladesh. Grameen opened in 1979 with $30 loans to 42 poor villagers. The borrowers paid back the loans, and the bank has gone on to lend a billion dollars to two million poor women in 35,000 villages (Useem 209). These small-scale programs benefit women directly, helping them start small businesses and climb out of poverty. In 1987, Nancy M. Barry left a high-paying position with the World Bank to become president of the Women's World Bank because she believed so strongly in these locally sponsored programs in microcredit for the poor. After seeing the poor results of the World Bank's structural adjustment programs, she asked herself, "Was there a future ... not only for building hydroelectric dams and reducing national deficits but also for directly investing in poor people?" (Useem 209). A typical loan made by the World Bank was for $250 million, while the Women's World Bank loans average $250. These grassroots programs drive not only development, but literacy, as women must learn the basics of accounting, managing, and communicating in order to run their businesses. Women's World Bank's development strategy is based on knowledge that men invest 40% of their income in their children's education and health, while women devote more than 90% (Useem 221). The Microcredit Summit organized in part by Barry has launched a campaign to reach 100 million of the poorest families by 2005.

However, the connections between large-scale debt and literacy need to be examined. Debt has been likened to "original sin" of the new millennium, a condition into which we are born and only leave when we die. The Jubilee 2000 Coalition organized to fight for cancellation of the unpayable debts of the most impoverished countries but had little success. African countries at the Jomtien, Thailand, Education for All conference linked debt relief and literacy, yet no action was taken. Recently, debt relief has again been considered, with more postive outcomes expected. Also in Africa, as well as other areas, the AIDS crisis causes widespread disruption to schooling and formal learning. Civil strife, famine, and war make learning impossible in many places. The intertwining of literacy gains and peace has long been noted in UN documents.

Since September, 2001, global literacy reports have linked literacy and education with the reduction of terrorism and the establishment of a culture of peace. The UN's attention has returned to the Universal Declaration of Human Rights, where education is listed as a human right. Indeed, "Education is one of the principal means to build the 'defences of peace' in the minds of men and women everywhere" (*World Education Report 2000* 5, paraphrasing the Preamble to the UNESCO Constitution). Currently, the UN is in a decade-long literacy campaign (2003–2012), the first years of which have been focused on women's literacy. That body's emphasis today is on the variety and quality of education over the lifespan. The centrality of literacy to personal and economic development has been recognized since the beginnings of studies in sustainable development, as well as in literacy studies. Around the globe, the right to education today must include not just quantitative aims, but also qualitative goals. World literacy workers also are beginning to concern themselves with disparities in technological literacies between not only men and women but also the global North and South.

Stromquist moves her literacy work toward citizenship, a key end for literacy both locally and globally:

> If we seek a world where access to print is a precondition to the development of assertive attitudes of feelings of belonging to one's society on more or less equal footing, it is necessary to help both women and men to develop competencies that with successive generations will translate into identities that claim citizenship and retain it. (*Literacy for Citizenship* 23)

Our literacy ideals run up against obstacles to survival in the world's poorest countries. As we work to aid women's survival, our literacy practice must always also aim to increase women's ability to participate freely in creating the conditions that make all our lives, both locally and globally, more than a struggle to survive.

NOTES

1. The year 2001 marked the 40th anniversary of Cuba's literacy campaign in which young people reduced Cuba's literacy rate to below 4% in one year alone. See Keeble, *In the Spirit of Wandering Teachers*, about those who worked in 1961with peasants, teachers, and organizers in the Cuban literacy campaign.
2. The website describes the study as an in-house survey taking a sample representative of the non-institutionalized population ages 16 and older who are living in households in the United States. The NAAL will describe the status of literacy in the nation and states. It will inform policymakers and educators about the factors believed to play critical roles in the development of adult literacy abilities and the use of literacy skills in workplace, family, and community settings. Knowledge about the roles, relationships, and impacts of such factors will help improve educational practices and programs.
3. In my own state, the cost of the state portion of the survey was too high in 1992 as well as during the recent economic crisis, so Oklahoma is not included in the detailed state literacy information. This is despite efforts of the federal government to have surplus welfare funds (supposedly unspent due to the declining welfare rolls) allocated by the states to gather information on literacy and the poor.
4. Of course, Scribner and Coles's earlier ethnography of the Vai in Liberia has provided valuable and, to some extent, unheeded wisdom about the complexities of literacy in Africa.
5. The term "multiliteracies" is valuable in talking about various literate knowledge today at home and is needed as well in discussing global literacies.

6. I rely heavily on the 1995 report because it focused on women's literacies. However, UNESCO's *World Education Report 2000*, its *Education for All Global Monitoring Report*, and UN statistics in general have also been consulted.

7. Brock-Utne believes the "rate of return" figures on primary education presented by the World Bank led to a narrowing of alternatives earlier proposed by Africans. Rate of return is difficult to figure in women's work, which has been invisible in world economic statistics, where housework is unvalued and women's agricultural work has gone uncounted.

8. Many including Brock-Utne use the terms "North" and "South" for the developed and developing world, although, of course, these do not work in every instance, for example, New Zealand and Australia.

WORKS CITED

Ballara, Marcella. *Women and Literacy*. [For Joint UN-NGO Group on Women and Development.] London: Zed Books, 1992.

Brandt, Deborah. *Literacy in American Lives*. New York: Cambridge UP, 2001.

Brecher, Jeremy, Tim Costello, and Brendan Smith. *Globalization from Below: The Power of Solidarity*. Cambridge, MA: South End, 2000.

Brock-Utne, Birgit. *Whose Education for All? The Recolonization of the African Mind*. New York: Falmer, 2000.

Coleman, Isobel. "The Payoff from Women's Rights." *Foreign Affairs* 83.3 (2004): 80–95.

Fish, M. Steven, and Matthew Kroenig. "Aiming to Keep Faith and Egomania in Check." *Newsday*. 14 Mar. 2004: Combined editions, A56.

Hobbs, Catherine. Introduction. "Cultures and Practices of U.S. Women's Literacy." *Nineteenth-Century Women Learn to Write*. Ed. Catherine Hobbs. Charlottesville: U Press of Virginia, 1995. 1–33.

Horsman, Jennifer. *Something in My Mind Besides the Everyday: Women and Literacy*. Toronto: Women's P, 1990.

———. *Too Scared to Learn: Women, Violence, and Education*. Mahwah, NJ: Lawrence Erlbaum Associates, 2000.

International Bank for Reconstruction and Development. *World Development Indicators, 2001*. Washington, DC: The World Bank Group, 2001.

Keeble, Alexandra. *In the Spirit of Wandering Teachers: Cuba's Literacy Campaign, 1961*. Melbourne, Australia: Global, 2001.

Kirsch, Irwin S., Ann Jungeblut, and Andrew Kolstad. *Adult Literacy in America: A First Look at the Results of the National Adult Literacy Survey*. Washington, DC: Office of Educational Research Improvement, U.S. Department of Education, 1993.

Nafisi, Azar. *Reading Lolita in Tehran: A Memoir in Books*. New York: Random House, 2003.

National Center for Education Statistics. *A First Look at the Literacy of America's Adults in the 21st Century*. Washington, DC: U.S. Department of Education, 2005.

Rideout, William M. "Globalization and Decentralization in Sub-Saharan Africa: Focus Lesotho." *Globalization and Education: Integration and Contestation across Cultures*. Stromquist and Monkman.

Rockhill, Kathleen. "(Dis)connecting Literacy and Sexuality: Speaking the Unspeakable in the Classroom." *Critical Literacy: Politics, Praxis and the Postmodern.* Ed. Colin Lankshear and Peter L. McLaren. Albany: State U of New York P, 1993. 335–66.

Scribner, Sylvia, and Michael Cole. *The Psychology of Literacy.* Cambridge: Harvard UP, 1981.

Scully, Nan. "Women and Structural Adjustment." *Peace and Freedom* July–Sept. 1996: 10–11.

Soltow, Lee, and Edward Stevens. *The Rise of Literacy and the Common Schools in the United States: A Socioeconomic Analysis to 1870.* Chicago: U of Chicago P, 1981.

Street, Brian V., ed. *Cross-Cultural Approaches to Literacy.* Cambridge, UK: Cambridge UP, 1993.

Stromquist, Nelly P., and Karen Monkman, ed. *Globalization and Education: Integration and Contestation across Cultures.* Lanham, MD: Rowman and Littlefield, 2000.

Stromquist, Nelly P., and Michael L. Basile. *Politics of Educational Innovations in Developing Countries: An Analysis of Knowledge and Power.* New York: Falmer, 1999.

Stromquist, Nelly P. *Increasing Girls' and Women's Participation in Basic Education.* Paris: UNESCO International Institute for Educational Planning, 1997.

——. *Literacy for Citizenship: Gender and Grassroots Dynamics in Brazil.* Albany: State U of New York P, 1997.

——. *"Women and Literacy: Promises and Constraints." Annals of the American Academy of Political and Social Science* 520 (1992): 54–65.

UNESCO [United Nations Educational, Scientific, and Cultural Organization]. *Statistical Yearbook.* Paris, UNESCO, 1996– .

——. *Education for All Global Monitoring Report 2001.* Paris: UNESCO, 2001.

——. *The State of the World's Children, 2003.* New York: UNESCO, 2002.

——. *World Education Report 1995.* Oxford: UNESCO, 1995.

——. *World Education Report 2000.* Paris: UNESCO, 2000.

Useem, Michael. *The Leadership Moment: Nine True Stories of Triumph and Disaster and their Lessons for Us All.* New York: Three Rivers P, 1998.

Segue

The daily news brings mixed messages about progress toward achieving the ideals that Catherine Hobbs addresses so well in her chapter. Of course, many of these messages embed assumptions about literacy's consequences that contributors to this collection are inclined to question, but nonetheless find instantiated in their research participants' experience. Still, some public discourse on the global status of women's literacy is better than none. Such discourse can evolve into meaningful dialogue on women and literacy—dialogue that has the potential to be widely legible and audible. But moving from potential to actual public dialogue is more easily imagined than enacted. Consider, then, the fate of two recent studies of girls' and women's literacy.

In April 2005, the UN Children's Fund (UNICEF) released a "report card on gender parity and primary education," one in a series of reports on progress toward goals that include universal primary education as a necessary step toward gender equality and women's empowerment. The report finds that girls' access to education has been expanding in countries around the world, but not quickly enough to meet the goal of gender parity in 2005. Still, girls' primary education has increased at an average annual rate since 2001 that points toward long-term success: projections from UNICEF point to many regions, and nations within regions, attaining gender parity in primary education by 2015. Nations in Africa (especially in the West/ Central and Eastern/Southern regions) and South Asia have furthest to go.

In the weeks after its release, the UNICEF report did not enjoy much mainstream media attention in the United States, perhaps because of its technical orientation, but more likely because its argument revolves around UN—and not U.S.—interests. Contrast the UNICEF report's lukewarm public reception in the U.S. with the U.S. news media's more eager embrace of a report issued in early May 2005 by Save the Children, self-described as "the leading independent organization creating real and lasting change for children in need in the United States and in more than 40 countries around the world" (ii). Unveiled the week before Mother's Day, the "State of the World's Mothers 2005: The Power and Promise of Girls' Education" greets its audience with a foreword by ABC News and National Public Radio commentator Cokie Roberts, a crisp recitation of findings and recommendations, and a willingness to examine gendered gaps in literacy both abroad and in the U.S.

Both reports take care to acknowledge that the education of girls is but one of many prerequisites to improving the conditions of life in developing and developed nations around the world. But both reports assert that among these prerequisites, literacy, attained through formal education, is the most likely agent by which individuals and groups can enjoy the fruits of economic modernization. For example, in her forward to the Save the Children report, Roberts sets up past as prologue:

> Take a look at parts of Asia. South Korea, Taiwan, Thailand and Indonesia not too long ago (back around 1950) looked a good deal like sub-Saharan Africa does today, statistically speaking. They were in the same state in terms of economics, literacy, health care and fertility rates. How did these so-called Asian tigers do it? Through education—particularly the education of girls.

> It's a simple and well-documented fact. A girl who goes to school and stays there is much more likely to postpone marriage and childbirth.

> Those decisions have a dramatic ripple effect. Later childbirth results in lowering the overall fertility rate, which means higher per capita income and the increased ability of a woman to earn a living for herself and her family. And educated women provide better health care for themselves and their children, meaning lower maternal and infant mortality rates. In fact, a country's investment in education leads to a whole host of results that promote economic and social development. (3)

It is this story—succinct, familiar, believable—that is retold in much news coverage of the Save the World report. Contributors to this volume tend to tell more complicated stories. They are skeptical of "simple" and "well-documented" "facts." Yet they remain committed to the idea that literacy creates opportunities that are critical to the advancement of women toward personal and social well-being. At the same time, they are aware that this very well-being can be compromised—sometimes radically—by the economic demands attendant upon the acquisition of literacy.

Min-Zhan Lu explores precisely this tension in her afterword, wherein she extends the argument she develops in "An Essay on the Work of Composition: Composing English against the Order of Fast Capitalism," which won the 2004 Braddock Award for best article in *College Composition and Communication*. Lu is concerned that "[t]he pressure to acquire and use English is increasingly becoming a lived reality for peoples stratified by labels such as Native-Speaking, Educated, Developed Countries, or Democracy and their Others" (20). *And their Others:* Whereas Roberts marvels at the advances in literacy made a generation ago by Other nations such as the "so-called Asian tigers," Lu is troubled that these advances have brought these nations' economic development to a place where literacy in Korean or Mandarin or Thai is under pressure from the "exclusivity and dominance of standardized U.S. english" (21). Consequently, while her afterword suggests that she sees gender parity in access to literacy as a laudable goal, she insists on asking, *literacy in whose language?*[1]

It is Lu's contention that scholars in composition and rhetoric should "redesign standardized U.S. English against the grain of fast capitalism" by "[w]orking alongside resistant users of English across the world" (46). Such "word-work," Lu writes, "can help to design a better world. By all. For all" (46). What does this mean? What does it mean to work collectively against the grain of fast capitalism?

In *The New Work Order*, James Gee, Glynda Hull, and Colin Lankshear examine "fast capitalist texts" that describe a work world that is being rapidly transformed by the global mobility of capital and the international transfer of technology. These texts advocate a new style of capitalism that is less about the production and consumption of commodities and more about *"privatization"*: the advocacy that "everything—business, social processes, private lives—ought to be *unregulated* except by the forces of competition ('markets') defined around *quality* as determined by 'customers' (where our family and our friends are, in our private lives, our 'customers')" (35). Against the privatizating impulse of fast capitalism, Gee, Hull, and Lankshear offer "a critical version of sociocultural literacy" that is meant to prepare students and workers to slow the damage done to humanity by the new economy (165).

Coming at the problem from a slightly different direction, Ben Agger explains in *Fast Capitalism* that "[c]apitalism today [nearly twenty years ago now] quickens the pace at which significance diminishes away from text and moves toward things themselves," a process that results in the mind being "short-circuited to the world without passing through the discursive media of speech and text" (6, 7). If this definition seems somewhat opaque, it is because Agger does not "want terms like fast capitalism to become mindless slogans substituting for thought

and analysis" (15). Rather, fast capitalism's meaning emerges as Agger
returns to the term throughout his book (and again in *Speeding Up Fast
Capitalism* [2004]) in a process of "self-reflection" that "constitutes an alternative to straightforward definitions" (16).

So it is that Lu reflects on the contents of *Women and Literacy*, building
as she goes a definition of fast capitalism that captures and illuminates
what could be lost if the plural meanings of literacy represented in this
book are allowed (or forced) to collapse into a singular, standard, stable
English-language literacy. Her reflection resists the conventions of a
stable or standardized literacy in various ways, the most obvious being
the capitalization of words and phrases that are implicated in the accel-
eration of capitalism's global reach. By engaging in such resistance, Lu
demonstrates "the necessity and possibility of responsive and responsible uses of language ... in a world rife with and riven by systems and relations of injustice" (18).

NOTE

1. David Crystal assesses the "dangers of a global language," finding some
   threats more credible than others (14). "Will those who speak a global language as a mother tongue automatically be in a position of power compared with those who have to learn it as an official or foreign language?"
   he asks (16). "The risk," he answers, "is certainly real." He notes, however, that "if proper attention is paid to the question of language learning,
   the problem of disadvantage dramatically diminishes." By proper attention, he means adherence to two principles: "Languages of identity need
   to be maintained. Access to the emerging global language—widely perceived as a language of opportunity and empowerment—needs to be
   guaranteed. Both principles demand massive resources. The irony is that
   the issue is approaching a climax at a time when the world financial climate can least afford it" (28). For an activist perspective on the subject, see
   the various contributions to Tove Skutnabb-Kangas and Robert
   Phillipson's edited collection, *Linguistic Human Rights*.

WORKS CITED

Agger, Ben. *Fast Capitalism: A Critical Theory of Significance*. Urbana: U of Illinois P,
     1989.
———. *Speeding Up Fast Capitalism: Cultures, Jobs, Families, Schools, Bodies*. Boulder:
     Paradigm, 2004.
Crystal, David. *English as a Global Language*. 2nd ed. Cambridge, UK: Cambridge UP,
     2003.
Gee, James Paul, Glynda Hull, and Colin Lankshear. *The New Work Order: Behind the
     Language of the New Capitalism*. Boulder: Westview, 1996.
Lu, Min-Zhan. "An Essay on the Work of Composition: Composing English against
     the Order of Fast Capitalism." *College Composition and Communication* 56 (2004):
     16–50.

Save the Children. *State of the World's Mothers 2005: The Power and Promise of Girls' Education.* Westport, CT: Save the Children, 2005.

Skutnabb-Kangas, Tove, and Robert Phillipson, eds. *Linguistic Human Rights: Overcoming Linguistic Discrimination.* New York: de Gruyter, 1994.

UNICEF. *Progress for Children: A Report Card on Gender Parity and Primary Education.* No. 2. New York: UNICEF, 2005.

Afterword: Reading Literacy Research Against the Grain of Fast Capitalism

Min-Zhan Lu

> No one today is unaware of this divide between the world's rich and poor. No one today can claim ignorance of the cost that this divide imposes on the poor and dispossessed who are no less deserving of human dignity, fundamental freedoms, security, food and education than any of us. The cost, however, is not borne by them alone. Ultimately, it is borne by all of us—North and South, rich and poor, men and women of all races and religions.   —*Kofi Annan*, Nobel Lecture (2001)

This is an invested reading motivated by two assumptions. First, all of us working in U.S. Composition—students as well as teachers and researchers—need to view English as enlivened and enlightened by the efforts of users/learners around the world (whether English has been tagged as their Native, First, Second, or Foreign Language) to make English limn the ever-changing, complex, different conditions of their lives which standardized englishes are not designed to serve. Second, how we address issues of language, literacy, and learning in U.S. Composition classrooms matters. It could have long-term impact on the present and future of not only one's own sense of self and life, one's relations with other users of English the world over, but also the lives of other users and the world we share.[1]

My premise rests on a story of the current world I've patched together from my reading of research on literacy and learning from a cultural materialist perspective.[2] We are currently witnessing a global restructuring of capitalism—the emergence of what critics have variously termed Fast capitalism, or a regime of flexible accumulation. The devastating effects of capitalism are intensifying, deepening the division of labor and widening the gap between rich and poor individuals, social collectives, institutions, cultures, nation/states, and continents. In this race for wealth and markets, the ability to design, market, and vary goods or services and to process and manipulate information becomes a critical measure of the intra- and international division of labor. Three broad categories of work are emerging: routine production services, in-person services, and symbolic-analytic services (Reich, in Gee, Hull, and Lankshear 44–45). Only those employed in conducting symbolic-analytic work are considered substantial Value Adders. Predictably, such jobs fall into the hands of a small number of people within a small number of countries which have benefitted and are increasingly benefitting from the regime of flexible accumulation. A majority of the people in the United States and across the world holding routine production and in-service jobs are progressively exploited and worse off, having to make do with part-time or temporary work, short-term individual contracts, fewer employment rights, and entitlements.

In the Discourse of Fast capitalism, social, economic, cultural, and technological Development (as it is defined according to the interests of Developed Countries such as the United States) serves as the overriding code for construing and constructing the world (in words and deeds). "Super-developed" countries like the U.S. mobilize all their geopolitical, military, technological, and economic capital to "recruit" governments and people across the world into subscribing to the myth that "marketization" is an unstoppable force for the natural good of the world. The geopolitical tension in Mao Tse-Tung's map of a "third" world against the "first" (U.S.-dominated Western Capitalist) world and "second" (Soviet-dominated Eastern Communist) world has been dissolved by the myth of a world united by its inevitable and unavoidable economic fate—finding a viable niche in a hyper-competitive and science- and technology-driven market. In fact, this fairytale plot banks on the assumption that development according to the logic of Fast capitalism will result in infinite advancement at both personal and national levels—it is the only viable and desirable form of "freedom" worth sweating for. By the same token, "being exploited for low wages and poor working conditions" are the "dues" required of the Underdeveloped or "undeveloped" regions in order to join the fated march towards a global Free Market economy (Gee, Hull, and Lankshear 45). In such a story of the world, peoples "unable" to find a niche in the Developing, Globalizing, Free Market will become inconsequential, irrelevant to the World Economy, and will thus face natural extinction (Gee, Hull, and Lankshear 46, 130).

Because Development is defined in terms of an economy centering on the buying and selling of symbolic products such as (spoken or written) words, graphs, charts, images, and software, skills with literacy or symbols show up in all aspects of production: literacy is capitalized as a productive force (labor power), a product (with use and exchange value), a means of production (tool), and raw material (texts out of texts, budgets out of numbers) (Brandt 171). The status of literacy in diverse languages (English and computer programming or their Others) and forms of English (standardized and its Others) is ordered according to its Free Market value. Standardized U.S. english and Internet exchanges in that english are becoming the major freeways of intra- and international geopolitical, economic, and cultural trafficking. Accordingly, literacy in English increasingly means fluency in the kinds of "usage" appearing to be "usual" and "useful" to people who qualify as Consumers (with the most buying power) and (most profit-generating) Value Adders—and in a demeanor pleasing to Consumers and Value Adders in Developed Countries.[3] Illiteracy in the standardized english of the United Kingdom or the U.S. becomes a liability: cutting individuals and peoples off as Suppliers, Producers, and Consumers and, by logical extension, turning them into the necessary casualties of the pilgrimage towards the Global Free Market.

U.S. media (from local newspapers such as the *Milwaukee Journal Sentinel* to PBS programs such as the *NewsHour with Jim Lehrer*) bombard us with coverage of the frenzy of peoples in Developing, Underdeveloped, and Undeveloped Countries trying to join the mad race for jobs, wealth, and markets through the learning of standardized U.S. english: an agency is hiring inner-city Brazilian teens ("hard-working" enough to take its offering of crash English courses) to act as guides to U.S. Tourists eager for an "insider" but "safe" taste of Rio. Young Indian women in pursuit of service jobs (outsourced from U.S.-based conglomerates and run by male Indian subcontractors) are busy taking pronunciation courses (offered by middle-aged male Experts) and learning about U.S. culture and current events through U.S. mass media so that they might sound Native to the U.S. Customers they serve through the phone and on the Internet. Women in Mexico are vying for computer station in-service work outsourced from U.S. corporations, their "strong" accent having excluded them from voice-mediated service jobs outsourced to their Indian (Free Market) compatriots. In short, women across the world are living under pressure to acquire "demeanors"—defined by accent, syntax, semantics, rhythm, pitch, and so on—deemed "pleasant" to and by Customers and Employers entitled to the distinction of Native or Fluent Speakers of the standardized english of the U.S. or UK by formal accreditation or birth.

A story on *BBC News World Edition* online (31 July 2002) reports that "[w]ith China's growing internationalization, people's determination to become more proficient in English has reached fever pitch" (Markus). More and more people in China, the BBC asserts, "are seeking tongue operations to *improve* their English" (emphasis mine), "a snip of the muscle under the tongue using local anesthetic" promising to "improve [the patient's] pronunciation almost overnight." A plastic surgeon is quoted as saying that he "is inundated with people begging for the operation because they want their English pronunciation to be *clearer,* freeing them from that *tongue-tied feeling,*" and "they're taking interpreters [*sic*] exams or wanting to go abroad or get a job here [in China] with a foreign company" (emphasis mine). In a section subtitled "Parental Pressure," the surgeon's claim is substantiated by the words of the father of a seven-year-old boy who had just undergone the operation: "With China becoming more and more international, if you can't communicate properly in English it will have a serious effect on your career prospects." Proof: Just recently, his "bright and lively" son "was rejected by a bilingual primary school, let down by his English pronunciation." Further proof: "In Shanghai's People's Park on a sweltering Sunday morning, the heat does not stop droves of people turning out to practice their English."

Another item of media coverage, "Accent Axed with a Snip," begins:

> It's a simple if gruesome procedure ... chop a centimeter or so off your tongue to become a fluent English speaker.

> That is the hope that recently drove one mother to take her six-year-old son for surgery aimed at ridding him of his Korean accent when speaking the language of choice in global business.

> Driven by a desire to give their kids an edge in an increasingly competitive society, a surprising number of South Koreans have turned to the knife in a seemingly drastic bid to help their offspring perfect their English. (Kim)

This report is accompanied by the following "information": The actual surgery takes about five minutes. But even after surgery, months of language training are needed "for those with ankyloglossia—the medical term for those with a short frenulum."

Under the subtitle "Excessive Enthusiasm," the report goes on to point out that "[u]sing surgery to *enhance* your looks is already very common in South Korea, where many resort to plastic surgery to make their eyes bigger, noses *shapelier* and even their calves slimmer" (emphasis mine). Under the subtitle, "Growing Foreign Participation," we learn that "[f]rom toddlers to students to office workers, learning English has become a national obsession" since the 1997–98 Asian financial crisis. Subsequently,

> Financial markets were ... flung open and foreign investment flowed in ....

Many Koreans believe an early start in English could give their children an edge and so do not hesitate to send them overseas or at least to evening classes.

Central bank data show that spending for overseas study by South Koreans, including those who leave purely for a language course, jumped to $1.43 billion in 2002 from $960 million in 2000. (Kim)

Read from the perspective of such media coverage, several of the chapters in this collection can be said to provide further evidence of this "enthusiasm." The Vietnamese women Crawford spoke to consistently said they believed that their hard work ("the schoolwork, the money invested in night classes, the viewing of pirated copies of American movies, and the individual efforts to practice reading and writing for a few minutes in between customers, on break, or in the evenings") in pursuit of "better" English, despite the many material constraints they encounter, would eventually prove beneficial (237). A woman selling coffee in Ho Chi Minh City's Ben Thahn market takes classes in Japanese and English classes to get a "well-paying office job" (238). A Tunisian woman of color tells Walters that she makes a point of working for Foreign families, which enables (and pressures?) her to pick up some French, Roman-script literacy, and some English from Native-Speaking employers (201).

Yet, by taking a cultural materialist approach to how individual women living in and outside the U.S. are addressing issues of language, literacy, and learning (in and out of school), the chapters in this collection pose a set of questions absent in and occluded by a majority of the media coverage of the kind of "fever," "obsession," and "excessive enthusiasm" over "proficiency," "fluency," or "proper communication" in the "language of choice in global business" sweeping over the Developing, Underdeveloped, and Undeveloped Worlds. By a "cultural materialist approach," I have in mind the efforts to treat terms such as the "world," "society," "history," "culture," "social collective" (what others called "community"), "economy," "knowledge," or "Discourse" as conflicting, living processes in the making and as processes which are constitutive of one another. Discourse, defined as a specific way of talking, listening, reading, writing, feeling, acting, interacting, believing, valuing, using tools, gesturing, clothing, carrying one's body and so on at specific times and places, is treated as a "dual coding": a formal tool and a form of "sociotechnical device" shaped by and shaping social processes and relations—historical, geopolitical, military, cultural, economic, technological, intellectual, etc. (Gee, Hull, and Lankshear xv). This approach focuses attention on the interrelations between historical changes in three areas of life generally considered to be separate and referred to as the Workplace (job sites), private space (everyday life in life worlds), and public space (including government or educational programs and institutions; Cope and Kalantzis 11, 16).[4] Given escalating U.S. interests in Developing a Global Free Market to encompass all areas of life, it makes sense that most of the chapters in this volume employ the concept of "sponsorship" as a critical lens "to connect literacy as an individual development to literacy as an economic development" (Brandt 19).

Brandt treats as sponsors "any agents, local or distant, concrete or abstract, who enable, support, teach, and model, as well as recruit, regulate, suppress, or withhold literacy—and gain advantage by it in some way" (19). Reading the chapters alongside the media coverage I bring to it, I find myself returning to three aspects of how Brandt uses the concept. She foregrounds the "reciprocal relationship" between the sponsor and the sponsored in terms of the lending of resources (or credibility) and gaining of these "whether by direct repayment or, indirectly, by credit of association" (19). She tracks the socioeconomic trafficking that underwrites "a range of human relationships and ideological pressures that turn up at the scenes of literacy learning—from benign sharing between adults and youths to euphemistic coercions in schools and workplaces to the most notorious impositions and deprivations by church or state" (20). Brandt contextualizes the lengths to which people will go to secure literacy for themselves and their children in the "competition to harness literacy, to manage, measure, teach, and exploit it," a competition shaping (and, I'd add, shaped by) the "incentives and barriers" that greet literacy learners in any particular time and place, while also making "the pursuit of literacy feel so turbulent and precarious for so many" (21).

Read alongside the cultural materialist moves emerging in these chapters, media coverage of the recent fever for tongue surgery loses its transparency as direct data on the "obsessive" and "excessive" lengths to which Asians will go to secure "clear," "proper" English for their children. The chapters encourage us to instead interrogate forms of trafficking that substantiate the diagnoses Developed Countries like the U.S. make concerning the "pathology" of their Others. The chapters remind us to ask questions such as what counts as "proper," "clear," "perfect" English in current day (U.S.-dominated) Free Trading of money, products, ideas, services, or Tourists? How and why is English being standardized in these particular forms, at this particular historical juncture, and at diverse scenes of learning intra- and internationally? What benign, euphemistically coercive, or notoriously oppressive forces and relations might have been and are sponsoring its standardizing? How does each of these forces and relations work at diverse scenes of literacy learning: bilingual schools as well as medical journals, operating rooms, homes, family gatherings, phone and Internet exchanges (among family and friends living locally or abroad), the media (intra- or international), job interviews, exams or interviews (for entrance into the U.S. and U.S. institutions of learning), (People's) parks, evening classes, and so on? Which forms of unequal access and reward might be shaping and shaped by such a standardized english? (For instance, which population in current-day China or South Korea is most likely to have heard about the tongue operation and to come up with the surgery fee? How might we make sense of the fact that both children featured in the coverage and both surgeons interviewed are male?) Besides being "rejected" from educational and job opportunities and feeling "tongue-tied," what emotional, visceral, ideological, and social material consequences might the hegemonic power of standardized U.S. or UK english have for individual learners in these and other parts of the world? Besides "career prospects" and "an edge in an increasingly competitive society," what might be the complex but diverse, conflicting motives for learning English among individual learners, such as ways of using English for purposes other than the ones endorsed by (U.S.-dominated) International Business?

Besides the media coverage, I've also brought three observations to my reading of these chapters: (1) U.S.-standardized english in its spoken form is defined according to the rules of the written English of the College Educated (Lippi-Green); (2) the teaching of English as a Second or Foreign Language within and outside the United States is dominated by various traditions, approaches, and philosophies of U.S. Composition (Canagarajah, *Linguistic*); and (3) Native Speakers of English (without or with advanced degrees in the field) have traditionally been and are still considered the most and only qualified teachers for ESL or EFL within and outside English (Canagarajah, *Geopolitics* 259). I add to these observations a speculation: a significant number of U.S. Customers and Value Adders—Tourists, Executives, Business People, Lawyers, Teachers, Politicians, Officers, Parents, Expatriates, and so on, people with the geopolitical, cultural, and economic currency to track the Free Trading of intellectual, consumer, technological, or military goods intra- and internationally—are the products of, are currently working in, or will soon be passing through a U.S. Composition classroom. This in turn adds two more questions to my reading. How might Composition sponsor literacy and learning in ways that call into question rather than padlock English "usage" with dominant U.S. notions of what counts as "usual" ("fluent," "proficient," "perfect," "clear," or "proper") and "useful" (pleasing-profitable) to a small population in a small number of countries benefitting the most from the move to Develop a Global Free Market? How might we link our efforts to "harness" literacy in English with the lived literacy experiences of individual learners of English in the U.S. and across the world, especially those labeled Foreign, First, or Second Speakers of English?

Let me share some highly partial but impassioned connections I see between the two reports on tongue surgery and some of the chapters in this collection. All of the chapters support the premise that "economic competition" is a major sponsor of literacy in the standardized english of the UK or U.S. in a world dominated by the Free Trading policies of the Developed Countries. However, these stories also ask us to reread media coverage of the "pathology" of Other learners of English by considering the intersection between economic and geopolitical relations between the Developed World and its Others, particularly in terms of the historical changes in these relations in the last quarter of the twentieth century. The "fever" for the english of Foreign Investors and Tourists is clearly government sponsored—driven by notorious impositions and deprivations. The national congress of the communist party of Vietnam implemented in 1986 a shift to a socialist market economy by allowing foreign trade and investment and promoting knowledge economies centered on the trading of information (Crawford 229). As Vietnam is turning into both a niche market and a resource for Developed Countries, information in Vietnam is overwhelmingly in other languages, particularly English. This has made language learning, including fluency in standardized U.S. english, necessary, even compulsory for many working women in Vietnam. In current day, postcolonial Tunisia, French is no longer the language of instruction but is now taught as a language. So literacy means "literacy in French for some Tunisians, literacy in Arabic for others, and literacy in both languages (and English) for yet others" (Walters 196).

These chapters remind us to put media coverage of South Korea's "excessive enthusiasm" to acquire the "choice language of international business" in the context of U.S. involvement in the Korean War and its excessive geopolitical enthusiasm to Develop South Korea into Asia's fourth-largest "economy" (while Under-developing North Korea through political and economic sanctions), as well as the direct and indirect role the New York Stock Exchange played in the 1997–98 Asian financial crisis. Furthermore, this complex history of U.S. geopolitical relations with South and North Korea cannot be separated from U.S. relations with China vis-à-vis Taiwan. Likewise, coverage of the "fever pitch" for "clear" English as a result of "China's growing internationalization" needs to be read against the background of the triangular power struggle between Mao Tse-Tung's First, Second, and Third Worlds, respectively presided over by the U.S., the former Soviet Union, and the People's Republic of China, including the U.S. rush to Develop Taiwan into a major Asian "economy" to ensure its "independence" from the People's Republic of China and, thus, dependence on U.S.'s "protection."

These chapters teach us to approach the learning "frenzy" in China and South Korea in terms of the intersection between gender, class, race, ethnicity, and other lines of injustice. As Brandt points out in her study of the literacy experiences of two learners of the same age, Raymond Branch and Dora Lopez, self-initiating the learning of a foreign language (computer programming for him and Spanish for her) at the same time and in the same geographical area, may "labor equally to acquire literacy but do so under systems of unequal subsidy and unequal compensation" (180). Of the women we encounter in these chapters, Safia El-Wakil, one of the co-authors of "Women and the Global Ecology of Digital Literacies" (Hawisher, Selfe, Coffield, and El-Wakil), seems to be the only one sharing the kind of relatively seamless, fluid, and steady network of sponsors depicted in Brandt's account of the self-initiated learning of Raymond Branch, the kind of network withheld from most of the people we encounter in Brandt's book, including his contemporary Dora Lopez (Brandt 169–86). Like Safia El-Wakil, most of the women we encounter in this volume experience equally intense ideological and socioeconomic pressure to learn English. They labor equally hard. But, like Brandt's Lopez, they face different but also equally uneven and contradictory pulls, often having little contact with any technological infrastructure (classroom, Internet, training sessions), (English or computer) user groups, or commercial facilities (retailers or manufacturers of English books, tapes, newspapers or computer hard- and software).

"Women and the Global Ecology of Digital Literacies" offers a comprehensive account of the complex, changing network of sponsors for the literacy activities of two of its authors, Kate Coffield and Safia El-Wakil. Given my concern here, a series of details concerning the literacy experience of Safia El-Wakil, who has taught writing for fifteen years at the American University of Cairo (AUC), caught my attention. Born in 1942 and brought up in a "well-to-do, educated, Muslim Egyptian family," El-Wakil entered a British school in Alexandria, Egypt, at the age of five (212–13). In addition to a year of high school in Switzerland, she received an MA from the American University of Beirut in Lebanon and an MLitt from St. Hugh's College of Oxford University in the UK (213). Upon returning to Egypt (from Lebanon after the death of her husband), El-Wakil worked for a few years as "chief administrator" in a teacher training program at the Fulbright Commission in Cairo and then took a teaching position in the "Writing Program" at the American University of Cairo. El-Wakil's consistent access to the englishes sponsored by U.S. and UK educational, governmental, and business interests took a further turn in the 1990s, when the writing program at the American University of Cairo where she had been working began experimenting with computers—some years after the

University of Illinois's English Department received a grant from IBM for "computer rhetoric classrooms" and when Michigan Tech was establishing its Center for Computer-Assisted Language Instruction. Around 1994, the Internet came to AUC. Such institutional restructuring legitimized a series of learning opportunities El-Wakil had already had, including a three-day tutorial in 1987 on how to use computers for word processing. Subsequently, she enjoyed a travel grant from the American University of Cairo to attend the two-week Computers in Writing- Intensive Classes Workshop at Michigan Technological University in 1995, and in 1999 American University of Cairo sponsored a technology symposium at which U.S. scholars Hawisher and Selfe gave papers (217).

Hawisher, Selfe, Coffield, and El-Wakil are also careful to detail the intersection between personal history and national, international histories on the educational, cultural, social, and geopolitical levels. As El-Wakil points out, "Education at the university, graduate and postgraduate level became very common during the years I grew up ...." (213). Furthermore, "[M]en in my family, my father and my husband (rather than my mother), were those who offered me the greatest support in pursuing higher levels of education" (213). This narrative is accompanied by an analysis of the network of social forces, historical events, economic patterns, material conditions, and cultural expectations sustaining her literacy endeavors, including the United States's geopolitical and economic interests in Egypt in terms of U.S competition with other Developed Countries; the unstable relations among Egypt, Great Britain, Soviet Union, Israel, and the United States; the change of governing forces in Egypt (Nasser, al-Sadat, Mubarak); the opportunities becoming available to women in Egypt and the United States as a result of feminist activism in both countries; and the time of her return to Egypt (in the early eighties, just when personal computers were making their appearance on the global market and Mubarak was attempting to revitalize the Egyptian economy (215).

Reading El-Wakil's literacy experience alongside discussions of the emotional effects of literacy learning and practices in chapters such as Crawford's research on Vietnam and Strickland's reading of Dorothy West's "The Typewriter," several bits of information in the two media stories take on new meaning for me. In the section of "Accent Axed with a Snip" titled "Excessive Enthusiasm," we learn that "many psychologists, professors, and native English speakers argue that there are many downsides" to tongue surgery. A professor at Seoul National University who specializes in issues of adolescent psychiatry worries that tongue surgery might cause a "speech impediment"—or worse, make the child "autistic" (Kim). This type of citing of Experts further pathologizes the "frenzy" of Chinese or South Korean Parents. Reading the Expert opinions, a side of me agrees with (what the reporter calls) the "somewhat traditional" approach of the "retired teacher" (an "old timer" to the English practicing gatherings at Shanghai's People's Park), who was quoted as calling it "a waste of time, waste of money" (Markus).

Another side of me identifies with the professor of English at a local university in Seoul, who was quoted as saying that the "surgery may be an extreme case but it reflects a social phenomenon": "English is now becoming a means of survival .... Entering a college, getting jobs, and getting promoted—many things hinge heavily on your mastery of English" (Kim). The story does not tell us whether the English of any of the psychologists, professors, or surgeons speaking against the "frenzy" for tongue surgery speak the kind of English that would qualify as "clear" or "proper" by the kind of entrance examinations and job interviews the parents and the professor of English anticipate for the younger generation.

But it does suggest that a network of factors—including academic credentials, occupation, generation, and Native (or Non-Native) Speaking status—does indeed affect one's sense of and the social assessment of one's English literacy and one's positions on issues of literacy and learning. What might be the intersecting as well as different material conditions shaping and shaped by one's sense of feeling (or not feeling) "tongue-tied" (whether one is with or without a strong Korean or Chinese Accent) and feeling (or not feeling) Literate, Semi-literate, or Illiterate in the (U.S.) "choice" language of Free Trade? I wonder how English users like El-Wakil might comment on such media stories. I know I speak English with a heavy Foreign Accent (which Experts have informed me is not *purely* Chinese). I also know that at different scenes of literacy learning, at different points of my life, when I'm interacting with users of English with different assumptions and attitudes toward the standardizing of english, I feel "tongue-tied" or loose, literate, semi-literate, or illiterate in English. I am also aware that my sense of the educational, income, gender, race, sex, and other inequities embedded in my relations with each of the people with whom I'm "communicating" at a given time and place, significantly affect my visceral, intellectual, and practical understanding of my English. The chapters in this collection have made me acutely aware of the need, when making sense of the "frenzy," to attend to the different networks of intra- and international sponsors available (and not available) to learners and users of English and of computer technology: learners and users such as myself, El-Wakil, each of the boys undergoing tongue surgery, each parent of each boy, each of the "psychologists, professors, and native English speakers" cited in the stories, each of the reporters working on the stories, and the person or persons at the two web sites in a position to place the stories online and in their specific sections or links.

The chapters in *Women and Literacy* render story after story of the complex effects on individual learners and users of English of with-holding the kind of relatively fluid and consistent network of sponsors available to El-Wakil. For instance, another of the four vignettes Walters draws from his research in postcolonial Tunisia involves a woman in her sixties identified as Fatiha (201). Fatiha was educated in the colonial school system of Tunisia, in French, because of her "father's commit-ment to education for his daughters and sons" (an attitude not shared by a man in his late twenties living in Korba whom Walters interviewed in 1986; 201–02). In college during the 1960s, Fatiha was "passed over for opportunities for study abroad" because "early Western develop-ment programs favored men" (201). Later, even when "international funding priorities became more gender neutral," younger women were chosen over women in Fatiha's generation (201). When Fatiha finally se-cured a one-year fellowship in the U.S., she turned it into a chance for a doctorate through "luck, pluck, and a great deal of hard work" (201–02). In the midst of writing her dissertation, she broke into sobbing during a conversation with Walters. It seems that her fear that all possibilities of funding would run out and she would have to return without a degree to Tunisia, "where marriage and family remain important to women" is a material, integral part of her learning she has to wrestle with from minute to minute (202).

The women in Crawford's research encounter a different set of withholdings and impositions with different kinds of conflicting pulls. Crawford's account of the frustrations, regrets, and irritations she notes from her contacts (in person and via e-mail) with women in Vietnam seems to suggest that these emotions result in part from the general absence and, at other times, coercive presence of sponsors of two kinds of English: reading-writing English vs. speaking-listening English, intersecting with the Specialized divisions of "literary" vs. "business" vs. "scientific" vs. "academic" englishes. To diminish Western ideological and cultural influences, only English textbooks and magazines featuring "politically neutral news events and cultural phenomena" are available to the general public (231). Classic litera-ture in English is most readily available in bookstores. Such state im-positions obviously conflict with the more euphemistic coercion from a globalizing Information Economy, which demands fluency in listen-ing-speaking and the ability to read-write forms of specialized, tech-nologically "developed" English such as Physics or Business Correspondence. The conflicting pulls cause layers of frustration for the women Crawford spoke to. Many of them owned few English books and magazines, which they found very expensive and had diffi-culty finding time to read (233). Adult foreign language classes are available, but tuition is an "enormous expense" (232). Again, "conversation practice" is not available, although women enrolled in the classes all cited economic advancement as their reason, which suggests that speaking-listening is their primary concern (232). For instance, Thuy Nga, a translator and secretary for a telecommunication company, takes English classes so that she can be her company's representative at trade shows and exhibits (236). The vast majority of Vietnamese people are cut off from Western television—a standard medium for picking up conversational English. However, pirated American movies are readily available and relatively cheap (233). Such "violation" of U.S. (-dominated) Free Trade laws ironically serves as a primary means for the general population to practice English comprehension and pronunciation. The Ben Thanh market in Ho Chi Minh City, located within walking distance of the major tourist hotels and a popular site for Native-Speaking Tourists, along with e-mail communication with Native Speakers (which is not available to a majority of the population) also serve as sites of "benign sharing," to borrow a term from Brandt, of the standardized englishes of the Developed Countries (20).

Against this general background, Crawford offers a detailed depiction of one "knowledge worker," Thuy Nga, to tease out the frustrations resulting from the contradictory forces and relations sponsoring her learning and use of English. Thuy "majored in economics and studied Japanese for four years at university" but currently "works for a company that sells telecommunications services, such as mobile phone access" (235). According to Thuy, her situation—holding a job outside her fields of training and interest—is common among university graduates (235). Thuy aspires someday to have a job related to economics or at least in international business, where she can resurrect her Japanese (236). Yet, the highly specialized English of the telecommunications industry eats up her free time by compelling her to read materials she takes home from work and thus deprives her of the time and energy she might spend keeping up her Japanese (236). At the same time, having to represent her company at exhibitions compels her to use her free time to catch up on listening-speaking and to do so despite the fact that opportunities for practicing "conversation" in formal (adult courses) and informal settings are seldom available. As in the case of Lopez in Brandt's account, a Globalizing (U.S.-dominated) Free Market sponsors the unequal status of, access to, and rewards for the language individual learners want (Spanish for Lopez and Japanese for Thuy) and the language of "choice" of intra- and international trading. Not only does Thuy have to compose in English at work when communicating with subsidiaries in Japan, she also has to live with the fact that Japanese-Vietnamese dictionaries with Japanese kanji are rare (232). To figure out the meaning of the kanji characters, learners like Thuy have to go through a two-step translation using a photocopied Japanese-English dictionary and an English-Vietnamese dictionary. The conflict between her self-initiated learning (of Japanese) and her job-imposed learning (of conversational and business written English), along with the euphemistic coercions of personal economic benefit, leave her feeling frustrated and resentful, ambivalent about her "improving" literacy in English, and regretful towards her eroding Japanese.

Details of the specific emotional effects of benign, euphemistic, and explicitly imposed pressures on learners like Thuy to acquire the standardized englishes of Developed Countries highlight two questions for rereading the media stories. Even if and when the two boys undergoing surgery do achieve the kind of "clear" English required for educational and job "competition" in a Free Market dominated by the interests of Developed Countries, besides "low self-esteem," "speech impediments," or becoming "autistic," what other effects on each boy's thoughts, feelings, and actions concerning learning and work might emerge along with such linguistic Development? The "frenzy" for tongue operations in countries like China and South Korea needs to be examined in relation to contradictions between the hegemonic status and economic rewards of standardized U.S. or UK English, on the one hand, and, on the other, the different levels and forms of availability of other sponsors, including technological infrastructures (classrooms, teaching practices, educational personnel, computer technology, Internet access), commercial facilities (bookstores or TV channels), or English user groups outside schooling and work in current day China and South Korea (in markets, parks, or on Internets), for learners with or without the economic resources and the knowhow to have access to the surgery.

Both Crawford and the Vietnamese women she talked to consistently attribute their frustration in learning English to their lack of opportunity to "work with" a Native Speaker of English and lack of (face-to-face or Internet) access to Native Speakers (232). This speaks to the residual power of an assumption shared by Native and Non-Native Speakers of English that Native Speakers (with or without special training) are the top choice authorities on the teaching and learning of English to Adult, Non-Native Speakers of English, even though that assumption has been challenged by research (Canagarajah, *Linguistic* 126). Given the tenacity of such an assumption, we need to treat all types of benign sharing between Native-Speaking U.S. Tourists, Expatriates, Researchers, Visiting Scholars, and learners on the streets, in the park, or in the markets of countries like China, South Korea, Vietnam, Ukraine, Brazil, or South Africa as instrumental to the standardizing of English. Feeling Literate (or not) and "tongue-tied" (or not) has as much to do with the conventions of academic argument promoted in U.S. universities, or the hiring and promotion practices of corporations as it has to do with our (often excessive) enthusiasm to speak to, get to know more about, and offer free lessons or conversational opportunities to Non-native, adult learners and users of English abroad and in the U.S. All of us with credentials to teach English as a Second Language (by formal education or rights of birth) should therefore be more vigilant toward the English we endorse in such benign sharing, especially the potential linkage between what we take to be "clear," "proper," or "common" usages and what have been and become "usual" and "useful" practices in systems and relations of injustice intra- and internationally.

For instance, I notice when reading Gwendolyn Gong's research on "Gender and Literacies: The Korean 'Comfort Women's' Testimonies" that we need to consider the validity and politics of a tendency to treat the relation between two terms in English, "comfort woman" and "military sex slave," as interchangeable. Despite its use, as Gong points out in her notes, by the women themselves and by sympathetic researchers and activists, the more common usage, "comfort woman," sponsors the viewpoint of Japanese Imperialists: it is more useful to those being "comforted" than to those being enslaved and undergoing violent bodily, emotional, and psychological pain and suffering as a result of such "comfort."

Vigilance toward the English we endorse can move us toward reflexive critique, but also, as the chapters in this collection illustrate, toward proactive efforts: practices which mobilize articulations (in words and deeds, that of our own and by the people we talk to, study, teach, and represent) aiming to make the standardized englishes of Developed Countries serve purposes and conditions of life critical to the learner/user but de-legitimized by the standardized englishes of Developed Countries. One such movement weaving through the chapters is a detailed attention to the actual, complex motives of learning beyond the concern to ensure and advance one's job status and economic returns in the Free Market. It is in concert with research such as Brandt's effort to validate the under-rewarded motives of Native English Speakers like Dora Lopez for learning a foreign language, such as acting as a "translator" in her janitorial job between her "supervisor" and the "largely Latina cleaning staff" (175), communicating with Spanish-speaking relatives, making sure that her children and niece are bilingual, and trying to get certified as a bilingual social worker (175, 179). Powell examines the letters of request by women residents of Virginia's Blue Ridge Mountains during the 1930s, when the Shenandoah National Park was being formed. As Powell cogently illustrates, their letter writing not only leaves us a record of the kinds of material issues confronting the rural poor at this particular time and place but also the efforts and ability of these women to employ a variety of rhetorical strategies to request services and resources, advocate and defend their own and others' honor, resist authority, and bring about changes in Park policy. Powell intervenes with the hegemonic power of the formal structures of standardized U.S. english by reminding us that surface errors in spelling and grammatical constructions do not directly equate to Unclear communication. Users of Improper english are often quite successful in articulating their awareness of the english of "government officials," mobilizing rhetorical conventions for evoking author/audience relations, and asserting their sense of their right to government official attention and its duty to provide assistance. In short, Illiteracy in standardized U.S. english does not equal ignorance, nor "the deprivation of the fullness of life," as Mary DeShazer, quoting Nadine Gordimer, puts it in her chapter (251). Rather, it can produce generative work—bending, reshaping English to serve the needs and desires of peoples living in Under- or Un-developed pockets of the world and, in the process, it can keep English alive by making it cogent for a whole range of lives and peoples dismissed by the standardized english of the Super-developed. Furthermore, in the past and present and around the world, women wrestling with interlocking systems and relations of oppression along lines of gender, race, class, etc. have been on the cutting edge of this generative work. Finally, one of the ways in which Native and Fluent Speakers of U.S.-standardized english can and should actively participate in this line of work is to enact reading-writing that constructs the material and formal logic of alternative uses of standardized Englishes in the past and present.

For instance, Strickland enacts a responsible use of her expertise and certification as a Native Speaker of standardized U.S. english in her reading of the resistant work produced by writers like Dorothy West in compositions such as "The Typewriter." Strickland calls attention to West's alternative use of English by performing a close reading of West's depiction of the unequal distribution of opportunities and rewards facing two generations of African Americans, Millie and her father, in their efforts to reckon with a New Technology (the typewriter) and by putting West's choice of character and plot in the context of the network of sponsorship available and withheld to a young, female writer of West's race, class, and generation.

In "Literacy on the Margins: Louisa May Alcott's Pragmatic Rhetoric," Roskelly and Ronald read Alcott's recently recovered anonymous and pseudonymous works alongside her better known novels to tease out the ways in which Alcott uses her writing and her career as a writer to fine-tune the meaning of the concept "pragmatism" endorsed by the all-male

Metaphysical Club, posing an alternative, sustainable notion of "pragmatism" sustained by women's desire for "independence" against the
historical, social, and cultural "givens" of their lived realities.

The literacy accounts of El-Wakil in "Women and the Global Ecology of Digital Literacies" likewise weave in details absent in media
stories of the internationalizing hegemonic power of English. Instead
of letting the New (computer literacy) displace the Traditional (such as
El-Wakil's passion for Arabic calligraphy and literature), El-Wakil designed an electronic pen with a sharp reed nib to capture the symmetry
and discipline of letters revered in the art of calligraphy to produce
"words that lighten the heart" (Hawisher, Selfe, Coffield, and El-Wakil
221). By taking the care to inform its readers of this "unusual" use that
El-Wakil has made of her (U.S.-sponsored) computer literacy, the
chapter depicts people needing aid for technological Development as
leading the effort to carve alternative spaces in a digital landscape
dominated by U.S. interests. Across this landscape, the U.S. interests
generally push to globalize the nation's Free Market, designing forms
of literacy that use the Goods of the powerful to support and invigo-
rate a wealth of technologies that do not serve the interests of peoples
and cultures labeled Traditional and Local. It also presents Non-Native Speaking teachers of English and computer literacy as cut-
ting-edge scholars, aiding-teaching Native and Non-Native speaking
teachers and learners alternative ways of using standardized U.S. digital literacy to serve the interests and needs peripheralized and at risk
of being erased by the logic of U.S.-dominated Free Trade. Such details
also indicate that U.S.-based training programs (such as the Michigan
Tech workshop El-Wakil attended in 1995) and the invitation of U.S.
scholars to international technology symposiums can perform—and,
indeed, have performed—work of resistance, initiating benign sharing that is "caring" (rigorously working to build a more just world for
all) rather than merely "kind" (in a manner to wittingly or unwittingly
turning the Other into Our kind of people). That is, U.S. Composition
can potentially produce unusual work more useful to English learners
and users Othered by U.S.-standardized English and perform unusual
work at scenes of teaching and learning subsidized by economic,
geopolitical, and cultural forces designed to promote the interests of
globalizing a (U.S.-dominated) Free Market.

I notice a similar move in DeShazer's analysis of "Post-Apartheid
Literacies: South African Women's Poetry of Orality, Franchise, and
Reconciliation": a "poetics of resistance" conjoining domestic workers, academics, comrades-in-arms, reworking diverse modes of literacy (oral and written, communal and single authored) and a variety of
"indigenous languages" and as well as Englishes. Such a generative

space poses "competing cultural genealogies" against the history of apartheid in South Africa by calling attention to how issues of gender, race, class, and postcoloniality shape and are shaped by scenes and forms of literacy. In "Sponsoring Clubs: Cultivating Rural Identities through Literacy," Charlotte Hogg interviews members of a Garden Club in Paxton, Nebraska, to highlight the alternative literacy practices emerging from its club activities. Against the top-down logic operating in two other forms of interaction available to rural women interviewed by Hogg—a Tupperware party format driven by corporate interest in customizing the consumer needs and desires of female "homemakers" and the Extension Club events dictated by the "lesson plans" of "home economics" specialists—members of the Garden Club sponsored literacy practices and knowledge production grounded in the specificity of the "local" concerns of its members. Dissatisfied with their designation in the Extension Club as the mere "transmitters or receivers" of discrete bits of information on what all female "homemakers" are supposed to know, desire, and do and thus, render rural women "underdeveloped" or needing "development," members of the Garden Club initiated a series of writings and readings to "carve identities as integral contributors and purveyors of local authority" (116). In "Reconsidering Power, Privilege, and the Public/ Private Distinction in the Literacy of Rural Women" by Kim Donehower, we encounter Pearl, who describes reading as a means to cope with the material hardship of having to raise six children during the Great Depression while her husband was away working on the railroad: "Something to—get my mind *interested in*, y'know. Cause that was a hard life then. You know" (104, emphasis mine). In "Crusader: Ethel Azalea Johnson's Use of the Written Word as a Weapon of Liberation" by Rhea Estelle Lathan, we meet Johnson, a working-class, single mother with no formal instruction in journalism or the convention of public writing (59). Analyzing the content and style of genres of writing Johnson authored for a weekly newsletter, *The Crusader,* for which Johnson serves as co-founder, editor, business manager, and columnist, Lathan reminds us once again of the breadth and depth of the collective efforts of African American women to make literacy practices serve their concern to fight racial, economic, and gender injustice.

The sorts of care these chapters give to the creative work produced by users of English (othered by the assumed authority of Native Speakers of standardized U.S. english) in circumstances designed to submerge them is both timely and much needed in U.S. Composition. It calls us to demand coverage of the actual, complex, and often contradictory motives and plans for uses of "clear" english not cited by the media ventriloquizing of Local Parents and Teachers. It also reminds us to create alternative "discourse maps," as exemplified by the collection of chapters here, which trace patterns of traffic conducted by users of English in the Un- and Under-developed Worlds within and outside the U.S. against the grain of U.S. interests to Globalize its version of Free Trade (rather than on remarking solely those Freeways working to Develop all forms of unjust trading—economic, geopolitical, cultural, digital, verbal, and so on).

As DeShazer points out in her reading of Gcina Mhlophe's poem "A Vote for Unity," Mhlophe "code-switches from a colonial language to an indigenous one that many 'superliterate' South Africans cannot read" to remind them that "they have much to learn" (251). I read Mhlophe's decision to pay homage in Zulu to the leaders of her country's liberation as also reminding her readers of the peoples, leaders, actions, languages, feelings, meanings, and ways of making sense that are bound to be made to disappear if all texts and all of the poems were written in the english of Superliterates.

As I've argued elsewhere, Composition needs more research on how to read-write in ways that acknowledge and learn from the work of resistant users of English, literacy practices that make English serve the needs and aspirations of peoples devalued in the (U.S.-dominated) Free Trading of words, images, products, knowledge, technology, etc. If "equity asks that we march in step with the needs of all students, to be responsive to their past histories and current aspirations" (Brandt 186), we need more research on the actual but complex histories and aspirations motivating and sustained by the specific literacy practices of all our students, especially those interested in formulating words, phrases, and sentences which are clearly in English but might not sound entirely "clear" or "proper" to U.S. Customers or Value Adders, forms of literacy practices aimed at making English serve peoples, languages, concepts, and contexts rendered irrelevant—fated to be erased—by the logic of Fast capitalism. We need more research like the work collected here to remind us of both the necessity and possibilities of sponsoring literacy learning and practices that would not drive parents and kids in China or South Korea to look for "scientific" and "technical" procedures like tongue surgery to dissolve "struggles" necessitated by geopolitical, economic, cultural as well as linguistic structures and relations of injustice. It would help us to acknowledge the justified refusal of learners and users across the world to yield their needs, desires, aspirations, and rights as they seek to build a more just world in words and deeds.

The chapters in this collection, in allowing me to raise these questions, offer readers like myself—and I hope, Composition in general—a sense of the gaps in our knowledge and practice that might be inadvertently sponsoring the kind of media coverage I've overtly critiqued. We need more discursive maps of intra- and international trafficking like the ones emerging from this volume, and we need to explore ways of using such research in our undergraduate and graduate courses to counter media coverage of the eagerness of Others to partake in a U.S.-dominated Global Free Market. As Suresh Canagarajah points out, the "communicative conventions"—textual and publishing—of academic research in Developed Countries such as the United States shape and are shaped by a particular set of "social conventions"—"the rituals, regulations, and relationships governing the interaction of members of the academic community as they engage in knowledge production and communication" (*Geopolitics* 6). These conventions require specific conditions of work and life not always available to all researchers within and outside the United States and almost never available to researchers (U.S.-based or not) doing work in Under- or Un-developed Worlds such as Jaffna, Sri Lanka, and other Asian, African, and South American communities (8–10).

For instance, when conceiving his project, Canagarajah had decided to "address publishing problems [facing his former colleagues in Sri Lanka] through a full-fledged study in its own right," using methods similar to the ones he had used when conducting ethnographic research of U.S. minority students for his Doctoral degree at the University of Texas at Austin. In spite of his U.S. academic preparation and "elaborate" plan (13), when he began to identify the subjects for his "longitudinal study" and schedule interviews, he ran into a series of "practical problems" (14). The hunger, scarcity, and heavy bombardment being experienced in the region made his project seem an "irrelevant, even heartless preoccupation" to some, and he often had to reschedule interviews or abandon the meeting because of a bombing raid or other emergency (14). He had difficulties obtaining and using equipment, such as finding electricity for his audiovisual taping (14), and he had to cancel his plans to distribute a lengthy questionnaire for lack of photocopying facilities (15). Instead of abandoning the project (as he had seriously considered), he decided to go ahead with whatever information he could get "as opportunities presented themselves" (15). Among the reasons he gave for continuing with the project was his realization that "condition[s] of social instability, economic deprivation, and technological backwardness" are not that "unusual" for learners and researchers in "periphery communities." If such a story "had to be suppressed simply because we didn't have the conditions and resources to undertake 'empirically valid' research, then this is a form of silencing that would indirectly suit center interests" (15).

I sense vestiges of and notice references to similar conditions in some of the chapters here. For instance, Crawford went to the Ben Thanh market "to shop and to meet merchants interested in being interviewed about their literacy practices" (233). On each occasion, women approached her to exchange basic greetings and questions in English (233). Crawford was only able to continue her interviews and correspondence with Hoang and Thuy over email because both have access to the Internet through work (233). She can only correspond by letter with a high school girl tutored by Thuy. The slow pace of the mail and the expense of postage have proven to be "insurmountable constraints" (234).

I end my reading with these two references to remind myself of the incredible labor, commitment, and ingenuity embedded in each bit of information concerning the lived experiences of women learners and users of English around the world gathered in this collection. Their work compels me to read against the grain of not only the media coverage of the tongue-snipping frenzy but also and more importantly, our existing notions of what counts as useful information for Composition students, researchers and teachers, the criteria we use to assess the validity of work like the chapters included in this collection, the usual— "clear" and "proper"—readings we are trained to produce of these texts, and the pedagogy we develop out of such readings.

CODA

This reading was composed using Microsoft Word 2000, which signaled (with a RED curly underline) my deviation from "clear" U.S. english vocabulary, including "english," "Latina," "literacies," "Lopez," "Thuy Nga," "DeShazer," and "Wakil."

NOTES

1. For a detailed discussion of the viability of such assumptions for composition studies, see Lu, "An Essay on the Work of Composition: Composing English against the Order of Fast Capitalism."
2. I have particularly in mind Brandt; Canagarajah; Cope and Kalantzis; and Gee, Hull, and Lankshear.
3. For a detailed discussion of the linkage between usage, the usual, and the useful, see Philip E. Lewis's discussion of Derrida's critique, in "La mythologie blanche," of the "us-system."
4. I prefer "job sites" to Workplace because of the tendency to treat only paid work as work, which has historically disadvantaged women's work at Home. By "life worlds," I have in mind those domains in which each of us is a culturally specific but "unspecialized" person.

WORKS CITED

Annan, Kofi. Nobel Lecture. Oslo, Norway, 10 Dec. 2001. Nobel Foundation. 3 Mar. 2003 <http://www.nobel.se/peace/laureates/2001/annan-lecture.html>.

Brandt, Deborah. *Literacy in American Lives.* New York: Cambridge UP, 2001.

Canagarajah, A. Suresh. *Critical Academic Writing and Multilingual Students.* Ann Arbor: U of Michigan P, 2002.

——. *A Geopolitics of Academic Writing.* Pittsburgh: U of Pittsburgh P, 2002.

——. *Resisting Linguistic Imperialism in English Teaching.* New York: Oxford UP, 1999.

Cope, Bill, and Mary Kalantzis, eds. *Multiliteracies: Literacy Learning and the Design of Social Futures.* London: Routledge, 2000.

Gee, James Paul, Glynda Hull, and Colin Lankshear. *The New Work Order: Behind the Language of the New Capitalism.* Boulder: Westview, 1996.

Kim, Kyoung-wha. "Accent Axed with a Snip." *Aljazeera.net.* 19 Oct. 2003. 17 Nov. 2003 <http://english.aljazeera.net/NR/exeres/4794AA93-CDAE-4E8C-BAEB-977E2DA59B0E.htm>.

Lewis, Philip E. "The Measure of Translation Effects." *The Translation Studies Reader.* Ed. Lawrence Venuti. London: Routledge, 2002. 264–83.

Lippi-Green, Rosina. *English with an Accent: Language, Ideology, and Discrimination in the United States.* New York: Routledge, 1997.

Lu, Min-Zhan. "An Essay on the Work of Composition: Composing English against the Order of Fast Capitalism." *College Composition and Communication* 56 (2004): 16–50.

Markus, Francis. "Chinese Find Learning English a Snip." *BBC News World Edition.* 31 July 2002. 17 Nov. 2003 <http://news.bbc.co.uk/2/hi/world/asia-pacific/2161780.stm>.

Author Index

Subject Index

A

Adult literacy programs, 284
Affective labor, 47
Africa, gender inequities in education, 291
African Americans, and literacy myth, 48–58
African American women
   critical intelligence, 67–69
   leadership roles, 59
   literacy and culture, 15
African Methodist Episcopal Church, 67
African National Congress, 246, 250
Afrikaans, 247, 254
Afrikaner nationalism, 250
Age, and literacy, 27–28
Ahab's Wife (Alcott), 135
AIDS crisis, 286
Algeria, 192
Alliance Building, 164–165
American Dream (DeParle), 20
Americanization movement, 182
American University of Beirut, 213, 215, 305
American University of Cairo, 211, 216–225, 305–306
   mission of, 223–224
   women in academic computing, 225n3
Ankyloglossia, 300
"Anniversary, The," 143, 145
Anti-apartheid poets, 243
Apartheid era, South Africa, 243; *see also*
   Post-apartheid literacies
Appalachia, 91
   people of, 72–75
   stereotypes of culture/illiteracy, 99, 102

Appalachian language, de-legitimization of, 95
Arabic
   diglossia, 194, 200
   publications/texts in, 194–195
Arab states
   enrollment ratios, 283
   illiteracy rates, 282
   women's rights, 199–202
"Ariel" (poem-Plath), 145
Art, revolutionary, 140–141
Artifacts, of literacy, 118–119
Assimilation, and literacy, 10
Assuming the Positions (Miller), 16
"At the Commission" (poem-de Kok), 253, 255
Aunt Jo's Scrapbook (Alcott), 130
Authority, writerly, 150

B

Baccalauréats, 195
Bac classique, 195
Bamaqli, 191
Bangladesh, literacy rates, 277
Basic literacy, 154
BBC News World Edition, 299
Belletrism, 175
Ben Thanh market, 233, 301, 317
Beyond Tomorrow, 121
Bible reading, 176
Bilingualism, Arabic/French, 194
Bint El-Nil, 215
Black accommodationist writing, 66–67
Black Power movement, 145

325